OXFORD MODERN LANGUAGES AND LITERATURE MONOGRAPHS

Editorial Committee

D. J. CONSTANTINE   D. E. EVANS
R. E. GOLDTHORPE   I. W. F. MACLEAN
E. M. RUTSON
G. C. STONE   R. W. TRUMAN
J. R. WOODHOUSE

Playing with Truth

LANGUAGE AND THE HUMAN CONDITION IN PASCAL'S *PENSÉES*

NICHOLAS HAMMOND

CLARENDON PRESS · OXFORD
1994

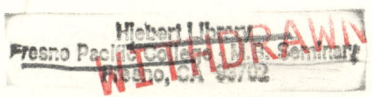

Oxford University Press, Walton Street, Oxford OX2 6DP
Oxford New York Toronto
Delhi Bombay Calcutta Madras Karachi
Kuala Lumpur Singapore Hong Kong Tokyo
Nairobi Dar es Salaam Cape Town
Melbourne Auckland Madrid
and associated companies in
Berlin Ibadan

Oxford is a trade mark of Oxford University Press

Published in the United States
by Oxford University Press Inc., New York

© Nicholas Hammond 1994

All rights reserved. No part of this publication may be reproduced,
stored in a retrieval system, or transmitted, in any form or by any means,
without the prior permission in writing of Oxford University Press.
Within the UK, exceptions are allowed in respect of any fair dealing for the
purpose of research or private study, or criticism or review, as permitted
under the Copyright, Designs and Patents Act, 1988, or in the case of
reprographic reproduction in accordance with the terms of the licences
issued by the Copyright Licensing Agency. Enquiries concerning
reproduction outside these terms and in other countries should be
sent to the Rights Department, Oxford University Press,
at the address above

British Library Cataloguing in Publication Data
Data available

Library of Congress Cataloging in Publication Data
Hammond, Nicholas.
Playing with truth: language and the human condition in Pascal's
Pensées/Nicholas Hammond.
(Oxford modern languages and literature monographs)
Includes bibliographical references and index.
1. Apologetics—17th century. 2. Catholic Church—Apologetic
works. 3. Certainty. 4. Belief and doubt. 5. Catholic Church—
Doctrines. 6. French literature—17th century—History and
criticism. [1. Pascal, Blaise, 1623–1662. Pensées.] I. Title.
II. Series.
B1901.P43H36 1994 230'.2—dc20 93–44417
ISBN 0–19–815893–9

1 3 5 7 9 10 8 6 4 2

Typeset by Cambrian Typesetters
Frimley, Surrey
Printed in Great Britain
on acid-free paper by
Bookcraft Ltd.,
Midsomer Norton, Bath

*FOR MY PARENTS
AND MY BROTHERS*

Acknowledgements

I am indebted above all to Richard Parish, who supervised the thesis on which this book is based. His continued advice and friendship have been of immense value. Peter Bayley and Denys Potts, the two examiners of the thesis, were most generous in their encouragement and recommendations. Ian Maclean was a painstaking reader, correcting a number of mistakes and offering many invaluable suggestions. Gareth Moore's patience and expertise were equally indispensable in overcoming the problems presented by my incompetence in the finer details of word-processing. For making available unpublished material, I am indebted to Andrew Brown of the Voltaire Foundation, Pol Ernst, Pierre Force, John Gallucci, Anthony McKenna, and Philippe Sellier. I am grateful to the Beit Fellowship for supporting me financially for the first three years of my research, and to the Taylor Institution, Oxford, for providing financial assistance to travel to libraries in France. My thanks are due to those at Oxford University Press, especially Vicki Reeve, Janet Moth, and Sarah Barrett, who provided willing assistance at the various editing stages of this book. I would also like to thank the following for their informed advice and support: Camilla Bingham, Todd Breyfogle, Elfrieda Dubois, Michael Hawcroft, Jeremy Robbins, and Ben Rogers. Finally, this book would never have appeared were it not for the inspired enthusiasm for Pascal of my undergraduate tutor, Jean-Louis Cattanéo.

N. H.

Pembroke College, Oxford
June 1993

Contents

ACKNOWLEDGEMENTS vii
ABBREVIATIONS xii

INTRODUCTION

État présent 1
Terminology 3
De l'esprit géométrique and Port-Royal 10

Part I. Language and Order in the *Pensées*

1. Language in the *Pensées* 25
   Parole/Mot 25
   The Tyranny of Speech: *Dire/Contredire* 33
   Interprétation 41

2. *Ordre* 50
   Ordonner 59
   Order and Fragmentation 60
   L532: 'Le Véritable Ordre' 63
   Ordre as *Dispositio* 69
   Memoria 74
   Order, Truth, and Language 76

Part II. *La Condition de l'Homme*

Introduction 81

3. *Inconstance* 86
   Inconstance and *Bizarrerie* 94
   Inconstant/Constant 96
   Constance 99

4. *Ennui* 103
   Ennui/Néant 107

Ennui and *Divertissement*   109
Ennui and the Possibility of Salvation   114

5. *Inquiétude*   118

    The Anxiety of Man's Fallen State   122
    Inquiétude and *Curiosité*   128
    Inquiétude and Continued Spiritual Endeavour   130

6. *Repos*   135

    L136   136
    Pyrrhonism and Stoicism   139
    Tranquillité   142
    Paix   143
    Human *Repos*   145
    Spiritual *Repos*   147

7. *Bonheur/Félicité*   150

    Sur la conversion du pécheur   151
    False Happiness   152
    Happiness and *Divertissement*   155
    Spiritual Happiness   162

8. *Justice*   166

    Injustice   168
    Human Justice   169
    Natural Justice   171
    Political Justice   178
    Les justes   182
    Divine Justice   184
    Christ as Mediator   193

Part III. Playing with Truth

9. *Playing with Truth*   197

    Truth and Play   201
    Vérité   203
    Truth and Corruption   209
    Raison des effets   216
    Figures and Miracles   219

CONCLUSION 226

TABLE OF TERMS 229
BIBLIOGRAPHY 230
INDEX OF PASCAL'S WORKS 243
INDEX OF NAMES 247

Abbreviations

Unless I indicate otherwise, quotations from Pascal's writings will be taken from *Œuvres complètes*, edited by Louis Lafuma (Paris, Éditions du Seuil, 1963). I shall refer to this edition simply as Seuil. All references to the *Pensées* will be to this edition. Individual fragments will be preceded by the letter L, e.g. L44. Original spelling has been maintained in quotations from early editions or facsimiles of early editions.

Introduction

ÉTAT PRÉSENT

From my first reading of Pascal, I was struck by the unique way in which language is used in the *Pensées*. The words within the fragmentary text and, indeed, in their own right seemed to have a dynamism and instability different from other texts of the period. It was not surprising, therefore, to find that during the last fifty years in particular, much attention has been paid to language, and especially to the language of persuasion, in the *Pensées*.

The majority of studies to have appeared on Pascal's use of language concentrate either on vocabulary and style, without drawing conclusions about the way in which the language operates within the persuasive structure of the text, or solely on different aspects of style as means of persuasion. Dom Michel Jungo in *Le Vocabulaire de Pascal* (1950), for example, examines in great detail Pascal's choice of words, considering both archaisms and neologisms, even the spelling and pronunciation of Pascal, and continues with remarks on aspects of style. Sister Mary Maggioni's *The 'Pensées' of Pascal: A Study of Baroque Style* (1950) deals specifically with the patterns of asymmetry and antinomy, where she sees the *Pensées* as 'intrinsically a product of the Baroque epoch'.[1] An extensive analysis of Pascal's style and vocabulary is given by Jean-Jacques Demorest in *Dans Pascal: Essai en partant de son style* (1953). Moreover, Demorest concentrates particularly on the effect of Pascal's use of language. As he puts it, 'partout [. . .] il [Pascal] crée une friction. Partout dans sa pensée éclate un dialogue qui est mouvement tangible.'[2] However, the role of persuasion is ignored overall.

The first major study devoted to language and persuasion came with Patricia Topliss's *The Rhetoric of Pascal* (1966). Topliss reassesses Pascal in the light of traditional rhetoric, examining especially aspects of style (*elocutio*). In *L'Image dans l'œuvre de Pascal* (1969), Michel Le Guern examines the effect of different

---

[1] (Washington, DC), 142.   [2] (Paris), 138.

kinds of imagery, concentrating particularly on the different influences on Pascal and on what he calls 'les deux fonctions de l'image'—*docere* (knowledge) and *movere* (persuasion).

The publication in 1979 of the proceedings of a conference held in Clermont-Ferrand in 1976, *Méthodes chez Pascal*, provided a major redirection of interest in the various persuasive methods in Pascal's works.[3] However, those articles devoted to lexical aspects of the *Pensées* tend not to consider the relationship between words and persuasion.[4] The appearance in the same year of Hugh Davidson's *The Origins of Certainty: Means and Meaning in Pascal's 'Pensées'* marks the first close examination of individual terms within the context of persuasion. Davidson concentrates particularly on words of epistemological concern, *raison*, *coutume*, and *inspiration*, relating them to different levels of proof. More recently, Buford Norman's *Portraits of Thought: Knowledge, Methods, and Styles in Pascal* (1988) takes up an analysis of epistemological terms like *sentiment*, *principes*, *instinct*, *nature*, *coutume*, and *raison*, developing from them an analysis of methods and styles in Pascal's writings.

Although Sara Melzer in *Discourses of the Fall* (1986) does not examine individual terms, her radical re-evaluation of language within the context of the doctrine of the Fall and within various post-structuralist critical traditions offers a new reading of the text which has provided a useful starting-point for this book. Also, despite a tendency to ignore the historical proofs of God's existence which Pascal clearly regarded as important, Melzer's article, 'Classicism and Conventions of Meaning in the *Pensées*', throws interesting light on the function of paradox in the *Pensées*:

Paradox [...] is not a function of the thought itself, but only of the language used to communicate it [...]. Paradox is possible only because language is flexible. It is this very flexibility that is the source of semantic confusion. The paradoxical play on the polyvalence of the word calls attention to language as containing gaps that the reader must fill in order to construct meaning.[5]

---

[3] See the Bibliography for individual articles of particular interest which appear in *Méthodes chez Pascal*. In matters of rhetoric and persuasion, the articles of Philippe Sellier and Le Guern are especially useful.
[4] See e.g. the articles by H. Davidson, E. Morot-Sir, and A. Robinet.
[5] *Papers on French Seventeenth Century Literature*, 14–15 (1981), 73–4.

Melzer concludes the article by stating that it is through the destruction of the reader's basic assumptions of his ability to attain truth and meaning in a fallen world that Pascal hopes to persuade the reader to search for truth in God.

Taking these studies into account, I realized that, although much valuable work had been devoted to epistemological concerns in the *Pensées*, the function of terms depicting the human condition were equally crucial to the persuasive process of the *Pensées* and had been largely unexplored. It is in this respect that my research differs from previous readings. Through an analysis of the language used by Pascal to portray man's status in the world, it is my aim to derive a model of interpretation which will show many different levels of persuasion at work in the *Pensées*.

TERMINOLOGY

Inseparable from the depiction of the human condition, the problems of language form an integral part of the persuasive process in the *Pensées*. In order to understand the framework in which this persuasion is effected, it is important to consider initially whether the *Pensées* can be viewed as an apology. Although the term 'apology' is one which has been widely assigned to describe the *Pensées*, a difficulty arises from the fact that Pascal himself makes no mention of 'apologie' in the *Pensées*, nor do Gilberte and Étienne Périer use it to describe their brother and uncle's work. Édouard Morot-Sir raises strong objections to the choice of the word. He claims that Pascal's perspective is much broader than that of the traditional apology, which is 'une annexe inférieure des théologies positive ou rationnelle, ou un appendice à une théodicée'.[6]

In recent years, two main perspectives with regard to the apologetic aspect of the *Pensées* have emerged: the first, where the notion of an apology is implicitly or explicitly denied;[7] and the

---

[6] 'Du nouveau sur Pascal?', *Romance Notes*, 18 (1977), 278.
[7] e.g. L. Goldmann, *Le Dieu caché: Étude sur la vision tragique dans les 'Pensées' de Pascal et dans le théâtre de Racine* (Paris, 1955); L. Marin, *La Critique du discours: Sur la 'Logique' de Port-Royal et les 'Pensées' de Pascal* (Paris, 1975), and '"Pascal": Text, Author, Discourse ...', *Yale French Studies*, 52 (1975);

second, where the apologetic plan is pivotal to all discussions of the *Pensées*.[8]

Those interpretations which reject the term 'apologie' tend to concentrate on the notions of language and fragmentation, without being constrained by literal or historical readings of the text. However, there are certain pitfalls in adopting such an approach. First, by rejecting the undoubted apologetic aspects of the text, as evidenced by the 'table des matières' and headings such as 'Preuves de Jésus-Christ', there is a danger of returning to the eighteenth-century interpretations of the *Pensées*,[9] where emphasis is placed upon the *pensées philosophiques* as opposed to the *pensées religieuses*. Secondly, by ignoring the historical proofs which dominate several fragments, there is a risk of assigning a fideistic position to the writer of the *Pensées*.[10] Thirdly, the fact that 'the dis-orderly and especially the fragmentary have been hailed as the hallmark of Modernism'[11] can lead to lifting the *Pensées* out of its seventeenth-century context and to treating it solely as a 'modernist' work.

The other approach has not only brought us nearer to the state of the fragments as left by Pascal at his death, through the editions of Lafuma and Sellier, but has demonstrated also the apologetic thread which runs through many passages. Yet there are numerous pieces which clearly were not intended as part of an apology, such as the *Mémorial* (L913), the passage entitled 'Le Mystère de Jésus' (L919), and the fragments concerned with miracles. The tendency to assume or to construct an apology, with claims that it comes closest to Pascal's intentions, must therefore be perceived as misguided. The fact remains that we have a collection of fragments

---

Morot-Sir, 'Du nouveau sur Pascal?'; D. Stanton, 'Pascal's Fragmentary Thoughts: Dis-order and its Overdetermination', *Semiotica*, 51 (1984); S. Melzer, *Discourses of the Fall: A Study of Pascal's 'Pensées'* (London, 1986).

[8] e.g. M. L. Hubert, *Pascal's Unfinished Apology: A Study of his Plan* (New Haven, Conn., 1952); P. Ernst, *Approches pascaliennes* (Gembloux, 1970); J. Mesnard, *Les 'Pensées' de Pascal* (Paris, 1976); P. Sellier, introd. to his 1976 and 1991 edns. of the *Pensées*; D. Wetsel, *L'Écriture et le reste: The 'Pensées' of Pascal in the Exegetical Tradition of Port-Royal* (Columbus, Oh., 1981); A. Pugh, *The Composition of Pascal's 'Apologia'* (Toronto, 1984).

[9] e.g. Voltaire, Letter 25 of *Lettres philosophiques* (1734) and Condorcet's *Éloge de M. Pascal* (1776).

[10] See Wetsel, *L'Écriture et le reste*, p. xx.

[11] Stanton, 'Pascal's Fragmentary Thoughts', 214. See also L. D. Kritzman (ed.), *Fragments: Incompletion and Discontinuity* (New York, 1981), 3–4.

which do not constitute a completed apology, and we can never hope to attain anything more than what lies before us, despite the undoubted apologetic purpose of many fragments.

The most significant steps towards discovering the chronological order in which Pascal wrote many fragments have been made by Pol Ernst in his 1990 thesis, 'Géologie et stratigraphie des *Pensées* de Pascal'.[12] Through painstaking research into the paper on which the fragments were written, with the different watermarks and the way the paper was cut both before and after Pascal's death, as well as through other factors such as the handwriting and lines separating fragments, Ernst has succeeded in reconstructing many of the original pages which Pascal would have used. Although Ernst identifies about sixty different types of paper, some 75 per cent of the fragments were written on eight varieties, 60 per cent of these appearing on only four kinds of paper (named by Ernst as the four 'strates majeures'). The study of the paper and the evidence gleaned from various fragments enables him to suggest that the first fragments of the *Pensées* (probably L922–4, which appear to constitute notes for Pascal's second letter to Charlotte de Roannez on 24 September 1656) were written in September 1656. These fragments were written on one of the minor *strates*, bearing the watermark 'Cadran 1 B cœur C'. Other early fragments also written on this paper are L901–2, on the miracle of the Holy Thorn, and L904 and L962, preparatory fragments for the fifteenth *Provinciale*, which was published on 25 November of that year.

Of the four 'strates majeures', the earliest (consisting of about 100 fragments) bears a coat of arms over a floweret, marked RC/DV, and can be dated from the end of 1656 to March 1657. Amongst these fragments appear some concerned with 'Raison des effets' (L98–100), with 'Tyrannie' (L58), as well as those included by Lafuma in the *liasse* entitled 'Soumission et usage de la raison'. The second major *strate* is the paper with a horn over the letters PH, mostly situated between March and May 1658. The greatest number of fragments on this paper forms the whole *dossier* XXV, L635–729. The two remaining 'strates majeures', 'France et Navarre' on PH (FNPH) and 'France et Navarre IC' (FNIC), can be

---

[12] (Univ. of Paris IV.) The thesis is divided into 2 clear sections, the 1st a discussion of Ernst's reconstruction work, the 2nd an Album of photocopied reconstituted pages. I shall hereafter refer to this second section simply as 'Album'.

placed between April and June 1658, which shows an acceleration of composition in those months.

The importance of Ernst's work cannot be underestimated, for his research enables us to look at the *Pensées* from another perspective. As he points out,

> Cette lecture mérite amplement d'être la première. N'est-elle pas la seule qui rende compte de la naissance et de l'évolution, dans la cohérence et l'approfondissement sans aucune rupture, de l'ensemble du projet apologétique pascalien? Ce parcours génétique, hier impensable, est aujourd'hui possible et donc nécessaire.[13]

However, whereas Ernst emphasizes the importance of his findings in establishing an understanding of the apologetic project, I contend that a knowledge of the order of the different *strates* and the reconstruction of those fragments which were composed concurrently can help us to move away from considerations of ordering which we will never know with any certainty. Rather, I intend to refer to Ernst's findings where the dating and pairing of fragments throw light on the meaning of important terms in the *Pensées*.

Since Ernst's work, Emmanuel Martineau has produced an edition of the *Pensées* which relies largely on chronological ordering. However, as Martineau himself admits, this chronology 'demeure relative et surtout conjecturale'.[14] Moreover, his decision to collate several shorter fragments into longer discourses represents, it would seem, an imposition of ordering which can never be claimed to approximate Pascal's own preferred method.[15]

A further problem concerned with reading the *Pensées*, inseparable from their unfinished state, is that of the speaker. The text is inhabited by a multiplicity of voices, some clearly defined, others purposely undefined, and many more rendered ambiguous by the lack of precise context. It is only during the last fifty years that the identity of the speaker in the *Pensées* has been questioned specifically. Jeanne Russier attempts to distinguish between Pascal and the *libertin*, which in turn earns the rebuff from Lucien Goldmann that 'une pareille méthode permet d'attribuer n'importe

---

[13] (Univ. of Paris IV.) i. 204.
[14] *Discours sur la religion et sur quelques autres sujets* (Paris, 1992), 10.
[15] I shall discuss this aspect more fully in Ch. 2.

quoi à n'importe qui'.[16] Louis Marin in ' "Pascal": Text, Author, Discourse' is the first to write of 'the author's effacement of the Self' in the *Pensées*, where the speaker/writer of the fragments cannot simply be designated as Pascal; rather, he sees the speaker as figured in the name Salomon de Tultie (from L745), itself an anagram of Pascal's pseudonym from the *Lettres provinciales*, Louis de Montalte:

> This proper name is thus double the cipher for 'Pascal', the proper name of he who writes the fragment and who succeeds through this twice removed disguise in making its referent, the Self, disappear, spent in the stages of its designation.[17]

However, Marin does not develop this argument, and makes no distinction between the Salomon de Tultie figure and those interlocutors who are given speaker status in the *Pensées*.[18]

Richard Parish in his article 'Mais qui parle? Voice and Persona in the *Pensées*',[19] gives the most detailed analysis of the complexities involved in the identification of the speaker, particularly through the use of personal pronouns. As far as the 'je' is concerned, he distinguishes between an authorial voice, an apologetic speaker (the apologist), and potential interlocutors (themselves divided into 'searchers' and 'non-searchers'). Furthermore, he rejects the possibility of 'a unifying entity called Pascal', because any attempt to assign the feelings of the different personae in the *Pensées* to Pascal himself would become a narrowly biographical problem: 'If we wish to construct a Pascal from the text, it will therefore be of our own making.'[20]

As I concur largely with Parish's categorization of the different speakers, I do not intend simply to retrace his analysis. However, I

---

[16] See J. Russier, *La Foi selon Pascal* (Paris, 1949), 7–12; Goldmann, *Le Dieu caché*, 190, n. 1.

[17] Marin, '*Pascal*: Text, Author, Discourse', 142.

[18] See also K. Schärer's discussion of the pseudonyms Salomon de Tultie, Louis de Montalte, and Amos Dettonville in 'Pascal und das Problem der Sprache', *Romanische Forschungen*, 92 (1980), 74–87.

[19] *Seventeenth-Century French Studies*, 8 (1986), 23–40. G. Leveillé-Mourin, in *Le Langage chrétien, anti-chrétien de la transcendance: Pascal–Nietzsche* (Paris, 1978), entitles the 1st chapter of the 2nd section 'Qui parle?', but does not discuss in any detail the different speakers in the *Pensées*. See also C. Meurillon, 'La Narration dans les *Pensées*', *XVIIᵉ Siècle*, 177 (Oct.–Dec. 1992), where different levels of narration rather than speakers are considered.

[20] Parish, 'Mais qui parle?', 32.

would like to elaborate on his depiction of the 'apologist' persona, which, he states,

> is in one sense an applied, argumentative aspect of the author, which enunciates the apologetic project both in its conception and elaboration, and in its didactic intentions to confront the human condition and propose a way forward.[21]

As I mentioned previously, the apologetic nature of many of the fragments is indubitable. Yet the diversity and different purposes of the *Pensées* must preclude one from calling them, without qualification, an 'apology'. Similarly, I believe that the term 'apologist' must be used with circumspection.[22] Through their content and their unfinished state, the *Pensées* transcend and deconstruct the purpose of most contemporary apologies. We can accept that the speaker acts as an apologist in certain contexts, but the term cannot be used in too wide a sense. It would appear that another word is needed to cover that broader scope, as it would be cumbersome to adopt a series of different titles for a 'je' who is fulfilling the same essential role *qua* voice if not *qua* purpose.

The term 'moraliste' might be applicable, but it also seems to be too narrow. Of the three main seventeenth-century dictionaries, the 1690 Furetière is the only one to define 'moraliste', as 'auteur qui escrit, qui traite de la morale', 'la morale' in turn being described as 'la doctrine des mœurs'. This definition would apply to the speaker as observer of human nature, but it ignores the importance which is attached to the Christian religion. Furthermore, the term 'moraliste' would be inadequate in expressing the strong elements of persuasion and presentation of arguments which are evident in the *Pensées*.

I have therefore chosen to use 'dialectician'. Pierre Magnard, in an article entitled 'Pascal Dialecticien', identifies many of the methods of Pascal as those of a dialectician (in the sense of one who considers contrasting arguments, as epitomized in the 'renversement continuel du pour au contre'), methods which I shall discuss in my analysis of key words in the *Pensées*: 'en l'occurrence, Pascal est à n'en pas douter dialecticien, dans cet éloignement de tout

---

[21] Parish, 29.

[22] e.g. J.-J. Demorest, in 'Pascal's Sophistry and the Sin of Poesy', in Demorest (ed.), *Studies in Seventeenth-Century French Literature* (Ithaca, NY, 1962), states that 'we would like to go further and suggest that the *Pensées* should not even be read as an Apology, but only as tactical projects and sketches' (p. 143), and yet continues to apply the term 'apologist' to the speaker (e.. p. 151).

dogmatisme, ce sens des antinomies, cet usage de la négativité
[...]'.[23] In *Les 'Pensées' de Pascal*, Jean Mesnard entitles the
second section 'La Dialectique des *Pensées*, and goes on to
distinguish between two principal senses of the word 'dialectique'.[24]
The first definition is 'l'art de l'argumentation, c'est-à-dire
l'ensemble des techniques qui permettent de conduire un raisonnement en vue de convaincre un interlocuteur et de réfuter ses
objections', which incorporates the close relation between 'dialectique' and 'dialogue'. The second meaning revolves around an
'opposition de contraires'; these contrasts are either non-
contradictory (which present no difficulties of interpretation), or
contradictory (the problematic nature of which Mesnard specifies).

Dialectics had a strong humanist tradition, stemming largely
from the need for analysis and use of ordinary language for formal
debating and clear thinking. The most significant teachers of
dialectics in this period were Lorenzo Valla (1407–57), Rudolph
Agricola 1444–85), and, latterly, Peter Ramus (1515–72). Valla
stressed that the major part of argumentation is concerned not with
certainty but with persuasion and probability;[25] this definition is
particularly germane to the *Pensées*, a text which deals centrally
with uncertainty and instability as means of persuasion, as I hope to
show. It is also significant that the term 'dialectique' had an
important role to play even in lesser-known apologetic writings of
the seventeenth century. René du Pont, for example, defines 'la
Dialectique' in his *La Philosophie des esprits* (first published in
1602) as

autrement Logique science de disputer, discerner le vray d'avec le faux. Elle
donne des lieux, des argumens, et des loix d'argumenter, et dispute
probablement de toute question proposée, aussi prompte à deffendre la
negative qu'à soustenir l'affirmative.[26]

I use the term, therefore, not in its sense of one who teaches Logic
but rather, as the Furetière dictionary calls the 'dialecticien', one
'qui sçait mettre les arguments en forme', or to quote the 1694
Dictionnaire de l'Académie Françoise, 'Un homme qui raisonne

---

[23] *Pascal présent* (Clermont-Ferrand, 1962), 289.
[24] See Mesnard, *Les 'Pensées' de Pascal*, 173–7.
[25] For a fuller account of the history of dialectics, see Lisa Jardine, 'Humanism and the Teaching of Logic', in N. Kretzmann *et al.* (eds.), *The Cambridge History of Later Medieval Philosophy* (Cambridge, 1982), 797–807.
[26] (1628, 1st edn. 1602), 231–2.

juste sur toutes choses'.[27] This term would have the advantage of taking into account both the direct authorial presence of fragments like L542, L627, and L656 and the wider role of the speaker in other contexts. I acknowledge the difficulties of choosing a word that is primarily associated with the human faculty of reason and which would seem to contradict Pascal's negation of the prominence of that very reason. However, where I use the term 'dialectician', I intend it to mean essentially 'one who presents an argument', without any implications of reason playing a greater role than, say, instinct. Moreover, I believe that the term 'dialectician' would be a feasible alternative to the other names given to the general speaker in the *Pensées*, and would better encapsulate what Parish calls 'an applied, argumentative aspect of the author' than would 'apologist'.

Where I use the term 'apologist', therefore, I shall intend it to be perceived within a specific context which I shall qualify. It would doubtless be misguided to apply the term 'dialectician' indiscriminately to all sections of the *Pensées*, but I hope that it will act as a clearer starting-point for my discussion of fragments which include the unspecified 'je', 'nous', or 'on'. In other categories of speaker, such as searchers and non-searchers, I intend to follow Parish's differentiation.

DE L'ESPRIT GÉOMÉTRIQUE AND PORT-ROYAL

The differing approaches to language in Port-Royal have been extensively covered by recent critical scholarship. As far as Pascal is concerned, there are some who see his analysis of language in the *Pensées* as largely coextensive with that found in Arnauld and Nicole's *Logique* and Arnauld and Lancelot's *Grammaire générale*. Hugh Davidson,[28] for example, assesses the reaction of Port-Royal against the restoration of rhetoric in the seventeenth century, and perceives Pascal as 'starting from principles like those of the Port-Royalists' (p. vii) in order to invent an art of persuasion. Although he recognizes differing subtleties in Pascal's use of language in the

---

[27] In this book, I shall refer frequently to definitions found in the various 17th-c. dictionaries. Despite their undoubted helpfulness, I intend only to use them as means to an end, for language in the *Pensées* operates from a notion of its own complexity.

[28] *Audience, Words, and Art* (Columbus, Oh., 1965).

Lettres provinciales and the *Pensées*, Davidson concludes that the *Pensées* consist of a combination of geometry and dialectic, which are not 'mutually exclusive' (p. 139). Buford Norman[29] takes the four main operations of the mind identified in *La Logique*, *concevoir, juger, raisonner*, and *ordonner*, as a starting-point in his analysis of methods and styles in the *Pensées*. His approach is both enlightening and intricate, but his use of Port-Royal logic implicitly negates the role of rhetoric in the *Pensées*.

On the other hand, there are those scholars who view Pascal's use of language as fundamentally opposed to the Arnauldian standpoint, and, instead, closely associated with the thought of Martin de Barcos. Goldmann[30] equates Pascal with Barcos, identifying them both as belonging to 'un courant extrémiste', as opposed to 'les courants centristes' (p. 9) to which Arnauld and Nicole belonged. Jean Mesnard has since successfully shown Barcos not to be the 'extrémiste' that Goldmann thought him, and, moreover, has made the important point that Barcos himself was deeply opposed to both the *Lettres provinciales* and the *Pensées*.[31] Sara Melzer[32] follows Goldmann's thesis, and goes on to state that both Pascal and Barcos 'place the notion of original sin at the center of their epistemology' (p. 27), thus making 'obscurity and distance' central to their linguistic theory (p. 27). Despite a tendency to omit aspects which would weaken her argument, such as the role of historical proofs in the *Pensées*, Melzer's reading is perceptive, and challenges the preconceptions of those who see clarity of language as central to an understanding of the *Pensées*.

Other critics have considered the influence of Pascal within the text of *La Logique*.[33] Louis Marin, for example, perceives *La Logique* as a reading of the tensions inherent in the *Pensées*. For

---

[29] *Portraits of Thought: Knowledge, Methods, and Styles in Pascal* (Columbus, Oh., 1988).

[30] *Correspondance de Martin de Barcos*, ed. L. Goldmann (Paris, 1956). See also Goldmann's *Le Dieu caché*.

[31] 'Martin de Barcos et les disputes internes de Port-Royal', *Chroniques de Port-Royal*, 26-8 (1977-9). Cf. also the comment by an anonymous writer in the *Recueil de choses diverses*, Bibliothèque Nationale, *nouvelles acquisitions françaises*, no. 4333: 'M. Barcos dit que M. Pascal a été foudroyé de Dieu comme un pygmée; que ce n'était pas à lui de parler de la religion', in *Œuvres complètes*, ed. J. Mesnard (Paris, 1964-91), i. 893.

[32] *Discourses of the Fall*.

[33] See esp. Marin, *La Critique du Discours*, and A. McKenna, *De Pascal à Voltaire* (Oxford, 1990), i. 1-184.

Antony McKenna, 'la pensée de Pascal joue un rôle important dans l'élaboration du texte de *La Logique* qui, sur certains points, constitue une véritable interprétation des *Pensées*' (*De Pascal à Voltaire*, p. 54). He explains the response of Arnauld and Nicole to 'l'univers pascalien', which he sees as 'le *pays* pyrrhonien de l'incertitude, de la vraisemblance' (p. 911).

One text by Pascal, *De l'esprit géométrique*, is crucial to an understanding of both his influence in Port-Royal and the way in which he moved towards the persuasive aims of the *Pensées*.[34] A fundamental misconception which has existed with respect to *De l'esprit géométrique* is that it consists of two separate parts, 'De l'esprit géométrique' and 'De l'art de persuader'. However, this separation is due solely to editors such as Lafuma and Chevalier who have tried to make some distinction between Pascal's examination of geometrical methods and the different elements involved in the art of persuasion. In fact, although it would seem that the original manuscript (which is lost) did consist of two fragments, it forms part of a single work, which is mentioned by Arnauld and Nicole in *La Logique* as 'un petit écrit non imprimé, qui avoit été fait par feu Monsieur Pascal, et qu'il avoit intitulé, *De l'esprit Geometrique*', and which is identified, along with the works of Descartes, whom they call 'un celebre philosophe de ce siecle, qui a autant de netteté d'esprit qu'on trouve de confusion dans les autres', as major influences on their work.[35] Furthermore, Pascal identifies two clear sections which bear no relation to those posited by editors:

l'une contiendra les règles de la conduite des démonstrations géométriques, c'est-à-dire méthodiques et parfaites, et la seconde comprendra celles de l'ordre géométrique, c'est-à-dire méthodique et accompli [. . .].[36]

In this work, as Buford Norman has explained, 'Pascal had two subjects to discuss—the method of demonstrating truths in

---

[34] Although the analysis of words in this book will be centred particularly on the *Pensées*, I shall refer frequently to Pascal's other writings both to examine important similarities and to underline significant differences. It is interesting, e.g. to see how certain terms are particularly suited to the apologetic aims contained within the *Pensées* as opposed to the polemical demands of a work like the *Lettres provinciales*.
[35] A. Arnauld and P. Nicole, *La Logique ou l'art de penser*, ed. P. Clair and F. Girbal (Paris, 1981; first published 1662), 21. See J. Mesnard's exhaustive commentary on the early edns. of *De l'esprit géométrique* in *Œuvres complètes*, iii. 360–89.
[36] Seuil, 348–9.

geometry and the way of ordering, or organizing them'.[37] With such an emphasis on geometry, another title which appears with the better known *De l'esprit géométrique*, 'Réflexions sur la géométrie en général', would seem to reflect more accurately its subject.

Thus, if we are to relate *De l'esprit géométrique* to the *Pensées*, it would seem misguided to associate the specifically mathematical concerns of rules for definitions, axioms, and demonstrations in the former with the use of language in the latter. Indeed, it is difficult to find ample direct use of geometrical reasoning in the *Pensées* other than in the Wager fragment, L418, and the passage on the 'Disproportion de l'homme', L199, which takes up the idea of 'deux infinis' as it appears in *De l'esprit géométrique*.[38] Whereas Arnauld and Nicole directly adopted these formulae in *La Logique* to discuss language and the replacement of rhetoric with logic,[39] nowhere in the *Pensées* do we find an evaluation of language in these terms.

Significantly, certain words which play an essential role in Pascal's mathematical writings and *De l'esprit géométrique*, as well as in *La Logique*, hardly feature in the *Pensées*. The word *axiome*, for example, does not appear at all. Even the noun *définition* is used only six times in its singular or plural form, three instances of which appear in L512, 'Différence entre l'esprit de géométrie et l'esprit de finesse', where the inadequacy of a purely geometrical method is emphasized:

Et ainsi il est rare que les géomètres soient fins et que les fins soient géomètres, à cause que les géomètres veulent traiter géométriquement ces choses fines et se rendent ridicules, voulant commencer par les définitions et ensuite par les principes, ce qui n'est pas la manière d'agir en cette sorte de raisonnement. (L512)[40]

---

[37] *Portraits of Thought*, 65.
[38] H. Davidson, in *The Origins of Certainty: Means and Meanings in Pascal's 'Pensées'* (Chicago, 1979), 12–27, distinguishes between different kinds of proof in the *Pensées*: 'geometrical', of which he admits there are very few to be found, 'syllogistic', 'dialectical', and 'pragmatic'. Cf. P. Topliss, in *The Rhetoric of Pascal* (Amsterdam, 1966), 187–238, who divides proofs into two categories, 'psychological proofs' and 'historical proofs'. [39] See e.g. I. ix; I. xii; IV.
[40] The other 3 appearances of 'définition' in the *Pensées*, in L66 and L830, seem also to be unrelated to the geometrical concerns in *De l'esprit géométrique*. In L66, the dialectician is attempting to evaluate the nature of human justice, and fragment L830 is devoted specifically to miracles.

Another term, *méthode*, which is used frequently in *De l'esprit géométrique* and which occurs exhaustively in Pascal's mathematical writings,[41] makes one solitary appearance in the *Pensées*, in a section concerned with the 'confusion' of Montaigne.[42] Rather, it is the word *ordre* which assumes a greater importance in the *Pensées*, as I shall go on to consider in Chapter 2.

It is evident, therefore, that the two works cannot easily complement each other. Thomas Carr, in a recent study on *Descartes and the Resilience of Rhetoric*, successfully identifies this division:

> Pascal's premature death left to scholars the task of harmonizing the theory found in *De l'esprit géométrique*, which explicitly does not apply to religious questions, with the conversion-oriented rhetoric of the *Pensées*. The first, as its title suggests, requires univocal definitions as the basis of tightly reasoned proofs, while the second allows for paradox, digression, and figures of speech.[43]

De l'esprit géométrique, along with *La Logique*, remains a work of Cartesian orientation, where rational demonstration prevails, and where the order of Charity (as named by Pascal in L298) plays no part.[44] It is no wonder that Arnauld and Nicole remained ambivalent towards the *Pensées*, as is evident in the omissions and additions in the 1670 Port-Royal edition. To quote Carr again, Arnauld and Nicole in *La Logique*, 'more confident than Pascal in the mind's power to know and to demonstrate truths, even those in religion, [. . .] have less need for persuasion'.[45] Rather, the concern with the precise definition of terms in the *Lettres provinciales* comes closer to the geometrical method of reasoning preferred in *La Logique*.[46]

---

[41] e.g. *Traité des ordres numériques* (Seuil, 68); *Des caractères de divisibilité des nombres déduits de la somme de leurs chiffres* (Seuil, 84); *Sommation des puissances numériques* (Seuil, 93–4).

[42] 'De la confusion de Montaigne, qu'il avait bien senti le défaut d'une droite méthode' (L780).

[43] T. M. Carr, *Descartes and the Resilience of Rhetoric: Varieties of Cartesian Rhetorical Theory* (Carbondale, Ill., 1990), 81–2.

[44] See M. Le Guern, *Pascal et Descartes* (Paris, 1971), 28–40, for a detailed account of the influence of Descartes on *De l'esprit géométrique*.

[45] p. 85. For a detailed analysis of the complexities involved in the 1st edn. of the *Pensées*, see McKenna, *De Pascal à Voltaire*, i. 1–159. See also L. Cognet's 'Le Jugement de Port-Royal sur Pascal', in *Blaise Pascal: L'Homme et l'œuvre*, 11–45.

[46] H. Davidson, in *Audience, Words and Art*, 118–35, provides a useful comparison between *De l'esprit géométrique* and the *Lettres provinciales*. See also

It should be noted, however, that despite the fact that *De l'esprit géométrique* is dominated by a belief in the clarity of geometric definitions, Pascal was even here acutely aware of the limitations of language. Not only are there some words 'incapables d'être définis', but they can be understood through means which are infinitely superior to language, 'parce que la nature nous en a elle-même donné, *sans paroles*, une intelligence plus nette que celle que l'art nous acquiert par nos explications'.[47] This 'intelligence' can be related to the function of *cœur* in L110. Elsewhere in *De l'esprit géométrique*, its superiority over language is reiterated, where it is described as 'une extrême clarté naturelle, qui convainc la raison plus puissamment que le discours'.[48]

If we are to discover any major parallels between *De l'esprit géométrique* and the *Pensées*, it is in the psychological assessment of persuasion, the role of 'agrément', an aspect which Pascal introduces but does not fully develop in *De l'esprit géométrique*. He acknowledges that, where reasoned demonstration (through 'entendement') is preferable in an ideal world (it is this ideal 'nature' to which he refers), man's 'volonté' is more difficult to assess but more in keeping with man's corrupt state and with the art of persuading others:

Personne n'ignore qu'il y a deux entrées par où les opinions sont reçues dans l'âme, qui sont ses deux principales puissances, l'entendement et la volonté. La plus naturelle est celle de l'entendement, car on ne devrait jamais consentir qu'aux vérités démontrées; mais la plus ordinaire, quoique contre la nature, est celle de la volonté; car tout ce qu'il y a d'hommes sont presque toujours emportés à croire non pas par la preuve, mais par l'agrément.[49]

This attempt to understand the *psychological* motivations of his readers counters the approach of Arnauld and Nicole in *La*

D. Descotes's 'Pascal, rhétoricien de la géométrie', *Cahiers de l'Association Internationale des Études Françaises*, 40 (1988), 251, where he provides the ingenious argument that Pascal's mathematical writings are as concerned with rhetoric as his later works: 'le souci de la mise en forme rhétorique et littéraire a orienté toute son œuvre.' Despite a useful analysis of the *Lettres de A. Dettonville*, Descotes does not make any distinction between the desire for clarity in the earlier writings and the deliberate use of ambiguity in the *Pensées*. See also Descotes, *L'Argumentation chez Pascal* (Paris, 1993), for a full discussion of the different kinds of rhetoric in Pascal's writings.

[47] Seuil, 350. My italics.
[48] Ibid. 352.
[49] Ibid. 355.

Logique. As Antony McKenna stresses, 'Pascal formule les principes psychologiques dont Arnauld et Nicole dénoncent les conséquences'.[50]

The notion in this section of *De l'esprit géométrique* of the complexities of the term 'volonté' and its necessary role in the art of persuasion finds a strong parallel in a 1609 translation by Jean Goulu of Epictetus, which Pascal is known to have used for his discussions in the *Entretien avec M. de Sacy*.[51] The similarities which can be found between *De l'esprit géométrique* and a chapter in the *Propos*, entitled 'De la faculté de bien dire', add plausibility to Jean Mesnard's hypothesis that the *Entretien* and *De l'esprit géométrique* are contemporary.[52] In the chapter on 'bien dire', Epictetus contrasts two 'puissances', 'la faculté de bien dire' and 'volonté', also called 'la puissance élective'. It is interesting that Pascal combines rather than contrasts these two concepts in his passage on the art of persuasion. Epictetus sees the dangers of 'la faculté de bien dire, qui pare et farde les paroles',[53] but recognizes also its necessity. Similarly, man's 'volonté' can be used to both positive and negative ends. Although Pascal was to reject the reliance of the Stoics on their own will and forbearance in the *Entretien* and the *Pensées*, we find here a foretaste of the major opposition between *misère* and *félicité* which dominates so many fragments, and an acknowledgement of the role which 'la faculté de bien dire', or, to use a Pascalian term, 'l'art d'agréer', can play:

> Bref c'est elle [la puissance élective] qui est cause de nostre misere si elle est negligée, et cause de nostre felicité si elle est bien et soigneusement cultivée. Mais de vouloir oster la faculté de bien parler, et dire qu'il n'y en a poinct en effect, ce seroit estre non seulement ingrat et mesconnaissant envers ceux qui nous l'ont donnee, mais aussi lasche et coüard.[54]

[50] *De Pascal à Voltaire*, ii. 714.
[51] See P. Courcelle's edn. of the *Entretien* (Paris, 1960); also J. Mesnard's notes in his introduction to the *Entretien*, *Œuvres complètes*, iii. 100.
[52] See Mesnard's introduction to *De l'esprit géométrique* in *Œuvres complètes*, iii. 372. See also his n. 2, p. 142, and n. 1, p. 143. H. Gouhier's suggestion, in *Cartésianisme et Augustinisme au XVIIe siècle* (Paris, 1978), 183, that part of *De l'esprit géométrique*, which he sees as two separate works, was written as late as 1660 (and therefore concurrent with later stages of the *Pensées*), seems to me implausible. L887, the only surviving original fragment which mentions Descartes directly, was written on the paper with the watermark 'Cadran1/B cœur C', which dates, according to P. Ernst, from Sept.–Oct. 1656. This would support Mesnard's hypothesis.
[53] *Les Propos et Le Manuel*, trans. J. Goulu (Paris, 1609), 298.
[54] Ibid. 301.

Pascal makes the point in *De l'esprit géométrique* that he will confine himself to mathematical reasoning, because he only feels capable of defining rules for such methods. But the 'art d'agréer' remains a subject of fascination for him:

> la manière d'agréer est bien sans comparaison plus difficile, plus subtile, plus utile et plus admirable; aussi, si je n'en traite pas, c'est parce que je n'en suis pas capable; et je m'y sens tellement disproportionné, que je crois la chose absolument impossible.[55]

Although Pascal felt incapable of defining rules for such an art in *De l'esprit géométrique*, I contend that the *Pensées* represent a different attempt to understand this other aspect of persuasion, through his use and analysis of language. The complexity of achieving this aim is reflected in the *Pensées* in the multiplicity of voices and in the fragmentation and constant preoccupation with the diverse meanings of words, which I intend to introduce in Chapter 1 and to develop in later sections as the central burden of my argument.

It would seem, therefore, that Pascal moved from the Cartesian basis of *De l'esprit géométrique* to a more anti-Cartesian stance in the *Pensées*. The root of the persuasive process in the *Pensées* comes not from those influenced by Descartes but rather from the inspiration of St Augustine.

It should be noted here that there were many instances in the seventeenth century, even at Port-Royal, of Cartesian thought being associated with Augustinianism. The Protestant Jurieu even went so far as to insinuate that 'les théologiens de Port-Royal ont autant d'attachement pour le Cartésianisme que pour le Christianisme'.[56] Henri Gouhier makes an important differentiation in his *Cartésianisme et Augustinisme au XVIIe Siècle* between what he calls the 'cartésianisme augustinisé' of some writers and the 'augustinisme cartésianisé' of others.[57] In the latter category, amongst whom he counts most significantly Antoine Arnauld, he writes of 'un augustinisme teinté de cartésianisme', where 'on va vers un augustinisme plus intimement cartésianisé lorsqu'il y a

---

[55] Seuil, 356.
[56] Quoted by G. Lewis in 'Augustinisme et Cartésianisme à Port-Royal', in J. Dijksterhuis (ed.), *Descartes et le Cartésianisme hollandais* (Amsterdam, 1951), 131.
[57] *Cartésianisme et Augustinisme au XVIIe siècle*, 14. These two categories become the titles of chs. 3 and 4 of the book.

volonté raisonnée et publiquement exprimée de retrouver saint Augustin dans Descartes'.[58] Even at Port-Royal, a distinction is made between 'l'admiration mitigée de Nicole pour la nouvelle philosophie et le cartésianisme militant d'Arnauld'.[59] Moreover, as Geneviève Lewis points out in her article 'Augustinisme et Cartésianisme à Port-Royal', despite the links between Cartesian and Augustinian thought, they should not be overestimated: 'l'affinité métaphysique entre le cartésianisme et l'augustinianisme ne portait que sur quelques points de départ'.[60]

Pascal, on the other hand, makes no direct connection in the *Pensées* between Descartes and Augustine. Only in *De l'esprit géométrique* does he refer to them both in the same passage, and even here it is in a way negative towards Descartes.[61] It is significant also that books like Louis de la Forge's *Traité de l'esprit de l'homme* and Jacques Rohault's *Entretiens sur la philosophie*, which, as Gouhier puts it, 'font de la parenté avec l'augustinisme un thème majeur de l'apologétique cartésienne',[62] were published only after Pascal's death. It is clear, therefore, that direct links in an apologetic context between Descartes and Augustine played no role in the *Pensées*. In Gouhier's words, neither Pascal's 'travaux ni les circonstances ne le portent à s'intéresser à la parenté possible de Descartes avec saint Augustin'.[63] Moreover, as can be seen in the explicit objections to Descartes in fragments L553, L887 and L1001,[64] he differed from his contemporaries at Port-Royal, even Nicole, who was less Cartesian in outlook than Arnauld. As E. D. James explains,

> Nicole's readiness to discuss and use Cartesianism in an apologetic context, and the very juxtaposition of intuition and rational argument in proving God's existence, contrast with Pascal's rejection of philosophical arguments and his restriction of the sphere of intuition to the recognition by man of his need of a Redeemer.[65]

---

[58] *Cartésianisme et Augustinisme au XVIIe siècle*, 89.
[59] Ibid. 89. Cf. J. Miel, 'Pascal, Port-Royal, and Cartesian Linguistics', *Journal of the History of Ideas*, 30 (1969), 262: 'Cartesianism was accepted at Port-Royal precisely insofar as it was found to be compatible with Augustinianism.'
[60] 'Augustinisme et Cartésianisme à Port-Royal', 181.
[61] See Seuil, 358.
[62] *Cartésianisme et Augustinisme au XVIIe siècle*, 142. [63] Ibid. 146.
[64] For an analysis of sections of the *Pensées* where the influence of Descartes can be discerned, see Le Guern, *Pascal et Descartes*.
[65] Pierre Nicole, *Jansenist and Humanist* (The Hague, 1972), 72.

Both Pascal and Nicole follow Augustine in their appeal to original sin as the explanation of man's condition, but it is Pascal who makes it the very foundation of his work. Indeed, as Philippe Sellier has put it, 'la théologie augustinienne de la grâce est le soleil de son œuvre'.[66] The *Écrits sur la grâce* show most clearly his fundamental Augustinianism:

Ils [Disciples de Saint Augustin] considèrent deux états dans la nature humaine:
L'un est celui auquel elle a été créée dans Adam, saine, sans tache, juste et droite, sortant des mains de Dieu, duquel rien ne peut partir que pur, saint et parfait;
L'autre est l'état où elle a été réduite par le péché et la révolte du premier homme, et par lequel elle est devenue souillée, abominable et détestable aux yeux de Dieu.[67]

It is this doctrine of the Fall which forms part of Catholic belief and which was made central by Augustine.

The notion of the two states of man was taken up in the seventeenth century with especial vigour by Jansenius in his *Augustinus* (1640). Moreover, the three books of his treatise *L'État de nature pure*, for example, were devoted to rejecting the idea that Augustine might perceive man's present state as emanating directly from God.[68] Similarly, another prominent Augustinian, Jean du Vergier de Hauranne, the abbé of Saint-Cyran, stressed in a letter to Arnauld d'Andilly the importance of man's fall from grace: 'il est besoin de savoir que le premier homme et tous les hommes dans lui sont tombés par le péché, non seulement dans un abîme de boue qui les a salis et noircis en toutes les parties de leurs corps et de leurs âmes, mais aussi sur des pointes de pierres qui les ont brisés et froissés en tous leurs corps et en toutes leurs âmes'.[69]

As we shall see in the course of this book, man's two states form the main thread both of Pascal's assessment of the human condition and of the language which depicts it. It is this central tenet which I shall call the Augustinian basis of the *Pensées*. Language belongs to

---

[66] *Pascal et Saint Augustin* (Paris, 1970), 619. Cf. Julien-Eymard d'Angers, who speaks of Pascal's 'augustinisme foncier', in *Pascal et ses précurseurs: L'Apologétique en France de 1580 à 1670* (Paris, 1954), 230. [67] Seuil, 312.
[68] See Sellier, *Pascal et Saint Augustin*, 236–7.
[69] Quoted by G. Delassault in *La Pensée janséniste en dehors de Pascal* (Paris, 1963), 31.

man in his fallen state and can only operate within the context of his corruption.

Augustine himself was deeply concerned with how far language communicates meaning about reality. In *De Magistro*, for example, he starts with the acknowledgement that it is only through words that human beings can discuss truth. However, words only convey meaning in an ambivalent and limited way and can be used to conceal and deceive. In this respect, language indicates man's corruption. He accepts the view that disputes are often conducted over words ('de verbo') and not that to which they refer ('non de re'); in the first case, a nominalistic (or stipulative) approach to definition is suggested; in the second, Augustine refers to scientific (or apodictic) definition, which cannot arise in language in view of the limitations placed on man's reason and perception.[70]

Augustine went on in other works like the *Soliloquia*,[71] *Sermones*,[72] and *Enarrationes in Psalmos*[73] to contemplate the communication of truth not through language, but through an internal sense which is intangible and inaudible. In *De Trinitate*, he calls it an internal word ('verbum') which existed before language and which relates directly to man's original perfection in God.[74] The individual thinker is deemed unable, in his fallenness, to attain truth by himself, but rather he is able to find the truth through Christ, the revealing Word of God, who is described as the 'magister interior', the inward teacher. As Jean-Claude Fraisse puts it, 'cette parole intérieure est identique chez tous les hommes, contrairement au langage [. . .]. Elle est ce que cherche toute pensée, et, lorsqu'elle y est parvenue, le désir originaire de vérité se convertit en amour de la chose connue.'[75]

This Augustinian notion of human language indicating man's

---

[70] See Augustine, *De Magistro*, xiii. 43. Where possible, all quotations of Augustine will be taken from 17th-c. translations. See H. Brinkmann's *Mittelalterliche Hermeneutik* (Tübingen, 1980), 24–6, for a fuller analysis of Augustine's distinction between *vox* and *res* in *De Magistro* and *De Doctrina christiana*.

[71] e.g. i. 9.   [72] e.g. 117. 7 onwards.   [73] e.g. 99. 5.

[74] See *De Trinitate*, xv. xi. 20.

[75] *Saint Augustin* (Paris, 1968), 30. See I. Maclean, *Interpretation and Meaning in the Renaissance: The Case of Law* (Cambridge, 1992), 158–64, for a useful study on the Renaissance application of *vox cordis*, *vox conceptus*, and *vox articulata*: 'In this tripartite scheme, three languages are distinguished: the language of the heart or of faith, which cannot lie and cannot be ambiguous; the language of intellectual life which can be deceptive, but which is unambiguous; and the fallible, fallen language of human communication which can be both deceptive and ambiguous' (p. 162).

fallen nature was taken up in the seventeenth century. Of the many writers influenced by Augustine, I have chosen in the course of this book to refer particularly to the Oratorian Jean-François Sénault. Two books in particular, *L'Homme criminel* (1644) and *L'Homme chrestien* (1648), throw light on the profoundly Augustinian foundation of his work, which is at once discernible in the subtitles: 'la Corruption de la Nature par le Peché, selon les Sentimens de S. Augustin', and 'la Reparation de la Nature par la Grace'. For Sénault, the fallibility of language was an extension of man's corrupt nature: 'comme la Nature est criminelle, il ne faut pas s'estonner que son langage soit corrompu'.[76]

Although the influence of scholasticism in seventeenth-century France cannot be underestimated, I have chosen not to concentrate closely on this aspect, given Pascal's own lack of training in scholastic thought,[77] and the fact that his quotation from or reference to writers such as Aristotle, Plato and Cicero is largely channelled through his reading of Montaigne and Augustine.[78] However, as there is no doubt that Pascal was thoroughly conversant with Latin, wherever a Latin term has clear authority over a French term, I shall refer to it. I shall draw upon many differing viewpoints, for each of them offers an interesting insight into the problems involved with the function of language in the *Pensées*. Two writers in particular who were widely read in the worldly circles, Montaigne and Charron, play an important part in the *Pensées*, and I shall refer to them often. Moreover, Pascal was working within the sphere of a strong apologetic tradition, and I shall relate Pascal's use of words to that of prominent apologists of the time.

In a study of this kind, where certain key words are studied in depth, there remains a danger in concentrating on individual terms at the expense of broader semantic fields.[79] However, I hope to

---

[76] *L'Homme criminel*, 403. See Ch. 1 for a fuller discussion of this passage.
[77] See the introduction to P. Sellier's 1991 edn. of the *Pensées*, 10.
[78] See B. Croquette, *Pascal et Montaigne* (Geneva, 1974), and Sellier, *Pascal et Saint Augustin*.
[79] See S. Ullmann's *Semantics* (Oxford, 1970; first published 1962), esp. ch. 9, pt. ii, for a discussion of associative and semantic fields. Cf. also G. Matoré, in *La Méthode en lexicologie: Domaine français* (Paris, 1953), who distinguishes between 'mots-témoins' and 'mots-clés', the latter being 'une unité lexicologique exprimant une société, [...] un être, un sentiment, une idée' (p. 68), and particularly useful in the study of stylistics.

show the particular significance and, in many cases, the autonomy of the words I have chosen within the context of the *Pensées*. Where individual terms are clearly linked to other words, I shall discuss those words.

The main body of this book is divided into three sections. In Part I, I shall explore the relevance of language and order to the persuasive process in the *Pensées*. The central section, Part II, will be devoted to a detailed examination of six key terms. The first three, *inconstance*, *ennui*, and *inquiétude*, are the nouns used by the dialectician in L24 to describe what at this stage we might call the 'negative' side of 'la condition de l'homme'. The second three, *repos*, *bonheur/félicité*, and *justice*, all relate back to the first three nouns and can be termed 'positive' aspects of the human condition. I have chosen these words as examples of how language depicting man's state is manipulated by the dialectician, not as an exhaustive survey of all central terms in the *Pensées*. At the end of each chapter devoted to the six central terms (Chapters 3–8), I shall include a tabled summary of the different categories of meaning which I have devised for each word. In Part III, I shall draw together the findings of Part II and relate them to the notion of truth, which underpins all aspects of the human condition in the *Pensées*.

Part I

Language and Order in the *Penseés*

1
Language in the *Pensées*

> PANCRACE. La parole a été donnée à l'homme pour expliquer sa pensée; et tout ainsi que les pensées sont les portraits des choses, de même nos paroles sont-elles les portraits de nos pensées. [...] Expliquez-moi donc votre pensée par la parole, qui est le plus intelligible de tous les signes.
> SGANARELLE. Peste de l'homme!
>
> (Molière, *Le Mariage forcé*, sc. iv)

PAROLE/MOT

Most dictionaries of the period do not explicitly differentiate *parole* from *mot*. However, the *Dictionnaire de l'Académie Françoise* gives a more detailed list of the possible meanings of *parole* than it does of *mot*, thereby distinguishing the one from the other. Among the definitions of *parole* offered by the dictionary, two in particular which underline its difference from *mot* apply to Pascal's use of the term in the *Pensées*. The one refers to *la parole* as 'l'Escriture sainte et les Sermons qui se font pour l'expliquer', appearing most often as 'la parole de Dieu'. It would seem that Pascal's use of *parole* in this context represents little more than the accepted usage of it as the Word of God in the Bible.[1]

However, the other definition of *parole* which distinguishes it particularly from *mot* clarifies the important function of *parole* in the *Pensées*. It is defined as 'Mot prononcé', with the example, 'Parole bien articulée mal articulée'. The fact that it is articulated suggests that it forms part of a discourse; this is supported by another definition of *parole* by the *Dictionnaire de l'Académie Françoise* as 'Mot, ou discours pris selon la qualité qu'il est'.[2]

---

[1] *Parole* used in this sense can be found in L272, L483, L485, L919, L965.
[2] The 1680 Richelet dictionary also links *parole* with 'discours', as well as defining *parole* as 'voix articulée'. However, the dictionary does not make any clear distinction between *mot* and *parole*, and describes *mot* as 'tout ce qui se prononce'. Similarly, the 1690 Furetière dictionary does not differentiate between the two, although *parole* is associated with articulation: 'mot articulé d'une ou de plusieurs syllabes, qui sert à expliquer la pensée, et que l'homme est capable de proférer'.

Whereas *mot* need not form part of any articulated discourse, *parole* is inseparable from the communication of a particular message. Indeed, this is substantiated by the dictionary's choice of such adjectives as 'civiles', 'obligeantes', 'amiables' [*sic*], 'facheuses', 'inciviles', 'outrageuses', and 'outrageantes' to accompany 'paroles' in its list of examples, for all presuppose some form of reaction or response. Taking into account this distinction between *mot* and *parole* as set down by the Académie dictionary, we may see more clearly how *parole* plays a significant role in the *Pensées*, for even many of the most incomplete fragments presuppose a reader or audience:[3] the beginning of L428, for example, which presents the undoubted apologetic aspect of many of the fragments, also shows the fact that the dialectician has an audience in mind:

Avant que d'entrer dans les preuves de la religion chrétienne, je trouve nécessaire de représenter l'injustice des hommes qui vivent dans l'indifférence de chercher la vérité d'une chose qui leur est si importante, et qui les touche de si près. (L428)

The noun 'preuves' is complemented by the verb 'représenter', both of which suggest the dialectician's concern to communicate a message to an implied reader, in this case so that he can attempt to provoke those men who are indifferent to their fate to search for truth. Furthermore, in another fragment devoted to miracles, 'paroles' are exposed as man's only means of persuading others of that truth:

Ce n'est point ici le pays de la vérité; elle erre inconnue parmi les hommes. Dieu l'a couverte d'un voile qui la laisse méconnaître à ceux qui n'entendent pas sa voix; le lieu est ouvert au blasphème et même sur des vérités au moins bien apparentes. Si l'on publie les vérités de l'Évangile on en publie de contraires, et on obscurcit les questions, en sorte que le peuple ne peut discerner. Et on demande: qu'avez-vous qui vous fasse plutôt croire que les autres, quel signe faites-vous? Vous n'avez que des paroles et nous aussi. Si vous aviez des miracles, bien. Cela est une vérité que la doctrine doit être soutenue par les miracles dont on abuse pour blasphémer la doctrine. Et si les miracles arrivent on dit que les miracles ne suffisent pas

---

[3] Cf. M. Le Guern, *Pascal et Descartes* (Paris, 1971): 'les notes rapides, qui étaient destinées à n'avoir d'autre lecteur que Pascal lui-même, voisinent avec les textes rédigés ou simplement ébauchés, mais qui constituent déjà, au moins à l'état embryonnaire, une œuvre littéraire, puisque l'auteur, en les écrivant, songe au lecteur éventuel' (p. 41).

sans la doctrine et c'est une autre vérité pour blasphémer les miracles. (L840)

In this fragment, 'paroles' form part of the argument furnished by 'le peuple'.[4] According to them, without the aid of miracles, words are the only means that either side of a debate possesses in order to present an argument.[5] Clearly, *parole* is used here as a 'mot prononcé' or part of a 'discours', in accordance with the definition offered by the *Dictionnaire de l'Académie Françoise*. Yet, in this context, words are seen to be easily corruptible. As with *interprétation*,[6] *paroles* are manipulated to communicate one's own viewpoint. Here, truth may be abused in order to blaspheme against doctrine just as it may also be abused to blaspheme against miracles. Conflicting truths are expressed in identical words; language on its own cannot act as an objective pointer to truth, an aspect of which is strongly conveyed in another fragment:

Ceux qui sont dans le dérèglement disent à ceux qui sont dans l'ordre que ce sont eux qui s'éloignent de la nature et ils la croient suivre, comme ceux qui sont dans un vaisseau croient que ceux qui sont au bord fuient. Le langage est pareil de tous côtés. (L697)[7]

Pascal's use of 'parole' and 'paroles' in Letter 16 of the *Lettres provinciales* further supports this sense of the failure of words to convey an unambiguous message. At the beginning of the letter, for

---

[4] In this complex fragment, with its varied use of the unspecified 'on', I have taken 'On demande' to refer back to 'le peuple'. I shall discuss this fragment at greater length in the final chapter.

[5] In another fragment on miracles, L830, words ('paroles') directed towards God are surpassed by the effects of miracles, a view which again suggests that words by themselves are not sufficient to lead man towards truth: 'S'il ne suffit pas qu'il soit au-dessus de la force naturelle des moyens qu'on y emploie; ma pensée étant que tout effet est miraculeux [lorsqu'il] surpasse la force naturelle des moyens qu'on y emploie. Ainsi j'appelle miraculeux la guérison d'une maladie faite par l'attouchement d'une sainte Relique, la guérison d'un démoniaque faite par l'invocation du nom de Jésus, etc., parce que ces effets surpassent la force naturelle des paroles par lesquelles on invoque Dieu et la force naturelle d'une relique [qui] ne peuvent guérir les malades et chasser les démons.'

[6] See my discussion on *interprétation*, esp. the section on L529.

[7] In Montaigne's *Apologie de Raimond Sebond*, we find a very similar approach to language; words are inherently deceptive: 'En la parole la plus nette, pure et parfaicte qui puisse estre, combien de faulceté et de mensonge a lon faict naistre? quelle heresie n'y a trouvé des fondements assez et tesmoignages, pour entreprendre et pour se maintenir? C'est pour cela que les autheurs de telles erreurs ne se veulent jamais departir de cette preuve, du tesmoignage de l'interpretation des mots', in *Essais* (*Œuvres complètes*, ed. M. Rat, Paris, 1962, II. xii. 569–70).

example, the writer condemns the Jesuits for their malicious abuse of Jansenius and of 'quelques paroles ambiguës d'une de ses lettres qui, étant capables d'un bon sens, doivent être prises en bonne part, selon l'esprit de l'Eglise, et ne peuvent être prises autrement que selon l'esprit de votre Société'.[8] Through the deliberate use of litotes, the writer asserts that the fact that a few words were ambiguous and that the Jesuits were able to misrepresent them shows that language can easily be misinterpreted for one's own ends. Later in the letter, the Jesuits are castigated for corrupting the words of Arnauld and are told that they ought to have 'révéré dans ses paroles ces saintes vérités, au lieu de les corrompre pour y trouver une hérésie qui n'y fut jamais, et qui n'y saurait être'.[9] Elsewhere in the letter, the polemicist[10] finds it necessary to qualify the truth of a statement, for 'paroles' in themselves do not seem adequate to prove his point:

Que répondez-vous, mes Pères, à des témoignages si évidents, non pas seulement de paroles, mais d'actions; et non pas de quelques actions particulières, mais de toute la suite d'une vie entièrement consacrée à l'adoration de Jésus-Christ résidant sur nos autels?[11]

Perhaps the major difference between the use of 'paroles' in this letter and the function of words in the *Pensées* lies in the fact that the polemicist, despite his recognition of the inadequacy of language, believes in the internal truth of words, as we saw in the above examples. In the *Pensées*, on the other hand, Pascal calls into question man's very ability to communicate truth through language, an aspect which I shall develop in the course of this section.[12]

---

[8] Seuil 446.   [9] Ibid. 450.

[10] I am following R. Parish in his use of the word 'polemicist'. See *Pascal's 'Lettres provinciales': A Study in Polemic* (Oxford, 1989), 131–45: 'the Montalte persona definitively sheds his disguise of ingenuousness (and thus his *raison d'être*) at the beginning of the eleventh letter, to be supplanted by the anonymous but direct and implicated epistoler (the polemicist), addressing the Society ('Mes Révérends Pères'), which is then specified further when a single addressee, Père Annat, is named in the seventeenth letter' (p. 131).   [11] Seuil 447.

[12] Towards the end of Letter 16 of the *Lettres provinciales*, the writer changes his line of fire from a defence of the truth of statements to an attack on the Jesuits' misuse of language: 'Mais qui ne sera surpris de l'aveuglement de votre conduite? Car, à qui prétendez-vous persuader, sur votre seule parole, sans la moindre apparence de preuve et avec toutes les contradictions imaginables, que des évêques et des prêtres qui n'ont fait autre chose que prêcher la grâce de Jésus-Christ, la pureté de l'Evangile et les obligations du baptême, avaient renoncé à leur baptême, à l'Evangile et à Jésus-Christ' (Seuil 452). Words alone cannot be hoped to prove the truth of such a statement.

It must be pointed out that Pascal does not always make a clear distinction between *mot* and *parole*. In L109, for example, 'mots' can easily be replaced by 'paroles'. A detailed analysis is not necessary at this stage,[13] but it would be useful to assess the status of words in this fragment. It is entitled 'Contre le pyrrhonisme', and clearly represents an attempt to show the weaknesses of the sceptics' opposition to the dogmatists. In examining the viewpoint of the dogmatists that there exists a natural link between words and things, Pascal acknowledges that some such regularity in the use of words does indeed seem to exist, certainly enough to discredit the systematic doubt of the 'pyrrhoniens'. However, there is still no guarantee that the use of the same word by different people would imply that they have the same idea, despite the likelihood of conformity of word and idea:

(C'est donc une chose étrange qu'on ne peut définir ces choses sans les obscurcir. Nous en parlons à toute heure.)[14] Nous supposons que tous les conçoivent de même sorte. Mais nous le supposons bien gratuitement, car nous n'en avons aucune preuve. Je vois bien qu'on applique ces mots dans les mêmes occasions, et que toutes les fois que deux hommes voient un corps changer de place ils expriment tous deux la vue de ce même objet par le même mot, en disant l'un et l'autre qu'il s'est mû, et de cette conformité d'application on tire une puissante conjecture d'une conformité d'idée, mais cela n'est pas absolument convaincant de la dernière conviction quoiqu'il y ait bien à parier pour l'affirmative, puisqu'on sait qu'on tire souvent les mêmes conséquences des suppositions différentes. (L109)

---

[13] See P. Force, *Le Problème herméneutique chez Pascal* (Paris, 1989), 146–7; A. Pugh, *The Composition of Pascal's 'Apologia'* (Toronto, 1984), 307–8; H. Gouhier, *Blaise Pascal: Conversion et apologétique* (Paris, 1986), 173–4; and Le Guern, *Pascal et Descartes*, 75–6, for further discussion of L109. P. Ernst's reconstruction of the paper on which the fragments were written shows that two other fragments concerned with the nature of language, L784 and L789, were written on the same paper type (with the mark of a bunch of grapes) as L109. I shall discuss both fragments in this chapter.

[14] These sentences in brackets were deleted by Pascal. A problem in analysing the *Pensées* stems from the many sections which Pascal himself crossed out, for it is debatable as to what value one should assign to them. As it is possible that he would have kept some deleted fragments to place elsewhere in the completed work, I have therefore decided to consider, on the whole, those longer deleted sections as of equal value as the undeleted fragments, although I shall point out all quotations from deleted passages. Particular words or phrases which were crossed out by Pascal provide a useful point of comparison, and I shall refer to certain terms which were replaced by others in the *Recueil original*.

Words, as they appear above, retain their ambiguity. Reason alone cannot attain truth, which adds impetus to the sceptics' arguments against the dogmatists. Yet, the sceptics fail to account for the role which 'la clarté naturelle',[15] however obscured, plays in all matters of reasoning:

> Cela suffit pour embrouiller au moins la matière, non que cela éteigne absolument la clarté naturelle qui nous assure de ces choses. Les académiciens auraient gagé, mais cela la ternit et trouble les dogmatistes, à la gloire de la cabale pyrrhonienne qui consiste à cette ambiguïté ambiguë, et dans une certaine obscurité douteuse dont nos doutes ne peuvent ôter toute la clarté, ni nos lumières naturelles en chasser toutes les ténèbres. (L109)

The argument in L109 shifts from one side to the other, and there is indeed a strong sense of ambiguity. As we have seen in the other fragments, words and ideas form part of this instability. We find, as Pierre Force puts it, that 'le caractère coutumier de l'usage des mots est, dans un premier temps, un argument contre le caractère naturel des relations de signification, et, dans un deuxième temps, un argument fort, quoique non décisif, en sa faveur'.[16]

Similarly, words by themselves, especially in the Bible, cannot suffice to establish the truth of a proposition. It is at this point that a third term, 'sens', must be brought into the argument. As Pascal writes in the *Écrits sur la grâce*, it is through meanings ('sens') that one can attempt to solve apparent contradictions:

> Car vous savez que la contrariété des propositions est dans le sens et non pas dans les paroles, autrement l'Écriture serait pleine de contradictions, comme quand il est dit: *le Père est plus grand que moi*; et qu'il est dit ailleurs que *Jésus-Christ est égal à Dieu*; *Si je me glorifie moi-même*, etc. De sorte que je me glorifie moi-même, etc. Et: *on est justifié par la foi sans les œuvres*. Et: *La foi sans les œuvres est morte*. Et tous les autres de cette espèce.[17]

On the other hand, the above use of 'paroles' would seem to be contradicted by L789: 'Un même sens change selon les paroles qui l'expriment. Les sens reçoivent des paroles leur dignité au lieu de la leur donner.' Here, changing meanings are perceived as

---

[15] I take 'la clarté naturelle' as analogous to 'le cœur', as used in L110. See Gouhier, *Blaise Pascal: Conversion et apologétique*, 60–65.
[16] *Le Problème herméneutique chez Pascal*, 147.
[17] Seuil 326. Cf. 322.

receiving their worth from unchanging words. Judging from Pascal's other uses of the word 'dignité' in the *Pensées*,[18] I take it that there is no intentional ambiguity in its appearance here. Indeed, as can be seen in the 1680 Richelet Dictionary, 'la dignité des paroles' occurs as an example of an accepted turn of phrase at that time, with the sense of 'Beauté, grandeur, éclat, noblesse de paroles, de sujet, de matiere'. As opposed to 'paroles' in the other passages which I have quoted, where words cannot stand alone without the influence of interpretation, in L789 'paroles' are used primarily in a theoretical capacity. Words as they are, without any corruptive interpretation, give dignity to meanings. In this fragment, an important distinction must be made between 'un même sens' and 'les sens'. Pierre Force gives a cogent analysis of this differentiation, and it would be useful to quote him at some length:

Il apparaît donc que lorsque Pascal énonce la règle selon laquelle 'un même sens change selon les paroles qui l'expriment', il donne successivement au mot *sens* deux significations différentes. Le sens unique qui est exprimé par des paroles différentes est ce que nous appellerons un sens virtuel. C'est le sens littéral d'une proposition avant son interprétation, catholique ou hérétique. C'est le sens des mots de l'Écriture qui contiennent en germe leur interprétation. Ce 'même sens' est celui sur lequel tous les interprètes tomberont d'accord s'ils suspendent leur interprétation. On voit donc que ce sens unique n'est pas un donné mais une construction. Dans la pratique, un lecteur n'aura pas affaire à des propositions hors contexte, mais au contraire à des phrases liées entre elles et qui se donnent mutuellement leur sens. Ce qui est donné, ce sont donc des sens différents, et non pas un même sens. Parler d'un 'même sens' n'est qu'un artifice d'exposition. Le vrai sens est le sens actuel, celui qui se manifeste dans une énonciation donnée. C'est pour cela que 'les sens reçoivent des paroles leur dignité au lieu de la leur donner'.[19]

Force's commentary serves to reiterate two major factors of Pascal's approach towards words (*paroles*) and meaning (*sens*):

---

[18] Cf. L113, L137, L200, L208, L620, L756, L788, L930, L950. See Z. Klein, *La Notion de dignité humaine dans la pensée de Kant et de Pascal* (Paris, 1968), esp. 93–5. Klein tends to underestimate the deliberate play on the ambiguity of meanings, but I would concur with her view on the unity of the meaning of 'dignité' in the *Pensées*: 'là où Pascal a mis *dignité*, c'est bien de dignité qu'il s'agit' (p. 94). She does recognize, however, the problems associated with the term in a fragment like L756, where the value of 'dignité' is clear but somewhat undermined by the subsequent questioning of the status of 'la pensée': 'Toute la dignité de l'homme est en la pensée, mais qu'est-ce que cette pensée? qu'elle est sotte?' (L756).

[19] *Le Problème herméneutique chez Pascal*, 261–2. See also 256–63.

first, that the meaning of words can only be ascertained within their context; and secondly, that they cannot exist without the presupposition of a reader. In other words, interpretation is integral to all words and meanings, whether it be an author attempting to impose his meaning through a particular arrangement of words or a reader's reaction to a particular text. These two aspects are present within Pascal's assertion that 'Les mots diversement rangés font un divers sens. Et les sens diversement rangés font différents effets' (L784). Words function within a continual 'jeu de différences', as Louis Marin describes it.[20] Indeed, there exists a distinctly theatrical element in Pascal's representation of words and meanings. The use of the word 'effets' in the above fragment strongly suggests an actor-like 'author' manipulating meanings in order to achieve certain effects.[21] However, this conscious theatricality should not be mistaken for frivolity: it forms part of the art of persuasion. As Pascal himself writes in *De l'esprit géométrique*,

L'art de persuader a un rapport nécessaire à la manière dont les hommes consentent à ce qu'on leur propose, et aux conditions des choses qu'on veut faire croire.[22]

Yet, as he stresses later in the same passage, he does not presume to be able to communicate divine truth through the art of persuasion, for God alone is capable of giving truth to human souls. Therefore, the use of theatrical effect, while being a means of persuasion, represents by the same token man's *difference* from God, his inability to impart truth through language. Indeed, it is a condition of man's fallen nature that word (*parole*) and intention, and word and 'effet' remain separate: only in God do they all meet, as is made clear in an important fragment:

En Dieu la parole ne diffère pas de l'intention car il est véritable, ni la

---

[20] *La Critique du discours: Sur la 'Logique' de Port-Royal et les 'Pensées de Pascal* (Paris, 1975), 379: 'L'identité des termes ou du tout est maintenue dans le jeu de différences: ce sont les *mêmes* pensées et les *mêmes* mots qui forment un autre corps de discours, d'*autres* pensées par leur différente disposition.' This in turn goes a long way to an understanding of L696, where Pascal asserts that 'la disposition des matières est nouvelle'. This fragment is discussed in the section on *Ordre*.

[21] I am here considering 'effets' in one particular sense. The meanings of the word as it appears in the *Pensées* are complex. See J. Molino's 'La Raison des effets' in *Méthodes chez Pascal*, and L. Thirouin's 'Raison des effets: Essai d'explication d'un concept pascalien', *XVIIe Siècle*, 134–7 (1982), 31–50.

[22] Seuil 355.

parole de l'effet car il est puissant, ni les moyens de l'effet car il est sage. (L968)[23]

The main function of language must be to convince man of his corruption, of his fall from truth, a fall which in turn explains the obscurities of language: 'Que conclurons-nous de toutes nos obscurités, sinon notre indignité?' (L445).

THE TYRANNY OF SPEECH: *DIRE/CONTREDIRE*

My discussion thus far of *mot*, *parole*, and *sens* leads to an important extension of the notion of language as communication. Speech and reported speech form an integral part of the dialectical process in the *Pensées*. The different verbal forms of *dire*, for example, excluding such related words as *contredire* and *médire*, appear 585 times in the *Pensées*.[24] When we consider that that is the equivalent number of times that the combination of *homme* and *hommes* appears, its full significance can be appreciated. In addition to this, there are 127 examples of different forms of the verb *parler*, some of which I intend to consider in conjunction with my analysis of *dire*.

To return to a fragment on language which I quoted earlier, we find that the verb *dire* is directly linked to the dialectician's depiction of the corruptive power of language: 'Ceux qui sont dans le dérèglement disent à ceux qui sont dans l'ordre que ce sont eux qui s'éloignent de la nature' (L697). Or, rather, the malleability of language lends itself to corruption. It is, like justice in L85, 'une qualité spirituelle', as opposed to a quality like force

---

[23] See my '"Levez le rideau": Images of the Theatre in Pascal's *Pensées*', *French Studies*, 47/3 (July 1993), for a greater development of theatrical imagery in the *Pensées*. The disparity between words and intention in man is captured well by Bourdonné in *Le Courtisan desabusé* (1658), where he asks the reader in the preface to 'considerer plutost mon intention que mes paroles, puis que je me suis laissé aller à escrire mes sentimens sans penser que je n'estois pas orateur'. However, Bourdonné differs from Pascal in that he presupposes a certain clarity in the reader's perception of meaning through intention. Cf. Jacqueline Pascal's letter to her brother just after his definitive conversion, where she stresses the need to 'vous endoctriner par exemple plus que de parole' (19 Jan. 1654, *Œuvres complètes*, ed. Mesnard, iii. 69).

[24] All statistical evidence of this kind is drawn from H. Davidson and P. Dubé's *A Concordance to Pascal's 'Pensées'* (Ithaca, NY, 1975).

which is 'palpable'; yet always it maintains the same appearance: 'le langage est pareil de tous côtés' (L697).[25]

If we compare briefly this approach to language with that of an apologist earlier in the seventeenth century, the difference is marked. In the Jesuit Antoine Sirmond's *La Deffense de la vertu*, which provoked strong opposition from both Arnauld and Jean-Pierre Camus, Bishop of Belley, and in which the views on the love of God are ridiculed in Letter 10 of the *Lettres provinciales*,[26] the value of *dire* and *parler* are perceived in a very different way: 'Que voulez-vous donc dire? qu'entendez-vous par ces mots [. . .]? Parlez clair, et on vous entendra.'[27] Significantly, this extract comes immediately after the first quotation which Pascal takes from *La Deffense de la vertu* in the *Lettres provinciales* and a few pages before the second quotation, so it is likely that he was aware of Sirmond's approach to language.

The abuse and manipulation of words lead to a state which is akin to tyranny. Language becomes an instrument of power:

Tyrannie.
La tyrannie est de vouloir avoir par une voie ce qu'on ne peut avoir que par une autre. On rend différents devoirs aux différents mérites, devoir d'amour à l'agrément, devoir de crainte à la force, devoir de créance à la science.

On doit rendre ces devoirs-là, on est injuste de les refuser, et injuste d'en demander d'autres. Ainsi ces discours sont faux, et tyranniques: je suis beau, donc on doit me craindre, je suis fort donc on doit m'aimer, je suis . . . Et c'est de même être faux et tyrannique de dire: il n'est pas fort, donc je ne l'estimerai pas, il n'est pas habile, donc je ne le craindrai pas. (L58)

It is this kind of tyranny which the dialectician attributes to eloquence in L584: 'Éloquence qui persuade par douceur, non par

---

[25] This was a point made in passing by L. Thirouin in his paper, 'Le Réalisme de Pascal', at the Clermont-Ferrand conference, *Droit et pensée politique autour de Pascal* (Sept. 1990); proceedings published as G. Feyerolles (ed.), *Justice et force: Politiques au temps de Pascal* (Paris, 1993).

[26] Seuil 418. Pascal uses and abridges 2 quotations from *La Deffense de la vertu* (1641), 11–12 and 18–19.

[27] Ibid. 13. Cf. Jean de Silhon in *Les Deux veritez* (1626): 'il y a des propositions et maximes revestues de tant de clarté, et portant en elles mesmes tant d'évidence, qu'à mesme qu'elles sont conceues, elles sont persuadées' (p. 16). However, cf. Silhon's *De l'immortalité de l'âme* (1634), 55, where he relates obscurity of propositions to 'la plus generalle condition du genre humain qui est l'ignorance'.

empire, en tyran non en roi' (L584).²⁸ Indeed, an example listed under 'Tyrannie' in the Académie dictionary accentuates the tyrannical force of eloquence: 'l'eloquence exerce une espece de tyrannie sur les esprits'. Language represents a corruption which extends to a form of tyranny.

This perception of language was especially prevalent in the writings of those who saw themselves as following the teaching of St Augustine. In *L'Homme criminel*, for example, the Oratorian Jean-François Sénault makes this point about language in the section, 'Que l'Eloquence est ennemie de la Raison, de la Verité, et de la Religion':

> Mais comme la Nature est criminelle, il ne faut pas s'estonner que son langage soit corrompu, et comme le Fils de Dieu souffre l'impureté de nostre vie, nous ne devons pas trouver estrange qu'il endure la vanité de nos paroles, jusqu'à ce qu'estant entrez dans la liberté de ses enfans, il nous délivre de la Tyrannie du peché, et de la servitude de l'Eloquence.²⁹

Whereas language by itself indicates natural corruption, the dialectician distinguishes a further kind of wilful tyranny which man can exercise through words. In L780, for example, Montaigne is identified as one such writer who misleads others by design:

> Le sot projet qu'il [Montaigne] a de se peindre et cela non pas en passant et contre ses maximes, comme il arrive à tout le monde de faillir, mais par ses propres maximes et par un dessein premier et principal. Car de dire des sottises par hasard et par faiblesse c'est un mal ordinaire, mais d'en dire par dessein c'est ce qui n'est pas supportable et d'en dire de telles que celles-ci ... (L780)

The deliberate wielding of language as an instrument of power leads to mutual deception. For man, the act of speech cannot be synonymous with human truth, because the truth in its turn can be

---

²⁸ Within this context, 'empire', viewed as justifiable, is used in a very different sense from that in L665: 'L'empire fondé sur l'opinion et l'imagination règne quelque temps et cet empire est doux et volontaire. Celui de la force règne toujours. Ainsi l'opinion est comme la reine du monde mais la force en est le tyran.' In his excellent paper, 'De la tyrannie', presented at Clermont-Ferrand in September 1990, P. Sellier quotes from the 1643 translation by J. Baudouin of Ripa's *Iconologie* to demonstrate the sense of 'empire' as legitimate: 'Elle [la tyrannie] est armée et se tient debout, pour montrer que la vigilance et la force lui sont nécessaires afin de se maintenir [...]. Au lieu de [sic] sceptre, qui est une marque d'empire et de gouvernement légitime, elle tient une épée nue, un mors et un joug' (Paris, 1643, 174). ²⁹ *L'Homme criminel* (1644), 403.

used against those who speak it: 'dire la vérité est utile à celui à qui on la dit, mais désavantageux à ceux qui la disent, parce qu'ils se font haïr' (L978). Consequently, *dire* coincides with deception. To quote Sénault again, 'Si nous parlons c'est plustost pour mesdire que pour edifier'.[30] In the final paragraphs of the fragment devoted to 'amour-propre', L978, it is significant how many times the verbs *dire* and *parler* accompany images of 'cette mutuelle tromperie':

> Ainsie la vie humaine n'est qu'une illusion perpétuelle; on ne fait que s'entre-tromper et s'entre-flatter. Personne ne parle de nous en notre présence comme il en parle en notre absence. L'union qui est entre les hommes n'est fondée que sur cette mutuelle tromperie; et peu d'amitiés subsisteraient, si chacun savait ce que son ami dit de lui lorsqu'il n'y est pas, quoiqu'il en parle alors sincèrement et sans passion.
> L'homme n'est donc que déguisement, que mensonge et hypocrisie, et en soi-même et à l'égard des autres. Il ne veut donc pas qu'on lui dise la vérité. Il évite de la dire aux autres; et toutes ces dispositions, si éloignées de la justice et de la raison, ont une racine naturelle dans son cœur. (L978)

Similarly, the thin line which exists between *dire* and *médire* is reiterated in L606. The advantages of friendship are undermined by language. Words spoken about others lead to mistrust and a sense of instability, only exacerbated by the presence of others:

> Un vrai ami est une chose si avantageuse même pour les plus grands seigneurs, afin qu'il dise du bien d'eux et qu'il les soutienne en leur absence. Même qu'ils doivent tout faire pour en avoir, mais qu'ils choisissent bien, car s'ils font tous leurs efforts pour des sots, cela leur sera inutile quelque bien qu'ils disent d'eux. Et même ils n'en diront pas de bien s'ils se trouvent les plus faibles, car ils n'ont pas d'autorité et ainsi ils en médiront par compagnie. (L606)

The corruptive power of language reaches such a point in this lack of communication, therefore, that even such key concepts as greatness and wretchedness become intermingled: 'Tout ce que les uns ont pu dire pour montrer la grandeur n'a servi que d'un argument aux autres pour conclure la misère' (L122).[31]

---

[30] *L'Homme criminel* (1644), 49.

[31] Pascal differs in his use of the lack of clarity of language from his friend Méré, who, while accepting the existence of ambiguity in language, also associated 'la justesse de l'expression' and 'la pureté du langage' with the notion of *honnêteté*, in his *Discours de la justesse*, *Œuvres*, ed. C. Boudhours (3 vols., Paris, 1930), i. 102–3. Cf. also Méré's *Discours de la Conversation*, *Œuvres*, ii. 116–17, where he stresses that an *honnête homme* should not allow for lack of clarity.

The deception which spoken language produces draws attention not only to the fallibility of words themselves but also to the way in which they are spoken, and indeed to the rhetorical dimension of their delivery. The word or thing becomes secondary to the manner in which it is expressed, a point which follows from my earlier comments about theatricality. This is precisely what the dialectician emphasizes in L928, when he speaks of 'la manière étant ainsi aussi importante que la chose, et peut-être plus'. The implied comparison of matter (*matière*) and manner (*manière*), and the role which each plays in the mutual deception of man is strikingly expressed in L655:

Les discours d'humilité sont matière d'orgueil aux gens glorieux et d'humilité aux humbles. Ainsi ceux du pyrrhonisme sont matière d'affirmation aux affirmatifs. Peu parlent de l'humilité humblement, peu de la chasteté chastement, peu du pyrrhonisme en doutant. Nous ne sommes que mensonge, duplicité, contrariété et nous cachons et nous déguisons à nous-mêmes. (L655)

The image of disguise (as seen here in the verb *déguisons* and in the noun *déguisement* in the passage which I quoted from L978) reiterates the significance of theatrical imagery in the depiction of man's corruption.[32] It is interesting to see a very similar approach to the notion of the importance which we attach to the manner, rather than the matter, of spoken language in 'L'Art de conférer' of Montaigne (indeed, Pascal calls Montaigne 'l'incomparable auteur de *L'Art de conférer*',[33] which shows admiration for this essay):

Autant peut faire le sot celuy qui dict vray, que celuy qui dict faux: car nous sommes sur la maniere, non sur la matiere du dire. Mon humeur est de regarder autant à la forme qu'à la substance [. . .].[34]

On a political level, *dire* and *contredire* are applied in the *Pensées* to evoke the instability of human justice. As the dialectician writes in L103, 'La justice sans force est contredite, parce qu'il y a toujours des méchants'. Because of man's corruption, there will *always* be evil in the world. Language alone cannot prove justice.

---

[32] Cf. L44, where two forms of 'déguisement' are used to show the deceptive power of the imagination.
[33] *De l'esprit géométrique*, Seuil 357.
[34] *Essais* III. viii. 906. See L. Thirouin's excellent article, 'Pascal et *L'Art de conférer*', *Cahiers de l'Association Internationale des Études Françaises*, 40 (1988), 199–218.

Indeed, words themselves can be subverted by force, a force which constitutes another form of tyranny: 'la force a contredit la justice et a dit qu'elle était injuste, et a dit que c'était elle qui était juste' (L103). For this reason, the dialectician argues that political power cannot be given to those who claim to deserve it, because language is such that all those desiring power will *say* that they merit it, and so will deceive people easily:

> Opinions du peuple saines.
> Le plus grand des maux est les guerres civiles.
> Elles sont sûres si on veut récompenser les mérites, car tous diront qu'ils méritent. Le mal à craindre d'un sot qui succède par droit de naissance n'est si grand, ni si sûr. (L94)[35]

Even the famous 'pensée de derrière' which is evoked in the fragments devoted to *Raison des effets* points to the inadequacy of spoken language, for, although those 'habiles' who make use of the 'pensée de derrière' are more sophisticated in their appraisal of reasons for honouring nobly born people, they still find themselves speaking 'comme le peuple' (L91).

Political deception extends to perceptions of the self. In two fragments (written on the same sheet and included as one fragment by Sellier) concerned with 'l'esprit boiteux', L98 and L99, we find how words lead to self-deception. Physical lameness, which is visible to all, is unambiguous, but mental lameness provokes misconceptions:

> D'où vient qu'un boiteux ne nous irrite pas et un esprit boiteux nous irrite? A cause qu'un boiteux reconnaît que nous allons droit et qu'un esprit boiteux dit que c'est nous qui boitons. (L98)

Moreover, the inadequacies of the human mind, and not the sight of physical defects, cause ambiguity and contradiction (itself another form of the verb *dire*): 'Il n'y a jamais cette contradiction dans les sens touchant un boiteux' (L99). Indeed, whereas spoken words indicate duplicity in man, silence represents the best way to counter such corruption, as the dialectician makes clear:

> L'homme est ainsi fait qu'à force de lui dire qu'il est un sot il le croit. Et à force de se le dire à soi-même on se le fait croire, car l'homme fait lui seul une conversation intérieure, qu'il importe de bien régler. *Corrumpunt*

---

[35] See Ch. 8 below for a fuller analysis of the roles of force and justice in the *Pensées*.

bonos mores colloquia prava. Il faut se tenir en silence autant qu'on peut et ne s'entretenir que de Dieu qu'on sait être la vérité, et ainsi on se le persuade à soi-même. (L99)[36]

The implied opposition between speech (as epitomized in the 'esprit boiteux') and sight (as represented by the 'boiteux') is made more explicit in other fragments. In one fragment entitled 'Orgueil', for example, man's vanity is depicted in the fact that his actions are more often prompted by a desire to speak about them than the mere enjoyment of seeing new vistas:

Curiosité n'est que vanité. Le plus souvent on ne veut savoir que pour en parler, autrement on ne voyagerait pas sur la mer pour ne jamais en rien dire et pour le seul plaisir de voir, sans espérance d'en jamais communiquer. (L77)[37]

The contrast between seeing (with its attendant meanings of understanding and knowing) and speaking is perhaps most forcefully highlighted in a fragment where different religions are compared. Other religions, the dialectician declares, make extravagant claims for themselves, marked in the text by the repetition of *dire*, whereas the act of *seeing* shows the Christian religion to be genuine:

Je vois plusieurs religions contraires et partant toutes fausses, excepté une. Chacune veut être crue par sa propre autorité et menace les incrédules. Je ne les crois donc pas là-dessus. Chacun peut dire cela. Chacun peut se dire prophète mais je vois la chrétienne et je trouve des prophéties, et c'est ce que chacun ne peut pas faire. (L198)

Just as we have seen the close relation between *dire* and man's corrupt language, so too is the term *contredire* inseparable from the fallen state of man, that 'sujet de contradictions' (L131). Whether it be the contradictory statements of the Jesuits,[38] of the Stoics,[39] or general comments concerning human nature,[40] man cannot escape

---

[36] Cf. L529: 'Il vaut mieux ne rien dire [...]'.
[37] Cf. the use of 'dire' in L185, which was written on the same sheet of paper as L77, as Pol Ernst has shown (Album, 44). In L185, the words of faith are placed above those of the senses: 'la foi dit bien ce que les sens ne disent pas'.
[38] e.g. L714: 'Il y a contradiction, car d'un côté ils disent qu'il faut suivre la tradition et n'oseraient désavouer cela, et de l'autre ils diront ce qu'il leur plaira.' Cf. L954 and L962. See also Letter 6 of *Lettres provinciales*.
[39] e.g. L147, concerning the 'Dispute du souverain bien': 'Il y a contradiction, car ils conseillent enfin de se tuer.'
[40] e.g. L123: 'Contradiction, mépris de notre être, mourir pour rien, haine de notre être.'

such inconsistencies. Only in God can they be resolved. As the dialectician accentuates in a fragment on the contradictory passages of writers, 'en Jésus-Christ toutes les contradictions sont accordées' (L257).

Where verbs describing speech are introduced in the *Pensées*, man's ambiguous use of words is contrasted with the clarity of God's language. This distinction is most vividly evoked in the concluding words of L303: 'Dieu parle bien de Dieu.'[41] Man cannot hope to emulate God in speaking about God. Indeed, when it comes to divine truths, as Pascal wrote in *De l'esprit géométrique*, 'Dieu seul peut les mettre dans l'âme, et par la manière qu'il lui plaît.'[42] The dialectician can only hope to speak of God through the medium of the Bible. In other words, to quote Philippe Sellier, 'l'apologiste chrétien ne peut qu'imiter Dieu pour parler de Dieu'.[43]

Words such as *dire*, *parler*, and *contredire* would therefore serve to confirm the hypothesis that, for Pascal in the *Pensées*, language is rooted in an Augustinian base. Far from the Cartesian foundation of *La Logique*, where Arnauld and Nicole believed that 'le meilleur moyen pour éviter la confusion des mots [...] est de faire une nouvelle langue',[44] the confusion of man's language is integral to the persuasive process in the *Pensées*. Although perfect clarity would be of *use* in situations where reason is predominant, it would lead to *abuse* in matters of the will, which, as the dialectician sees it, is of much greater importance in an apologetical context: 'Dieu veut plus disposer la volonté que l'esprit, la clarté parfaite servirait à l'esprit et nuirait à la volonté' (L234).

Through his deliberate use of the ambiguity of words and changing meanings, therefore, the dialectician intends his reader to remain aware of the weakness and instability which indicate man's

---

[41] This fragment forms the basis of an ample commentary by Étienne Périer in the preface to the Port-Royal edn. of the *Pensées*. See Seuil 498–9. Cf. Méré's *De l'éloquence et de l'entretien*, where he writes, 'voïez comme le Sauveur du monde traite simplement de l'autre vie, et quelle différence de son langage à celui des Prédicateurs', *Discours* III, in *Œuvres*, ed. C. Boudhours (Paris, 1930), iii. 117. Cf. also L309 and L403. See also P. Sellier, 'Rhétorique et apologie: *Dieu parle bien de Dieu*', in *Méthodes chez Pascal*, 373–81. Cf. also L328, where the speech of prophecy is shown to transcend exterior proofs: 'Prophétiser c'est parler de Dieu, non par preuves de dehors, mais par sentiment intérieur et immédiat.'
[42] Seuil 355.   [43] 'Rhétorique et apologie...', 375.
[44] *La Logique ou L'Art de penser*, ed. P. Clair and F. Girbal (Paris, 1981, first published 1662), I. xii. 86.

corruption. The fact that the *Pensées* are filled with so many fragments which relate directly to the act of writing itself demonstrates not only Pascal's preoccupation with style and the art of persuasion but also the incongruities and contradictions of language itself. Indeed, the very incompleteness of the *Pensées* adds to this sense of ambiguity and paradoxicality. One apparently self-referential fragment perhaps best reflects the dialectician's recognition of man's weakness through the communication of language:

En écrivant ma pensée elle m'échappe quelquefois; mais cela me fait souvenir de ma faiblesse que j'oublie à toute heure, ce qui m'instruit autant que ma pensée oubliée, car je ne tiens qu'à connaître mon néant. (L656)

This forgetfulness calls into question the very essence of words. As the Jansenist friend points out to the Jesuit father in the *Lettres provinciales*, words themselves are without substance; to agree on a word such as *suffisante* does not necessarily presuppose unanimity of meaning:

il y a deux choses dans ce mot de *grâce suffisante*: il y a le son, qui n'est que du vent, et la chose qu'il signifie, qui est réelle et effective. Et ainsi, quand vous êtes d'accord avec les Jésuites touchant le mot de *suffisante*, et contraires dans le sens, il est visible que vous êtes contraires pour la substance de ce terme, et que vous n'êtes d'accord que du son.[45]

It would seem, then, that, because the inadequacy of language as portrayed in the *Pensées* persuades the *reader* of his own inability to attain a transcendent meaning, *interpretation* of the text represents a possible way of moving from what Sara Melzer calls 'absorption in meaning itself towards the interpreting act required by its production'.[46] It is therefore necessary to proceed to an analysis of Pascal's own treatment of the word 'interprétation'.

INTERPRÉTATION

In its definition of the noun *interprétation*, the *Dictionnaire de l'Académie Françoise* distinguishes between 'l'interpretation de l'Escriture sainte' and that of more secular concerns, such as a 'passage', 'songe', 'discours', or 'action'.

[45] Letter 2, Seuil 377.
[46] Melzer, 'Classicism and Conventions of Meaning in the *Pensées*', *Papers on Seventeenth Century French Literature*, 14–15 (1981), 72.

Pascal, in the course of the *Pensées*, makes use of the noun only four times, and the verb *interpréter* once. Three main categories of interpretation emerge from these uses: biblical, casuistic, and textual. It is clear that, despite three examples where the noun refers to the Bible, the word is not specifically associated with biblical exegesis: two simply form part of notes which he took from the Book of Daniel (L485), and the other focuses on a particular Jewish mystical interpretation of the Old and New Testaments: 'Preuves par l'interprétation mystique que les Rabbins mêmes donnent de l'Écriture' (L274). Furthermore, it is interesting to note that, in the *Recueil original*, Pascal chose to replace 'interpréter' with 'prendre' in a short fragment which is concerned primarily with biblical interpretation: 'Deux erreurs. 1.prendre tout littéralement. 2.prendre tout spirituellement' (L252). This would suggest that he saw the neutral *prendre* as being preferable within this biblical context to *interpréter*. In other words, he appears to reserve the term *interprétation* for a different purpose, away from the biblical framework.

The one case where *interpréter* appears in the *Pensées* relates specifically to the casuists. Yet, it provides a clear indication of Pascal's perception of human judgement, which is seen as easily corruptible:

Casuistes.
Une aumône considérable, une pénitence raisonnable.
Encore qu'on ne puisse assigner le juste, on voit bien ce qui ne l'est pas. Les casuistes sont plaisants de croire pouvoir interpréter cela comme ils font. (L729)

The casuists are able to distort meanings for their own ends. *Interpréter*, as it occurs here, corresponds closely to the use of the verb in the *Lettres provinciales*. It might be useful to follow Pierre Force's assertion that *interprétation* in the *Lettres provinciales*, dealing as it does with biblical questions, begins from the premiss that the Bible is infallible, whereas the Bible is treated as a literary text in the *Pensées*.[47] However, in many cases, a profound irony

---

[47] 'S'il est nécessaire d'interpréter l'Écriture [in the *Lettres provinciales*], c'est parce que la parole de Dieu est infaillible. Les passages qui contredisent les données des sens doivent être accordés à celles-ci. La nécessité d'interpréter n'est donc pas fondée, comme dans les *Pensées*, sur l'hypothèse de la cohérence du texte, mais bien

underlies the word. In Letter 6, for example, the Jesuit Father explains to Montalte 'l'utilité des interprétations',[48] which are in effect a convenient excuse for the Jesuits to interpret such unquantified terms as *superflu* to their own advantage. As the Jesuit Father puts it, he is concerned to find 'la manière d'interpréter favorablement' tracts such as the papal bulls. He concludes that, 'soit par l'interprétation des termes, soit par la remarque des circonstances favorables, soit enfin par la double probabilité du pour et du contre, on accorde toujours ces contradictions prétendues, qui vous étonnaient auparavant, sans jamais blesser les décisions de l'Ecriture, des conciles ou des papes'.[49]

This leads us to the third and most important category of interpretation in the *Pensées*, which I have called textual, concerning the general interpretation of texts and meaning. Although the noun appears only once in this context, it warrants our particular attention:

Qu'il est difficile de proposer une chose au jugement d'un autre sans corrompre son jugement par la manière de la lui proposer. Si on dit: je le trouve beau, je le trouve obscur ou autre chose semblable, on entraîne l'imagination à ce jugement ou on l'irrite au contraire. Il vaut mieux ne rien dire et alors il juge selon ce qu'il est, c'est-à-dire selon ce qu'il est alors, et selon que les autres circonstances dont on n'est pas auteur y auront mis. Mais au moins on n'y aura rien mis, si ce n'est que ce silence n'y fasse aussi son effet, selon le tour et l'interprétation qu'il sera en humeur de lui donner, ou selon qu'il le conjecturera des mouvements et air du visage, ou du ton de voix selon qu'il sera physionomiste, tant il est difficile de ne point démonter un jugement de son assiette naturelle, ou plutôt tant il en a peu de ferme et stable. (L529)

sur la présupposition de sa vérité'; *Le Problème herméneutique chez Pascal*, 160. I offer Force's hypothesis with some reservation, as it is only after the 11th letter that the infallibility of the Bible is taken as a given. However, for the purposes of this argument, Force's assertion is helpful. See Letter 18 of the *Lettres provinciales*, pp. 466–7. For a detailed analysis of biblical interpretation in the *Lettres provinciales* and the *Pensées*, see Force's book, especially pt. ii, ch. 3. D. Wetsel's *'L'Écriture et le reste': The 'Pensées' of Pascal in the Exegetical Tradition of Port-Royal* (Columbus, Oh., 1981) also assesses the role of the Bible in the *Pensées*.

[48] Seuil 392.
[49] Ibid. 393. See B. Woshinsky's article, 'Pascal's *Pensées* and the Discourse of the Inexpressible', *Papers on French Seventeenth Century Literature*, 14–15 (1981), 62–3, for a comparison between interpretation of human and biblical discourse. See also D. Descotes, *L'Argumentation chez Pascal* (Paris, 1993), 231–65, for a discussion of interpretation as an 'extension du modèle géométrique', as he entitles the 3rd part of his book.

Clearly, interpretation and judgement are for Pascal inseparable from the weaknesses inherent in man. In this fragment alone, two key concepts in the *Pensées* are introduced: *imagination* and *inconstance*. Interpretation cannot remain untouched by external factors. Imagination, one of the *puissances trompeuses*, will either help to persuade or dissuade, according to one's reaction to the way in which the argument is presented: 'Ou on entraîne, ou on irrite' (L528). Furthermore, the very inconstancy and instability of our existence makes no human judgement inviolate, 'tant il est difficile de ne point démonter un jugement de son assiette naturelle, ou plutôt tant il en a peu de ferme et stable'.[50]

In addition to the variable effects of imagination, the word *interprétation* in this passage is coupled with the noun *tour* (both nouns in this context indicating the sense of inference), and is subject to the whims of mood (*humeur*). Moreover, it is associated with conjecture ('selon qu'il le conjecturera des mouvements et air du visage'). Being dependent upon all these external factors, it is shown, in Pierre Force's words, to be 'une activité parasitaire':

l'interprétation est l'opération de l'esprit qui rend signifiants toutes sortes d'éléments extérieurs à l'ouvrage qu'on doit juger, et fait entrer ceux-ci dans le jugement qu'on porte sur l'ouvrage.[51]

As a result of its dependence upon imagination, interpretation acts as an inevitable influence on the mind. Seemingly insignificant factors, such as tone of voice or facial expression, can transform a just judgement into a false interpretation. As the dialectician expresses elsewhere, with reference to the *esprit de finesse*, false conclusions can easily be reached:

dans l'esprit de finesse, les principes sont dans l'usage commun et devant les yeux de tout le monde. On n'a que faire de tourner la tête, ni de se faire violence; il n'est question que d'avoir bonne vue, mais il faut l'avoir

---

[50] The vocabulary at the end of this fragment corresponds closely to the words used in Pascal's celebrated depiction of the inconstancy of man in the fragment entitled 'Disproportion de l'homme': 'Nous brûlons du désir de trouver une assiette ferme, et une dernière base constante pour y édifier une tour qui s'élève à (l')infini, mais tout notre fondement craque et la terre s'ouvre jusqu'aux abîmes. Ne cherchons donc point d'assurance et de fermeté; notre raison est toujours déçue par l'inconstance des apparences: rien ne peut fixer le fini entre les deux infinis qui l'enferment et le fuient' (L199). In L529, Pascal uses parallel terms to depict the instability of human judgement.

[51] *Le Problème herméneutique chez Pascal*, 168.

bonne: car les principes sont si déliés et en si grand nombre, qu'il est presque impossible qu'il n'en échappe. Or l'omission d'un principe mène à l'erreur; ainsi il faut avoir la vue bien nette pour voir tous les principes, et ensuite l'esprit juste pour ne pas raisonner faussement sur des principes connus. (L512)

Furthermore, interpretation is always coloured by a reasoning which cannot remain untouched by external factors such as opinion or feeling (*sentiment*) and imagination or fantasy (*fantaisie*):

> Tout notre raisonnement se réduit à céder au sentiment.
> Mais la fantaisie est semblable et contraire au sentiment; de sorte qu'on ne peut distinguer entre ces contraires. L'un dit que mon sentiment est fantaisie, l'autre que sa fantaisie est sentiment. Il faudrait avoir une règle. La raison s'offre mais elle est ployable à tous sens.
> Et ainsi il n'y en a point. (L530)[52]

Following on from these words, Pascal's own ideas of the *art de persuader* underlie many of these fragments which are concerned with style. In L529, Pascal cannot be unaware that the vagaries of human interpretation can be attributed equally to his own judgement and to the interpretation of his work by his reader. Indeed, he shows such an awareness of himself in relation to his reader in a fragment which concerns man's vanity:

> La vanité est si ancrée dans le cœur de l'homme qu'un soldat, un goujat, un cuisinier, un crocheteur se vante et veut avoir ses admirateurs et les philosophes mêmes en veulent, et ceux qui écrivent contre veulent avoir la gloire d'avoir bien écrit, et ceux qui les lisent veulent avoir la gloire de les avoir lus, et moi qui écris ceci ai peut-être cette envie, et peut-être que ceux qui le liront ... (L627)

Like an actor upon the stage, he knows in his capacity as the 'persuader' or 'apologist' that his words are being scrutinized and interpreted; in his turn he influences through tone of voice or attitude just as his 'spectator' can be influenced by other external elements. This theatricality is clearly discernible in L529, where Pascal evokes images such as 'mouvements', 'air du visage', and 'ton de voix'. Indeed, he never loses sight of his audience. Persuasion, as we saw in the opening lines of the section on the 'art de persuader'

---

[52] See B. Norman's discussion of *sentiment* in *Portraits of Thought: Knowledge, Methods, and Styles in Pascal* (Columbus, Oh., 1988), 3–17. Norman sees *sentiment* in L530 as primarily a mental operation.

in *De l'esprit géométrique*, requires in the writer both a sensitivity to his reader's requirements and a knowledge of his own priorities in communicating his ideas. Yet the fact that man must resort to such means of persuasion as theatrical imagery reinforces the reader's awareness of his inability to communicate or interpret truth, and, as I showed earlier in my discussion of L784, exposes man's difference from God.

It would seem, then, that the term *interprétation* is strongly associated with the contradictions and weaknesses inherent in fallen man.[53] Significantly, when explaining the literal and figurative meanings of the Bible in the *Pensées*, the dialectician does not introduce the actual term *interprétation*: he tends to confine himself to nouns like *sens*, and, as we saw before, to neutral verbs such as *prendre*.

A brief analysis of some other fragments may help to throw further light on the dangers which the dialectician sees as accompanying any question of judgement. Two fragments in particular, which draw their inspiration from Montaigne, incorporate the image of perspective in painting. In L21, Pascal shows the instability of man's judgement. With paintings, the 'point indivisible' can be found; but in the pursuit of truth such a point is more difficult to attain:

> Si on est trop jeune on ne juge pas bien, trop vieil de même.
> Si on n'y songe pas assez, si on y songe trop, on s'entête et on s'en coiffe.
> Si on considère son ouvrage incontinent après l'avoir fait on en est encore tout prévenu, si trop longtemps après on (n')y entre plus.
> Ainsi les tableaux vus de trop loin et de trop près. Et il n'y a qu'un point indivisible qui soit le véritable lieu.
> Les autres sont trop près, trop loin, trop haut ou trop bas. La perspective l'assigne dans l'art de la peinture, mais dans la vérité et dans la morale qui l'assignera? (L21)

The passage from Montaigne's *Apologie de Raimond Sebond* which influenced the first lines of this fragment has been well documented.[54] However, the lines which immediately follow this

---

[53] Cf. P. De Man's assessment of interpretation as 'nothing but the possibility of error', in 'The Rhetoric of Blindness', from *Blindness and Insight: Essays in the Rhetoric of Contemporary Criticism* (New York, 1971), 141.

[54] *Essais* II. xii. 585: 's'il [un juge] est vieil, il ne peut juger du sentiment de la vieillesse, estant luy mesme partie en ce debat; s'il est jeune, de mesme; sain, de mesme; de mesme, malade, dormant et veillant'.

passage clarify the difficulties of interpretation which are presented in the *Pensées*:

> Pour juger des apparences que nous recevons des subjects, il nous faudroit un instrument judicatoire; pour verifier cet instrument, il nous y faut de la demonstration; pour verifier la demonstration, un instrument: nous voilà au rouet.[55]

Montaigne's image of a scientific 'instrument' used to judge appearances validates Pascal's distinction between the 'esprit de géométrie' and the 'esprit de finesse', for it is clear that a geometrical approach cannot successfully explain moral judgements. Following Montaigne's thoughts on judging appearances, elsewhere in the *Pensées* the dialectician accentuates 'l'inconstance des apparences' (L199); and indeed, inconstancy and instability remain central to his perception of interpretation.

The second fragment, L558, concentrates first on the wide diversity which is evident everywhere, such as in the fact that no two grapes are alike.[56] Similarly, no two interpretations are ever the same. Pascal concludes the fragment with another image of perspective in painting:

> Je n'ai jamais jugé d'une chose exactement de même, je ne puis juger d'un ouvrage en le faisant. Il faut que je fasse comme les peintres et que je m'en éloigne, mais non pas trop. De combien donc? Devinez ... (L558)

Interpretation for Pascal cannot therefore be defined under the 'esprit de géométrie', if indeed it can be defined at all. It is too diverse and too complicated for classification. Indeed, the approach towards interpretation in the *Pensées*, with its emphasis upon the variability and inconstancy of human judgement, comes close to Montaigne's assessment of human nature in the lines which immediately precede the passage quoted above:

> je m'effarouche de voir de la discordance de mes jugemens à ceux d'autruy, et que je me rende incompatible à la société des hommes pour estre d'autre sens et party que le mien: qu'au rebours, comme c'est la plus generale façon que nature aye suivy que la varieté [...] je trouve bien plus rare de voir convenir nos humeurs et nos desseins.[57]

---

[55] Ibid.
[56] Montaigne's essay, II. xxxvii. 766, is a likely source of L558: 'Et ne fut jamais au monde deux opinions pareilles, non plus que deux poils ou deux grains. Leur plus universelle qualité, c'est la diversité.'   [57] Ibid.

In this respect, Pascal's understanding of interpretation remains close to that of Montaigne.

It is in the *Entretien avec M. de Sacy* that we see most clearly the influence of Montaigne on the notion of interpretation in the *Pensées*. Although the excessive doubt and uncertainty, which 'roule sur elle-même dans un cercle perpétuel et sans repos',[58] are perceived ultimately to be self-defeating, the way in which Montaigne 'se moque de toutes les assurances' helps to avoid complacency about the powers of the human mind. Moreover, for Montaigne, 'les obscurités se multiplient par le commentaire', and 'le plus sûr moyen pour entendre le sens d'un discours est de ne le pas examiner et de le prendre sur la première apparence'.[59]

In the final analysis, the dialectician exposes the many perils which accompany all facets of interpretation. He does not confine himself solely to the way in which others, such as the casuists, interpret texts; rather, he recognizes the fact that he too is fashioning his own arguments through his judgement, just as his readers will interpret his writings through their own judgement. Indeed, the many interpretative approaches to the *Pensées* which have emerged in the three centuries following their publication vindicate this presentation of the complexities of interpretation. Yet it is clear that we are not supposed to reject entirely the notion of interpretation, and it is in this respect that Pascal differs most markedly from Montaigne, for it forms an essential part of the art of persuasion, as we have seen. While Montaigne states that many interpretations are unnecessary, interpretation for the dialectician in the *Pensées* forms a central part of the persuasive process, in order to show the fallen and corrupt state of man. Although the dialectician cannot claim to give man divine truth through persuasion (that being the prerogative of God), he knows that it is only through an agreeable way of presenting his argument or interpretation (*agrément*), as contrary to nature and as dangerous as it may be, that he can hope to appeal to man's will (*volonté*):

Personne n'ignore qu'il y a deux entrées par où les opinions sont reçues dans l'âme, qui sont ses deux principales puissances, l'entendement et la

---

[58] Seuil 293.
[59] Ibid. 294. This passage is taken mainly from a section in the *Essais*, III. xiii. 1044, where Montaigne states that 'il se sent par expérience que tant d'interprétations dissipent la vérité et la rompent'.

volonté. La plus naturelle est celle de l'entendement, car on ne devrait jamais consentir qu'aux vérités démontrées; mais la plus ordinaire, quoique contre la nature, est celle de la volonté; car tout ce qu'il y a d'hommes sont presque toujours emportés à croire non pas par la preuve, mais par l'agrément.[60]

Thus, as so often occurs in the vocabulary of the *Pensées*, the dialectician applies the 'renversement du pour au contre' to *interprétation*, for, like *agrément*, it is 'basse, indigne et étrangère',[61] and yet it is also indispensable for the expression of his argument in his planned work. Even language has its *grandeur*.

Therefore, interpretation must be approached with caution, for, as we saw with the obscurity of human discourse, the very fact of interpretation is perceived as a sign of man's fallen nature and of his lack of direct communication with God. Yet, paradoxically, it is through a recognition of this obscurity, of this corruption, that one can begin to perceive the truth of religion:

Reconnaissez donc la vérité de la religion dans l'obscurité même de la religion, dans le peu de lumière que nous en avons, dans l'indifférence que nous avons de la connaître. (L439)[62]

[60] *De l'esprit géométrique*, Seuil 355.   [61] Ibid. 355.
[62] It is in this respect that I differ from S. Melzer's reading of an *aporia* within the text of the *Pensées*; see *Discourses of the Fall: A Study of Pascal's Pensées* (London, 1986), 3–4.

2
Ordre

M. de la Chaise a fait la préface des fragments de M. Pascal. M. de Roannez veut achever ses discours. M. Périer, son neveu, les veut donner tels qu'ils sont: chacun en tirera tel usage qu'il lui plaira.[1]

If the very fallenness of language in the *Pensées* acts as a persuasive force, we are led to question the status of its ordering, its *dispositio*. Does order matter in a world where words act as a constant reminder of man's corruption? The noun *ordre* plays an important part in the *Pensées*, for not only does it form the heading of the first *liasse*, but also its prominent position in many fragments and its frequency (70 occurrences) testify to its significance.[2]

It is not my purpose in this chapter to give a comprehensive analysis of *ordre* in all its manifestations, for it is a term which has been extensively covered by recent scholarship.[3] Rather, I intend first to look briefly at its different meanings and the way in which these meanings shift, and then to consider order in relation to fragmentation.

There are six main categories into which it is convenient to divide the usage of *ordre* in the *Pensées*, some of which are interconnected: arrangement, plane of understanding, divine and world order, orderliness, command, and priestly succession.[4]

---

[1] *Bibliothèque Nationale*, nouvelles acquisitions françaises, no. 4333. Quoted by Jean Mesnard in his edition of the *Œuvres complètes* (3 vols., Paris, 1964–91), i. 891.
[2] See H. Davidson and P. Dubé, *A Concordance to Pascal's 'Pensées'* (Ithaca, NY, 1975).
[3] For full analyses of *ordre* as a chapter title and as a dominant concept in the *Pensées*, see H. M. Davidson, *The Origins of Certainty: Means and Meanings in Pascal's 'Pensées'* (Chicago, 1979), ch. 2; P. Ernst, *Approches pascaliennes* (Gembloux, 1970), 17–47; A. Pugh, *The Composition of Pascal's 'Apologia'* (Toronto, 1984), pt. i, ch. 1; P. Bayley, 'A Reading of the First *Liasse*', in D. L. Rubin and M. B. Mckinley (eds.), *Convergences* (Columbus, Oh., 1989), 196–207. For the mathematical significance of *ordre*, see D. Descotes, *L'Argumentation chez Pascal* (Paris, 1993), 47–103.
[4] Davidson, in ch. 2 of *The Origins of Certainty*, outlines only 3 different meanings of *ordre* in the *Pensées*: sequence, domain, and imperative.

The first grouping (which I shall call O1) relates principally to Pascal's notes on the ordering of his text, and concerns *ordre* as 'arrangement, disposition des choses mises en leur rang', as defined by the *Dictionnaire de l'Académie Françoise*. The word appears most frequently in the *Pensées* within this context, usually as a heading for what seems to be a working note.[5] This sense of *ordre* will be the main focus of this chapter.

The second grouping of *ordre* (O2) is closely related to the first, as we shall see, but it operates on a different level. It is concerned with particular planes of understanding or living, often in strict hierarchy or gradation to each other. The theme of the three orders in two fragments in particular, L308 and L933, has been viewed by most critics as central to an understanding of the *Pensées*. Jean Mesnard, for example, calls it 'une clef irremplaçable'.[6] In L933, the dialectician distinguishes between the three 'concupiscences':

> Concupiscence de la chair, concupiscence des yeux, orgueil, etc.
> Il y a trois ordres de choses. La chair, l'esprit, la volonté. (L933)[7]

Another three *ordres*, *l'esprit*, *le cœur*, and *la charité*, are identified in L298. It would seem that Pascal associates the problems concerning the ordering of texts with these three levels of interpretation:

> L'ordre. Contre l'objection que l'Écriture n'a pas d'ordre.
> Le cœur a son ordre, l'esprit a le sien qui est par principe et

---

[5] In the following fragments from the Lafuma edn., *ordre* is used in this sense, that of the ordering of material: 2, 5, 8, 11, 12, 387, 427, 467, 511, 532, 620, 683, 684, 694, 970. The word occurs in L58 and L733 with a slightly different meaning, but is still related to the sense of ordering.

[6] 'Le Thème des trois ordres dans l'organisation des *Pensées*', in L. M. Heller and I. M. Richmond (eds.), *Pascal thématique des 'Pensées'* (Paris, 1988), 55. For another recent analysis of the 3 orders, see P. Sellier's seminar in D. Wetsel (ed.), *Meaning, Structure and History in the 'Pensées' of Pascal* (Paris, 1990), 75–83. See also A. W. S. Baird, *Studies in Pascal's Ethics* (The Hague, 1975), chs. 1, 5, and 7; G. Ferreyrolles, 'L'imagination en procès' and A. McKenna, 'Pascal et le corps humain', *XVIIe Siècle*, 177 (Oct.–Dec. 1992).

[7] The biblical source of this fragment comes from 1 John 2: 16: 'Car tout ce qui est dans le monde est ou concupiscence de la chair, ou concupiscence des yeux, ou orgueil de la vie.' Cf. also Augustine's distinction between *libido sciendi*, *libido sentiendi*, and *libido dominandi*. See *De Civitate Dei*, xiv. 15 and xiv. 28; and *Confessions*, iii. 8. For a full discussion of the Augustinian origins of Pascal's conception of the 3 orders, see P. Sellier, *Pascal et Saint Augustin* (Paris, 1970), 170–1, 191–6.

démonstration. Le cœur en a un autre. On ne prouve pas qu'on doit être aimé en exposant d'ordre les causes de l'amour; cela serait ridicule.
J.-C., saint Paul ont l'ordre de la charité, non de l'esprit, car ils voulaient échauffer, non instruire.
Saint Augustin de même. Cet ordre consiste principalement à la digression sur chaque point qui a rapport à la fin, pour la montrer toujours. (L298)[8]

In L308, the different orders are also shown to have clear hierarchical value:

La distance infinie des corps aux esprits figure la distance infiniment plus infinie des esprits à la charité, car elle est surnaturelle. (L308)

It should be noted here that this concern for categorization of different planes of understanding is evident in both Pascal's mathematical and spiritual writings. However, as Janet Morgan has rightly pointed out, the notion that a doctrine of *three* orders underpins all his writings is misdirected.[9] In the *Préface sur le traité du vide*, for example, Pascal distinguishes between two modes of proof, 'autorité' and 'raison'.[10] Similarly, in the letter in which Pascal dedicated his *machine arithmétique* to Christina of Sweden in June 1652, he compares two orders, 'les esprits' and 'les corps'.[11] In the later *Trois discours sur la condition des grands*, there is another twofold distinction, this time between 'des grandeurs d'établissement' and 'des grandeurs naturelles'.[12] Recently, Philippe Sellier has even suggested that the concept of three orders began as four orders.[13] In the two fragments numbered L58, on 'Tyrannie', the dialectician considers four spheres: 'force', which produces 'crainte'; 'agrément', which is linked to 'amour'; 'science', on which 'créance' depends; and, finally, true 'piété'. Those fragments devoted to *Raison des effets* reveal also different levels of

---

[8] I follow the Sellier and Le Guern edns. in reading 'échauffer' instead of 'rabaisser'. Le Guern in particular gives invaluable background information to this fragment; see his edn., i. 318. See also Sellier, *Pascal et Saint Augustin*, 559–62, and Pugh, *The Composition of Pascal's 'Apologia'*, 533–4, n. 12. M. Warner, in *Philosophical Finesse: Studies in the Art of Rational Persuasion* (Oxford, 1989), suggests that *cœur*, together with its associated order, 'plays for Pascal a role analogous to that of dialectic in Aristotle's thinking' (p. 154).
[9] 'Pascal's Three Orders', *Modern Language Review*, 73 (1978), 755–6.
[10] Seuil 230–1.   [11] Ibid. 280.
[12] Seuil 367. I shall discuss the *Trois Discours* at greater length in Ch. 8 below.
[13] In his 'De la *Tyrannie*', in G. Ferreyrolles (ed.), *Justice et force: Politiques au temps de Pascal* (Actes du colloque de Clermont-Ferrand, Sept. 1990) (Paris, 1993).

perception, although they are not named as *ordres*. In L90, for example, we find a 'gradation' between five levels, 'le peuple', 'les demi-habiles', 'les habiles', 'les dévots', and 'les chrétiens parfaits'.[14]

Pascal's famous distinction between the 'esprit de géométrie' and the 'esprit de finesse' in fragments L511–13 undoubtedly is closely linked to this category of order (O2). In L511, for example, the dialectician distinguishes between different orders of understanding: 'Diverses sortes de sens droit, les uns dans un certain ordre de choses et non dans les autres ordres où ils extravaguent' (L511). It should be noted that in L511 a fundamental distinction is made between 'l'esprit de justesse' and 'l'esprit de géométrie', whereas in L512 we find the juxtaposition of 'l'esprit de finesse' and 'l'esprit de géométrie'. Each of these *esprits* is acknowledged as a 'sorte de raisonnement' (L512), and so in this regard they represent different categories within the second intellectual order of the three orders. In this respect, the 'esprit de finesse' goes beyond the functions of the heart in that it, like the other two *esprits*, is involved in drawing conclusions, which the heart does not do, as Buford Norman has pointed out.[15]

In *De l'esprit géométrique*, we find further use of different orders in the sense of O2, where the distinction is made between a supernatural order, 'la charité', and a natural order, 'l'esprit', which is corrupted by the need for 'agrément', dictated by the will:

il paraît que Dieu a établi cet ordre surnaturel, et tout contraire à l'ordre qui devait être naturel aux hommes dans les choses naturelles. Ils ont néanmoins corrompu cet ordre en faisant des choses profanes ce qu'ils devaient faire des choses saintes, parce qu'en effet nous ne croyons presque que ce qui nous plaît. Et de là vient l'éloignement où nous sommes de consentir aux vérités de la religion chrétienne, tout opposée à nos plaisirs. 'Dites-nous des choses agréables et nous vous écouterons', disaient les Juifs à Moïse; comme si l'agrément devait régler la créance! Et c'est pour punir ce désordre par un ordre qui lui est conforme, que Dieu ne verse ses

---

[14] L. Thirouin, in his elegant article, 'Pascal et le savoir-vivre', in T. Goyet *et al.* (eds.), *Pascal, Port-Royal, Orient, Occident* (Paris, 1991), has shown how, in these fragments, 'la pensée de derrière' relates closely to what he calls 'l'ordre d'apparences' (p. 273).

[15] *Portraits of Thought: Knowledge, Methods, and Styles in Pascal* (Columbus, Oh., 1988), 53. For a more detailed examination of this aspect, see ibid. 53–9, and Davidson, *The Origins of Certainty*, 43–5.

lumières dans les esprits qu'après avoir dompté la rébellion de la volonté par une douceur toute céleste qui la charme et qui l'entraîne.[16]

Placed at the opposite pole of man's 'désordre' is this supernatural order, which remains obscure to man in his fallen state until he can acknowledge the corruption of his condition.

Another field of meaning of the word *ordre*, and strongly linked to the differentiation which we have just seen between divine and human order, consists of divine will or divine order in relation to the order of the world (O3). One of the fragments which uses *ordre* in this sense is concerned primarily with the Cartesian theory of *raison naturelle*, that the natural order of the world reflects and proves God's existence. In fragment L449, Pascal writes of the two truths of the Christian religion: 'et qu'il y a un Dieu, dont les hommes sont capables, et qu'il y a une corruption dans la nature, qui les en rend indignes'. It is this double tension and not Descartes's *raison naturelle* which he sees as the true source of the order of the world:

> Qu'on examine l'ordre du monde sur cela, et qu'on voie si toutes choses ne tendent pas à l'établissement des deux chefs de cette religion: Jésus-Christ est l'objet de tout, et le centre où tout tend. Qui le connaît connaît la raison de toutes choses. (L449)

K. Kawamata, in his article, 'Saint-Cyran inspirateur de Pascal', quotes this short passage from the first abbé de Saint-Cyran, Jean Du Vergier de Hauranne, and equates it to a section of L149:

> Par quelles marques le (Dieu) connoist-on? Par trois principales; Par la lumière et le sentiment imprimé naturellement dans nos ames, par la beauté et l'ordre du monde: et beaucoup plus par l'instruction que Dieu mesme nous a donnée par sa grace.[17]

The parallels between the two writers are evident. However, Saint-Cyran's inclusion of 'l'ordre du monde' as proof of God's existence clearly contradicts the assertions in L449, as well as in L148, L463, and L3, where the dialectician considers, in a dialogue, the view that the sky and birds (in other words, Nature) prove God's

---

[16] Seuil 355. Other fragments in which *ordre* is used in this 2nd sense (that of a level or plane) are L106 (cf. L118) and L199. Two of the *Lettres provinciales* use *ordre* in this same sense: 8, p. 405, and 16, p. 449. See T. Harrington's *Vérité et méthode dans les 'Pensées' de Pascal* (Pascal, 1972), 93–4, for an analysis of *volonté*.

[17] *Méthodes chez Pascal*, 48.

existence.[18] In fact, Pascal is responding to the commonplace argument in apologies of the seventeenth century that the order of the world was perceived to mirror God's order. It is evident also that these apologists were relying on the fifth of the five traditional proofs of God, as set down by Thomas Aquinas in his *Summa Theologiae* (1a. 2, 3): 'an orderedness of actions to an end is observed in all bodies obeying natural laws. [...] Everything in nature, therefore, is directed to its goal by someone with understanding, and this we call God.'[19] In L449, the dialectician counters those who mistake Christianity for a form of deism, and it is possible that Pascal had in mind an apologist like Père Mersenne, who, as the title of his *L'Impieté des déistes refutée* (1624) suggests, was himself attempting to attack deist doctrines. Mersenne makes the point that,

veritablement quand on contemple le bel ordre qui est au monde, et qu'on voit que chaque chose retient son rang, et son lieu, nonobstant tous les desordres, qui semblent arriver, il faut conclure qu'il y a quelqu'un qui gouverne tout le monde, et qui maintient toutes choses en bon ordre [...].[20]

Similarly, Yves de Paris in *La Theologie naturelle* (1633) advocates the presence of 'une main toute puissante' in the order of the world,[21] and heads his chapters with 'De l'ordre et du mouvement des Cieus' (xii), 'De l'ordre general du monde' (xv), and 'L'ordre est un efet de la raison. Et l'ordre du monde supose une Raison universelle' (xvi).

---

[18] D. Wetsel, in *L'Écriture et le reste: The 'Pensées' of Pascal in the Exegetical Tradition of Port-Royal* (Columbus, Oh., 1981), 114–19, relates Pascal's use of 'l'ordre du monde' to De Sacy's interpretation of 'l'ordre du monde' as confirming the doctrine of the Fall. Furthermore, Wetsel points out that the folly of searching for God in created things was already a recurrent theme in the writings of St Paul (e.g. Acts 17: 24–7), St Augustine, Jansenius, and the theologians of Port-Royal (p. 119).
[19] 'Videmus enim quod aliqua quae cognitione carent, scilicet corpora naturalia. [...] Ergo est aliquis intelligens a quo omnes res naturales ordinantur ad finem, et hoc dicimus Deum.' The 4 other traditional proofs of God are: change (*motus*); causation (*ex ratione causae efficientis*); what need not be and what must be (*ex possibili et necessario*); gradation (*ex gradibus qui in rebus inveniuntur*).
[20] p. 81. Cf. p. 334.
[21] p. 174. Cf. pp. 214–15, 217–18. Cf. Jean de Silhon, *Les Deux veritez* (1626): 'Il faut donc voir si par la lumiere de la nature nous pouvons penetrer ce sien [= de Dieu] dessein, et si dans l'ordre et la disposition de l'Univers et de ses parties, il nous a laissé des impressions et marques suffisantes, pour le nous persuader' (pp. 12–13).

In L449, on the other hand, the dialectician deliberately undertakes at this point not to prove God in this manner, for, as he emphasizes, 'le Dieu des chrétiens ne consiste pas en un Dieu simplement auteur des vérités géométriques et de l'ordre des éléments'. In this latter sense, *ordre* refers back to its association with 'l'esprit de géométrie and 'l'esprit de finesse'. Indeed, just as God cannot be seen simply as a God of 'géométrie', so He cannot be proved solely through mathematical means. In other fragments where divine order and order of the world are linked, Pascal interprets *ordre* either as divine will or the worldly order which God determines. The sense of divine will is inseparable from the harmony which God alone can maintain, enigmatic as it may seem:

> Je puis bien aimer l'obscurité totale, mais si Dieu m'engage dans un état à demi obscur, ce peu d'obscurité qui y est me déplaît, et parce que je n'y vois pas le mérite d'une entière obscurité il ne me plaît pas. C'est un défaut et une marque que je me fais une idole de l'obscurité séparée de l'ordre de Dieu. Or il ne faut adorer qu'en son ordre. (L926)[22]

The order of the world is perceived by Pascal through the divine nature of prophecies and through history, and it is in this context that he uses *ordre* in a number of fragments, such as L594:

> Conduite générale du monde envers l'Eglise. Dieu voulant aveugler et éclairer.
>
> L'événement ayant prouvé la divinité de ces prophéties le reste doit en être cru et par là nous voyons l'ordre du monde en cette sorte. (L594)

In this fragment, the word 'ordre' is crossed out at the beginning, and replaced by 'conduite'. The *Recueil original* makes it clear that 'ordre' was not initially intended as a title of this fragment, as 'conduite' is placed immediately above the deleted word. Furthermore, Pascal clearly intended at first to write 'l'ordre général du monde', as the adjective 'général' remains in the masculine. Thus, Lafuma is wrong to imply that 'ordre' was originally intended as a title by placing it at the head of the fragment. It is tempting to

---

[22] Other fragments where *ordre* can be translated as divine will are: L14, L919, L945, and a section of L965 which Pascal deleted: 'ces choses [sont si conformes à l'ordre de la conduite divine et] sont si clairement prédites et qu'il a été annoncé depuis si longtemps...'. Cf. Gilberte Périer's *La Vie de Monsieur Pascal*, in Œuvres complètes, ed. Mesnard, ii. 634. See also L. Thirouin, *Le Hasard et les règles: Le Modèle du jeu dans la pensée de Pascal* (Paris, 1991), 79–84. I shall consider God's order in the world on a political level in the Ch. 8 below.

compare Pascal's association of 'ordre' and 'conduite' with L68, where he writes, 'Par l'ordre et la conduite de qui ce lieu et ce temps a[-t-]il été destiné à moi?' However, it is improbable that he planned *ordre* to be used in the sense of a command in L594, as it is in L68.[23]

The fourth aspect of *ordre* (O4) is the most difficult to define: perhaps the term 'orderliness' is the nearest we can come to categorizing it. In both fragments where the word is used in this way, Pascal contrasts 'ordre' with 'désordre'. The first fragment clearly constitutes a metaphor of the disorder which emanates from man's inability to look beyond himself:

Si les pieds et les mains avaient une volonté particulière, jamais ils ne seraient dans leur ordre qu'en soumettant cette volonté particulière à la volonté première qui gouverne le corps entier. Hors de là ils sont dans le désordre et dans le malheur; mais en ne voulant que le bien du corps, ils font leur propre bien. (L374)

In the other passage, Pascal again sees disorder as the natural result of inclination towards the self. His list of examples is particularly revealing, because, in addition to referring again to the image of the human body, the allusion to wider issues of human existence, such as war and government, show that he views *ordre* here as the orderly structure of society. It relates in particular to one of the three *concupiscences*, 'concupiscence de la chair' (*ordre* in the sense of O2), and on a political and social level can be termed what Gérard Ferreyrolles calls 'la concupiscence collective',[24] thus inviting association with 'l'ordre du monde' (O3):

Car tout tend à soi: cela est contre tout ordre.
Il faut tendre au général, et la pente vers soi est le commencement de tout désordre, en guerre, en police, en économie, dans le corps particulier de l'homme. (L421)

Apart from these two examples of *désordre*, the word occurs in the singular in only one other fragment, L532, which I shall discuss at length later. It is obvious that the singular form of *désordre* is employed by Pascal to contrast it with its antonym; hence it contains many of the tensions which we find within the word *ordre*. However, its plural form, which appears in L281, L700, L905, and

---

[23] For further examples of *ordre* seen in relation to prophecies and history, see L329, L451, L489.
[24] *Pascal et la raison du politique* (Paris, 1984), ch. 3.

L991, clearly has none of these associations; in all cases it contains the association of social, political, or religious disturbances. In the *Lettres provinciales*, this latter sense pertains to both the singular and plural forms of *désordre*.[25]

The image of the order of the body mirrored in the orderliness of one's life finds a vivid precedent in St Augustine's *De Civitate Dei*, where peace is seen to emanate from the ordered proportion of components of one's life:

> la paix du corps est donc une juste temperature de ses parties; la paix de l'ame sensitive, un repos bien reglé des appetits. La paix de l'ame raisonnable est le juste accord de la connoissance et de l'action.[26]

Augustine goes on to perceive understanding between man and God as part of the same orderliness.

Two other distinct semantic usages of *ordre* can be discerned in the *Pensées*: a command (O5), as evidenced in L68, L453, the third occurrence of the word in L489, L503, L609, L706, L846, and L945;[27] and holy orders (O6), as seen in both cases of the word in L950. There remains one fragment where Pascal's use of *ordre* can be linked to this last category; it constitutes a quotation from the Bible, and does not represent Pascal's own semantic usage (as in L950, which is a quotation from the papal bull of Paul IV): 'Qu'il devait y avoir un nouveau Testament qui serait éternel, qu'il devait y avoir une autre prêtrise selon l'ordre de Melchisedech [...]' (L609). 'L'ordre de Melchisedech' refers to Ps. 109: 4, familiar in the canon of the Mass, as well as to Gen. 14: 18, and, in the New Testament, Heb. 5: 6, 10; 6: 20; 7: 1, and can best be defined as Melchisedech's elevated priestly line or succession. The writer of the Epistle to the Hebrews refers to Melchisedech in order to prove the superiority of the priesthood of Christ, prefigured by Melchisedech, over that of Aaron and the Levites.

It is significant that the emphasis of the word *ordre* in the *Lettres*

---

[25] See Letters 5, p. 388; 6, p. 395; 7, p. 401; 9, p. 408; 10, p. 414; 11, p. 421; 13, p. 433; 16, pp. 447, 453; 18, p. 466.
[26] *De la cité de Dieu*, trans. by Ceriziers (1655), XIX. xiii. 647.
[27] At times this meaning of *ordre* (a command) overlaps with the sense of divine will, which I discussed in the previous paragraphs. However, the meanings are generally clear, especially where *ordre* is associated with human beings (e.g. 'l'ordre du roi' in L706).

provinciales differs markedly from that in the *Pensées*, for it lacks the variety and tension which we find in the *Pensées*, appearing almost exclusively in the context of a command or law (O5),[28] or of a religious order (O6).[29] This would mean that, for Pascal, the term, with all its associations, plays a much more central role in an apologetical than in a polemical context. With this distinction in mind, I intend later to consider 'Ordre' as a chapter title of a possible planned apology.

ORDONNER

But first, an examination of the verb *ordonner* and its relation to the noun *ordre* is necessary. In Arnauld and Nicole's *Logique*, *ordonner* is named as one of man's four 'principales operations de l'esprit', along with *concevoir*, *juger*, and *raisonner*:

> On appelle ici *ordonner* l'action de l'esprit, par laquelle ayant sur un même sujet, comme sur le corps humain, diverses idées, divers jugemens, et divers raisonnemens, il les dispose en la maniere la plus propre pour faire connoître ce sujet. C'est ce qu'on appelle encore *méthode*.[30]

Significantly, Lancelot and Nicole, in their *Grammaire*, omitted *ordonner* while maintaining the other three 'operations', and it is clear that, from the space devoted to each of these mental operations in the *Logique*, *ordonner* was considered the least important. If we are to relate the use of the verb to any of the categories in the *Pensées*, it would clearly be associated with O1, the ordering of materials, and O2, a plane of experience, in the context of 'ordre géométrique'. The *Logique* equates this sort of ordering with the term *méthode*, and the juxtaposition of the terms *méthode* and *ordre* in *De l'esprit géométrique*, a text which Arnauld and Nicole acknowledge as influencing them,[31] supports

---

[28] See Letters 5, pp. 387, 391; 8, pp. 403, 407; 12, p. 429; 13, pp. 433, 434; 14, pp. 435, 438, 439, 440; 15, p. 444; 16, p. 451. Although *ordre* is used frequently in the *Lettres provinciales* as 'l'ordre de Dieu', in each case it can be interpreted as the law or order of God, unlike in the *Pensées*, where it is used predominantly in juxtaposition with 'l'ordre du monde'.
[29] See Letter 2, Seuil 378; Letter 15, Seuil 442.
[30] A. Arnauld and P. Nicole, *La Logique ou L'Art de penser* (1662), ed. P. Clair and F. Girbal (Paris, 1981), 38.
[31] Ibid. 21.

this view. However, as I have already indicated,[32] the word *méthode* does not appear at all in the *Pensées* with this meaning, and Pascal's choice to use *ordre* and not *méthode* in this sense indicates a difference of approach from that in *De l'esprit géométrique*. It should also be noted that all examples of the verb *ordonner* in the *Pensées* (eighteen in all) can be related to the category O5, a command, and not to the way in which Arnauld and Nicole use it. Thus, although I will compare some uses of *ordre* in the *Pensées* with *De l'esprit géométrique*, it must be remembered that *ordre* in an apologetical, and indeed rhetorical, context differs in its totality from *ordre* as used in the *Logique* and *De l'esprit géométrique*.[33]

If at this stage we are to draw any insight from the multiplicity of uses of *ordre* in the *Pensées*, it is in their inter-referentiality. Not only is there interplay between the three orders in the sense of O2, but we have seen how some categories overlap. Martin Price introduces his study, *To the Palace of Wisdom*, with the example of Pascal's conception of order (largely with respect to the three orders), so as to show 'the dramatic way in which he raises the question of orders and all but subverts the more traditional idea of Order'.[34] As with the instability of language in the *Pensées*, the reader is led to question and indeed to overturn the notion of a single and irreversible order in a fallen world.

ORDER AND FRAGMENTATION

As it has been established with a fair degree of certainty that the list of chapter headings was in fact dictated by Pascal,[35] and that he intended to place his fragments into a particular order, it is

[32] See my discussion of *De l'esprit géométrique* in the Introduction.
[33] See Norman, *Portraits of Thought*, 118, and A. McKenna, *De Pascal à Voltaire* (Oxford, 1990), i. 44–5.
[34] *To the Palace of Wisdom: Studies in Order and Energy from Dryden to Blake* (Edwardsville, Ill., 1964), 27.
[35] See e.g. A. Barnes, 'La Table des titres de la copie des *Pensées* est-elle de Pascal?', *French Studies* (1953), 140–6. Cf. P. Sellier's enlightening comment in 'L'Ouverture de l'apologie pascalienne', *XVIIe Siècle*, 177 (Oct.–Dec. 1992), that we should consider the list of titles not as the order in which Pascal would have placed his *liasses* but rather as 'un simple récapitulatif de dossiers, un outil commode qui permettait à l'écrivain de trouver aisément la liasse dont il avait besoin, dans le dispositif d'une bureaucratique assez compliquée' (p. 437).

necessary here to consider the way in which fragmentation can be linked to the notion of order in the *Pensées*. From the fragments themselves, it is easy to perceive that Pascal intended to use 'lettres' (L4, L5, L7, L9, L11), 'chapitres' (L45), and 'dialogues' (L2). Yet it is more difficult to know in what state he would have left his collected thoughts. As a starting-point, I have chosen to consider the contrasting views of two prominent commentators, Lucien Goldmann and Jean Mesnard.

Goldmann's *Le Dieu caché* examines the tragic vision of both the *Pensées* and Racine's theatre. It is in this context that he appraises the question of fragmentation in the *Pensées*: according to him, the fragment represents the only adequate means of communicating man's paradoxical nature:

Chercher le 'vrai' plan des *Pensées* nous paraît ainsi une entreprise antipascalienne par excellence, une entreprise qui va à l'encontre de la cohérence du texte, et méconnaît implicitement ce qui constitue aussi bien son contenu intellectuel que l'essence de sa valeur littéraire. Il peut y avoir un plan logique pour un écrit rationaliste, un ordre de la persuasion pour un écrit spirituel; il n'y a, pour une œuvre tragique, qu'une seule forme d'ordre valable, celui du fragment, qui est recherche d'ordre, mais recherche qui n'a pas réussi, et ne peut pas réussir, à l'approcher.[36]

It would indeed seem to be wrong to assign a definitive structure to the *Pensées*. But, to justify their fragmentariness by the fact that they constitute 'une œuvre tragique' seems to me equally misguided. The importance which Pascal attributed to the word *ordre* and the authentication of the 'table des matières' both contradict Goldmann's attempt to subsume the question of fragmentation and order into his larger concern, the tragic vision of the *Pensées*. Furthermore, Goldmann concludes his discussion of paradox and the fragment by stating his preference for the Brunschvicg edition ahead of the Lafuma edition. He quotes Brunschvicg's declaration that this edition aims to avoid 'toute idée préconçue sur ce qu'aurait pu être l'*Apologie* de Pascal'.[37] However, Brunschvicg's edition, while not speculating upon the possible order which Pascal would have given to his completed work, still imposes thematic structures, and indeed strictures, upon the *Pensées*, and attempts to assign to them a coherence which arguably contradicts Pascal's aims and which in turn would seem to counter Goldmann's assertions.

[36] p. 220.   [37] Ibid. 227.

Mesnard, on the other hand, in his discussion of fragmentation cites L784 to justify order in the *Pensées*:

'Les mots diversement rangés font différents effets' (L784)
Comment une telle obsession de l'ordre ne se serait-elle pas traduite par l'établissement d'un plan détaillé tel que le présentent les *Copies*? Marque d'un génie dialectique, plutôt que tragique.[38]

Mesnard's claim that L784 supports the importance which Pascal attaches to ordering of fragments is misplaced, for it is ordering of *words* with which he is concerned in this particular fragment. Mesnard goes on:

L'œuvre étant demeurée inachevée, dira-t-on encore, le plan proposé ne saurait être que provisoire. Soit; mais là n'est pas la question. Le texte des fragments n'est pas moins provisoire. L'important n'est pas que le plan soit définitif, mais qu'il soit de Pascal. L'œuvre étant inachevée, nous ne pouvons disposer que d'un plan provisoire: acceptons-le.[39]

All that is expressed here is perfectly justified, but it is essential to make a distinction between 'le texte' and 'le plan'. While we can study the text which Pascal wrote without necessarily making suppositions about how it would have fitted into an apology, it would be impossible to analyse the provisional plan with the same degree of objectivity. Thus, we can accept that Pascal himself dictated the list of chapter titles, but we cannot with justice incorporate everything which he wrote into a provisional structure. Mesnard's more recent assertion in his article, 'Pourquoi les *Pensées* de Pascal se présentent-elles sous forme de fragments?', that the composition of the fragment relies on 'une fonction dynamique'[40] which is applied to a particular form of fragmentary composition, comes closer to my view of fragmentation in the *Pensées*, although he still insists on a more rigorous ordering of the text.[41]

[38] *Les 'Pensées' de Pascal* (Paris, 1976), 46. [39] Ibid.
[40] *Papers on French Seventeenth-Century Literature*, 18–19 (1983), 643. Cf. L. Thirouin, 'Les Premières Liasses des *Pensées*: Architecture et signification', *XVIIe Siècle*, 177 (Oct.–Dec. 1992), who rejects 'une rationalité thématique' (p. 453) in the ordering of the *liasses* and argues instead that 'la pensée de Pascal se déploie selon un mode musical, faite de thèmes qui sont exposés puis développés et maintes fois repris en des variations systématiques' (p. 456).
[41] Cf. V. Carraud in *Pascal et la philosophie* (Paris, 1992): 'la table des titres qui figure dans les deux Copies est moins le sommaire d'une future *Apologie de la religion chrétienne* qu'elle ne présente l'état [. . .] de la réorganisation que Pascal fait entre 1659 et 1662 [. . .] des papiers dont il dispose' (p. 100).

L532: 'LE VÉRITABLE ORDRE'

One fragment, L532, which is widely perceived as central to the question of order, and which has, by the same token, provoked many varied responses, deserves particular attention:

Pyrr.

J'écrirai ici mes pensées sans ordre et non pas peut-être dans une confusion sans dessein. C'est le véritable ordre et qui marquera toujours mon objet par le désordre même.

Je ferais trop d'honneur à mon sujet si je le traitais avec ordre puisque je veux montrer qu'il en est incapable. (L532)

The main problem centres on the enigmatic heading, 'Pyrr'. On the one hand, critics such as Jean Mesnard claim that the title, standing for 'Pyrrhonisme', proves the importance which Pascal placed on a definitive ordering of his text as opposed to the sceptics' exclusion of all order.[42] On the other hand, those writers who are at pains to demonstrate Pascal's deliberate use of fragmentation in the *Pensées*, such as Lucien Goldmann, and, more recently, Sara Melzer and Buford Norman, tend to ignore or to dismiss the significance of the title.[43] In his edition of the *Pensées* (*Discours sur la religion et sur quelques autres sujets*), Emmanuel Martineau makes the somewhat vague remark about the title that 'je présume que *pyrrhonisme* est une façon d'évoquer l'*Apologie*'.[44] It is not surprising that he underestimates this fragment, as all shorter and fragmentary passages are collated in his edition into longer, continuous sections. Anthony Pugh attempts to side-step the difficulty of the fragment by declaring that it was 'plainly written at an early stage, when

---

[42] See 'Pourquoi les *Pensées* de Pascal se présentent-elles sous forme de fragments?', 637–8; also his *Les 'Pensées' de Pascal*, 290.

[43] Goldmann, *Le Dieu caché*, 223; S. E. Melzer, *Discourses of the Fall: A Study of Pascal's 'Pensées'* (London, 1986), 65–6; Norman, *Portraits of Thought*, 201 n. 28. See also M. J. Maggioni, in *The 'Pensées' of Pascal: A Study in Baroque Style* (Washington, DC, 1950), 52, who passes over the title without examining it in any detail. See also F. Mariner, 'The Order of Disorder: The Problem of the Fragment in Pascal's *Pensées*', *Papers on French Seventeenth-Century Literature*, 20/38 (1993), 171–82, for a rehearsal of some of the differing critical readings of L532.

[44] *Discours sur la religion et sur quelques autres sujets*, ed. E. Martineau (Paris, 1992), 258.

Pascal decided to amass a large number of disconnected fragments'.[45] This view clearly belittles the importance of L532.

In his edition of the *Pensées* and elsewhere,[46] Michel Le Guern offers the ingenious explanation that the heading does not represent 'Pyrrhonisme' but rather 'Principes', an abbreviation of Descartes's *Principes de la philosophie*. His hypothesis that L532 constitutes a note on the 'Lettre-Préface' of the *Principes*, where Pascal contrasts his proposed order with the methodical order of Descartes, is indeed plausible. He claims that Pascal imposed a capital 'P' over a small 'p', hence explaining in his view earlier editors' mis-reading of the first two letters as 'Py'. However, a close examination of this and other fragments has convinced me that Le Guern's thesis cannot be followed. First, the fact that Pascal heads another two fragments, L518 and L905, with 'Pyrr' or 'Pyrrhonisme' makes it more likely that L532 is entitled 'Pyrr': nowhere in the *Pensées* do we find any heading abbreviated to 'Prin' or any direct reference to the title *Principes de la philosophie*. Secondly, although the formation of the word 'Pyrr' in L532 is different from that in L518 (see Figs. 1 and 2), the second letter is no more discernible as a small 'p' than as a 'y'; the capital 'P', which Le Guern assumes to be written over another letter, is formed in a very similar way in other fragments, such as L158, where there is no question of superimposition (see Fig. 3). Thirdly, most other fragments where Pascal writes the word 'principes', such as L158 and L698 (see Figs. 3 and 4), show that he dots the 'i' clearly and separates the 'i' distinctly from the 'n', neither of which is at all discernible in the title of L532.

If, therefore, we take it that the more likely reading of the heading is indeed an abbreviation of 'Pyrrhonisme', we have still to attempt to understand its significance in this fragment. One question which is closely related to that of the title is the identity of the speaker. Can we say that it is Pascal himself, the dialectician or the voice of a sceptical interlocutor? It is unlikely that the fragment

---

[45] *The Composition of Pascal's 'Apologia'* (Toronto, 1984), 45. Although L532 was written on the earliest paper type, 'cadran1/ B cœur C', as Ernst has shown, the fact that a fragment like L780 (to be discussed later), which shows a similar radical approach towards ordering, was written on one of the latest paper types, FNIC, indicates that the idea of a new way of ordering material was one that informed both early and late stages of composition.

[46] (Paris, 1977), ii. 302–3; and Le Guern, *Pascal et Descartes* (Paris, 1971), 48.

represents a working note intended only for Pascal, for such a coherent and polished statement of intent presupposes a reader other than the writer himself. Jean Mesnard interprets L532 as 'une sorte de parodie de la doctrine exposée',[47] where presumably he sees the speaker as Pascal himself or an invented character parodying the sceptics' approach to disorder. However, the persuasive eloquence of the fragment implies a greater seriousness than mere parody.

There remains the possibility, especially with the word 'Pyrrhonisme' heading the passage, that the speaker is a sceptic proclaiming his doctrine of disorder, especially as this would be in keeping with the dialectician's depiction in L131 of the sceptical doctrine of 'l'incertitude de notre origine qui enferme celle de notre nature'. Yet, the words 'et non pas une confusion sans dessein' immediately contradict a pyrrhonist belief in the impossibility of all order. This use of the disjunctive 'et' followed by a negative statement is commonly found in the *Pensées*, implying 'mais'. In L525, for example, Pascal originally wrote 'mais' but replaced it with 'et', obviously to avoid the repetition of 'mais' within the sentence:

La coutume ne doit être suivie que parce qu'elle est la coutume, *et non* parce qu'elle est raisonnable ou juste, mais le peuple la suit par cette seule raison qu'il la croit juste. (L525)[48]

To return to L532, therefore, within the apparent confusion there exists a design: the seventeenth-century use of *dessein* incorporates the traditional sense of *intention* and *projet*, as the Academy dictionary of 1694 defines it, with the sense of what we now know as *dessin*, that of ordering and structure, perhaps best defined by the 1690 Furetière dictionary as 'la pensée qu'on a dans l'imagination de l'ordre, de la distribution et de la construction d'un tableau, d'un Poëme, d'un livre [...]'.[49] A similar tension between these

---

[47] 'Pourquoi les *Pensées* de Pascal se présentent-elles sous forme de fragments?', 638.

[48] My italics. Cf. also L505: 'C'est le consentement de vous à vous-même et la voix constante de votre raison et non des autres qui vous doit faire croire'; and L512: 'Il faut tout d'un coup voir la chose, d'un seul regard et non pas par progrès de raisonnement.'

[49] L. Marin gives an insightful reading of these words, in 'Pascal: Text, Author, Discourse...' *Yale French Studies*, 52 (1975), 131: 'It is pointed out that disorder is and will be the principle of writing that speaks of human disorder, but in addition,

meanings can be found in the use of *dessein* in L780, the fragment in which the 'divisions de Charron' and, significantly, 'la confusion de Montaigne' are criticized:

> Le sot projet qu'il [Montaigne] a de se peindre et cela non pas en passant et contre ses maximes, comme il arrive à tout le monde de faillir, mais par ses propres maximes et par un dessein premier et principal. (L780)

Dessein in this context not only means 'intention', as A. J. Krailsheimer translates it, but also contains the sense of ordering in relation to Montaigne's 'confusion', which is evoked in the previous paragraph of L780. The speaker's reference to writing 'non pas peut-être dans une confusion sans dessein' in L532, therefore, distinguishes it from the confusion of Montaigne's ordering.[50] Perhaps therein lies the key to the mysterious 'Pyrrhonisme' which heads L532. Both other fragments which are entitled 'Pyrrhonisme', L518 and L905, contain references to Montaigne's *Essais*.[51] Indeed, in Pascal's perception of Pyrrhonism, Montaigne was, to use Michel Le Guern's phrase, 'le représentant le plus remarquable'.[52] Therefore, it is conceivable that in L532 Pascal is referring to the sceptical doctrine of disorder and, in particular, to Montaigne's own lack of ordering. The speaker, whom we can now assume to be the dialectician, acknowledges a method of disorder as his own but distinguishes it from the complete disorder of the sceptics and of Montaigne in particular. It is indeed possible that the discussion of the pyrrhonist notion of disorder in L532 contains a reference to a passage in the *Essais* where Montaigne speaks of his lack of concern for order:

> that this disorder of discourse must be distinguished from the disorder of the object of discourse, of which the former is but the mark. Its confusion is not without design (*dessein*); it is not without intention or project, nor without design (*dessin*), that is, without structure. The true order of the discourse is an intentional structure of disorder, whose function is less to signify than to indicate its referent.' See also D. C. Stanton's 'Pascal's Fragmentary Thoughts: Dis-order and its Overdetermination', *Semiotica*, 51 (1984), 211–35.

[50] It is difficult to concur with Carraud in *Pascal et la philosophie*, who suggests that 'le reproche adressé à Montaigne n'est pas d'être confus, mais de ne l'être pas assez' (p. 291).

[51] B. Croquette, in *Pascal et Montaigne* (Geneva, 1974), lists L518 as being inspired by *Essais* II. xii. 471, and III. xiii. 1090–1, and L905 deriving its influence from II. xx. 655 and III. i. 781. Moreover, both L518 and L905 were written on the same paper type (defined by Ernst as 'cadran I/ B cœur C') as L532, which further emphasizes their affinity.   [52] In his edn. of the *Pensées*, ii. 300 n. 3.

Les belles matieres tiennent tousjours bien leur reng en quelque place qu'on les seme. Moi, qui ay plus de soin du poids et utilité des discours que de leur ordre et suite, ne doy pas craindre de loger icy un peu à l'escart une très-belle histoire.[53]

Moreover, we find in the worldly circle of Pascal a similar notion of order in a text. Méré, in the posthumously published *De l'éloquence et de l'entretien*, writes,

Je ne m'attache pas à mettre dans un ordre bien exact tout ce que j'écris en cet Ouvrage, [. . .] je n'ai pour toute méthode, qu'un ordre naturel, et même selon mon caprice ou mon goût [. . .].[54]

It is possible that Pascal was again reacting against just such a conception of order, but, as with Méré, some sort of order is acknowledged through the apparent disorder.

Thus, although disorder is seen as a dominant principle, it is not the random formlessness which a sceptical interlocutor would advocate. Perhaps the *dessein* which the speaker contemplates relates to non-sequential discourse as opposed to the long chapters which, as in the case of Charron, 'attristent et ennuient' (L780).

In *De l'esprit géométrique*, Pascal attempts 'l'explication du véritable ordre, qui consiste [. . .] à tout définir et à tout prouver'.[55] He then immediately rejects such an ideal order as 'absolument impossible', because 'les hommes sont dans une impuissance naturelle et immuable de traiter quelque science que ce soit, dans un ordre absolument accompli'.[56] Yet he acknowledges geometric order, although inferior to perfect order, as a feasible way of appealing to the human mind. It is this distinction which is made between 'l'esprit de géométrie' and 'l'esprit de finesse' in L513: 'La finesse est la part du jugement, la géométrie est celle de l'esprit'.[57] Thus, the prevailing disorder of the *Pensées* would seem to be tempered by aspects of geometric order, which would distinguish it from the complete disorder upheld by the sceptics.

However, it is important to note that *désordre* cannot be

---

[53] II. xxvii. 678.
[54] *Œuvres*, ed. C. Boudhours (3 vols., Paris, 1930), iii. 103.
[55] Seuil 349.   [56] Ibid. 350.
[57] See Norman, *Portraits of Thought* for a useful analysis of terms such as *jugement*, *sentiment*, and *raisonnement*, esp. in relation to *De l'esprit géométrique*. See also M. Warner, *Philosophical Finesse: Studies in the Art of Rational Persuasion* (Oxford, 1989), 153–4.

perceived as an alien concept to Pascal. In fact, the Académie dictionary defines *désordre* as 'renversement', and the 1680 Richelet dictionary reads it as 'dérèglement', both of which are terms that play a very important part in the *Pensées*. Sara Melzer, despite not taking into account the aspects of order which distinguish it from the sceptics' view of it, offers an enlightening interpretation of disorder in L532:

> The highlighting of disorder in the narrator's discourse has four effects. First, it emphasizes the chaotic nature of the subject matter. To impose order on an inherently disorderly subject matter would be false and misleading. Second, it shows that all discourse is by nature mechanical and conventional and thus there can be no order. Any order that one chooses can be reversed. Third, it serves a specific persuasive purpose: the discourse of disorder turns the reader against the proud rationalism of Descartes which deludes itself into thinking that it can possess a true order. Fourth, it creates the desire for a transcendent order.[58]

This reading of the fragment certainly comes closer to Pascal's conception of the 'renversement continuel du pour au contre' (L93) than does the rigid order which many critics have attempted to assign to the *Pensées*. Man in his fallen state cannot attain true order by himself. As the dialectician asserts in fragment L530, 'Il faudrait avoir une règle. La raison s'offre mais elle est ployable à tous sens. Et ainsi il n'y en a point' (L530).

Such a notion of order is not peculiar to Pascal, for we find similar ideas in writings of the Jansenist circle which Pascal frequented. Martin de Barcos, abbé de Saint-Cyran, for example, wrote to la Mère Angélique in a letter dated December 1652 the following words, which throw fascinating light upon the Jansenist view of order:

> Permettez moy de vous dire que vous avez tort de vous excuser du desordre de vos discours et de vos pensées, puis que s'ils estoient autrement ils ne seroient pas dans l'ordre, surtout pour une personne de votre profession. Comme il y a une sagesse qui est folie devant Dieu, il y a aussy un ordre qui est desordre; et par consequent il y a une folie qui est sagesse, et un desordre qui est un reglement veritable [...].[59]

---

[58] *Discourses of the Fall*, 66.
[59] Letter of 5 Dec. 1652, taken from *Correspondance*, ed. L. Goldmann (Paris, 1956), 140. P. Sellier, in *Pascal et Saint Augustin*, 560–1, claims that Pascal's ideas on order were influenced by the apparent haphazard state of a number of

In L532, therefore, when the speaker stresses that both his broader objective (the *objet*), which is presumably the eventual depiction of man's happiness with God, and his more specific subject matter (the *sujet*), which in this case would be a discussion of scepticism and man's fallen state, are dominated by disorder, it represents an acknowledgement of fallen man's inability to attain perfect order.[60] Only Christ on this earth was able to achieve true clarity:

J.-C. a dit les choses grandes si simplement qu'il semble qu'il ne les a pas pensées, et si nettement néanmoins qu'on voit bien ce qu'il en pensait. Cette clarté jointe à cette naïveté est admirable. (L309)

Thus, in his role as dialectician or persuader, Pascal cannot hope to attain the order of divine truth. As he asserts in the section on the art of persuasion in *De l'esprit géométrique*,

Je ne parle pas ici des vérités divines, que je n'aurais garde de faire tomber sous l'art de persuader, car elles sont infiniment au-dessus de la nature: Dieu seul peut les mettre dans l'âme, et par la manière qu'il lui plaît.[61]

It is in God alone that ultimate order can be attained.

ORDRE AS DISPOSITIO

However, despite the evidence that Pascal did not intend a rigid structure for his work, not to discuss the proposed ordering which Pascal set down in the chapter headings and in the first *liasse* would be to ignore the central problem of order in the *Pensées*. Most

---

Augustine's works, such as his Commentaries on the Psalms and on St John: 'Pourtant ce désordre n'est pas plus réel que celui des astres qui semblent vagabonder dans le ciel. Tout gravite autour du Dieu biblique. L'univers augustinien a la profondeur et l'unité d'une vision poétique: c'est une sphère dont le centre est partout. Toute l'apologie pascalienne obéit au même principe de composition.' However, it must be added that Pascal's own observations on order and disorder, which I have cited, indicate that he viewed disorder as an inherent part of fallen man's state. This in turn corresponds with Barcos's comments on order. At the same time, as Mesnard has successfully shown in 'Martin de Barcos et les disputes internes de Port-Royal', *Chroniques de Port-Royal*, 26–8 (1977–9), 73–94, we should not overestimate the proximity of Barcos's and Pascal's thought. Barcos was deeply opposed to both the *Lettres provinciales* and the *Pensées*.

[60] The juxtaposition of *objet* and *sujet* can also be found in L427 and L449.
[61] Seuil 355.

commentators of the dossier entitled 'Ordre' either interpret it simply as rough working notes[62] or see it as an embryonic introduction.[63] It is significant that adherents of this second theory, such as Pol Ernst and Anthony Pugh, strongly advocate a coherent structure in what they perceive to be the unfinished apology. To do otherwise would immediately undermine the main thrust of their thesis. Pol Ernst's recent reconstruction work on the state of the fragments has since proved that many of the fragments in this *liasse* were written at a late stage and do not constitute early jottings.[64] These findings show how Pascal was as preoccupied as ever with the problem of ordering as he neared the end of his life. However, the state of fragments such as L2, L5, L8, L11, and L12 still suggests that the *liasse* formed the basis of working notes on the complexities of ordering. It is particularly revealing to find that the idea of using an epistolary format in the fragments (as we see in L5, L7, L9, and L11) was a relatively late thought.

This leads to the problem of the title, 'Ordre'. Pugh argues that the fragment L694 proves Pascal's intention to write a 'discours d'ordre':

Ordre.—J'aurais bien pris ce discours d'ordre comme celui-ci: pour montrer la vanité de toutes sortes de conditions, montrer la vanité des vies communes, et puis la vanité des vies philosophiques, pyrrhoniennes, stoïques; mais l'ordre n'y serait pas gardé. (L694)

Yet it would seem that the speaker here is not discussing a 'discours' *on* order, as Pugh suggests,[65] but rather the uselessness of treating his subject in a particular order, which he then elaborates.[66]

---

[62] e.g. H. Gouhier, *Blaise Pascal: Commentaires* (Paris, 1966), 181: 'La liasse I groupe des textes sur *Ordre* qui sont des notes de travail, hors série, et non celles d'une introduction ou d'un premier chapitre.' See also A. Adam, 'Sur les *Pensées* de Pascal', *Information littéraire*, 9 (1957), 6; P. Sellier (ed.), *Pensées* (Paris, 1976), 35.

[63] See Ernst, *Approches pascaliennes*, 17–47; Pugh, *The Composition of Pascal's 'Apologia'*, 29–45. P. Bayley neatly combines both readings in 'A Reading of the First *Liasse*', in D. L. Rubin and M. B. McKinley (eds.), *Convergences*, calling it a 'start to an apology' (p. 200), but also recognizing the need to consider it at first as 'notes' rather than as a 'project' (206 n. 1).

[64] See 'Géologie et stratigraphie des *Pensées* de Pascal' (4 vols., thesis, Univ. of Paris IV, 1990), 192–3. Fragments L5, L7, L8, L9, L11 as well as L387 were written on the paper FNIC, which dates from the spring of 1658 and represents the last of the 'strates majeures'.

[65] See Pugh, *The Composition of Pascal's 'Apologia'*, 43.

[66] In this interpretation I concur with A. J. Krailsheimer's translation of the fragment in *Pensées*; he translates the passage on *discours d'ordre* as: 'I could easily have treated this discourse in this kind of order'.

L694 represents, then, another working note on possible ways of approaching the proposed subject-matter, whether it be an apology or not. Therefore, can the title of the dossier be regarded as another guiding note for Pascal? It seems unlikely that, even if Pascal did intend an introduction on how he was going to treat his topic, he would have entitled it 'Ordre', a word which indicates the heading of a rough plan, intended for the writer alone. Moreover, a *sententia* which first appeared in the Port-Royal edition of the *Pensées* may testify to the fact that, in its incomplete state, we cannot know how Pascal would have introduced his projected apology: 'La dernière chose qu'on trouve en faisant un ouvrage est de savoir celle qu'il faut mettre la première' (L976).

After questioning the likelihood of 'Ordre' being used as a chapter title in the final version of an intended apology, it would be inevitable for us to continue by considering the other chapter headings. It is clear that Pascal was aware of the fact that ordering can obscure an argument, as can be seen in his comment about the 'divisions de Charron, qui attristent et ennuient' (L780). Yet the three headings which follow 'Ordre' in the title page, 'Vanité', 'Misère', and 'Ennui', are all used as chapter headings by Charron in his *De la sagesse*, which would seem to contradict his statement. Perhaps these headings also represent guiding notes for Pascal and not final chapter headings, despite the probability that many of the titles would still have played an important part in the completed work.

The fragment L696 has been cited as further proof of the importance which Pascal attached to ordering in the *Pensées*, and it merits our particular attention:[67]

> Qu'on ne dise pas que je n'ai rien dit de nouveau, la disposition des matières est nouvelle. Quand on joue à la paume c'est une même balle dont joue l'un et l'autre, mais l'un la place mieux.
> J'aimerais autant qu'on me dise que je me suis servi des mots anciens. Et comme si les mêmes pensées ne formaient pas un autre corps de discours par une disposition différente, aussi bien que les mêmes mots forment d'autres pensées par leur différente disposition. (L696)

Yet the very examples which Pascal uses here show that he is not concerned with the *order* in which he puts his fragments so much as

---

[67] Indeed, Pugh uses this fragment in his evidence for Pascal's ordering in the *Pensées* (*The Composition of Pascal's 'Apologia'*, 45).

the way in which he organizes his thoughts. Thus, in the first image, it is the *way* in which each player places the same ball which is more important. A passage from Montaigne's chapter 'Des livres' is a possible source of this passage. Significantly, Montaigne does not concern himself with the ordering of material but rather with 'la façon' in which he treats it: 'Qu'on ne s'attende pas aux matieres, mais à la façon que j'y donne.'[68] Furthermore, it is significant that in L696, in the *Recueil original*, Pascal wrote the words 'l'ordre de' before deleting them and substituting them with 'la disposition des matières'. This would suggest that he felt the word 'ordre' to be incorrect in the fragment, perhaps because it implies a too rigorous ordering, as opposed to the more abstract meaning attached to 'disposition'. If we take into account the sense of 'disposition' as *dispositio*, one of the five parts of rhetoric,[69] especially in conjunction with the tennis image in the same fragment, it would be plausible to read the word not as the ordering of material into chapters but rather the arrangement of ideas within fragments. Pierre Force has shown how in this fragment *dispositio* is opposed to *inventio*:

> On sait que dans l'ancienne rhétorique, l'ordre du discours (*dispositio*) est distingué de son style (*elocutio*) et de son contenu (*inventio*). La revendication d'originalité de Pascal porte sur l'ordre et non pas sur le contenu. Plus précisément, cette revendication d'originalité est double: elle est d'abord stylistique (même si Pascal n'y insiste pas). Pascal déclare avoir utilisé la langue (les 'mots anciens') d'une manière nouvelle. Les thèses de saint Augustin ou de Montaigne, par le simple fait d'être formulées autrement, prennent une signification nouvelle. Mais le sens des prédécesseurs de Pascal est surtout changé par le bouleversement que Pascal fait subir à l'ordre des arguments.[70]

Moreover, *dispositio* can be used to convey the impression of the *disorder* of language in a way that the simple ordering of themes into coherent chapters could not. Ralph Heyndels makes this point

---

[68] *Essais*, II. x. 387.
[69] The other 4 parts of rhetoric are *inventio, elocutio, memoria*, and *actio*. See P. Topliss, *The Rhetoric of Pascal* (Amsterdam, 1966), 13. See also P. Kuentz, 'Le Rhétorique ou la mise à l'écart', *Communications*, 16 (1970), 143–57, who discusses these 4 parts with reference to *La Logique*.
[70] 'Ordre et signification chez Pascal', in D. Wetsel (ed.), *Meaning, Structure and History in the 'Pensées' of Pascal* (Paris, 1990), 45. See also Force's *Le Problème herméneutique chez Pascal* (Paris, 1989), 273–81.

in his work, *La Pensée fragmentée*: 'le discours discontinu actualise sa propre *dispositio*: il n'est pas l'expression seconde d'une pensée antérieure'.[71] Philippe Sellier even goes so far as to say that 'Pascal avait mis au point une véritable stratégie d'anéantissement par la *dispositio*'.[72] The dialectician uses *dispositio* to manipulate his reader's responses. This interpretation also helps to clarify fragment L532, where the dialectician sees lack of order in language as 'le véritable ordre et qui marquera toujours mon objet par le désordre même'. This new attitude towards order, as he asserts in L696, would also counteract earlier apologists, such as René du Pont in *La Philosophie des esprits* (1602), who claims that rhetoric 'enseigne la disposition de toutes harangues et discours en si bel ordre, que rien ne s'y trouve de confus'.[73] For Pascal, obscurity plays an essential role in the *dispositio* of the *Pensées*.

John Gallucci, in an illuminating paper entitled 'Politique et écriture: La *Disposition* pascalienne comme principe de liberté',[74] examines both the verb *disposer* and the noun *disposition* as they appear in the *Pensées*. Following the definition of *disposer*, given by the Furetière dictionary as 'ordonner en maître', Gallucci shows how the verb 'signale un acte qui est la manifestation et la preuve de la liberté et du pouvoir du sujet', evident in fragments such as L708 and L836.[75] Similarly, the noun as it appears in L696 has a dynamic function which goes beyond mere ordering. As Gallucci puts it, 'Surtout, la disposition est un acte. Les mots de Pascal sont là; mais leur disposition demande une interprétation, une lecture.' This point leads back to my discussion of *interprétation*, where I

[71] *La Pensée fragmentée: Discontinuité formelle et question du sens* (Brussels, 1985), 28.
[72] 'Imaginaire et rhétorique dans les *Pensées*', in L. M. Heller and I. M. Richmond (eds.), *Pascal thématique des 'Pensées'* (Paris, 1988), 129. See esp. '*Dispositio et memoria*' (pp. 128–35).
[73] (1628 edn.), 231–2. Cf. Jean-Pierre Camus in *Les Diversitez* (1609), who follows the Platonist conception that *l'ordre* is 'l'ame de l'univers [...] par sa belle disposition', so as to show that 'la methode est une des principales parties d'un discours net et bien tissu, autrement ce n'est qu'une chimere informe' (ii. 313).
[74] Presented at Clermont-Ferrand in Sept. 1990, and published in G. Ferreyrolles (ed.), *Justice et force: Politiques au temps de Pascal* (Paris, 1993). My quotations from this paper come from a copy kindly supplied by the author.
[75] See also how the verb *disposer* is used to convey the notion of power (*potestas*) and legal terms (*leges* and *jus*) in Pascal's translation from the Latin of his *Histoire de la roulette*: 'Car je n'ai pas mis des conditions à la dispensation de l'honneur, dont je ne dispose pas, mais seulement à celle des prix dont j'ai pu disposer à mon gré' (Seuil 121).

showed that the need for interpretation acts as a sign of man's fallen nature. Like *interprétation, disposition* is an act which reminds the reader of the disorder of his corrupt state and yet which pushes him to continue searching for true understanding and true order. Jean-François Sénault uses *disposition* in just this way; it acts as a reminder of our corruption and yet points towards the possibility of a positive end: 'le sentiment de nostre mal sera une disposition à nostre guerison'.[76]

MEMORIA

In addition to the re-evaluation of the traditional rhetorical use of *inventio* and *dispositio*, we find in the *Pensées* a radical reassessment of the fourth part of rhetoric, *memoria*, which is closely connected to the new ordering. The traditional use of *memoria* was to help orators remember the speeches they had composed, but, as Philippe Sellier has pointed out,

> par un de ces 'renversements' auxquels il excelle, Pascal a métamorphosé le champ de la *memoria*. La question que lui se pose est la suivante: comment écrire des textes qui s'impriment immédiatement et durablement dans la mémoire des lecteurs? La *memoria* pénètre ainsi jusqu'au plus intime de l'écriture littéraire.[77]

The use of fragmentary quotation from other texts (in itself a new form of ordering), notably from the Bible, St Augustine, and Montaigne, serves immediately to introduce into the reader's memory a wider context. A few words, often familiar to the informed reader, will provoke thought which goes beyond the immediate confines of the text. Memory will in itself act, like the fragmentary *dispositio* of the *Pensées*, as a persuasive device to

---

[76] Preface to *L'Homme criminel*.
[77] Introduction to Sellier's 1991 edn. of the *Pensées*, 77. This part of Sellier's argument is largely a recapitulation of his 'Imaginaire et rhétorique dans les *Pensées*', 128–35. In this article, he formulates different techniques which Pascal uses: (1) 'la recherche du discontinu et de la cassure' (pp. 122–4); (2) 'privilégier une panoplie de figures que la plupart des théoriciens du temps dénonçaient comme excessive' (pp. 124–7); (3) 'l'imitation originale des prophètes d'Israel' (pp. 127–8); (4) 'l'usage de la citation comme coup de fouet ou coup de massue' (p. 128); (5) 'le réglage du rire' (p. 128); and (6) 'la mathématisation des images et des arguments' (pp. 129–30).

search beyond the self. Indeed, in a fragment devoted to the inadequacies of the self, L688, memory and the self are identified as separate entities; our memory is named as a quality, distinct from the essence of our being: 'si on m'aime pour mon jugement, pour ma mémoire, m'aime-t-on? *moi*? Non, car je puis perdre ces qualités sans me perdre moi-même' (L688). Moreover, in L646, memory is seen as a *sentiment*, which in this context, as Buford Norman has shown,[78] means an operation of the mind: 'la mémoire, la joie sont des sentiments' (L646). This sense is made more apparent in L651: 'la mémoire est nécessaire pour toutes les opérations de la raison'.

Memory as a mental operation is crucial to the dialectician's purposes, for it is through this process that the reader can retain the thoughts expressed in the *Pensées*. The way that these thoughts can best be remembered is central to the form and content of the work. Significantly, written on the other side of a fragment in which the dialectician makes the maxim-like statement, 'lorsqu'on ne sait pas la vérité d'une chose il est bon qu'il y ait une erreur commune qui fixe l'esprit des hommes' (L744), we find an important consideration of the nature of writing and *memoria*. The dialectician, typically distancing himself by adopting the persona of Salomon de Tultie, names Epictetus and Montaigne as two examples of writers whose styles are particularly well suited to being imprinted in the reader's memory:

> La manière d'écrire d'Epictète, de Montaigne et de Salomon de Tultie est la plus d'usage, qui s'insinue le mieux, qui demeure plus dans la mémoire et qui se fait le plus citer, parce qu'elle est toute composée de pensées nées sur les entretiens ordinaires de la vie, comme quand on parlera de la commune erreur qui est dans le monde que la lune est cause de tout, on ne manquera jamais de dire que Salomon de Tultie dit que lorsqu'on ne sait pas la vérité d'une chose il est bon qu'il y ait une erreur commune, etc. (L745)[79]

Significantly, the dialectician stresses the fact that all three writers are concerned with 'les entretiens ordinaires de la vie'. The human

---

[78] *Portraits of Thought*, 14.
[79] Cf. Pascal's mention of 2 other successful writers, in L403: 'Salomon et Job ont le mieux connu et le mieux parlé de la misère de l'homme [. . .]'. As Sellier stresses in the introduction to his 1991 edn. of the *Pensées* (p. 79), it is the simple and clear expression of their language which is particularly effective. Cf. also L302, where Christ 'a dit les choses grandes si simplement qu'il semble qu'il ne les a pas pensées'.

condition lies at the foundation of their writing. Moreover, as the word *entretien* implies, human language is equally fundamental, accentuated in L745 by the repetition of the verbs *parler* and *dire*. As we saw earlier, language acts as a continual sign of man's fallenness, but it is through a recognition of this corruption that the dialectician can begin to persuade the reader of the necessity to search for a superior being beyond the obscurities of human language.

The memory is therefore receptive to simplicity as well as to the precision and concision of maxims. Similarly, the poetic quality of many of the fragments makes them more readily memorable. As La Harpe stressed in his *Cours de littérature*, 'le privilège de l'harmonie poétique est de graver dans la mémoire tout ce qu'elle exprime, ce que ne peut faire la meilleure prose'.[80]

ORDER, TRUTH, AND LANGUAGE

With 'le véritable ordre' in the *Pensées* being governed by disorder, and with the hope of attaining such perfection inherent in a recognition of our fallen nature, there exists the problem of order coexisting with a form of ultimate truth. I shall consider this problem at length in the final chapter, but it is necessary at this stage to consider briefly the way in which order and truth function together, for, as with language and order, the difficulty of applying a stable meaning even to such a transcendent concept as truth is immediately apparent. There exists an initial problem of distinguishing between geometrical truths, as described in *De l'esprit géométrique*, and those truths which are understood through the 'esprit de finesse'. Furthermore, man with his imperfect perception cannot hope to attain something as subtle as truth:

> La justice et la vérité sont deux pointes si subtiles que nos instruments sont trop mousses pour y toucher exactement. S'ils y arrivent ils en écachent la pointe et appuient tout autour plus sur le faux que sur le vrai. (L44)

For man in his fallen state, truth itself becomes corrupted by reason and the senses:

---

[80] Jean-François La Harpe, *Lycée ou Cours de littérature* (Paris, 1798–9), iv. 444.

L'homme n'est qu'un sujet plein d'erreur naturelle et ineffaçable sans la grâce. Rien ne lui montre la vérité. Tout l'abuse. Ces deux principes de vérité, la raison et les sens, outre qu'ils manquent chacun de sincérité, s'abusent réciproquement l'un l'autre [. . .]. (L45)

The words 'sans la grâce' would seem to point to the possibility of unambiguous truth through the grace of God, just as perfect order can only hope to be found in God. Yet, even in faith, there remain truths which appear to contradict each other. In L733, for example, after depicting the contrary errors which abound in the Church, Pascal asserts that faith embraces many seemingly contradictory truths:

Il y a donc un grand nombre de vérités, et de foi et de morale qui semblent répugnantes et qui subsistent toutes dans un ordre admirable. (L733)

Ordre here would seem to be used on a transcendent level: beyond man's inability to attain coherent order, there exists in the orthodox interpretation of Christian theology an 'ordre admirable' which is divinely inspired.

Thus, although it is not within man's capacity to resolve the contradictions which abound in a fallen world, he must hope for the possibility of their resolution through faith. Truth, as ambiguous a concept as it may be, must in its transcendent sense contain the hope of perfect order, and it is this aspect which Pascal stresses in L974: 'La vérité est donc la première règle et la dernière fin des choses' (L974).

I hope to have shown in my consideration of language and order in the *Pensées* that the only way to portray the fragmentation and obscurity of language is in a fragmentary text. As Buford Norman puts it, 'the self is discontinuous, and so is the text of the *Pensées*'.[81] This disorder in itself acts as a persuasive force for the reader as he is made aware of the fragmentariness of his being in a fallen world, pushing him to search for coherence and true order elsewhere. It is in this respect that the dialectician in the *Pensées* differs markedly from both the sceptics' doctrine of total disorder and the belief in natural and rational order as advocated by many apologists of the day.

Filleau de la Chaise, warning readers in his *Discours sur les 'Pensées' de M. Pascal* of the lack of order in the *Pensées*, writes

---

[81] *Portraits of Thought*, 212.

that: 'Quantité de gens seront sans doute choqués d'y trouver si peu d'ordre, de ce que tout y est imparfait, et de ce qu'il y a mesme quantité de Pensées sans suite ny liaison, et dont on ne voit point où elles tendent.'[82] It does not occur to him that just such a shock in the reader might be a deliberate persuasive ploy on the part of the dialectician.

Following my discussion thus far of language and order in a fallen context, the question is therefore posed of how the dialectician uses language to describe the very terms which depict man's corruption in the *Pensées*. In the next sections, I shall examine closely in the framework which I have established those words which epitomize the human condition, as set down in L24: *inconstance*, *ennui*, and *inquiétude*.

[82] *Discours sur les 'Pensées' de M. Pascal* (Paris, 1672), 6. Cf. La Harpe in his *Cours de littérature* (1798–9) on the lack of cohesion in the *Pensées*: 'la liaison des idées est nécessairement perdue: c'est une force principale, qui manque pour le but de l'ouvrage' (vii. 200).

Part II

La Condition de l'Homme

Introduction
La Condition de l'Homme

> Condition de l'homme.
> Inconstance, Ennui, Inquiétude. (L24)

L24 constitutes the only fragment where 'la condition de l'homme' is directly named.[1] The dialectician's use of asyndeton gives the three nouns a sense of finality, as if they encapsulate the entire spectrum of the human condition.[2] Moreover, the *Recueil original* clearly shows that Pascal wrote each term with a capital letter, a point which all editors have ignored. Yet, at the same time, the lack of any subordinate clauses leaves the fragment open-ended: each of the nouns is open to interpretation, an activity in itself which, as I showed in the previous chapters, indicates man's corruption. Thus, the combination of these factors leads the enquiring reader to look elsewhere in the fragmentary text for examples where the terms *inconstance, ennui,* and *inquiétude* are more fully developed. The definitive terseness of L24 represents the dialectician's subtle means of coaxing his reader to continue an interpretative search which may in turn become a pursuit of something more profound.[3] As he states in L427, 'c'est au moins un devoir indispensable de chercher'. Moreover, the habit of searching, whether it be simply textual or

---

[1] The sentence 'C'est l'image de la condition des hommes', which concludes L434 in many edns., is a spurious addition. See J. Mesnard, *Les 'Pensées' de Pascal* (Paris, 1976), 320 n. 1.

[2] It is a common method of Montaigne to list several nouns together in a sentence. However, nowhere does he write such a terse description of the human condition. See e.g. in *Essais* the *Apologie de Raimond Sebond*, (Œuvres complètes, ed. M. Rat, Paris, 1962), II. xii. 465, where several nouns which play an important role in the *Pensées* are listed together: 'nous avons pour nostre part l'inconstance, l'irresolution, l'incertitude, le deuil, la superstition, la solicitude des choses à venir, voire, après nostre vie, l'ambition, l'avarice, la jalousie, l'envie, les appetits desreglez, forcenez et indomptables, la guerre, la [sic] mensonge, la desloyauté, la detraction et la curiosité'. It is interesting to note that a number of these nouns are directly related to the words from L24 which I shall be discussing: in addition to 'inconstance', 'incertitude', 'irresolution', and 'curiosité' are closely linked to 'inquiétude'.

[3] I therefore dispute J. Deprun's assertion, in *La Philosophie de l'inquiétude en France au XVIIIe siècle* (Paris, 1979), that the list of nouns in L24 constitutes '[une] brève table de matières d'une *Lettre sur la condition de l'homme*' (p. 127).

not, can also lead to the perception of something beyond the imperfection of our worldly existence. It is in this respect too that *coutume* constitutes one of the 'trois moyens de croire' (L808).

The patterning of L24 should also be considered. It has been well established that word order and patterning play an essential stylistic role in the *Pensées*.[4] Philippe Sellier has even called a number of fragments 'poems in prose'.[5] In L24, it would seem more appropriate to order the three nouns in increasing or decreasing numbers of syllables; for example, *ennui, inconstance, inquiétude*, or the other way around. However, Pascal chose a word of three syllables, followed by two syllables and then four syllables. A consideration of the Latin root of the words may help to establish the reasoning behind the order *inconstance, ennui, inquiétude*. The 1614 French–Latin dictionary gives the translation of the two outer nouns as 'inconstantia' and 'instabilitas' (*inconstance*), and 'inquietudo' and 'inquies' (*inquiétude*). Not only are both nouns expressed as direct negatives of other nouns (*inconstance* of *constance* and *inquiétude* of *quiétude*) but both depict an essential restlessness and movement. *Ennui*, on the other hand, translated, amongst other terms, as 'odium', 'satietas', and 'taedium', has no direct contrary concept and reflects stasis rather than movement. Thus, the ordering of the three nouns in L24 shows a progression from movement (*inconstance*) to stasis (*ennui*) back to movement (*inquiétude*). We shall see in many respects how the terms depicting restlessness, *inconstance* and *inquiétude*, are closely related to each other, but also how both nouns point towards *ennui* and *ennui* refers back to them.

The Académie dictionary distinguishes between a number of different meanings of 'condition', many of which appear in the *Pensées*.[6] The widest application of the term, and the most

---

[4] See e.g. P. Topliss, *The Rhetoric of Pascal* (Amsterdam, 1966), 239–311; J.-J. Demorest, *Dans Pascal: Essai en partant de son style* (Paris, 1953); M. Le Guern, *L'Image dans l'œuvre de Pascal* (Paris, 1969).

[5] 'Sur les fleuves de Babylone', in D. Wetsel (ed.), *Meaning, Structure and History in the 'Pensées' of Pascal* (Paris, 1990), 33. For a more detailed discussion of these poetic qualities, see Demorest, *Dans Pascal*; M. J. Maggioni, *The 'Pensées' of Pascal: A Study in Baroque Style* (Washington, DC, 1950); M. Jungo, *Le Vocabulaire de Pascal* (Paris, 1950); M. Le Guern, *L'Image dans l'œuvre de Pascal* (Paris, 1969); Topliss, *The Rhetoric of Pascal*.

[6] Neither the Furetière nor the Richelet dictionary gives as comprehensive a list of definitions. Cf. V. Carraud, in *Pascal et la philosophie* (Paris, 1992), who makes the distinction between *condicio*, which 'désigne la manière par laquelle Dieu a créé

important for our purposes at this stage, is defined as 'la nature, l'estat et la qualité d'une chose ou d'une personne'. One of the examples furnished by the dictionary best reflects 'condition' as it is found most often in the *Pensées*: 'la condition des hommes semble plus malheureuse que celle des animaux'.[7] The overwhelming impression that the term gives initially in the *Pensées* is indeed that it is associated exclusively with the wretchedness of man's fallen nature. In L70, for example, the dialectician writes: 'Si notre condition était véritablement heureuse il ne faudrait pas nous divertir d'y penser.'[8] Elsewhere, the sceptical interlocutor speaks of 'l'incertitude de l'éternité de ma condition future' (L427), and perhaps the most striking image of man's wretchedness can be found in L434:

Qu'on s'imagine un nombre d'hommes dans les chaînes, et tous condamnés à la mort, dont les uns étant chaque jour égorgés à la vue des autres, ceux qui restent voient leur propre condition dans celle de leurs semblables, et, se regardant les uns et les autres avec douleur et sans espérance, attendent à leur tour. (L434)[9]

However, if we look more closely at other fragments where 'condition' is used, it becomes clear that the term is not as one-dimensional as it might seem. In L208, for example, Pascal writes of 'les effets de notre déplorable condition'. And yet an inspection of the original draft of the fragment shows that he had crossed out the words 'la dignité de notre condition', thereby unearthing an essential dichotomy in his use of the term, akin to the Augustinian

---

l'homme' (p. 127), and *conditio*, which 'signifie d'abord la création, en tant qu'action de créer, puis le résultat de cette action, la créature' (p. 128).

[7] A glance at its other meanings might also be useful. On one level, it is defined as 'la qualité que donne la naissance'; this sense occurs most frequently in *Trois discours sur la condition des grands* (to be discussed more fully in Ch. 8 below), where Pascal urges those of noble birth to 'entrer dans la véritable connaissance de votre condition' (Seuil 366). Cf. 'le bonheur des personnes de grande condition' (L136). Another related meaning of 'condition' refers specifically to 'la profession ou vacation dont on est', and the plural form of the noun is largely used in this sense in the *Pensées* (see L35, L148, L544, and L634) and the single form is used with this meaning in L193. Finally, the Académie dictionary also makes the point that '*Conditions*, au pluriel, se prend quelquefois pour les mœurs, les habitudes'. This category would apply to the plural noun in L693, L694, and L800.

[8] L70 is almost exactly repeated in L889. This aspect of man's condition will form a part of my discussion of both *ennui* and *bonheur/félicité*. See also L117.

[9] See n. 1 above. Cf. L33, where 'condition' is linked to man's 'faiblesse'.

conception of man's two natures. This awareness of the contradictoriness of the human condition is apparent in L208:

> n'est-il pas plus clair que le jour que nous sentons en nous-mêmes des caractères ineffaçables d'excellence et n'est-il pas aussi véritable que nous éprouvons à toute heure les effets de notre déplorable condition?
>
> Que nous crie donc ce chaos et cette confusion monstrueuse sinon la vérité de ces deux états avec une voix si puissante qu'il est impossible de résister? (L208)

The two fragments in which we find the most frequent and interesting use of the word *condition* are L136 and L131 (which will be an important focus of my study of various terms in later chapters). In L136, *condition* is used in several contexts. Not only are we reminded of 'le malheur naturel de notre condition faible et mortelle', but also in other sections it signifies both elevated birth and a profession. The major function of *condition* in the fragment is in the assertion that man seeks diversions in order to avoid contemplating 'notre malheureuse condition'. But, the fact that he thinks he is searching for happiness and restfulness through these *divertissements* points to 'un autre instinct secret qui reste de la grandeur de notre première nature'. Man's condition is not entirely clouded by corruption.

In three deleted sections of L131, the two-sided condition of man is reiterated: 'N'est-il donc pas clair comme le jour que la condition de l'homme est double?', 'Concevons donc que la condition de l'homme est double', and 'Car qui ne voit que sans la connaissance de cette double condition de la nature on était dans une ignorance invincible de la vérité de sa nature.' The word recurs four times in undeleted sections, each one pointing to the need for man to recognize the doctrine of Original Sin as the basis of his double condition. The dialectician condemns those men who try to understand their 'véritable nature' through 'raison naturelle', and urges them instead to acknowledge 'quel paradoxe vous êtes à vous-même', thereby understanding 'votre condition véritable que vous ignorez'. While the human condition is underpinned by corruption, there remains a reminder of former perfection before the Fall:

> Car enfin si l'homme n'avait jamais été corrompu il jouirait dans son innocence et de la vérité et de la félicité avec assurance. Et si l'homme n'avait jamais été que corrompu il n'aurait aucune idée ni de la vérité, ni de

la béatitude. Mais malheureux que nous sommes et plus que s'il n'y avait point de grandeur dans notre condition, nous avons une idée du bonheur et nous ne pouvons y arriver. (L131)

As we saw in the section on language and order, it is the hope of perfection that must prompt the reader to search beyond the limitations of his corruption. Yet, the recognition of Original Sin, 'ce mystère', is also the key to self-knowledge: 'le nœud de notre condition prend ses replis et ses tours dans cet abîme'.

Thus, these two natures lie behind man's condition in the world. As the dialectician emphasizes in L444, 'tout instruit l'homme de sa condition'. In this way, leading to the search for God, 'les hommes sont tout ensemble indignes de Dieu et capables de Dieu: indignes par leur corruption, capables par leur première nature' (L444). This dichotomy informs all the fragments, giving the reader a sense of instability in this world. Moreover, it is Jesus Christ whom the dialectician posits as the one figure to make sense of the human condition in all its complexities. It is Christ who 'a pris cette malheureuse condition pour pouvoir être en toutes personnes et modèle de toutes conditions' (L946).

3
Inconstance

> A de vagues desseins l'Homme est tousjours en proye,
> Son instabilité ne meurt qu'avecque luy,
> Et nous voyons, Seigneur, que sa plus douce joye
> Dégenere souvent en son plus grand ennuy.
>
> (Brébeuf, 'De l'inconstance humaine')

Of the three nouns which appear together in L24, *inconstance* occurs the least number of times in the *Pensées*, with only six examples of the noun and two instances of its adjectival form.[1] However, in addition to its prominent placing in L24, it is used as a heading in three other fragments, L17, L54, and L55. It also assumes an important position in the structure of L73. Situated as the final word, it offsets the structural symmetry of the fragment, thereby drawing particular attention to it:

⟨Le sentiment⟩ ⟨de la fausseté⟩ ⟨des plaisirs présents⟩
et
⟨l'ignorance⟩ ⟨de la vanité⟩ ⟨des plaisirs absents⟩
cause
l'inconstance.

The scarcity of the use of *inconstance* in other fragments serves to highlight its significance in those passages where it appears in a prominent position.[2]

A major context in which *inconstantia* traditionally appears is in its contrast to the Stoic and neo-Stoic conception of *constantia*. In Pascal's time, the neo-Stoic treatises on constancy by writers such as Justus Lipsius (who greatly influenced both Montaigne and

---

[1] See H. Davidson and P. Dubé, *A Concordance to Pascal's 'Pensées'* (Ithaca, NY, 1975). Neither noun nor adjective is used in the *Lettres provinciales*.

[2] The Furetière dictionary gives the most complete definition of *inconstance* amongst the 17th-c. dictionaries, for it considers not only physical and mental instability but also inconstancy of time: 'Manque de fermeté, de durée, de resolution'. One example which is cited can be applied particularly to Pascal's consideration of the human condition: 'la foiblesse de l'esprit humain est la cause de son inconstance'.

Charron) and Du Vair were still widely read. As Anthony Levi has pointed out, Lipsius's *De Constantia* represents 'a genuine attempt to give a Christian interpretation to a truly stoic ethic'.[3] Moreover, constancy was attributed by the neo-Stoics to the *ratio* and seen to be opposed by the passions.

The theme of inconstancy, of the changeability of all earthly things is one which recurs throughout writings known to Pascal. As Philippe Sellier has clearly shown,[4] the Bible, especially Psalms 101 and 136 and St Augustine's commentaries on them, were a major source of inspiration to Pascal. In them, through the repetition of the Latin terms *inconstantia* and *instabilitas*, the mutability of human life is contrasted with the constancy of God. We find particularly vivid echoes of this theme in what Sellier calls 'les écrits les plus personnels [de Pascal]',[5] such as *Sur la conversion du pécheur* and *Prière pour le bon usage des maladies*. In the latter work, for example, the speaker contrasts himself with God: 'vous êtes toujours le même, quoique je sois sujet au changement'.[6]

In French writing, too, from the time of Montaigne, *inconstance* was commonplace in the depiction of man's fragility. Jean Rousset identifies *inconstance* as a widespread baroque theme from 1580 to 1670,[7] and in many respects Pascal's use of the term forms part of the same literary tradition. Jean-Pierre Camus, for example, whose writings were probably known to Pascal and whom Pascal opposed in the Saint-Ange affair,[8] emphasizes in *Les Diversitez*, in a chapter

---

[3] *French Moralists: The Theory of the Passions, 1585–1649* (Oxford, 1964), 67. See also M. Morford, *Stoics and Neostoics: Rubens and the Circle of Lipsius* (Princeton, NJ, 1991), 160–8. Cf. Montaigne's 'De la constance', *Essais*, I, 12.

[4] *Pascal et Saint Augustin* (Paris, 1970), 22–38, and 'Sur les fleuves de Babylone', in D. Wetsel (ed.), *Meaning, Structure and History in the Pensées of Pascal* (Paris, 1990), 33–44. Cf. L918, L545, L199 for images of instability drawn from the Bible and Augustine. [5] *Pascal et Saint Augustin*, 22.

[6] Seuil 362. Cf. *Sur la conversion du pécheur*, Seuil 290: 'l'âme, étant immortelle comme elle est, ne peut trouver sa félicité parmi des choses périssables'.

[7] *La Littérature de l'Âge Baroque en France* (Paris, 1953), 8. See pts. i and ii for Rousset's discussion of the theme of inconstancy in the works of various baroque poets.

[8] For discussion of the Saint-Ange affair and the possible influence of Camus on Pascal, see Julien-Eymard d'Angers, *Pascal et ses précurseurs: L'Apologétique en France de 1580 à 1670* (Paris, 1954), 147–8, 163; H. Brémond, *Histoire littéraire du sentiment religieux en France* (Paris, 1928), i. 155–6; J. Descrains, *Jean-Pierre Camus (1584–1652), et ses 'Diversités' (1609–1618), ou La Culture d'un évêque humaniste* (Lille, 1985), i. 310, 319, 337, 376–7 (where Descrains attributes to Pascal the 'angoisse' of the speaker in L201), 492.

entitled 'De l'incertitude', that 'tout n'est qu'inconstance, changement, Incertitude'.[9] Elsewhere, he compares man's inconstancy to a sea-like flux: 'cette vie humaine est sujette à tant de mutation, pleine de tant d'inconstance, puis que ce n'est qu'un flux et reflux de miseres'.[10] This juxtaposition of changeability and the image of flux, which recurs in both L734 and L771, and in a deleted passage of L27, can be found elsewhere. Bourdonné, in *Le Courtisan desabusé*, which was first published in 1658, and which was therefore contemporaneous with the composition of a number of the fragments,[11] writes in a chapter entitled 'De l'inconstance des choses du monde',

Il n'y a rien si déraisonnable que de croire pouvoir trouver du repos et de la stabilité dans le monde, puis qu'on n'y voit que des revolutions continuelles et des changemens perpetuels. Le ciel roule tousjours sur nos testes: l'air se couvre à toute heure de nuages: la mer a sans cesse son flux et reflux: la terre change continuellement de face: tous les elemens se font une guerre perpetuelle: et ainsi on peut dire avec verité qu'il n'y a rien de plus constant dans le monde que l'inconstance.[12]

No claims for originality can therefore be assigned to Pascal in his choice of the term *inconstance*. However, it is in the way in which he uses the word, especially in association with *ennui* and *inquiétude*, that we can assess its importance in the depiction of the human condition.

Both Montaigne and Charron play an integral part in the formation of the concept of *inconstance* in the *Pensées*. Of Montaigne's writings, two essays, 'De l'inconstance de nos actions' (II. i) and *L'Apologie de Raimond Sebond* (II. xii), appear to serve as Pascal's primary source. As Bernard Croquette has observed, there are numerous references to both essays in the *Pensées*.[13] For

---

[9] *Les Diversitez*, i. (1612; 1st edn. 1609), 294.   [10] Ibid. 144.
[11] L17, for example, where *inconstance* appears as a heading and which I shall discuss later, was written on paper named by Ernst as FNIC and identified by him as being written between May and June 1658.
[12] *Le Courtisan desabusé ou Pensées d'un gentil-homme qui a passé la plus grande partie de sa vie dans le Cour et dans le guerre* (Paris, 1658), 404. Cf. pp. 23, 299, 306–7.
[13] *Pascal et Montaigne* (Geneva, 1974), 108–9. He cites 6 references to 'De l'inconstance de nos actions' and 77 references to the *Apologie*. Unless I state otherwise, my allusions to Montaigne's influence on particular fragments have been signalled but not discussed by Croquette.

the most part, the portrayal of *inconstance* in these essays differs markedly from other essays, where the word is often used to describe either his own physical discomfort,[14] or the infidelity of women,[15] or the erratic behaviour of servants.[16] Rather, in these two essays, *inconstance* is portrayed on a broader, more generalized level, where it is seen as a part of human nature. The same can be said for Charron's use of the term. Like Montaigne, who incorporates *inconstance* into the title of one of his chapters, he heads a chapter of *De la sagesse* 'Inconstance' (I. xxxviii), and the theme of man's instability recurs throughout the first book.[17]

To turn to the *Pensées*, there are three main categories into which *inconstance* appears to fall (see the Key at the end of this chapter): the first, which I shall call Inc. 1, relates directly to man's fallen condition; the second, Inc. 2, concerns man's restlessness as a sign of both his wretchedness and his attempts to move away from that state; and the third, Inc. 3, is connected to man's positive search for spiritual fulfilment. I shall consider first those fragments where *inconstance* is prominently placed, then I shall move to an examination of *inconstance* in conjunction with the term *bizarrerie*, after which I shall assess the status of the adjective, *inconstant*, before concluding with an analysis of the terms *constance* and *constant*.

In one unfinished fragment, L55, where *inconstance* is used as a title, and in the sense of Inc. 1, the image of an organ is applied to the changeability of man:

Inconstance.
On croit toucher des orgues ordinaires en touchant l'homme. Ce sont des orgues à la vérité, mais bizarres, changeantes, variables. (Ceux qui ne savent toucher que les ordinaires) ne seraient pas d'accord sur celles-là. Il faut savoir où sont les [touches]. (L55)[18]

Significantly, it would seem that Pascal took this image from Montaigne's 'De l'inconstance de nos actions':

---

[14] e.g. *Essais*, III. xiii. 1076, 1082.   [15] e.g. ibid. v. 864, 868.
[16] e.g. ibid. iii. 801.
[17] See e.g. *Essais*, I. 18. 65–6; I. xxxvi. 109–11; I. xxxvii. 114–15.
[18] The phrase in brackets was crossed out by Pascal. The Brunschvicg and Sellier edns. give different wordings of this fragment, adding after 'variables', 'dont les tuyaux ne se suivent pas par degrés conjoints'. Also, instead of 'ne seraient pas d'accord', they read 'ne feraient pas d'accords'.

Le discours en seroit bien aisé à faire, comme il se voit du jeune Caton; qui en a touché une marche, a tout touché; c'est une harmonie de sons très-accordans, qui ne se peut démentir.[19]

Although Montaigne's image in itself does not refer directly to the inconstancy of man, the central subject of the essay, its impact is reworked and enhanced by the dialectician. It is also possible that Pascal developed an image used by Charron in a chapter entitled 'Vraye et essentielle preud'hommie; premiere et fondamentale partie de sagesse' from *De la sagesse*:

> La prud'hommie est semblable au bon joüeur d'orgue, qui touche bien et justement selon l'art: la grace et l'esprit de Dieu est le souffle et le vent qui exprime les touches, anime et fait parler l'instrument, et produit la melodie plaisante.[20]

Whereas both Montaigne and Charron evoke the organ on a generalized level to depict a sense of harmony, Pascal recreates the image with scientific detail to portray, not the coherence, but rather the complexity of man. Indeed, he shows a more informed awareness of the technical capabilities of the organ than do his predecessors, thus transforming a possibly undefined and colour-less image into a finely observed portrait. It is indeed probable that Pascal himself was well acquainted with music: not only did he write a treatise on sounds at the age of eleven, as his sister Gilberte reported in her *Vie de Monsieur Pascal*,[21] but also evidently he considered music as a science, as we see in his *Préface sur le Traité du Vide*:

> C'est ainsi que la géométrie, l'arithmétique, la musique, la physique, la médecine, l'architecture, et toutes les sciences qui sont soumises à l'expérience et au raisonnement, doivent être augmentées pour devenir parfaites.[22]

Placed as it is (along with L54) in the *liasse* entitled 'Misère', *inconstance* in L55 epitomizes the wretched side of man's condition

---

[19] II. i. 317.
[20] P. Charron, *De la sagesse* (*Œuvres*; Geneva, 1970, facsimile of the 1635 Paris edn.), II. iii. 43.
[21] Seuil 18.
[22] Ibid. 230–1. The likelihood of Pascal having an informed knowledge of the workings of an organ are further supported by the fact that Père Mersenne dedicated the 6th book of his *Harmonie universelle*, entitled *Des Orgues*, to Pascal's father. For more evidence of Pascal and his father's association with music, see J. Mesnard, 'Pascal et la musique', in *Textes du tricentenaire* (Paris, 1963), 195–205.

(Inc. 1). Yet, for all the complexity and changeability of human nature, the dialectician posits the potential for greater wholeness within that inconstancy. As he emphasizes, 'il faut savoir où sont les [touches]' in order to reach true harmony. In this way, *inconstance* contains also the sense of Inc. 2. Like the fragmentary text, man in himself is inconsistent and incoherent, but the possibility remains for him to reach beyond himself and to bring together all the variable aspects of his condition. Just as a notion of the inadequacy of language is manipulated by the dialectician for persuasive purposes, so too is this recognition of inconstancy used to convince the reader of the need to attain self-understanding. No solution other than the will to comprehend the intricacies of the self, like the complexities of the organ, is offered.

The combination of the musical image in L55 with the adjective *bizarre* is paralleled in L805, where the noun *bizarrerie* is used to depict the misguided view which man holds of his own good:

En sachant la passion dominante de chacun on est sûr de lui plaire, et néanmoins chacun a ses fantaisies contraires à son propre bien dans l'idée même qu'il a du bien, et c'est une bizarrerie qui met hors de gamme.

Just as man's nature is perceived in L55 as too variable to achieve true harmony, here man's changeability is depicted, through the image of the musical scale, as being beyond consistent assessment. Because of the instability of the human predicament, the dialectician cannot take purely rational lines in order to convince his reader; he must take into consideration the very vagaries which he is describing.

In the other fragment from the same *liasse* where *inconstance* appears as a heading, L54, the generalized depiction in L55 is directed towards a more particular consideration of the inconstancy of the human soul, but largely used again with the sense of Inc. 1:

Inconstance.
Les choses ont diverses qualités et l'âme diverses inclinations, car rien n'est simple de ce qui s'offre à l'âme, et l'âme ne s'offre jamais simple à aucun sujet. De là vient qu'on pleure et qu'on rit d'une même chose.

The final sentence of the fragment is an evident reference to the title of Montaigne's 'Comme nous pleurons et rions d'une mesme chose'.[23] Despite the fact that Montaigne does not use *inconstance*

[23] *Essais*, I. xxxviii.

in this essay, thematically he discusses the diversity of the human soul, with a vocabulary very similar to that used in L54:

> il faut considerer comme nos ames se trouvent souvent agitées de diverses passions. Et tout ainsi qu'en nos corps ils disent qu'il y a une assemblée de diverses humeurs, desquelles celle là est maistresse qui commande le plus ordinairement en nous, selon nos complexions: aussi, en nos ames, bien qu'il y ait divers mouvemens qui l'agitent, si faut-il qu'il y en ait un à qui le champ demeure. [...] D'où nous voyons non seulement les enfans, qui vont naifvement après la nature, pleurer et rire souvent de mesme chose [...] Nulle qualité nous embrasse purement et universellement.[24]

Apart from Montaigne's use of 'pleurer et rire [...] de mesme chose', other words, such as 'ame', 'diverses', and 'qualité', clearly anticipate Pascal's choice of vocabulary. The direct linking of this image with a consideration of man's inconstancy may come from Charron's words in the chapter entitled 'Inconstance' from *De la sagesse*:

> L'homme est l'animal de tous le plus difficile à sonder et cognoistre, car c'est le plus double et contrefait, le plus couvert et artificiel [...]. Tout son branler et mouvoir n'est qu'un cours perpetuel d'erreur: le matin naistre, le soir mourir; tantost aux cepts, tantost en liberté, tantost un Dieu, tantost une mouche. Il rit et pleure d'une mesme chose.[25]

The contradictoriness within man is exemplified by his attitude towards pleasure. I shall discuss this aspect at length in the section concerned with *divertissement* in Chapter 4, but it can also be related directly to *inconstance*, as is clear in L73: 'Le sentiment de la fausseté des plaisirs présents et l'ignorance de la vanité des plaisirs absents cause l'inconstance' [Inc. 1].[26] Here inconstancy is

---

[24] Ibid. 229–30.   [25] I. xxxviii. 125.
[26] In 2 sections of the *Apologie de Raimond Sebond* (II. xii), *inconstance* and *vanité* are placed together, as in L73. In the 1st, the essayist speaks of 'une si grande inconstance, varieté et vanité d'opinions' (p. 493); and in the 2nd, in a passage which directly inspired L60, 'il est croyable qu'il y a des loix naturelles, comme il se voit ès autres creatures; mais en nous elles sont perdues, cette belle raison humaine s'ingerant par tout de maistriser et commander, brouillant et confondant le visage des choses selon sa vanité et inconstance' (pp. 564–5). Cf. also Charron's use of *vanité* and *inconstance* together, in *De la sagesse*, I. xxxvi. 109: 'La vanité est la plus essentielle et propre qualité de l'humaine nature. Il n'y a point d'autre chose en l'homme, soit malice, mal-heur, inconstance, irresolution (et de tout cela il y en a tousjours à foison) tant comme de vile inanité, sottise et ridicule vanité.' In another of the *Essais*, 'De la diversion' (III. iv), which we know to have been integral to Pascal's formulation of *divertissement* (see J. Mesnard's 'De la *diversion* au

seen to be the direct result of the discrepancy which exists between man's realization of the futility of his present diversions and his aspiration towards other pleasures. Moreover, the fact that each person's perception of pleasure differs both within himself at different times and from that of his fellow man only serves to intensify the sense of inconstancy. This is emphasized in a section of *De l'esprit géométrique* concerned with the difficulties of applying rules to the art of persuasion which, significantly, drew its inspiration from Montaigne's 'De l'inconstance de nos actions':[27]

La raison de cette extrême difficulté vient de ce que les principes du plaisir ne sont pas fermes et stables. Ils sont divers en tous les hommes, et variables dans chaque particulier avec une telle diversité, qu'il n'y a point d'homme plus différent d'un autre que de soi-même dans les divers temps. Un homme a d'autres plaisirs qu'une femme; un riche et un pauvre en ont de différents; un prince, un homme de guerre, un marchand, un bourgeois, un paysan, les vieux, les jeunes, les sains, les malades, tous varient; les moindres accidents les changent.[28]

In the paragraphs preceding this section on pleasures, the dialectician acknowledges the difficulties of finding rules for the 'art d'agréer', and, importantly, he states that 'je ne sais s'il y aurait un art pour accommoder les preuves à l'inconstance de nos caprices'.[29] Because of the inconstancy of human nature, one cannot apply rational methods to activities such as *agrément* which are perceived by the dialectician to exemplify man's corruption.[30] Similarly, because of the fallenness of language, words cannot adequately express intention. A few paragraphs later, the dialectician uses almost identical terms to stress such an impossibility: 'je ne sais s'il y a moyen de donner des règles fermes pour accorder les discours à

divertissement', in *Mémorial du Premier Congrès Internationale des Études Montaignistes* (Bordeaux, 1964), 123–8), Montaigne writes of 'le benefice de l'inconstance', explaining that 'la variation soulage, dissout et dissipe' (p. 813).

[27] Cf. *Essais*, II. i. 318–19: 'Non seulement le vent des accidens me remue selon son inclination, mais en outre je me remue et trouble moy mesme par l'instabilité de ma posture; et qui y regarde primement, ne se trouve guere deux fois en mesme estat. Je donne à mon ame tantost un visage, tantost un autre, selon le costé où je le couche. Si je parle diversement de moy, c'est que je me regarde diversement. Toutes les contrarietez s'y trouvent selon quelque tour et en quelque façon.'
[28] *De l'esprit géométrique*, Seuil 356. In this section, Pascal broadens Montaigne's essentially personal comments to make a general observation on 'tous les hommes'.
[29] Seuil 356.
[30] Cf. *De l'esprit géométrique*, 353, where the dialectician, referring to 'agrément', emphasizes that 'cette voie est basse, indigne et étrangère'.

l'inconstance de nos caprices'.[31] It is in this regard that *inconstance* is so central to the dialectician's assessment of the human condition (Inc. 1): all our attempts to attain true coherence in the world are undermined by our inconstancy.

INCONSTANCE AND BIZARRERIE

The third fragment in which *inconstance* appears as a heading, L17, also leads to my examination of the juxtaposition of *inconstance* and *bizarrerie*:

> Inconstance et Bizarrerie.
> Ne vivre que de son travail et régner sur le plus puissant état du monde sont choses très opposées. Elles sont unies dans la personne du grand seigneur des Turcs.

This fragment refers to the popular legend of the day that the 'Grand Turc' laboured on the land (despite doubt thrown on such a story as early as 1560 by Guillaume Postel in his *La République des Turcs*).[32] It would seem that the choice of *inconstance* at the head of the passage indicates another aspect of the inconsistencies of man (Inc. 1). The 'choses très opposées' described by the dialectician are brought together in the 'grand seigneur des Turcs', who is used as a particular example. However, the title of the fragment evokes generally the human condition, showing man's *vanité*, which is the title of the second *liasse* in which L17 appears.

A possible source of L17 can be found in Montaigne's 'De la vertu'. The paragraph in which the term *bizarre* is used depicts the contradictions of an eminent acquaintance of Montaigne, indirectly introducing the theme of the inconstancy of man, which may provide an initial indication of Pascal's linking *inconstance* with *bizarrerie*:

> Un personage, grand d'ans, de nom, de dignité et de doctrine, se vantoit à moy d'avoir esté porté à certaine mutation très-importante de sa foy par

---

[31] Seuil 356.
[32] This reference is widely made by most editors. M. Le Guern, in his edn. (Paris, 1977), i. 251–2, gives examples of sultans in the 17th c. who were known to work with their hands, and cites Tavernier's *Nouvelle relation de l'intérieur du sérail du Grand Seigneur* (Paris, 1675), 239–242, to support this.

une incitation estrangere aussi bizarre et, au reste, si mal concluante que je la trouvoy plus forte au revers: luy l'appelloit miracle, et moy aussi, à divers sens.[33]

Words such as *mutation, étranger, bizarre, revers,* and *divers* are terms which recur in both the *Essais* and the *Pensées*, especially in relation to the theme of inconstancy.[34] Moreover, in the paragraph preceding the above passage from 'De la vertu', Montaigne writes of 'Un jeune Seigneur Turc', whose tale of the vagaries of hunting shows 'combien nostre raison est flexible à toute sorte d'images'.[35] This depiction of the 'Seigneur Turc' and the introduction of the term *bizarre* in relation to the theme of inconstancy might provide a clue to the source of the combination of *inconstance* and *bizarrerie* in L17.

In addition to L17, we have already seen how *inconstance* and *bizarrerie* are juxtaposed in L55, and, by association with the musical image, in L805. All three seventeenth-century dictionaries define *bizarre* as 'fantasque', with *bizarrerie* variously interpreted as 'extravagance' (Académie), 'caprice' (Richelet and Furetière), 'fantaisie' and 'folie' (Richelet). The Richelet and Furetière dictionaries also give a definition of the noun with a positive connotation, connected with 'variété bizarre et agréable' (Richelet). It would seem that the meaning of diversity, showing the instability of man, points to the connection between *inconstance* and *bizarrerie* in the *Pensées*. The two words appear together in another fragment, where the varieties of beliefs and customs throughout the world are perceived as proof of human unreliability and contrasted with the Jewish faith:

Mais en considérant aussi cette inconstante et bizarre variété de mœurs et de créances dans les divers temps je trouve en un coin du monde, un peuple particulier séparé de tous les autres peuples de la terre, le plus ancien de tous et dont les histoires précèdent de plusieurs siècles les plus anciennes que nous ayons. (L454)

---

[33] *Essais,* II. xxix. 688.
[34] Cf. ibid. I. xxxiv. 217; I. lxix. 285; II. i. 315–19; II. xii. 493; III. xiii. 1054, 1085; and Pascal, L54, L55, L199, L454, L803.
[35] II. xxix. 688. Croquette does not mention the parallels between II. xxix and L17. Cf. the one case in the *Essais* where Montaigne uses the noun *bizarrerie,* in 'De l'affection des peres aux enfans' (II. viii. 364). Here, he links the 'bizarrerie' and 'dessein farouche et extravagant' of his writing to his 'humeur melancolique' and 'chagrin de la solitude', which is not unlike *ennui* as described in L136.

In this fragment, inconstancy is portrayed as unstable both in time ('dans les divers temps') and in place, conforming with the Furetière definition of *inconstance* as 'manque de fermeté, de durée, de resolution'. The description of the 'inconstante et bizarre variété de mœurs' in L454 finds an echo in Montaigne's 'De l'inconstance de nos actions', where the instability of society is seen as a primary cause of *inconstance*:

> Il y a quelque apparence de faire jugement d'un homme par les plus communs traicts de sa vie; mais, veu la naturelle instabilité de nos meurs et opinions, il m'a semblé souvent que les bons autheurs mesmes ont tort de s'opiniastrer à former de nous une constante et solide contexture [. . .]. Je croy des hommes plus mal aiséement la constance, que toute autre chose, et rien plus aiséement que l'inconstance.[36]

INCONSTANT/CONSTANT

As is clear in the use of the adjective *inconstant* in L454, despite its less central positioning in the fragment, its meaning conforms to that of the noun as it appears in the *Pensées* in the sense of Inc. 1. The same can be said of the only other occurrence of the adjective, in L803:

> Mais parce que les songes sont tous différents et que l'un même se diversifie, ce qu'on y voit affecte bien moins que ce qu'on voit en veillant, à cause de la continuité qui n'est pourtant pas si continue et égale qu'elle ne change aussi, mais moins brusquement, si ce n'est rarement comme quand on voyage et alors on dit: il me semble que je rêve; car la vie est un songe un peu moins inconstant.

Life itself is portrayed as fantasy, hardly more stable than dreams. Again the source of this fragment comes directly from Montaigne:

> Ceux qui ont apparié nostre vie à un songe, ont eu de la raison, à l'avanture plus qu'ils ne pensoyent. Quand nous songeons, nostre ame vit, agit, exerce toutes ses facultez, ne plus ne moins que quand elle veille [. . .].
> Nous veillons dormans, et veillans dormons. Je ne vois pas si clair dans le sommeil; mais, quand au veiller, je ne le trouve jamais assez pur et sans nuage. Encores le sommeil en sa profondeur endort par fois les songes.

[36] II. i. 315–16.

Mais nostre veiller n'est jamais si esveillé qu'il purge et dissipe bien à point les resveries, qui sont les songes des veillants, et pires que songes.[37]

This same passage from the *Essais* is developed elsewhere in the *Pensées*, in a fragment devoted to the sceptics and dogmatists:

> De plus que personne n'a d'assurance, hors de la foi—s'il veille ou s'il dort, vu que durant le sommeil on croit veiller aussi fermement que nous faisons. Comme on rêve souvent, qu'on rêve entassant un songe sur l'autre. Ne se peut-il faire que cette moitié de la vie n'est elle-même qu'un songe, sur lequel les autres sont entés, dont nous nous éveillons à la mort, pendant laquelle nous avons aussi peu les principes du vrai et du bien que pendant le sommeil naturel. Tout cet écoulement du temps, de la vie, et ces divers corps que nous sentons, ces différentes pensées qui nous y agitent n'étant peut-être que des illusions pareilles à l'écoulement du temps et aux vains fantômes de nos songes. On croit voir les espaces, les figures, les mouvements, on sent couler le temps, on le mesure, et enfin on agit de même qu'éveillé. De sorte que la moitié de la vie se passant en sommeil, par notre propre aveu ou quoi qu'il nous en paraisse, nous n'avons aucune idée du vrai, tous nos sentiments étant alors des illusions. Qui sait si cette autre moitié de la vie où nous pensons veiller n'est pas un autre sommeil un peu différent du premier. (L131)[38]

The images of 'écoulement', 'agitation', and 'diversité', which are depicted here, all parallel the portrayal of *inconstance* as we have seen it in L54, L55, L454, and L803. There remains one other example of the noun in the *Pensées*, in the fragment entitled 'Disproportion de l'homme', which perhaps epitomizes most strongly the centrality of *inconstance* to the dialectician's perception of the human condition, and yet also points to man's desire to escape from that state. There is a play between the term as Inc. 1 and Inc. 2. Although the word itself is used only once, the image of instability recurs throughout the long fragment. At the point where the term appears, the dialectician has reiterated the disparity between man's inclination towards constancy and the fact of his unstable condition. In the preceding paragraph, for example, an

---

[37] II. xii. 580–1. In the lines which immediately precede this passage, we find the words 'A un homme ennuyé et affligé, la clarté du jour semble obscurcie et tenebreuse' (580), indicating an initial link between *inconstance* and *ennui*, which perhaps was taken into account by Pascal.

[38] Cf. Epictetus, *Les Propos et Le Manuel*, trans. J. Goulu (Paris, 1609), i. 5; and also Descartes *Méditations*, I, in *Œuvres et Lettres*, ed. A. Bridoux (Paris, 1952), 268–9.

image used by Montaigne in the *Apologie de Raimond Sebond* is developed to accentuate this discrepancy:

> Voilà notre état véritable. C'est ce qui nous rend incapables de savoir certainement et d'ignorer absolument. Nous voguons sur un milieu vaste, toujours incertains et flottants, poussés d'un bout vers l'autre; quelque terme où nous pensions nous attacher et nous affermir, il branle, et nous quitte, et si nous le suivons il échappe à nos prises, nous glisse et fuit d'une fuite éternelle; rien ne s'arrête pour nous. C'est l'état qui nous est naturel et toutefois le plus contraire à notre inclination. Nous brûlons du désir de trouver une assiette ferme, et une dernière base constante [Inc. 2] pour y édifier une tour qui s'élève à (l')infini, mais tout notre fondement craque et la terre s'ouvre jusqu'aux abîmes. (L199)[39]

The appearance in this paragraph of the by then archaic verb *branler* again shows Pascal's debt to Montaigne, who uses both noun and verb frequently.[40] The verb only appears once elsewhere in the *Pensées*, in another fragment strongly influenced by Montaigne, L60. It would seem that Pascal was concerned not to use archaic terms as employed by Montaigne, because the noun *branle*, which is used often by Montaigne and particularly in conjunction with *inconstance*, does not appear at all in the *Pensées*.[41] This concern is evident in the *Recueil original*, where, at the beginning of L47, Pascal even deleted the words 'si bien accoutumés au branle' and substituted 'Nous ne nous tenons jamais

---

[39] Cf. Montaigne: 'Si noz facultez intellectuelles et sensibles sont sans fondement et sans pied, si elles ne font que floter et vanter, pour neant laissons nous emporter nostre jugement à aucune partie de leur operation, quelque apparence qu'elle semble nous presenter; et la plus seure assiete de nostre entendement, et la plus heureuse, ce seroit celle là où il se maintiendroit rassis, droit, inflexible, sans bransle et sans agitation' (II. xii. 544–5). Cf. also II. xii. 553, where the nouns *assiette* and *constance* appear together.

[40] R. E. Leake, in his *Concordance de Montaigne* (Geneva, 1981), finds 44 examples of the noun and 16 of the verb.

[41] In the *Essais*, *branle* and *inconstance* appear directly together in 'La fortune se rencontre souvent au train de la Raison' (I. xxxiv. 217); and 'De l'inconstance de nos actions' (II. i. 316), which is particularly enlightening: 'Ce que nous avons à cett'heure proposé, nous le changeons tantost, et tantost encore retournons sur nos pas; ce n'est que branle et inconstance [. . .]. Nous n'allons pas; on nous emporte, comme les choses qui flottent, ores doucement, ores avecques violence, selon que l'eau est ireuse ou bonasse.' In this regard I disagree with Dom M. Jungo, in *Le Vocabulaire de Pascal* (Paris, 1950), 74, who uses *branle* as an example of 'le goût de l'archaïsme' which Montaigne inspired in Pascal. One occurrence of the noun, in the 18th letter (p. 468), represents the only appearance of the term in the *Lettres provinciales*.

au temps présent'. Pascal's choice of the words 'une dernière base constante' highlights the difference between man's desire and his actual state. The use of the adjective *constant* forms an effective opposition to *inconstance* in the following paragraph:

> Ne cherchons donc point d'assurance et de fermeté; notre raison est toujours déçue par l'inconstance [Inc. 1] des apparences: rien ne peut fixer le fini entre les deux infinis qui l'enferment et le fuient. (L199)[42]

Like man's inability to attain true coherence in the world, constancy remains a distant goal which only serves to remind man of his present state of inconstancy. Indeed, the dialectician's juxtaposition of this elusive aspiration and the fact of man's present weakness generates a further sense of instability in the reader. Significantly, we find a very similar persuasive ploy in the use of *constant* elsewhere in L199, in a deleted section, where the constancy and eternity of God and nature are contrasted with man's inconstancy and ephemerality:

> L'éternité des choses en elles-mêmes ou en Dieu doit encore étonner notre petite durée. L'immobilité fixe et constante de la nature, comparaison au changement continuel qui se passe en nous doit faire le même effet.

As we see here, the dialectician makes skilful use of antithesis to unsettle the reader and thereby to prompt him to seek stability beyond his own state, implying also the need for a spiritual search, in the sense of Inc. 3. We find similar techniques in other fragments where *constant* and *constance* appear.

CONSTANCE

Like *inconstance*, *constance* recurs relatively few times in the *Pensées*: the noun appears only once, and the adjective and adverb fifteen times. As I mentioned at the beginning of the chapter, Pascal's contemporaries were still reading neo-Stoic treatises on

---

[42] It is possible that these words evoke a section from ch. 18 of the first book of *De la sagesse*, 'Des passions en general', where Charron writes: 'aussi les sens pour ne pas comprendre tout ce qui est de la raison, sont souvent deçeus par l'apparence'. Pascal's inclusion of *inconstance* gives more focus to the generalized statement of Charron.

constancy, and the *constantia/inconstantia* opposition was a dominant one at the time.[43]

In L767, *constant* is used in the context of fantasy in opposition to reality, similar to the example of *inconstant* in L803. Human laws and institutions of authority are perceived as contradictory and randomly chosen:

> Comme les duchés, et royautés, et magistratures sont réelles et nécessaires (à cause de ce que la force règle tout) il y en a partout et toujours, mais parce que ce n'est que fantaisie qui fait qu'un tel ou telle le soit, cela n'est pas constant, cela est sujet à varier, etc. (L767)[44]

In this example, *constant* might best be translated as 'consistent', but it still relates to *inconstance* in its association with the variety and instability of human laws. Inconstancy is therefore seen as an integral part of man's fall from truth. Just as we noted the desire for constancy in fragments like L199 and L55, man has an innate capacity for truth and happiness, but is unable by himself to attain those goals. As a result of this disparity between desire and ability, inconstancy remains part of his nature, as is made clear in the other fragment where *constant* is used in a negative clause:

> Qu'il se haïsse, qu'il s'aime: il a en lui la capacité de connaître la vérité et d'être heureux; mais il n'a pas de vérité, ou constante, ou satisfaisante. (L119)

This concept of the inaccessibility of truth recalls a deleted passage from L131, which we have seen already to be closely connected to *inconstance*. Opposing the contradictory doctrines of the sceptics and dogmatists, the dialectician argues that only the Christian doctrine of the Fall can explain man's contradictoriness. Whereas human philosophies exemplify inconstancy, the truths which are offered by the authority of religion are shown to be constant:

> Ces fondements solidement établis sur l'autorité inviolable de la religion nous font connaître qu'il y a deux vérités de foi également constantes.
> L'une que l'homme dans l'état de la création, ou dans celui de la grâce,

---

[43] It should be added that my analysis of *constance* here is derived from its contrast with *inconstance* in the *Pensées*, and I have not attempted to encapsulate all its complexities.

[44] Cf. L60: 'Et les législateurs n'auraient pas pris pour modèle, au lieu de cette justice constante, les fantaisies et les caprices des perses et allemands.' I shall discuss this fragment at length in Ch. 8 below.

est élevé au-dessus de toute la nature, rendu comme semblable à Dieu et participant de la divinité. L'autre qu'en l'état de la corruption, et du péché, il est déchu de cet état et rendu semblable aux bêtes. Ces deux propositions sont également fermes et certaines.

The choice of adjectives such as *constant*, *fermes*, and *certaines* accentuates the strong sense of certainty in matters pertaining to God and religion, as opposed to words such as *incertitude* and *mensonge*, which are used to describe the sceptics and dogmatists in the same fragment. Moreover, unlike the inconstancy of human reason by itself, as was emphasized in L199 ('notre raison est toujours déçue par l'inconstance des apparences'), in matters of faith, reason can, on the contrary, be redirected towards constancy: 'C'est le consentement de vous à vous-même et la voix constante de votre raison et non des autres qui vous doit faire croire' (L505). It is in this regard that philosophers like Epictetus are seen to be misguided, for they assume the constancy of Christianity to be easily attained: 'Epictète conclut de ce qu'il y a des chrétiens constants que chacun le peut bien être' (L146).

Judging from the one fragment in which the noun *constance* appears, its function differs from the use of the adjective because of its association with pagan virtues. Here, the status of words is thrown into doubt through the example of passions which can be mastered to become virtues. Similarly, terms generally considered to be virtues can be misused to become passions:

Abraham ne prit rien pour lui mais seulement pour ses serviteurs. Ainsi le juste ne prend rien pour soi du monde, ni des applaudissements du monde, mais seulement pour ses passions dont il se sert comme maître en disant à l'une: Va et viens, *sub te erit appetitus tuus*. Ses passions ainsi dominées sont vertus; l'avarice, la jalousie, la colère, Dieu même se les attribue. Et ce sont aussi bien vertus que la clémence, la pitié, la constance qui sont aussi des passions. Il faut s'en servir comme d'esclaves et leur laissant leur aliment empêcher que l'âme n'y en prenne. Car quand les passions sont les maîtresses, elles sont vices et alors elles donnent à l'âme de leur aliment, et l'âme s'en nourrit et s'en empoisonne. (L603)

The dialectician asserts here that a stoic virtue like *constance*, generally considered to be firm and unimpeachable (the Académie dictionary, for example, defines *constance* as 'Vertu par laquelle l'ame est affermie contre les choses qui sont capables de l'esbranler'), can be overturned just as passions can be redirected to become virtues. In other words, even a concept which is the antonym of *inconstance* is subject to the inconstancy which permeates the human condition. By the same token, this ability to transfer passions to virtues suggests that there remains the possibility that *inconstance*, like the passions, can be mastered to attain a state of *constance*, not as a pagan virtue, but one related to the Christian doctrine (Inc. 3).

We have seen, therefore, how the dialectician manipulates *inconstance* as well as *constance* to unsettle the reader and to provoke searching beyond the instability of the self. Although *inconstance* is perceived largely to represent the wretchedness of the human condition (Inc. 1), it is also clear that its association with other terms points towards something more positive (Inc. 2 and Inc. 3). I shall turn now to a consideration of *ennui* to find how it relates back to *inconstance* and forward towards *inquiétude*.

Key to *Inconstance*

Inc. 1   *inconstance*: wretchedness of man's fallen state
Inc. 2   *inconstance*: restlessness of human condition
Inc. 3   *inconstance*: spiritual searching

4
Ennui

> Il faut que nous disions à Dieu, que nous prenons plaisir à nostre ennuy, afin de nous point ennuyer.
>
> (Saint-Cyran)[1]

The long tradition of the use of the word *ennui* in French literature, and indeed its Greek and Latin roots, have been thoroughly documented.[2] I do not intend, therefore, to explore the history of the term other than in those circumstances where it is possible that Pascal was influenced in his usage of the word. Let it suffice to mention that all general studies of *ennui* recognize the original and central importance which Pascal brought to it. As Antoine de la Garanderie puts it, 'Si l'évolution du mot ennui est apparente depuis le xve siècle, elle atteint avec Pascal un sommet.'[3]

The significance of *ennui* in the *Pensées* would seem to be diminished by the relatively small number of times that it is used, only 29 times in its nominal and verbal forms (there are no examples of the adjective *ennuyeux*). However, its prominent position in many of those fragments underlines the central importance which Pascal accords the term. Not only is it listed with *inconstance* and *inquiétude* in L24 as encapsulating '[la] condition de l'homme', but also it appears as one of the projected chapter headings, *liasse* IV in the Lafuma edition.[4]

Of the three major seventeenth-century dictionaries, neither the Richelet nor the Furetière defines *ennui* as anything more than 'tristesse' and 'déplaisir' (Richelet) or 'chagrin' and 'fâcherie que donne quelque discours, ou quelque accident desplaisant'

---

[1] Jean du Verger de Hauranne, *Maximes saintes et chrestiennes* (1648), 145.
[2] See A. Bianchini Fales, 'Le Développement du mot *ennui* de la Pléiade jusqu'à Pascal', *Cultura neolatina*, 12 (1952), 223–8; A. de la Garanderie, *La Valeur de l'ennui* (Paris, 1968), 71–121; M. Bouchez, *La Valeur de l'ennui* (Paris, 1971); P. Dumonceaux, *Langue et sensibilité au XVIIe siècle: L'Évolution du vocabulaire affectif* (Geneva, 1975), 241–84.
[3] *La Valeur de l'ennui*, 119.
[4] For a thematic analysis of *ennui*, see my article, 'The Theme of Ennui in Pascal's *Pensées*', *Nottingham French Studies*, 26/2 (1987), 1–16.

(Furetière). Only the Académie dictionary makes a distinction between these generalized definitions and a more specialized meaning, namely 'lassitude d'esprit, causée par une chose qui déplaist par elle-même ou par sa durée'. This definition implies not only a state which turns in upon itself but also one which is tied to the notion of time. Furthermore, the examples of *ennui* which are given to support this particular sense are used exclusively in the singular form: 'On ne sçauroit entendre cela sans ennuy, sans mourir d'ennuy.' This is significant because, with only one exception (which itself is expanded in scope by the preceding 'beaucoup de'), all examples following the generalized definitions of 'Fascherie, chagrin, déplaisir, souci' are in the plural: 'Un homme accablé d'ennuis, les ennuis de la vieillesse, de mortels ennuis, cette affaire luy a donné beaucoup d'ennuy, cela sert à adoucir les ennuis, à charmer les ennuis.' Overall, then, 'ennuis' (in the plural) would seem to be associated with a more frivolous form of boredom, as the examples offered by the Furetière dictionary demonstrate: 'le vin, la bonne compagnie charment les ennuis, dissipent les ennuis'.

I have chosen to make this comparison between the singular and plural forms of *ennui* because in the *Pensées* every example of the noun is in the singular, which would seem to promote the more specialized meaning of the term. Indeed, to a large extent we find an important distinction between the use of the singular and plural forms in all key terms associated with the human condition.[5] A deletion which Pascal made in the original manuscript of L136 shows that he was careful to avoid using *ennui* as a plural noun, which inevitably would have diminished the impact of the fragment, where *ennui* is central. In the passage, he began to write 'tous nos ennu ...', before crossing out 'ennuis' and replacing it with 'malheurs':

Mais quand j'ai pensé de plus près et qu'après avoir trouvé la cause de tous nos [ennu] malheurs j'ai voulu en découvrir les raison[s] [. . .]. (L136)

In addition to the lack of plural nouns, *ennui* in the *Pensées* never appears with the indefinite article; all examples of the term are used either with the definite article, as in L79, L136, L414, L622, and

---

[5] Cf. J. Rohou, who, writing of the term *tourment* in Racine's theatre, stresses that 'le singulier tend à désigner un état permanent, par opposition à des manifestations particulières', in *L'Évolution du tragique racinien* (Paris, 1953), 159 n. 27.

L919, or without any article, as in the heading to L622 and in L24, L36, and L136. As Pierre Dumonceaux emphasizes, 'l'utilisation de l'article défini fait même entrevoir une certaine fixité du sentiment',[6] a 'fixité' which is further expanded in those fragments where no article is used. Both its individuality and its strength are encapsulated in the phrase, 'l'ennui de son autorité privée', from fragment L136, which I shall discuss at greater length later in this chapter. All these aspects point to the weight which Pascal undoubtedly wished to attach to *ennui*.[7]

It is inevitable that the impact of the verbal form would seem to be less than that of the noun, rather as the plural noun would lack the weight of the singular. However, there is a clear difference when the verb is used in its reflexive form. The reflexive *se* suggests a turning in of the verb onto its subject, which, in the case of *s'ennuyer* in the *Pensées*, is appropriate to Pascal's notion of the connection between *ennui* and the human condition: only humans 's'ennuient', not animals or tables and chairs. This point is best illustrated by a fragment where the verb is used in both its reflexive and non-reflexive forms:

> L'éloquence continue ennuie.
> Les princes et rois jouent quelquefois. Ils ne sont pas toujours sur leurs trônes. Ils s'y ennuient. La grandeur a besoin d'être quittée pour être sentie. (L771)

Whereas the first use of the verb implies a more general question of style, the second use, in the reflexive, centres upon the humanity of kings and princes, and on their need for diversity. Indeed, it is interesting to note that all instances of the non-reflexive verb (except for one case in L136, where *ennui* and *divertissement* are clearly central) show the dialectician's stylistic concerns rather than

---

[6] *Langue et sensibilité au XVIIe siècle*, 242.
[7] A useful comparison to be made is between the *Lettres provinciales* and the *Pensées*. The fact that the noun does not appear in the *Lettres provinciales* in either singular or plural form underlines the importance of *ennui* to the apologetic and dialectical context of the *Pensées* rather than to the polemical debate of the *Lettres provinciales*. As I hope to show, the state of *ennui* in the *Pensées* is essential to the dialectician's portrayal of man's fallen condition, a portrayal which focuses primarily on the psychology of his reader. The only form of *ennui* to appear in the *Lettres provinciales* is the verb *ennuyer* in the 12th letter (p. 425), where its use is entirely conventional: 'j'essaierai de vous ennuyer le moins qu'il se peut en ce genre d'écrire'.

the depiction of the human condition: for example, in addition to the above 'éloquence continue' which 'ennuie', elsewhere the dialectician specifies the 'divisions de Charron, qui attristent et ennuient' (L780), and in another fragment, L528, the phrase 'je crains de vous ennuyer' is cited as a 'compliment' which the dialectician finds difficult to accept. In all these cases, *ennuyer* would appear to be unconnected to the portrayal of man's state.

All uses of *s'ennuyer* in the *Pensées*, on the other hand, tend to correspond explicitly or implicitly to the noun *ennui* or to the human condition as a whole. In L136, for example, the verb is introduced both to complement and to oppose the noun. In L941, *s'ennuyer* is introduced as a counterfoil to man's need for spiritual hunger:

> On ne s'ennuie point de manger, et dormir, tous les jours, car la faim renaît et le sommeil, sans cela on s'en ennuierait.
>
> Ainsi sans la faim des choses spirituelles on s'en ennuie; faim de la justice, béatitude 8ᵉ.

Even L534, where the phrase 'Vous vous ennuyez' carries no particular weight by itself, concerns man's perception of time, a theme which is closely linked to *inconstance, ennui,* and *inquiétude* in the *Pensées*.

I now intend to concentrate mainly on uses of the noun and on those fragments where it is coupled with or played off against the verb.

Of all uses of *ennui* in the *Pensées*, only one seems to fit the more generalized meaning offered by the seventeenth-century dictionaries, that of *déplaisir*:

> L'ennui qu'on a de quitter les occupations où l'on s'est attaché. Un homme vit avec plaisir en son ménage; qu'il voie une femme qui lui plaise, qu'il joue 5 ou 6 jours avec plaisir, le voilà misérable s'il retourne à sa première occupation. Rien n'est plus ordinaire que cela. (L79)

Paradoxically, this sole example of *ennui* used in a more conventional sense is the only fragment with the word *ennui* to appear in the *liasse* entitled 'Ennui'. However, the subject of the fragment contains the seed of the longer *divertissement* fragment, L136, and it is possible that the meaning of *ennui* here would have been intensified in a longer draft.

All other appearances of *ennui* in the fragments contain greater weight. As with so many of the key terms in the *Pensées*, the meaning is not static. Yet *ennui* differs to the extent that a word denoting a sense of nothingness must necessarily attain greater significance through its association with other terms. There are two main levels on which *ennui* in a human context operates, and which in many respects overlap. The first, which I shall call E1, is *ennui* in association with the concept of *néant*, and the second, E2, is *ennui* combined with *divertissement*. There is a third element, E3, which stems directly from the first two and which, again, points towards a spiritual solution.

ENNUI/NÉANT

The fragment which perhaps best encapsulates the role of *ennui* in the *Pensées* is L622:

Ennui.
Rien n'est si insupportable à l'homme que d'être dans un plein repos, sans passions, sans affaires, sans divertissement, sans application.
Il sent alors son néant, son abandon, son insuffisance, sa dépendance, son impuissance, son vide.
Incontinent il sortira du fond de son âme, l'ennui, la noirceur, la tristesse, le chagrin, le dépit, le désespoir.

Not only does this passage expand our perception of the term through its association with other concepts, but also the patterning of six parallel nouns in the final two sentences links *ennui* with *néant*:

néant	ennui
abandon	noirceur
insuffisance	tristesse
dépendance	chagrin
impuissance	dépit
vide	désespoir

A clear distinction can be made between the nouns in the first sentence (listed in the left column) and those in the second sentence (on the right). The first nouns would seem to present an objective state, whereas the second nouns communicate a subjective response to that situation. Therefore, in order to distinguish between *néant* and *ennui*, while *néant* expresses the physical and spiritual *state* of emptiness and nothingness, *ennui* conveys the *sense* or perception of that void. This distinction between the two terms is best illustrated in L36, where the dialectician specifies that young people's pursuit of *divertissement* clouds their view of the vanity of the world:

> Mais ôtez leur divertissement vous les verrez se sécher d'ennui. Ils sentent alors leur néant sans le connaître, car c'est bien être malheureux que d'être dans une tristesse insupportable, aussitôt qu'on est réduit à se considérer, et à n'en être point diverti.

As can be seen here, *ennui* is a *néant* which men 'sentent'.

So strong is the sense of *ennui* which the *néant* produces that it becomes all-engulfing. This aspect is most amply shown in the short *Opuscule, Sur la conversion du pécheur*, where the progress of man's soul is charted, from a state of false repose, through an awareness of overwhelming *néant*, followed by a stage of self-abasement, culminating in the approaching communion with God. Significantly, the *néant* which the soul reaches comes only as a result of a heightened self-awareness granted by God:

> La première chose que Dieu inspire à l'âme qu'il daigne toucher véritablement, est une connaissance et une vue tout extraordinaire par laquelle l'âme considère les choses et elle-même d'une façon toute nouvelle.[8]

This self-knowledge leads the soul to an acknowledgement of the transitoriness of everything connected with the human condition. All becomes part of the *néant*:

> De là vient qu'elle [l'âme] commence à considérer comme un néant tout ce qui doit retourner dans le néant, le ciel, la terre, son esprit, son corps, ses parents, ses amis, ses ennemis, les biens, la pauvreté, la disgrâce, la prospérité, l'honneur, l'ignominie, l'estime, le mépris, l'autorité, l'indigence, la santé, la maladie et la vie même [. . .].[9]

This accumulation of antitheses intensifies the all-engulfing sense of *ennui* which the *néant* produces. Not only do our minds but also our bodies become nothing, not only wealth but poverty, not only health but sickness, culminating in the terrifying realization that life itself is as transitory as all the other aspects, and thus showing that all such terms are relative. Far from being an entirely negative awareness, this state of self-knowledge can, on the contrary, be seen

---

[8] Seuil 290. [9] Ibid.

to be positive, for it marks an important stage in the conversion of the soul.

But, to remain with *ennui* on a human level, it is inevitable that man, in order to escape from the all-encompassing sense of *ennui* which his state of nothingness produces, should seek diversions to distract himself.

ENNUI AND DIVERTISSEMENT

Thus far, we have seen *ennui* only in the sense of E1 (see the Key at the end of this chapter), that of *ennui-néant*, which is represented primarily as a *passive* state. However, the *active* side of *ennui* is encapsulated in *divertissement*. As with *ennui*, which encapsulates the human condition as a whole, *divertissement* comprises, as D. C. Potts puts it, 'not only the pursuit of particular pleasures such as gambling and hunting, but a whole way of life'.[10] The combination of these two terms, E2, makes one of the most central and original concepts in the *Pensées*. I intend, therefore, to consider the pivotal fragment on *divertissement*, L136, in conjunction with a number of texts which may have acted as a source for Pascal and also with some contemporary responses to the fragment.

Jean Mesnard has elegantly documented the proximity of Pascal's *divertissement* to Montaigne's 'De la diversion', showing how Pascal returns to the etymological sense of *divertir*, that of 'action de détourner, de se détourner', a meaning which was hardly apparent in seventeenth-century usage of the term.[11] However, he makes no comment on the relation between *ennui* and *divertissement*, and rather chooses to define Montaigne's *diversion* as an 'acte' and Pascal's *divertissement* as an 'état'.[12] As I have indicated,

---

[10] 'Pascal's Contemporaries and Le Divertissement', *Modern Language Review*, 57 (1962), 31–40.
[11] See 'De la *diversion* au *divertissement*', in *Mémorial du Premier Congrès International des Études Montaignistes*, 1964), 123–8. For other useful discussions of *divertissement*, see P. Sellier, *Pascal et Saint Augustin* (Paris, 1970), 164–7, who relates *divertissement* to Augustine's *aversio*; Dumonceaux, *Langue et sensibilité au XVIIe siècle*, ch. 4, who sees in the ambiguity of the term for Pascal 'sa force expressive, et une originalité de style incomparable' (p. 218); and D. Jaymes, 'Play in Pascal's *Pensées*', *Papers on French Seventeenth Century Literature*, 14–15 (1981), 39–49, who interprets the dialectical use of *divertissement*. I shall discuss some of these views at greater length in the final chapter.
[12] 'De la *diversion* au *divertissement*', 128.

if one considers the difference between *ennui* and *divertissement* in the *Pensées*, *divertissement* would seem to be the active form of the state of *ennui*. In other words, while *ennui* is an 'état', *divertissement* is an 'acte'.

The famous lines towards the beginning of the fragment, 'j'ai dit souvent que tout le malheur des hommes vient d'une seule chose, qui est de ne savoir pas demeurer en repos dans une chambre', find a clear echo in one of Seneca's Dialogues, *De Tranquillitate Animi*. Indeed, the notions of both *ennui* and *divertissement* are suggested in the text. In a 1598 translation of the work, Simon Goulart translates 'taedium' as 'chagrin':

l'esprit ne peut durer en maison ni en solitude quelconque, les parois le faschent, et estant ainsi abandonné à soy-mesme il se regarde de travers et à contrecœur. De là vient ce chagrin, ce mépris de soy [*Hinc illud est taedium et displicentia sui*], ceste perpetuelle agitation d'esprit, ceste triste et foible patience en repos. [...] Voilà ce qui engendre ces ennuis, ces rides interieures [*maeror marcorque*], et mille flots en la conscience vagabonde [...].[13]

It is significant that Goulart chooses the term *chagrin* in the singular and *ennuis* in the plural, for clearly *ennui* in the singular form does not have the weight which Pascal was to attach to it. In L136, for example, we find a similar use of verb and noun as in the last sentence quoted, but *ennui* (here used in the sense of E1) appears in the singular:

Ainsi s'écoule toute la vie; on cherche le repos en combattant quelques obstacles et si on les a surmontés le repos devient insupportable par l'ennui [E1] qu'il engendre.

I make the point about Goulart's omission of the singular noun *ennui*, because there is another passage in L136, probably influenced by Montaigne, where Pascal replaces Montaigne's *chagrin* with *ennui*:

---

[13] *Les Œuvres morales et meslees de Seneque*, trans. S. Goulart (1598), 334. Cf. Mersenne's *L'Impiété des déistes réfutée* (1624), where *ennui* is linked to solitude, but without the importance which is attached to the concept for Seneca and Pascal: 'j'ai hâté le pas pour vous joindre, et consoler dans la douceur de votre compagnie, si vous l'avez pour agreable, l'ennuy qu'apporte d'ordinaire avec soy la solitude du chemin' (p. 1). Cf. Saint-Evremond's reaction against such a conception of *ennui* and *divertissement* in his essay, 'Sur les plaisirs', *Œuvres meslées* (Paris, 1680), vi. 59, 64, 65.

Car ou l'on pense aux misères qu'on a ou à celles qui nous menacent. Et quand on se verrait même assez à l'abri de toutes parts l'ennui [E1] de son autorité privée ne laisserait pas de sortir du fond du cœur où il a des racines naturelles, et de remplir l'esprit de son venin.

Montaigne, in his *Apologie de Raimond Sebond*, writes:

Ou l'humeur melancholique me tient, ou la cholerique; et de son authorité privée à cet'heure le chagrin prédomine en moy, à cet'heure l'alegresse.[14]

I would argue that Pascal invests *ennui* with a power which far surpasses that of the term *chagrin* in the *Pensées*. Indeed, the word *chagrin* appears in only two fragments, L136 and L622, both in conjunction with *ennui* and *divertissement*. In L622, as I showed above, the patterning of the two final sentences would link *chagrin* with *dépendance*, but neither noun achieves any prominence in the fragment or in the *Pensées* as a whole. As far as L136 is concerned, it is significant that in the *Recueil original* the word *chagrin* was crossed out at three points in the fragment, once in the same sentence as 'l'ennui de son autorité privée'. This would indicate that Pascal found it inappropriate to apply to *chagrin* a strength of meaning which he would use with *ennui*. The one section of L136 where *chagrin* remains unscored shows the subservience of the term to *ennui* and contains the sense of mere unhappiness, in contrast to the pervasive effects of *ennui*:

L'homme, quelque plein de tristesse qu'il soit, si on peut gagner sur lui de le faire entrer en quelque divertissement le voilà heureux pendant ce temps-là, et l'homme quelqu'heureux qu'il soit s'il n'est diverti et occupé par quelque passion ou quelque amusement, qui empêche l'ennui de se répandre, sera bientôt chagrin et malheureux.

The use of the reflexive verb *se répandre*, accentuates the 'autorité privée' of *ennui*.

This pervasive influence of *ennui* is vividly captured in another section of L136, where the dialectician makes skilful use of polyptoton, playing off the verb *ennuyer*, with its weaker meaning, against the noun:

Ainsi l'homme est si malheureux qu'il s'ennuierait même sans aucune cause d'ennui par l'état propre de sa complexion. Et il est si vain, qu'étant plein

---

[14] *Essais* (in *Œuvres complètes*, ed. M. Rat, Paris, 1962), II. xii. 549.

de mille causes essentielles d'ennui, la moindre chose comme un billard et une balle qu'il pousse, suffisent pour le divertir.

The introduction of *s'ennuyer*, denoting a more conventional form of boredom, serves to accentuate the importance of the noun *ennui*, not only providing a contrast but also giving the sense of an accumulation of its all-engulfing force. This is also found in a passage which closely follows the above quotation, and which shows the reality of *ennui*, despite man's attempts to explain his need for diversions:

Tel homme passe sa vie sans ennui en jouant tous les jours peu de chose. Donnez-lui tous les matins l'argent qu'il peut gagner chaque jour, à la charge qu'il ne joue point, vous le rendez malheureux. On dira peut-être que c'est qu'il recherche l'amusement du jeu et non pas le gain. Faites-le donc jouer pour rien, il ne s'y échauffera pas et s'y ennuiera. Ce n'est donc pas l'amusement seul qu'il recherche. Un amusement languissant et sans passion l'ennuiera.

For Charron, on the other hand, whom Pascal undoubtedly read and whose use of *ennui* may provide a useful link between Montaigne and Pascal, *ennui* comes not from an awareness of the wretchedness of one's present condition but from the repetition of pleasures or *divertissements*:

L'homme ne peut gueres durer au plaisir, le plaisir du corps est feu de paille: s'il enduroit il apporteroit de l'ennuy et deplaisir.[15]

Moreover, for Charron, in addition to the *ennui* which a surfeit of pleasures brings, he sees man as being overcome with *ennui* from his past, not present, wretchedness:

Bref, il [l'homme] est si fort et incessamment agité de soin, et pensemens, non seulement inutiles et superflus, mais espineux, penibles et dommageables, tourmenté par le present, ennuyé du passé, angoissé pour l'advenir, qu'il semble ne craindre rien plus, que de ne pouvoir pas estre assez miserable [. . .].[16]

As we have seen with the first two meanings of *ennui* in the *Pensées* (E1 and E2), Pascal's perception of the term differs markedly, not only because it is an all-embracing sense of one's present *néant* but

---

[15] *De la sagesse*, in *Œuvres* (Geneva, 1970; facsimile of the 1635 Paris edn.), i. 127–8.   [16] Ibid. 129–30.

also because *divertissement* provides a spurious attempt to escape from that *néant*.

The combination of these terms, along with the idea of solitude, as we saw in L136, is in no way new, but the way in which it becomes central to his argument about the corruption of man shows the originality of Pascal. If we compare this to the juxtaposition of *ennui, solitude,* and *divertissement* in the work of an earlier seventeenth-century apologist, Jean de Silhon, for example, the difference is striking. Speaking of his apology, *Les Deux veritez*, Silhon explains, 'j'ay tasché de flatter mes ennuis, et addoucir ma solitude par ce divertissement'.[17] For him, his work acts as a positive *divertissement* to escape from his solitude. In no way does solitude make him aware of his wretched condition. In the work of another humanist apologist, Yves de Paris, solitude is perceived in completely the opposite way to Pascal. He sees in solitude greatness rather than weakness: 'si nous nous enfonçons dans la profonde solitude d'une forest, parmy le silence [. . .], nostre cœur sent des emotions inaccoutumees; et tout le corps qui fremit d'une crainte respectueuse, nous advertit de la presence d'une grandeur infinie'.[18]

To return to Pascal, in a similar way to the distinction which I made earlier between *ennui* and *chagrin,* the function of the word *tristesse* differs greatly from that of *ennui* in the *Pensées*. Despite Nicole's claims in a letter to the Marquis de Sévigné that Pascal confused *ennui* with *tristesse,* nowhere is the word *tristesse* used with a significance equal to or greater than that of *ennui*.[19] Although no direct distinction between the two nouns is made by Pascal, Nicole evidently underestimates the important link between *ennui* and *divertissement* in the *Pensées*:

Il [Pascal] suppose dans tout le discours du divertissement ou de la misere de l'homme, que l'ennui vient de ce que l'on se voit; de ce que l'on pense à

---

[17] *Les Deux veritez* (Paris, 1626), 263. Cf. the 'Advertissement', where Silhon writes to his reader, 'j'ay à t'advertir que ces discours que je te presente sont des fruits d'une solitude dans laquelle je m'estois reduit, comme ceux qui pour se garantir de la tourmente gaignent un bord desert et rude. Pour adoucir ce cruel loisir je m'amusay les premiers mois à ranger avec quelque ordre et entregent [sic] les matieres que j'avais choisies pour mon entretien.'

[18] *La Theologie naturelle ou Les Premieres Veritez de la foy sont eclaircies par raisons sensibles et moralles* (Paris, 1633), 69.

[19] See L36, L136, and L622, where *tristesse* appears with *ennui* and *divertissement*, as well as L281 and L483.

soi, et que le bien du divertissement consiste en ce qu'il nous ôte cette pensée. Cela est peutêtre plus subtil que solide. Mille personnes s'ennuyent, sans penser à eux. Ils s'ennuyent, non de ce qu'ils pensent, mais de ce qu'ils ne pensent pas assez. Le plaisir de l'ame consiste à penser vivement et agréablement. Elle s'ennuye sitôt qu'elle n'a plus que des pensées languissantes; ce qui lui arrive dans la solitude, parce qu'elle n'y est pas si fortement remuée. C'est pourquoi ceux qui sont bien occupés d'eux-mêmes peuvent s'attrister, mais ne s'ennuyent pas. La tristesse et l'ennui sont des mouvemens differens. L'ennui cherche le divertissement, la tristesse le fuit. L'ennui vient de la privation du plaisir, et de la langueur de l'ame, qui ne pense pas assez; la tristesse vient des pensées vives, mais affligeantes. Monsieur Pascal confond tout cela.[20]

Nicole's own discussion of *ennui* and *divertissement* here would seem to be 'plus subtil que solide', for he ignores the positive aspect of *ennui* (E3) which is contrasted with the negative side of *divertissement* in the *Pensées*. Indeed, quite the opposite of Nicole's statement elsewhere that *ennui* is 'un état que je croi qu'on est obligé d'éviter',[21] *ennui* for Pascal is *necessary* to make man search for something more lasting. This point is emphasized in a fragment entitled 'Misère':

La seule chose qui nous console de nos misères est le divertissement. Et cependant c'est la plus grande de nos misères. Car c'est cela qui nous empêche principalement de songer à nous et qui nous fait perdre insensiblement. Sans cela nous serions dans l'ennui, et cet ennui [E3] nous pousserait à chercher un moyen plus solide d'en sortir, mais le divertissement nous amuse et nous fait arriver insensiblement à la mort. (L414)

Whereas *divertissement* can cloud man's judgement and make him ignore his true state, *ennui* alerts him to the reality of his condition and so can prompt him to look beyond mere diversion towards a possible spiritual solution.

ENNUI AND THE POSSIBILITY OF SALVATION

Up to now, I have mentioned the presence of *ennui* in the sense of E3 in other fragments, especially where acknowledgement of *ennui*

---

[20] Letter 88 in P. Nicole, *Essais de morale* (Paris, 1733–71; repr. Geneva, 1971), viii. 242. [21] Letter 97, ibid. 326.

can encourage man to search beyond his own temporary needs. However, there remains one fragment where *ennui* appears in a different context, in the semi-autonomous passage known as 'Le Mystère de Jésus', L919: 'Jésus dans l'ennui'.[22]

In this fragment we encounter a dramatic and lyrical account of Jesus spending his final hours in the Garden of Gethsemane while his disciples are asleep, the latter half taking the form of a prosopopoeia, with a dialogue between an unidentified 'je', whom I take to be the dialectician as searcher, and Jesus. Jesus, taking upon himself the burden of those human beings who are asleep, undergoes an awareness of a *néant* which is not unlike fallen man's sense of *ennui*. Indeed, the spiritual state of Jesus who endures 'cette peine et cet abandon dans l'horreur de la nuit' (L919) is similar to the speaker's terror at 'le silence éternel de ces espaces infinis' in L201. Finding himself in this state before he leaves the earth, Jesus contemplates the void of 'ce délaissement universel' (L919). However, there exists a significant difference between the depiction of man's *ennui* and the state in which Christ is portrayed here, for, whereas elsewhere *ennui* is related to man's own frailty, here it signifies Christ's 'délaissement', his abandonment by earthly support. In brutal contrast to the image of the sleeping disciples, the insomnia of Jesus is expanded into a symbol of universal affliction: 'Jésus sera en agonie jusqu'à la fin du monde; il ne faut pas dormir pendant ce temps-là' (L919). Yet, Jesus, in facing this 'agonie', is effecting man's salvation:

Jésus pendant que ses disciples dormaient a opéré leur salut. Il l'a fait à chacun des justes pendant qu'ils dormaient, et dans le néant avant leur naissance, et dans les péchés depuis leur naissance. (L919)

It is at this point that the dialectician depicts 'Jésus dans l'ennui', for it is clear that *ennui* forms part of that path towards spiritual salvation. After these lines, Jesus, taking account of his sleeping friends and vigilant enemies, 'se remet tout entier à son Père'.

This spiritual implication of *ennui* can also be found elsewhere, in works which Pascal would very probably have known. St François de Sales, for example, relates *ennui* to the experience of

---

[22] In my discussion of this fragment, I am restating a number of the observations which I made in 'The Theme of Ennui in Pascal's *Pensées*'.

Christ. In *L'Introduction à la vie dévote*, Philotée is exhorted to remember the suffering of Christ on the cross:

> Voyez souvent de vos yeux intérieurs Jésus-Christ crucifié, nu, blasphémé, calomnié, abandonné, et enfin accablé de toutes sortes d'ennuis, de tristesse et de travaux [. . .].[23]

However, clearly there is no positive aspect of *ennui* in this usage. Elsewhere, in the *Traité de l'amour de Dieu*, *ennui* is related to the 'délaissement' of Christ, as in 'Le Mystère de Jésus'; it is significant that *ennui* belongs to his life on earth but that God has touched him with his eternal happiness:

> Notre-Seigneur aussi, élevé en la croix entre la terre et le ciel, n'était, ce semble, tenu de la main de son Père que par l'extrême pointe de l'esprit, et, par manière de dire, par un seul cheveu de sa tête, qui, touché de la douce main du Père éternel, recevait une souveraine affluence de félicité, tout le reste demeurant abîmé dans la tristesse et ennui; c'est pourquoy il s'écrie: Mon Dieu, mon Dieu, pourquoi m'as-tu délaissé?[24]

Perhaps the best indication of the *necessity* of *ennui* in François de Sales's writings, and which we can compare to Pascal's similar use of the term, comes in a letter which he wrote to Mme Bourgeois, the abbesse of the Puits d'Orbe:

> il est force que nous souffrions de l'ennuy interieur quand Dieu arrache la derniere peau du vieil homme pour le renouveller en l'homme nouveau qui est créé selon Dieu.[25]

It would seem that *ennui* must be experienced before God can save man from his inner corruption.

Altogether, therefore, in the *Pensées*, *ennui* plays a significant part in the apologetic process. It remains inextricably linked to the human condition, and yet an acknowledgement of its centrality can lead man to search for a spiritual solution. The coexistence of *ennui* and spiritual need is perhaps best encapsulated in De Sacy's translation of Psalm 118: 'Mon âme s'est assoupie d'ennui, fortifiez-moi par vos paroles.'[26] In *ennui* there resides a reminder of man's condition and the hope of fulfilment.

---

[23] *Œuvres*, ed. A. Ravier (Paris, 1969), III. iii. 137.
[24] Ibid. IX. v. 772.
[25] Written between 15 and 18 Apr. 1605.
[26] Ps. 118, v. 28.

Key to *Ennui*

E1 *ennui-néant*: wretchedness of man's fallen state
E2 *ennui-divertissement*: restlessness of human condition
E3 *ennui*: possible salvation

5
Inquiétude

> Ce que vous dites sur les inquiétudes que nous avons si souvent et si naturellement sur l'avenir, et comme insensiblement notre inclination se change et s'accommode à la nécessité, est la plus juste matière d'un livre comme celui de Pascal.
>
> (Mme de Sévigné to Mme de Grignan, 9 August 1671)

Inquiétude completes the triad of terms depicting the human condition in L24. Jean Deprun calls *inquiétude* in this fragment 'l'antonyme fraternel de l'ennui, la phase B d'un incessant et vain processus d'oscillation'.[1] Indeed, not only does it frame the fragment, along with *inconstance*, with a sense of movement as opposed to the stasis of *ennui*, but, as we have seen, *ennui* itself points strongly towards the movement inherent in both *inconstance* and *inquiétude*. The Latin root of *inquiétude*, *inquies* (meaning literally lack of rest), and its antonym *quies*, will be shown in both this and the following chapter to play a significant role, most particularly with reference to the influence of Augustine. Central to the very first chapter of the *Confessions*, for example, are the words 'inquietum est cor nostrum' (i. 1), which, as we shall see, form the inspiration of a number of Pascalian writings. As Pierre Courcelle states, 'l'inquiétude pascalienne est fille de l'inquiétude augustinienne'.[2] Antoine de la Garanderie makes a useful distinction between *ennui* and *inquiétude*, which shows this inner tension between stasis and movement: 'l'inquiétude, c'est l'absence de repos, alors que l'ennui est comme l'inquiétude du repos'.[3] It refers back also to *inconstance* in its status as a negative noun. In fact, the Académie dictionary reinforces the analogy between the two terms in defining *inquiétude* as 'inconstance d'humeur', as well as 'trouble, agitation d'esprit' and 'impatience causée par quelque passion, quelque indisposition'. The Furetière dictionary, on the

---

[1] *La Philosophie de l'inquiétude en France au XVIIIe siècle* (Paris, 1979), 127.
[2] *Les Confessions de Saint Augustin dans la tradition littéraire* (Paris, 1963), 434. See also n. 16 below.
[3] *La Valeur de l'ennui* (Paris, 1968), 118.

other hand, equates *inquiétude* with *ennui*, defining it as 'chagrin, ennuy, trouble et affliction d'esprit'.

Of the eleven times that the noun *inquiétude* appears in the *Pensées*, it is used in all cases as a singular noun either with no accompanying article or with a definite article. The fact that there are no examples of the plural noun or indefinite article indicates that the dialectician uses the term in a generalized context, depicting a condition, as in L24, rather than in the more personalized sense of a particular worry.[4] The noun also predominates over all other forms of the word: we find only one example of the verb (L929) and one example each of the adjectival forms *inquiet* (L744) and *inquiétant* (L522).[5]

I have discussed already the direct bearing of Montaigne and Charron on the formulation of *inconstance* and *ennui* in the *Pensées*. Although the influence on particular fragments where *inquiétude* appears is not as strikingly discernible, a brief examination of some uses of the word in the *Essais* and in *De la sagesse* should throw light on the term in the *Pensées*. Pascal's enlargement of the term into a symbol of the human condition in L24, for example, finds a parallel in Montaigne's chapter 'Que philosopher c'est apprendre à mourir' (i. 20), where *inquiétude* is linked implicitly to 'l'humaine condition'. The soul, in surpassing man's condition, is deemed to be capable of escaping from such states as 'l'inquietude, le tourment, la peur' which are inextricably part of that humanity:

Le corps, courbe et plié, a moins de force à soustenir un fais; aussi a nostre ame: il la faut dresser, et eslever contre l'effort de cet adversaire. Car, comme il est impossible qu'elle se mette en repos pendant qu'elle le craint: si elle s'en asseure aussi, elle se peut venter, qui est chose comme surpassant l'humaine condition, qu'il est impossible que l'inquietude, le tourment, la peur, non le moindre desplaisir loge en elle [. . .].[6]

---

[4] In 2 letters Pascal uses *inquiétude* in the plural. I shall examine these examples at the end of the chapter.

[5] The fact that the noun does not appear at all in the *Lettres provinciales* would suggest, as we have seen already with *inconstance* and *ennui*, that it is specifically suited to the apologetic dimensions of the *Pensées* rather than to polemical argument. The verb is the one form of *inquiétude* used in the *Lettres provinciales*, the only example of which appears in a quotation of Pope Alexander III, in the 18th letter (Seuil 466).

[6] *Essais* (in *Œuvres complètes*, ed. M. Rat, Paris, 1962), I. xx. 89.

Elsewhere in the *Essais*, *inquiétude* is associated with terms and concepts which are found regularly in the *Pensées*. However, in almost all cases, the meaning is essentially specialized. In 'Divers evenemens de mesme conseil', for instance, Montaigne places *inquiétude* with *incertitude*, but both nouns are concerned with particular precautions ('provisions') which one can take:

> D'appeller les mains ennemies, c'est un conseil un peu gaillard si croy-je qu'encore vaudroit-il mieux le prendre que de demeurer en la fievre continuelle d'un accident qui n'a point de remede. Mais, puisque les provisions qu'on y peut aporter sont pleines d'inquietude et d'incertitude, il vaut mieux d'une belle asseurance se preparer à tout ce qui en pourra advenir, et tirer quelque consolation de ce qu'on n'est pas asseuré qu'il advienne.[7]

Similarly, in another essay, 'De la vanité', where Montaigne's assertion that 'je me plonge la teste baissée stupidement dans la mort' prefigures Pascal's image of death for the godless man,[8] *inquiétude* is linked to a state of inconstancy. However, the term refers specifically to the dangers of travel:

> Je sçay bien qu'à le prendre à la lettre, ce plaisir de voyager porte tesmoignage d'inquietude et d'irresolution. Aussi sont ce nos maistresses qualitez, et praedominantes. Ouy, je le confesse, je ne vois rien, seulement en songe et par souhait, où je me puisse tenir; la seule varieté me paye, et la possession de la diversité, au moins si aucune chose me paye.[9]

Other examples of *inquiétude* in the *Essais* also show it to be related to specific people's worries.[10]

Although *inquiétude* does not occupy as prominent a place in *De la sagesse* as *ennui* and *inconstance* (both of which are utilized as titles of chapters), it nevertheless assumes a generalized role which

---

[7] Ibid. xxiv. 132.
[8] Ibid. ix. 949. See L133: 'les hommes n'ayant pu guérir la mort, la misère, l'ignorance, ils se sont avisés, pour se rendre heureux, de n'y point penser'. Although this conception of death in a godless existence bears the influence of Montaigne, it must be added that, from a Christian standpoint, the dialectician distances himself from Montaigne's thoughts on death: 'on ne peut excuser ses sentiments tout païens sur la mort' (L680).   [9] *Essais*, III. ix. 966.
[10] Cf. ibid. I. xiv. 61; I. xxiv. 124; II. xxxi. 693. Of the verbal forms of *inquiétude*, Montaigne makes one interesting use in linking *inquiétée* to the cares of life as a whole: 'C'est en fin tout le soulagement que je trouve en ma vieillesse, qu'elle amortist en moy plusieurs desirs et soins de quoy la vie est inquietée. Le soing du cours du monde, le soing des richesses, de la grandeur, de la science, de la santé, de moy' (I. xxviii. 682).

appears to be less derivative of Montaigne than anticipatory of Pascal. In the chapter entitled 'Misere', for example, Charron introduces *inquiétude* together with concepts such as *ennui* and *divertissement* (although he does not name the latter) in his depiction of man's state:

Ce n'est pas encores assez; car afin qu'il ne luy manque jamais matiere de misere, voire qu'il y en aye tousjours à foison, il va tousjours furetant et recherchant avec grande estude les causes et alimens de misere: il se fourre aux affaires de gayeté de cœur, et tels que quand ils s'offriroient à luy, il leur devroit tourner le dos, ou bien par une inquietude miserable de son esprit, ou pour faire l'habile, l'empesché, et l'entendu: c'est à dire le sot et miserable, il entreprend et remue besongne nouvelle, ou s'entre-mesle de celle d'autruy. Bref, il est si fort et incessamment agité de soin, et pensemens, non seulement inutiles et superflus, mais espineux, penibles et dommageables, tourmenté, par le present, ennuyé du passé, angoissé pour l'advenir, qu'il semble ne craindre rien plus [....].[11]

Charron's expansion of words such as 'inquietude', 'miserable', 'tourmenté', 'ennuyé', and 'angoissé' into metaphors of the human condition clearly paves the way for Pascal's concise manipulation of similar terms. In this passage, the use of the indefinite article with *inquiétude* restricts its sense; but, in the chapter, 'Des passions en general', for example, the word appears without any article, thus attaining the image of a general state rather than a specific complaint: 'elle [imagination] nous remplit de trouble et d'inquietude'.[12] Nevertheless, the infrequency of the use of *inquiétude* and its insignificant position within the text show that it

[11] P. Charron, *Œuvres* (Geneva, 1970; facsimile of the 1635 Paris edn.), I. 1. xxxix. 129–30. See my discussion of this passage in Ch. 4 above. Cf. Bourdonné, *Le Courtisan desabusé* (Paris, 1658): 'il y a tousjours quelque souvenir qui nous inquiete, quelque tristesse qui nous afflige, et quelque crainte qui nous trouble. Non seulement le present nous fasche, mais nous nous tourmentons encore de l'avenir' (pp. 301–2). For Bourdonné, *inquiétude* characterizes court life. Cf. Nicolas Faret, in *L'Honneste-Homme ou l'Art de plaire à la cour* (Paris, 1630), who speaks of the 'inquiétudes de la Cour' (p. 69). Cf. also Mme de Lafayette, *La Princesse de Clèves*, ed. A. Adam (Paris, 1966), where individuals within the court constantly experience it: e.g. pp. 38, 48, 60, 62, 75, 100, 101, 109, 119, 127, 143, 149, 161.

[12] *Œuvres*, I. xviii. 66. Cf. the very different use of imagination by Pascal in L44, where it 'remplit ses hôtes d'une satisfaction bien autrement pleine et entière que la raison' (L44). Cf. also Charron's more specialized use of *inquiétude* in *Les Trois veritez*, concerning tyrans: 'le tyran est tousjours le plus miserable, et qui a moins d'aise et de repos, que le plus chetif de ceux qu'il opprime. Il craint tous ceux qui le craignent et le hayssent. Inquietude continue, que la tyrannie et la prosperité des meschans' (*Œuvres*, II. i. 53).

cannot be regarded as a central term in *De la sagesse*. We must look to the *Pensées* to perceive the importance which Pascal assigns to it. In the course of this chapter, I intend to examine three categories of meaning into which *inquiétude* falls (see the Key at the end of this chapter): the anxiety of man's fallen state (I1), *inquiétude* as linked directly to fallen man's spiritual searching (I2), and within the context of the Christian's continued spiritual endeavours (I3).

THE ANXIETY OF MAN'S FALLEN STATE

Inquiétude in its first sense (I1) involves all the worries that man faces in the world, with, as Louis A. Mackenzie puts it,

the seamless slide from the psychological to the metaphysical, from everyday cares to everyman's questions of self-identity and self-worth. In his anxious condition—Pascal will refer to it as *inquiétude*—man faces the void as he senses his own loss and deprivation.[13]

This sense of loss reflects man's loss of innocence after the Fall. Indeed, another Augustinian writer, Sénault, not only links *inquiétude* to *inconstance*, but also sees it as resulting directly from original sin:

J'excuserois l'ignorance de l'esprit humain, si elle n'estoit accompagnée d'inquietude. [. . .] Son inquietude est une preuve de son inconstance; s'il estoit plus ferme il seroit plus arresté, et s'il n'avoit perdu la suprême verité, il ne seroit pas en queste de son ombre: son inquietude est tout ensemble la marque, et la peine de son peché [. . .].[14]

In the *Pensées*, this notion of *inquiétude* epitomizing man's corrupt nature (in the sense of I1) finds its most vivid expression in a fragment where what I take to be a non-believing interlocutor communicates his bewilderment at a world enveloped by anxiety and doubt:

---

[13] 'To the Brink: The Dialectic of Anxiety in the *Pensées*', *Yale French Studies*, 66 (1984), 58.
[14] *L'Homme criminel* (Paris, 1644), 142–3. Cf. St François de Sales, in a chapter from his *Introduction à la vie dévote* entitled 'De l'inquiétude': 'l'inquiétude est le plus grand mal qui arrive en l'âme, excepté le péché' (pt. iv, ch. 11). I shall discuss de Sales's use of *inquiétude* later in this chapter.

Voilà ce que je vois et ce qui me trouble. Je regarde de toutes parts, et je ne vois partout qu'obscurité. La nature ne m'offre rien qui ne soit matière de doute et d'inquiétude [I1]. Si je n'y voyais rien qui marquât une Divinité, je me déterminerais à la négative; si je voyais partout les marques d'un Créateur, je reposerais en paix dans la foi. Mais, voyant trop pour nier et trop peu pour m'assurer, je suis dans un état à plaindre, et où j'ai souhaité cent fois que, si un Dieu la soutient, elle le marquât sans équivoque [. . .]. (L429)

Here, *inquiétude* is closely linked to the sense of uncertainty which the dialectician depicts as underlying all man's thoughts and actions in a godless universe. However, confusing as the signs may be as to the situation in which the unbeliever finds himself, this very worry and doubt induce him to search for a 'divinité'.

It would seem that the appearance of *inquiétude* in two other fragments is peripheral to the central preoccupations of the *Pensées*. Both examples are concerned with style, but do not seem to be related to the depiction of man's wretchedness. Yet if we examine these passages more closely, we find that both relate to *inquiétude* in the sense of I1. In L583, the dialectician clarifies *inquiétude* as being integral to man's very nature rather than simply part of the mind: 'J'ai l'esprit plein d'inquiétude; je suis plein d'inquiétude vaut mieux.' The repetition of *inquiétude* here accentuates the difference of meaning between each example of the word. The first is more specialized, similar to the sense in which Montaigne uses it; its connection with the noun *l'esprit* suggests 'disquiet', as Cotgrave translates *inquiétude* in the 1611 and 1673 editions of his French and English Dictionary. The second, on the other hand, undoubtedly contains an enlarged perception of anxiety, more akin to the Pascalian definition of wretchedness. By juxtaposing these two meanings, not only does the dialectician bring out the instability of meaning, but also he underlines the status of *inquiétude* as an integral part of man's condition: it is not simply our minds which are governed by *inquiétude* but our whole beings. It is in this respect that Pascal differs from Sénault, whose reflections upon *inquiétude* I quoted earlier. While Sénault's observations focus on man's mind, Pascal deliberately expands his conception of the term to include the essence of post-Fall humanity.

In the other fragment, the dialectician considers two phrases and evaluates their worth:

Éteindre le flambeau de la sédition: trop luxuriant.
L'inquiétude de son génie: trop de deux mots hardis. (L637)

It would seem here that the dialectician is pointing out the inappropriateness of diminishing the scope of *inquiétude* by coupling it with the word *génie*, just as the juxtaposition of *inquiétude* and *esprit* had been deemed unacceptable. It is in this respect that the two terms together are described as 'mots hardis'.

If we consider a fragment where *inquiétude* is used in apparently the most negative sense of I1, it is interesting to note that it still contains the possibility of searching beyond the anxiety of one's present state:

Rien n'est si important à l'homme que son état; rien ne lui est si redoutable que l'éternité. Et ainsi, qu'il se trouve des hommes indifférents à la perte de leur être et au péril d'une éternité de misères, cela n'est point naturel. Ils sont tout autres à l'égard de toutes les autres choses: ils craignent jusqu'aux plus légères, ils les prévoient, ils les sentent; et ce même homme qui passe tant de jours et de nuits dans la rage et dans le désespoir pour la perte d'une charge ou pour quelque offense imaginaire à son honneur, c'est celui-là même qui sait qu'il va tout perdre par la mort, sans inquiétude [I1] et sans émotion. C'est une chose monstrueuse de voir dans un même cœur et en même temps cette sensibilité pour les moindres choses et cette étrange insensibilité pour les plus grandes. C'est un enchantement incompréhensible, et un assoupissement surnaturel, qui marque une force toute-puissante qui le cause. (L427)

In this paragraph, the dialectician depicts man's blindness to his essential condition. Man remains 'sans inquiétude et sans émotion' when faced with fundamental major concerns, and yet worries needlessly about trifling matters. Nevertheless, the fact that he is blind without *inquiétude* implies that a recognition of *inquiétude* can lead him to embark upon a spiritual search.[15] Indeed, the recurrence of the words 'sans inquiétude' in another fragment suggests this very need to apply *inquiétude* as a motivating force

---

[15] Cf. the use of the adjectival form *inquiétant* in L522, a deleted fragment which represents a variation of L427: 'Cet homme si affligé de la mort de sa femme et de son fils unique, qui a cette grande querelle qui le tourmente, d'où vient qu'à ce moment il n'est point triste et qu'on le voit si exempt de toutes ces pensées pénibles et inquiétantes? Il ne faut pas s'en étonner. On vient de lui servir une balle et il faut qu'il la rejette à son compagnon' (L522). Although this variant inevitably carries less force than the noun, again we find it implied that recognition of these 'pensées pénibles et inquiétantes' is a more positive step than the *divertissements* with which man attempts to avoid his condition.

towards an investigation of spiritual concerns such as death and eternity; this need for spiritual questioning is intensified by the association of the word *réflexion* with *inquiétude*:

> Que l'on juge donc là-dessus de ceux qui vivent sans songer à cette dernière fin de la vie, qui se laissent conduire à leurs inclinations et à leurs plaisirs sans réflexion et sans inquiétude [I1], et, comme s'ils pouvaient anéantir l'éternité en en détournant leur pensée, ne pensent à se rendre heureux que dans cet instant seulement. (L428)

The sense of the need to search which is implied within the use of the preposition *sans* is supported by three fragments where the verb *chercher* is directly associated with *inquiétude* (I2): L400, L430, L477. In the *Pensées*, the act of searching in itself is perceived to be positive, as is again clear in 'Le Mystère de Jésus', where, through the prosopopoeia, Jesus is portrayed as saying, 'Console-toi, tu ne me chercherais pas, si tu ne m'avais trouvé' (L919). However, the reader is never allowed to rest in complacency. Whatever the positive connotations of searching and recognition of *inquiétude*, man's fall makes him unable *by himself* to regain his original state:

> L'homme ne sait à quel rang se mettre, il est visiblement égaré et tombé de son vrai lieu sans le pouvoir retrouver. Il le cherche partout avec inquiétude [I2] et sans succès dans des ténèbres impénétrables. (L400)

Moreover, even though *inquiétude* can prompt man to look beyond himself, this search can be misguided. As the dialectician emphasizes, *all* men seek in some way to regain original perfection:

> Voilà un étrange monstre, et un égarement bien visible. Le voilà tombé de sa place, il la cherche avec inquiétude [I2]. C'est ce que tous les hommes font. Voyons qui l'aura trouvée. (L477)

The dialectician's ironical retort at the end of the demonstration, 'Voyons qui l'aura trouvée', wryly accentuates man's misdirected attempts to find truth, and yet it does not exclude the *possibility* of attaining truth. Man's 'égarement' is echoed in L430:

> Que deviendra donc l'homme? Sera-t-il égal à Dieu ou aux bêtes? Quelle effroyable distance! Que serons-nous donc? Qui ne voit par tout cela que l'homme est égaré, qu'il est tombé de sa place, qu'il la cherche avec inquiétude [I2], qu'il ne la peut plus retrouver. Et qui l'y adressera donc? Les plus grands hommes ne l'ont pu. (L430)

The tension within Pascal's use of language, accentuated by the antithesis between God and beast, keeps the reader alert and ever moving onwards.

It is most significant that the three fragments just quoted were all probably inspired by the first chapter of St Augustine's *Confessions*, especially the lines: 'Tu excitas ut laudare te delectet; quia fecesti nos ad te, et *inquietum* est cor nostrum, donec requiescat in te.'[16] 'This neo-Platonic expression of the duality of restfulness and restlessness is one which we have seen recur in the *Pensées*.[17] The clear message of this sentence is that our hearts will remain restless until we find peace in God. However, on another level, the movement inherent in the word *inquietum* is mirrored in the dynamism of the accusative *ad te*, leading to the restfulness figured in *in te*. In other words, just as *inquiétude* proves man's fallen nature, so too can it prompt man to search for God. A similar point is made in the same chapter of the *Confessions*: 'ceux qui le [le Seigneur] cherchent le trouvent, et, l'ayant trouvé, le louent'.[18]

François de Sales, who himself was greatly influenced by Augustine, makes similar use of *inquiétude*, acknowledging both its closeness to sin and its persuasive force. On the one hand, in his *Introduction à la vie dévote*, in a chapter entitled 'De l'inquiétude', he asserts that 'l'inquiétude est le plus grand mal qui arrive en l'âme, excepté le péché'.[19] According to him, 'l'inquiétude n'est pas une simple tentation, mais une source, de laquelle et par laquelle plusieurs tentations arrivent', and that it 'provient d'un désir déréglé d'être délivré du mal que l'on sent',[20] a desire which, although misdirected, at least contains a recognition of evil in the world. Indeed, he makes an important distinction at the end of the

---

[16] *Confessions*, trans. R. Arnauld d'Andilly (Paris, 1659), I. i. 1: 'Et c'est vous-même, ô mon Dieu! qui lui inspirez cette pensée et lui faites goûter un plaisir secret dans ces louanges qu'il vous donne, parce que vous nous avez créés pour vous, et que notre cœur est toujours agité jusqu'à ce qu'il trouve son repos en vous.' Cf. the following passages influenced by the same extract: '[l'âme] ne peut arrêter son cœur qu'elle ne se soit rendue jusqu'au trône de Dieu, dans lequel elle commence à trouver son repos', *Sur la conversion du pécheur* (Seuil 291); 'Mon cœur, que vous n'aviez formé que pour vous', *Prière pour demander à Dieu le bon usage des maladies* (Seuil 363). Cf. also L399.

[17] See P. Sellier, *Pascal et Saint Augustin* (Paris, 1970), 36–8; Deprun, *La Philosophie de l'inquiétude*, 124–6.   [18] I. i. 2.

[19] *Introduction à la vie dévote*, IV. xi. 272. Deprun points out that in the earliest (1608) edn. the chapter was entitled 'De l'inquiétude qu'il faut éviter', but I would not go so far as to suggest, as does Deprun, that the original title 'laisse entendre que l'inquiétude n'est pas mauvaise en soi' (p. 281).   [20] Ibid. 272.

chapter. If we acknowledge our *inquiétude* to ourselves and to appropriate people, we can attain a sense of peace:

> Si vous pouvez découvrir votre inquiétude à celui qui conduit votre âme, ou au moins à quelque confident et dévot ami, ne doutez point que tout aussitôt vous ne soyez accoisée [tranquillisée] [...].[21]

In his *Traité de l'amour de Dieu*, which, as Cognet points out, contains more than seventy direct quotations from Augustine,[22] and a copy of which we know to have been in the Port-Royal library of Sacy,[23] we find an even more positive approach to the use of *inquiétude*. Not only does he refer approvingly to the passage on *inquietum est cor nostrum*,[24] but also he names *inquiétude* as a motivating force in the search for the sovereign good:

> nous avons une inclination naturelle au souverain bien, en suite de laquelle notre cœur a un certain intime empressement et une continuelle inquiétude [...].[25]

Perhaps the most remarkable passage devoted to *inquiétude* in the *Traité* comes in chapter 10 of book iii, where it is perceived as 'admirable' and 'aimable' in its role of never allowing man's 'soif extrême du vrai bien'[26] to be assuaged on this earth:

> O admirable, mais aimable inquiétude du cœur humain! Soyez, soyez à jamais sans repos ni tranquillité quelconque en cette terre, mon âme, jusques à ce que vous ayez rencontré les fraîches eaux de la vie immortelle et la très sainte Divinité, qui seules peuvent éteindre votre altération et accoiser [calmer] votre désir.[27]

This examination of *inquiétude* in François de Sales's writings should clarify the positive persuasive function of *inquiétude* in the *Pensées*, as seen especially in those fragments used in the sense of I2.

---

[21] Ibid. 273.
[22] L. Cognet, *La Spiritualité moderne* (Paris, 1947), 289; he adds, 'la pensée [de S. François] est bien plus augustinienne que thomiste'.
[23] See O. Barenne, *Une grande bibliothèque de Port-Royal: Inventaire inédit de la bibliothèque d'Isaac-Louis Le Maistre de Sacy (7 avril 1684)* (Paris, 1985), 162.
[24] 'O Dieu, dit saint Augustin, vous avez créé mon cœur pour vous, et jamais il n'aura repos qu'il ne soit en vous', in François de Sales, *Œuvres*, ed. A. Ravier (Paris, 1969), III. vi. 500.   [25] Ibid. II. xv. 453.   [26] Ibid. II x. 512.
[27] Ibid. III. x. 511. See Deprun, *La Philosophie de l'inquiétude*, 124, 264–5.

INQUIÉTUDE AND CURIOSITÉ

The one fragment where the adjectival form *inquiet* appears perhaps reveals the most interesting development of the concept of *inquiétude*:

> Lorsqu'on ne sait pas la vérité d'une chose il est bon qu'il y ait une erreur commune qui fixe l'esprit des hommes comme par exemple la lune à qui on attribue le changement des saisons, le progrès des maladies, etc., car la maladie principale de l'homme est la curiosité inquiète des choses qu'il ne peut savoir et il ne lui est pas si mauvais d'être dans l'erreur que dans cette curiosité inutile. (L744)

Here, 'la curiosité inquiète' is identified as man's main illness:[28] man prefers to remain in error than confront this 'curiosité'. Louis A. Mackenzie has given an ingenious interpretation of this fragment, and especially the term 'curiosité inquiète':

> by exploiting the etymological resonance of the term curious—*cura* denoting among other things anxiety—we are able to propose something like anxious anxiety ('curiosité inquiète'). This radical formulation suggests an anxiety which is self-generating, a yearning which arrives only at yearning.[29]

Moreover, Pascal equates 'curiosité inquiète' with 'curiosité inutile', which suggests the uselessness of anxiety, leading to, as Mackenzie puts it, 'a tragic pointlessness'.[30]

Before we take Mackenzie's assertions too far, it should be stressed that Pascal was following a long tradition connecting *curiositas* with a (usually pernicious) desire for knowledge. More specifically, this view formed the basis of the Augustinian attitude towards *curiosité*. Augustine himself always uses the term in a pejorative sense,[31] and just such a condemnation of *curiositas* is

---

[28] Cf. the juxtaposition of illness and *inquiétude* in Pascal's *Prière pour demander à Dieu le bon usage des maladies*: 'je reconnais, mon Dieu, que mon cœur est tellement endurci et plein des idées, des soins, des inquiétudes et des attachements du monde, que la maladie non plus que la santé, [...] ne peuvent rien du tout pour commencer ma conversion, si vous n'accompagnez toutes ces choses d'une assistance tout extraordinaire de votre grâce' (Seuil 363). [29] 'To the Brink', 61.
[30] Ibid. 62.
[31] See e.g. *Confessions*, x. xxxv. 408: 'Outre cette concupiscence de la chair qui se rencontre dans tous les plaisirs des sens [...], il y a dans l'âme une passion volage, indiscrète et curieuse [*vana et curiosa cupiditas*], qui, se couvrant du nom de science,

quoted by Pascal in L190: '*Quod curiositate cognoverunt, superbia amiserunt.*'[32] The most prominent followers of Augustine in the seventeenth century use the word in a similarly negative light. Jansenius, for example, like Augustine, names *curiosité* as a concupiscence of the mind:

> Elle [la curiosité] a mis le siege de son empire dans l'esprit, et c'est là qu'ayant ramassé un grand nombre de differentes images, elle le trouble par mille sortes d'illusions, et ne se contente pas d'agir sur luy, mais se produit encore au dehors par tous les organes des sens.[33]

Pascal makes similar use of *curiosité* in the *Pensées*, naming it in both major fragments devoted to the three orders, L308 and L933, as belonging to the realm of the mind: 'les curieux et savants, ils ont pour objet l'esprit' (L933). Elsewhere in the *Pensées*, *curiosité* is unequivocally condemned.[34]

Another rigorous Augustinian of the seventeenth century, Martin de Barcos, also denounces man's curiosity, but makes an interesting distinction in a letter written in 1657, probably (as Lucien Goldmann suggests) addressed to Pascal:

> Gardons donc de doubter jamais de la justice de Dieu quelque incomprehensible qu'elle nous soit en bien des choses, souvenons nous que nous sommes dans un lieu de tenebres, que c'est maintenant le temps de croire, que celuy de voir n'est pas encore venu, et que nous ne devons pas anticiper par une curiosité mal reglée.[35]

Barcos's mention of 'une curiosité mal reglée' implies that 'une curiosité bien réglée' can possibly be attained. In the *Pensées*, we find one fragment where *curiosité* is used with a similar suggestion

la porte à se servir des sens, non plus pour prendre plaisir dans la chair, mais pour faire des épreuves et acquérir des connoissances.' Cf. also pp. 410–11. See Sellier, *Pascal et Saint Augustin*, 175–82.

[32] 'What they gained by curiosity, they lost through pride', *Sermons*, CXLI, as translated and identified by A. J. Krailsheimer in his translation of the *Pensées*.

[33] *Traduction d'un discours de la reformation de l'homme interieur* (Paris, 1659), 40–1. See Wetsel, *L'Écriture et le reste: The 'Pensées' of Pascal in the Exegetical Tradition of Port-Royal* (Columbus, Oh., 1981), 23, for a discussion of De Sacy's attitude towards *curiosité*.

[34] e.g. L77: 'Curiosité n'est que vanité'; L199, where *curiosité* is linked to the noun *présomption*; L919, where *curiosité* is juxtaposed with *vanité* and *orgueil*. Cf. the very different use of *curiosité* and the mind by Silhon: 'nous devrions brusler sans cesse d'une saincte curiosité d'en [de nos esprits] connoistre les perfections', *Les Deux veritez* (Paris, 1626), 230.

[35] *Correspondance*, ed. L. Goldmann (Paris, 1956), 265.

of a positive use of *curiosité*. Significantly, the noun is coupled with the term 'diversité', which incorporates a sense of both *inconstance* and *inquiétude*. Having emphasized that 'l'unique objet de l'Écriture est la charité', the dialectician shows how man's love for diversity can be reconciled in God's charity:

> Dieu diversifie ainsi cet unique précepte de charité pour satisfaire notre curiosité qui recherche la diversité par cette diversité qui nous mène toujours à notre unique nécessaire. Car une seule chose est nécessaire et nous aimons la diversité, et Dieu satisfait à l'un et à l'autre par ces diversités qui mènent au seul nécessaire. (L270)

As we have seen with *inquiétude*, *curiosité* can be redirected towards more positive ends. Similarly, the 'curiosité inquiète' of L744, while epitomizing 'la maladie principale de l'homme', can contain a possible cure within a recognition of its own restlessness. As it stands, it is 'inutile', but, with a realization of its pointless circularity, man can attempt to leave the entrapment of this state and search elsewhere. In *inquiétude* and *curiosité*, therefore, there lies both the reminder of man's corruption and the restlessness to move beyond that corruption.

INQUIÉTUDE AND CONTINUED SPIRITUAL ENDEAVOUR

It is significant that Pascal makes his only use of the verb *inquiéter* at a point in his dialectic where acceptance of the Christian faith is assumed. Worldly anxiety gives way to a spiritual restfulness. With the genuine search and possession of God undertaken, the three verbs *chercher*, *posséder*, and *inquiéter* become coextensive: 'Tu ne me chercherais pas si tu ne me possédais. Ne t'inquiète donc pas' (L929). It is here that *inquiétude* is introduced within the context of the Christian's continued endeavours (I3). Two letters which Pascal wrote to the Roannez family in December 1656 show that even the true Christian who has accepted God is not immune to *inquiétude*. Searching, of which *inquiétude* is an irrevocable part, never ceases. Indeed, this very state of anxiety acts as a sign that the Christian is on the genuine path towards salvation. As Pascal writes, quoting from the Bible,

> Saint Paul a dit que *ceux qui entreront dans la bonne vie trouveront des peines et des inquiétudes en grand nombre* [Acts 14: 22]. Cela doit consoler

ceux qui en sentent, puisque étant avertis que le chemin du ciel qu'ils cherchent en est rempli, ils doivent se réjouir de rencontrer des marques qu'ils sont dans le véritable chemin.[36]

Furthermore, Pascal, upon hearing of the *inquiétude* of a Christian woman, expresses no surprise, for he perceives *inquiétude* as a reminder of man's fallen state:

> Je plains la personne que vous savez dans l'inquiétude où je sais qu'elle est, et où je ne m'étonne pas de la voir. C'est un petit jour du jugement qui ne peut arriver sans une émotion universelle de la personne, comme le jugement général en causera une générale dans le monde, excepté ceux qui se seront déjà jugés eux-mêmes, comme elle prétend faire; cette peine temporelle garantirait de l'éternelle, par les mérites infinis de Jésus-Christ, qui la souffre et qui se la rend propre; c'est ce qui doit la consoler. Notre joug est aussi le sien, sans cela il serait insupportable.
> [...] Je lui voudrais dire qu'elle se souvienne que ces inquiétudes ne viennent pas du bien qui commence d'être en elle, mais du mal qui y est encore et qu'il faut diminuer continuellement [...][37]

It is significant that in both letters we find instances of *inquiétude* being used in the plural form. Once faith has been attained, *inquiétude* is diminished from an all-engulfing image of the human condition to temporary worries which recall man's corrupt state but which do not deter the Christian from the quest for ultimate communion with God. The 'petit jour du jugement' described in the letter evokes the words at the end of the *Mémorial*: 'Éternellement en joie pour un jour d'exercice sur la terre' (L913).

Inquiétude, therefore, acts as a reminder of corruption and yet a stimulus in the search for perfect peace. The many facets of the term are perhaps best encapsulated in a poem by Jacqueline Pascal, 'Prière sur le Miracle de la Sainte Épine', where ultimately *inquiétude* is deemed to be 'heureuse' and 'sainte':

> Je me trouve, Seigneur, dans ce pénible état;
> Je suis dans cette heureuse et sainte inquiétude.
> Mon cœur veut témoigner qu'il ne t'est pas ingrat;
> Mais mon peu de pouvoir trahit ma gratitude.[38]

---

[36] Dec. 1656 (Seuil 269).   [37] 24 Dec. 1656 (Seuil 270).
[38] *Œuvres complètes*, ed. L. Brunschvicg (Paris, 1904–14), vi. 113. B. Beugnot, in 'Apologétique et mythe moral: La Méditation pascalienne sur le repos', in L. M. Heller and I. M. Richmond (eds.), *Pascal, thématique des 'Pensées'* (Paris, 1988), 57–78, makes an interesting comparison between the use of *sollicitudo* and *requies*

The restlessness within *inquiétude*, on all its levels, always points in the *Pensées* towards its antithesis, *repos* (the noun *quiétude* is not used at all). Moreover, as we have seen with the tension between stasis and movement in *inconstance*, *ennui*, and *inquiétude*, the notion of *repos* is always implicit. I shall be devoting a full chapter to an examination of the term in its own right.

Now that I have analysed each of the three nouns placed in L24 under the heading 'Condition de l'homme', it would be useful to draw some partial conclusions from their use in the *Pensées*. The juxtaposition of the terms in L24, their interaction with each other, and their development in other fragments (aspects which have been largely ignored by critical scholarship) are pivotal not only to the depiction of humanity but also to Pascal's persuasive methods and purpose.

For each of the terms, it is clear that the meaning is never completely stable. Rather, the dialectician exploits their instability in order to unsettle the reader, just as we saw in Part I the obscurity of language itself being used to remind the reader of his fallen nature. However, as with the dialectician's notion of order, the shifting fields of meaning do not reflect 'une confusion sans dessein' (L532). There remains a strong sense of method, an *esprit géométrique*, within them. It is perhaps no coincidence that I determined for each of *inconstance*, *ennui*, and *inquiétude* three main categories of meanings. It would be wrong to oversimplify the different meanings, many of which overlap, of each of the three nouns. However, there is a distinct pattern in the way in which they are used by the dialectician.

The first category of each noun (Inc. 1, E1 and I1) relates directly to the wretchedness of man in his fallen state. It is significant that each noun on this level depicts human blindness and self-deception. Inc. 1 reflects man's general instability, while E1 is associated with the *néant* of human existence, and I1 shows the anxiety of man's fallen state.

The second meaning of each word in turn contains a sense of movement: within Inc. 2, E2, and I2 we find the restlessness needed

in the New Testament: 'la *sollicitudo* biblique oscille en effet entre le négatif et le positif, tantôt elle est pur trouble et instabilité de l'homme séparé de Dieu, tantôt elle est vigilance et attention, attente de Dieu' (p. 63). Jacqueline Pascal's use of *inquiétude* would seem to be related to this 2nd sense of *sollicitudo*.

for man to try and escape from his corrupt state. Inc. 2 and I2 are both inherently unstable, but a recognition of that instability provides a primary motivation to move from the inner wretchedness of Inc. 1 and I1 to the spiritual purpose of Inc. 3 and I3. E2, which is central to all three terms, is characterized particularly by its association with *divertissement*, the active form of *ennui*. Man's need for *divertissement* is shown to be crucial in the redirection of man towards self-knowledge.

For the third category, Inc. 3, E3, and I3 are all directly connected to positive spiritual searching. Inc. 3 corresponds closely to its antithesis, *constance*, and through the juxtaposition of the two terms, the dialectician indicates how restlessness can be mastered to move beyond the instability of the self and towards God's constancy. Both E3 and I3 go even further, in that the Christian still experiences *ennui* and *inquiétude* as part of the ongoing endeavour to seek eternal peace in God. However, Inc. 3, E3, and I3 also act as a continual reminder for the Christian of his former state and the corruption of the world in which he lives.[39]

In many respects, each register of meaning can be linked to one of the three orders, as seen in L298, L308, and L933. Although the complexities of every word depicting the human condition cannot be wholly subsumed into the three orders, which themselves are far from simple, they at least provide a useful model which throws light on the three levels of meaning which I have outlined. The first category is firmly rooted in the concupiscence of man's fallen nature, described as 'les corps' in L308 and 'la chair' in L933. The second category, in its association with self-knowledge, can be likened to the second order, *l'esprit*. However, this sense incorporates not only human reason but also *le cœur*, the intuitive understanding which leads beyond the limitations of reason. The third category points towards the order of *charité*, which, as the dialectician emphasizes in L298, is personified in Christ, St Paul, and St Augustine.

Only a detailed examination of each of the terms enables us to arrive at such distinct categorization. It is the fragmentary text, on the other hand, which gives the terms both their dynamism and their instability. By moving from one category to another in a

---

[39] For a summary of the different categories, see the table of terms at the end of the book.

'renversement continuel du pour au contre' (L93), the dialectician manipulates fragmentation in order to obtain the maximum persuasive effect, an effect which he would not achieve in a conventionally ordered discourse.

From such apparently 'negative' words as *inconstance*, *ennui*, and *inquiétude*, I intend to turn now to three terms which, by contrast, would seem to be 'positive': *repos*, *bonheur/félicité*, and *justice*.

Key to *Inquiétude*

I1   *inquiétude*: anxiety of man's fallen state
I2   *inquiétude*: fallen man's searching
I3   *inquiétude*: continued spiritual endeavour

6
Repos

> Nous ne serons jamais en repos en cette vie. Ceux que nous croyons estre le plus en repos le sont le moins.
>
> (Saint-Cyran)[1]

As I hope to have shown in the chapters on *inconstance*, *ennui*, and *inquiétude*, these terms are in almost all cases held in implicit and explicit contrast to the notion of *repos* (*quies*). However, *repos* also functions on its own terms in the dialectical process of the *Pensées*.

A number of useful studies of *repos* in the *Pensées* and in literature of the seventeenth century have appeared, most notably articles by Bernard Beugnot and Domna Stanton.[2] However, despite the invaluable nature of these two analyses, I believe that another study is necessary. Stanton, for example, keeps to a thorough and penetrating reading of the *ideal* of *repos* in the seventeenth century as a whole, and therefore does not consider closely the subtleties and ambiguities of the term in the *Pensées*. Furthermore, her misinterpretation of the use of *repos* in L136 as being merely synonymous with 'the good life' needs correction.[3] Beugnot provides an enlightening analysis of the different kinds of *repos* in the *Pensées*, but his assertion that the use of the term shows 'le souci de Pascal de lever les confusions et les ambivalences'[4] clearly contradicts my reading of the function of language in the *Pensées*, and indeed, as I hope to show in this chapter, the particular role of *repos*.

---

[1] *Maximes saintes et chrestiennes tirées des lettres de Messire Jean du Verger de Hauranne, Abbé de Saint Cyran* (Paris, 1648), 160.
[2] B. Beugnot, 'Apologétique et mythe moral: La Méditation pascalienne sur le repos', in L. M. Heller and I. M. Richmond (eds.), *Pascal thématique des 'Pensées'* (Paris, 1988), 57–78. D. C. Stanton, 'The Ideal of *Repos* in Seventeenth-Century French Literature', *L'Esprit créateur*, 15 (1975), 79–104. See also Beugnot, 'Morale du repos et conscience du temps', *Australian Journal of French Studies*, 13 (1976), 183–96; P. Sellier, *Pascal et Saint Augustin* (Paris, 1970), 36–8; M. Vigouroux, *Le Thème de la retraite et de la solitude chez quelques epistoliers du XVIIe Siècle* (Paris, 1972). [3] 'The Ideal of *Repos*', 79.
[4] 'Apologétique et mythe moral', 62.

The seventeenth-century dictionaries show that the word operated in a number of different ways.[5] On its simplest level, it denoted 'Cessation de peine et de travail' (Richelet).[6] Although this would serve as a literal definition of *repos* in a number of fragments in the *Pensées*, it would at no point adequately explain the multi-layered resonances of the term. Another acceptation of the word by the Académie and Furetière dictionaries was conceived 'quelquefois seulement par opposition au mouvement, à l'agitation corporelle' (Académie). As we have seen in earlier chapters, the use of *repos* as a contrast is reiterated throughout the *Pensées*, and my examination of the word will take this aspect into account. On another level again, *repos* is viewed by all three dictionaries as synonymous with the words *paix* and *tranquillité*. It will therefore be necessary to consider the different applications of these two terms as they appear in the *Pensées*, especially with the connotation of spiritual *repos*. Indeed, it is this final sense which the Académie dictionary in particular underlines as 'le repos des ames, le repos éternel'. However, at this stage it would be appropriate to turn to the central fragment on *divertissement*, L136, for the use of *repos* here shows up the many extensions of the term as it appears throughout the *Pensées*.

L136

The fragment revolves around the famous lines from the first paragraph, which refer to man's inability to attain *repos* by himself:

j'ai dit souvent que tout le malheur des hommes vient d'une seule chose, qui est de ne savoir pas demeurer en repos dans une chambre.

These words strongly recall the Stoic notion of *repos*, of which Seneca was the principal exponent. Indeed, the Senecan ideal of *repos* was one which influenced and shaped many interpretations of the term in the seventeenth century, and which had undoubtedly inspired the Church Fathers, despite the obvious difference of the

---

[5] See also Stanton, 'The Ideal of *Repos*', 80, where she refers to the common addition of intensifiers and superlatives to *repos* in literature of the period, 'in an effort to distinguish their more serious conception from casual, superficial usage'.

[6] Richelet's definition reflects the standard scientific usage of *quies*, and is probably taken from Aristotle's *Metaphysics*, 4. 1012^{b}16 ff.

Stoics' deification of man.[7] One of the more likely sources of this sentence is Montaigne's paraphrase of a passage from Seneca's letters, in the chapter entitled 'De la solitude': 'la plus grande chose du monde, c'est de sçavoir estre à soy'.[8] Moreover, it is possible that Pascal referred directly to Seneca, for *repos* was central to the Stoic notion of the sage's search to find lasting tranquillity through an indifference to the manifold agitations of man's outward existence. In an extract taken from the 1598 translation of Seneca's *De Tranquillitate Animi* (entitled in French by the translator, Simon Goulart, *Traité du repos et contentement de l'esprit*; mentioned in a different context in the chapter on 'ennui'), for example, there is a passage which bears a striking resemblance to L136:

l'esprit ne peut durer en maison ni en solitude quelconque, les parois le faschent, et estant ainsi abandonné à soy-mesme il se regarde de travers et à contrecœur. De là vient ce chagrin, ce mespris de soy, ceste perpetuelle agitation d'esprit, ceste triste et foible patience en repos.[9]

Thus, on a human level, both Seneca and Pascal show man's inability to avoid agitation. Yet, whereas Stoic tradition would suggest that happiness and rest must be sought within ourselves, and others would try to attain them through *divertissements*, the dialectician's response is more equivocal, as can be seen in another fragment which is closely related to L136:

Les stoïques disent: rentrez au-dedans de vous-même, c'est là où vous trouverez votre repos. Et cela n'est pas vrai.
Les autres disent: sortez dehors et cherchez le bonheur en un divertissement. Et cela n'est pas vrai, les maladies viennent.
Le bonheur n'est ni hors de nous ni dans nous; il est en Dieu et hors et dans nous. (L407)[10]

---

[7] See Stanton, 'The Ideal of *Repos*', 83, 90, 92, 97–101. Of the Church Fathers, I shall consider St Augustine at a later stage in this chapter.
[8] Montaigne, *Essais* (in *Œuvres complètes*, ed. M. Rat, Paris, 1962), I. xxxix. 236.
[9] Seneca, *Les Œuvres morales et meslees*, trans. S. Goulart (Paris, 1598), 334.
[10] P. Ernst's reconstruction of the page on which L407 appeared reveals fascinating insights (see his *Album*, 33): not only do we find other fragments, L405 and L620, incorporating the notion of *divertissement*, but the contrast between Stoics and Sceptics is intensified (L405). Moreover, fragments with strong Augustinian resonance, L399 and L400, were written on the same page. The connection between L407 and L400 underlines Pascal's juxtaposition of *repos* and *inquiétude*.

This notion that happiness resides in several different places (which I shall discuss at greater length in the section on *bonheur* and *félicité*) returns in a section of L136 which was crossed out. Furthermore, *repos* here, while excluding explicit reference to spiritual happiness, functions on two distinct levels. The first use comes near to the dictionary definition of 'Cessation de peine et de travail' (what I shall call R1; see the Key at the end of this chapter), a state which he endeavours to evade but which is in itself part of the fallen world and, therefore, false, whereas the second relates to man's inner sense of tranquillity (R2), a state which he believes himself to be seeking:

> Dire à un homme qu'il soit en repos [R2], c'est lui dire qu'il vive heureux. C'est lui conseiller [. . .] d'avoir une condition toute heureuse et laquelle il puisse considérer à loisir, sans y trouver sujet d'affliction.[. . .]
> Aussi les hommes qui sentent naturellement leur condition n'évitent rien tant que le repos [R1]; il n'y a rien qu'ils ne fassent pour chercher le trouble.

This double conception of *repos* is encapsulated in the image of Pyrrhus, taken from Montaigne,[11] where he is advised to embrace a *repos* which he believes he is seeking (R2) but which in fact he is always avoiding (R1): 'Et ainsi le conseil qu'on donnait à Pyrrhus de prendre le repos qu'il allait chercher par tant de fatigues, recevait bien des difficultés.' This dichotomy within *repos* is also evident in the words, 'Ils [les hommes] croient chercher sincèrement le repos et ne cherchent en effet que l'agitation.'[12] This concept also has biblical roots. In L889, for example, Pascal quotes the book of Ecclesiasticus, 'In omnibus requiem quaesivi',[13] adding, 'si notre condition était véritablement heureuse, il ne nous faudrait pas divertir d'y penser pour nous rendre heureux'.

However, in L136, there remains another dimension to *repos*, closer to R2 than to R1, which is firmly implanted in Augustinian tradition. Man's pure nature before the Fall gives him, now in his

---

[11] *Essais*, I. xlii. 259.
[12] Cf. Filleau de la Chaise's remark, 'C'est à cet étrange repos que Monsieur Pascal en voulait principalement', *Discours sur les 'Pensées' de M. Pascal* (Paris, 1672), 20.
[13] Eccles. 24: 11, translated by de Sacy as 'parmi toutes ces choses j'ai cherché un lieu de repos'.

state of corruption, an instinct of a *repos* (R3) which relates closely to his original perfection and thereby to a unity with God:[14]

> Et ils [les hommes] ont un autre instinct secret qui reste de la grandeur de notre première nature, qui leur fait connaître que le bonheur n'est en effet que dans le repos [R3] et non pas dans le tumulte. Et de ces deux instincts contraires il se forme en eux un projet confus qui se cache à leur vue dans le fond de leur âme qui les porte à tendre au repos [R3] par l'agitation et à se figurer toujours que la satisfaction qu'ils n'ont point leur arrivera si en surmontant quelques difficultés qu'ils envisagent ils peuvent s'ouvrir par là la porte au repos [R3].
> Ainsi s'écoule toute la vie; on cherche le repos [R2] en combattant quelques obstacles et si on les a surmontés le repos [R1] devient insupportable par l'ennui qu'il engendre. Il en faut sortir et mendier le tumulte.[15]

The deliberate shift between different kinds of *repos* in L136 characterizes its function throughout the *Pensées*. The instability of language is exploited by the dialectician to give the reader a sense of the very agitation which he is trying to escape in seeking *repos*.

The problems which L136 uncovers will inform my study of *repos* in the *Pensées* as a whole. First, I shall examine more closely the pyrrhonist conception of *repos* in relation to the Stoics, then I shall consider the terms *tranquillité* and *paix* (identified by the seventeenth-century dictionaries as largely synonymous with *repos*), going from there to an analysis of human *repos* (R1 and R2), before analysing *repos* within a specifically spiritual context (R3).

PYRRHONISM AND STOICISM

As my discussion of L136 has shown, the Stoic idea of *repos* plays a significant role in the *Pensées*. Although the Stoic belief that ultimate tranquillity can be attained within the self is deemed by the

---

[14] It is precisely this corruption which J.-F. Sénault in *L'Homme criminel* (Paris, 1644) sees as preventing man from attaining *repos* (in the sense of R3): 'son [l'esprit] inquietude est tout ensemble la marque, et la peine de son péché, il ne peut trouver le repos parce qu'il ne le cherche pas en Dieu' (p. 142).
[15] *Repos* in the sense of R1, and closely related to *ennui* and *divertissement*, reappears in L622: 'Ennui. Rien n'est si insupportable à l'homme que d'être dans un plein repos, sans passions, sans affaires, sans divertissement, sans application.'

dialectician to be wrong (as we saw in L407), there are certainly positive parallels to be drawn from L136 and from Seneca's treatment of *repos*. The fact that the Stoic looks for peace within himself rather than in external pleasures is in itself positive. Indeed, it is precisely this fact which Pascal accentuates in his praise of another great Stoic philosopher, Epictetus, in the *Entretien avec M. de Sacy*:

> Je trouve dans Epictète un art incomparable pour troubler le repos [R2] de ceux qui le cherchent dans les choses extérieures [. . .].[16]

This evocation of Epictetus is used particularly to oppose the false *repos* of Montaigne, who represents the pyrrhonist doctrine in the *Entretien* as well as in the *Pensées*. The *repos* of the Sceptics is based principally upon ignorance and an avoidance of agitation rather than the attainment of self-knowledge.[17] As Pascal explains in the *Entretien*, in a passage where the terms *repos* and *tranquillité* are used synonymously,

> considérant combien il y a que l'on cherche le vrai et le bien sans aucun progrès vers la tranquillité, il [Montaigne] conclut qu'on en doit laisser le soin aux autres; et demeurer cependant en repos [R1], coulant légèrement sur les sujets de peur d'y enfoncer en appuyant [. . .].[18]

Moreover, the pyrrhonist *repos* is directly contrasted with 'cette vertu stoïque':

> Il se fait aussi quelque violence pour éviter certains vices; et même il garde la fidélité au mariage, à cause de la peine qui suit les désordres; mais si celle qu'il prendrait surpasse celle qu'il évite, il y demeure en repos [R1], la règle de son action étant en tout la commodité et la tranquillité. Il rejette donc bien loin cette vertu stoïque qu'on peint avec une mine sévère, un regard

---

[16] Seuil 297. As P. Courcelle points out in his edn. of the *Entretien* (Paris, 1960); this section is inspired by a passage from Epictetus's *Propos*, 4. 4, 1: 'Souvenez-vous que non seulement le desir des estats et des richesses rend les hommes vils et abjets et soumis aux autres, mais aussi que le desir desordonné du repos, de l'oisiveté, de voyager et d'estudier, a le mesme effet' (p. 62).

[17] Cf. L428: 'Ce repos dans cette ignorance est une chose monstrueuse [. . .]'. It is in this respect that Jean de Silhon, in *De l'immortalité de l'ame* (Paris, 1634), stresses that 'il faut qu'il y ait un repos actif, et non pas une indolence morte' (p. 4). Cf. Montaigne's use of the story of the pig in the storm, taken from Diogenes Laertius, *Pyrrho*, 9. 68, in *Essais*, I. xiv. 54–5: 'A quoy faire la cognoissance des choses, si nous en perdons le repos et la tranquillité [. . .], et si elle nous rend de pire condition que le pourceau de Pyrrho?'
[18] Seuil 295.

farouche, des cheveux hérissés, le front ridé et en sueur, dans une posture pénible et tendue, loin des hommes, dans un morne silence, et seul sur la pointe d'un rocher: fantôme, à ce qu'il dit, capable d'effrayer les enfants, et qui ne fait là autre chose, avec un travail continuel, que de chercher le repos [R2], où elle n'arrive jamais. La sienne est naïve, familière, plaisante, enjouée, et pour ainsi dire folâtre; elle suit ce qui la charme, et badine négligemment des accidents bons ou mauvais, couchée mollement dans le sein de l'oisiveté tranquille, d'où elle montre aux hommes, qui cherchent la félicité avec tant de peine, que c'est là seulement où elle repose, et que l'ignorance et l'incuriosité sont deux doux oreillers pour une tête bien faite, comme il dit lui-même.[19]

This *paresse* which informs Montaigne's philosophy comes directly from Pyrrho's doctrine of *ataraxia*. It is in the *Apologie de Raimond Sebond*, the essay which most encapsulates Montaigne's scepticism, that the words *repos* and *ataraxie* appear in conjunction with each other. In describing the beliefs of the 'Pyrrhoniens', for example, he defines their *ataraxia*:

Or cette assiette de leur jugement, droicte et inflexible, recevant tous objets sans application et consentement, les achemine à leur Ataraxie, qui est une condition de vie paisible, rassise, exempte des agitations que nous recevons par l'impression de l'opinion et science que nous pensons avoir des choses.[20]

Pascal himself paraphrases a later section from the *Apologie* in a fragment (later crossed out) which implicitly condemns the Sceptics' *ataraxia* as one of many misguided attempts to attain the sovereign good:

L'un dit que le souverain bien est en la vertu, l'autre le met en la volupté, l'autre à suivre la nature, l'autre en la vérité—*felix qui potuit rerum cognoscere causas*—, l'autre à l'ignorance totale, l'autre en l'indolence, d'autres à résister aux apparences, l'autre à n'admirer rien—*nihil mirari prope res una quae possit facere et servare beatum*—, et les braves pyrrhoniens en leur ataraxie, doute et suspension perpétuelle. Et d'autres plus sages qu'on ne le peut trouver, non pas même par souhait. Nous voilà bien payés. (L76)[21]

It is evident, then, that both the Stoic conception of *repos* (close to R2), for all its positive values, and the pyrrhonist notion (akin to

---

[19] Ibid. 296. See Montaigne, *Essais*, I. xxvi. 160, and III. xiii. 1050–1.
[20] *Essais*, I. xii. 483. [21] Cf. ibid. 562.

R1) are deemed to be false. Attention to *tranquillité*, *paix*, and further examples of *repos* as they appear in the *Pensées* is needed to establish the dialectician's perception of the concept.

TRANQUILLITÉ

Although the noun *tranquillité* and its adjectival and adverbial forms appear only once each in the *Pensées*, they play an important role in establishing the human and self-deluding dimension of *repos*. In L806, for example, the use of *tranquillité* accentuates a central problem which informs the function of language throughout the *Pensées*. How are we to distinguish between our true selves and the image which our 'vie imaginaire' attempts to portray? Even a concept such as tranquillity is purposefully made ambiguous by the dialectician:

> Nous travaillons incessamment à embellir et conserver notre être imaginaire et négligeons le véritable. Et si nous avons ou la tranquillité ou la générosité, ou la fidélité nous nous empressons de le faire savoir afin d'attacher ces vertus-là à notre autre être et les détacherions plutôt de nous pour les joindre à l'autre.

The two other uses of *tranquillité* in the *Pensées* refer to the Stoic and Sceptic notions of *repos*, which I have just introduced. In L533, Plato and Aristotle are named as two thinkers for whom '[la partie] la plus philosophe était de vivre simplement et tranquillement', which in turn refers to the Stoic perception of *repos* or *tranquillitas animi*.[22] In L427, *tranquille* is linked to the *oisiveté* of the sceptics, as we found in the *Entretien avec M. de Sacy*:

> celui qui doute et qui ne recherche pas est tout ensemble et bien malheureux et bien injuste. Que s'il est avec cela tranquille et satisfait, qu'il en fasse profession, et enfin qu'il en fasse le sujet de sa joie et de sa vanité, je n'ai point de termes pour qualifier une si extravagante créature.

Thus *tranquillité* is introduced in the *Pensées* to illustrate the inadequacy of human forms of *repos*. It is therefore implied that another form of tranquillity must be sought, one that is separated from the corruption of humanity.

---

[22] See Beugnot, 'Apologétique et mythe moral', 61.

PAIX

The term *paix* is used in many more different ways than *tranquillité* in the *Pensées*. I shall concentrate principally on its relation to *repos*.

On one level, *paix* is strictly synonymous with *tranquillité* in the different forms of *repos* which various sects claim to attain. In L410, the dialectician contrasts the Stoics with the Epicureans. The terms *paix* and *repos* are used interchangeably to evoke this spurious sense of tranquillity:

> Cette guerre intérieure de la raison contre les passions a fait que ceux qui ont voulu avoir la paix se sont partagés en deux sectes. Les uns ont voulu renoncer aux passions et devenir dieux [*the Stoics*], les autres ont voulu renoncer à la raison et devenir bête brute [*the Epicureans*]. Des Barreaux. Mais ils ne l'ont pu ni les uns ni les autres, et la raison demeure toujours qui accuse la bassesse et l'injustice des passions et qui trouble le repos [R1] de ceux qui s'y abandonnent. Et les passions sont toujours vivantes dans ceux qui y veulent renoncer.[23]

On a political and social level, the opposition between peace and war is made explicit throughout the *Pensées*. Within this context, *paix* has the sense, in the words of the Académie dictionary, of 'Repos, estat d'un peuple qui n'est point en guerre'.[24] Politically, peace is perceived as 'le souverain bien' (L81). However, the contrast between war and peace does not remain only on a human level in the *Pensées*. The dialectician exploits the imagery to apply it to a spiritual framework. On earth, war is condemned for the disruption which it brings, and peace is deemed preferable.[25] But, in a spiritual context, it is important to distinguish between true and false peace, just as a distinction must be made between true and false war:

> La plus cruelle guerre que Dieu pût faire aux hommes en cette vie est de les laisser sans cette guerre qu'il est venu apporter. Je suis venu apporter la

---

[23] Cf. the use of *paix* in L621, which evokes the 'Guerre intestine de l'homme entre la raison et les passions'. The reference to Des Barreaux in L410 relates to his Epicurean beliefs and to the lines from a song which he composed: 'Et, par ma raison, je bute | A devenir bête brute.'
[24] For examples of the contrast between war and peace on a political level, see L29, L485, L750.   [25] See Ch. 8 below.

guerre, dit-il, et pour instrument de cette guerre je suis venu apporter le fer et le feu. Avant lui le monde vivait dans cette fausse paix. (L924)

It is in the *Écrits des curés de Paris* that we find the most elaborate distinction between false peace (typified by the Casuists) and true spiritual peace. There seem to be three distinct uses of *paix* in the following passage: false human peace (P1), justified human peace (P2), and true spiritual peace (P3). Significantly, *repos* (R1) is introduced to demonstrate another form of false restfulness:

Notre amour pour la paix [P2] a assez paru par la longueur de notre silence; nous n'avons parlé que quand nous n'eussions pu nous taire sans crime. Ils ont abusé de cette paix [P2] pour introduire leurs damnables opinions, et ils voudraient maintenant en prolonger la durée pour les affermir de plus en plus. Mais les vrais enfants de l'Église savent bien discerner la véritable paix [P3] que le Sauveur peut seul donner, et qui est inconnue au monde, d'avec cette fausse paix [P1] que le monde peut bien donner, mais qui est en horreur au Sauveur du monde. Ils savent que la véritable paix [P3] est celle qui conserve la vérité en la possession de la créance des hommes, et que la fausse paix [P1] est celle qui conserve l'erreur en possession de la crédulité des hommes. Ils savent que la véritable paix [P3] est inséparable de la vérité, [. . .] et que ce qui serait une paix [P1] devant les hommes, serait une guerre devant Dieu. Ils savent aussi que bien loin de blesser la charité par ces corrections, on blesserait la charité en ne les faisant pas, parce que la fausse charité est celle qui laisse les méchants en repos [R1] dans les vices, au lieu que la véritable charité est celle qui trouble ce malheureux repos [R1] [. . .].[26]

This juxtaposition of political and spiritual imagery is also found in L974, where the need to conserve peace in the Church (protecting its property, which is spiritual truth) is likened to a need to maintain peace in a State (protecting its own goods).[27] Within a spiritual context, 'Il y a donc un temps où la paix est juste et un autre où elle est injuste'.

Peace in its purest spiritual sense appears at the end of the *Mémorial* (L913), where the speaker communicates his sense of joy, certainty, and inner peace: 'Certitude, certitude, sentiment, joie, paix'.

---

[26] 'Réponse des curés de Paris', Seuil 478.
[27] In L974, *repos* is used as an exact synonym of *paix* in its sense of civil peace. Conversely, *paix* appears as a substitute for *repos* (R1) in L919: 'Nous implorons la miséricorde de Dieu, non afin qu'il nous laisse en paix dans nos vices, mais afin que Dieu nous en délivre.'

Thus, *paix* functions in a very similar way to *repos*, oscillating between human and spiritual referents. Up to this point, through my analysis of L136 and a brief study of *tranquillité* and *paix*, we find that the notion of *repos* is always shifting. Despite man's instinct for spiritual restfulness, he finds himself trapped between a desire to search for peace and a need to escape the 'cessation de travail' that causes *ennui*.

HUMAN *REPOS*

On earth, therefore, any *repos* which man thinks he has achieved can only be false. An indifference to a knowledge of the truth, for example, can provide a certain sense of peace:

Si vous ne vous souciez guère de savoir la vérité, en voilà assez pour vous laisser en repos [R1]. Mais si vous désirez de tout votre cœur de la connaître ce n'est pas assez regardé au détail. (L150)

However, whatever peace such indifference may provide, it can only be temporary. The dialectician accentuates this in L428, the fragment in which he wishes to represent 'l'injustice des hommes qui vivent dans l'indifférence de chercher la vérité d'une chose qui leur est si importante':

Ce repos [R1] dans cette ignorance est une chose monstrueuse, et dont il faut faire sentir l'extravagance et la stupidité à ceux qui y passent leur vie, en la leur représentant à eux-mêmes, pour les confondre par la vue de leur folie.

Within a purely human context, man can have no hope of genuine *repos*: 'Notre nature est dans le mouvement, le repos entier est la mort' (L641). The rest which death brings represents simply the end of such agitation on earth. Yet there remains some ambiguity within the notion of *repos* here: death and restfulness must point implicitly to the possibility of spiritual peace. For Christ, who 'n'a point où se reposer sur la terre qu'au sépulchre' (L560), it is his death which takes him away from the restlessness of the world and joins him to eternal peace.[28] This continual reiteration of the lack of true rest on earth provokes in the reader

[28] For further discussion of the relationship between *repos* and death, see Stanton, 'The Ideal of *Repos*', 97, and Beugnot, 'Morale du repos et conscience du temps', 195.

what Beugnot calls 'l'indispensable inquiétude',[29] hence the thematic link of *repos* with death:

> Nous sommes plaisants de nous reposer dans la société de nos semblables, misérables comme nous, impuissants comme nous; ils ne nous aideront pas: on mourra seul. (L151)[30]

Man is forced to look beyond himself and the limited time of his earthly life. This tension within human *repos* finds its roots in biblical tradition, through the pairing of *requies* and *sollicitudo*. As Beugnot points out,

> La *sollicitudo* biblique oscille en effet entre le négatif et le positif, tantôt elle est pur trouble et instabilité de l'homme séparé de Dieu, tantôt elle est vigilance et attention, attente de Dieu. Ainsi le repos peut être l'état d'une âme qui a renoncé à toute vigilance, donc à la vie spirituelle, ou le désir qui exprime un malaise fécond.[31]

As we have seen, the lack of 'vigilance' of those who seek forgetfulness in *repos* contrasted with the uneasiness of those who wish to escape their present state (depicted in L136) fit into this biblical model. Man is trapped between his natural inconstancy and a desire for rest. It is within this framework that I believe we should read *repos* in the famous fragment on the disproportion of man, L199. After the passage devoted to man's inner instability ('nous voguons sur un milieu vaste') and the incapacity of human reason ('notre raison est toujours déçue par l'inconstance des apparences'), the dialectician argues that 'cela étant bien compris je crois qu'on se tiendra en repos, chacun dans l'état où la nature l'a placé'. However, this *repos* is as spurious as any restfulness attained by the pyrrhonists, for, as the dialectician explains in the following paragraph, it would constitute only a very brief state of motionlessness in the eternity of time: 'la durée de notre vie n'est-elle pas également infime de l'éternité pour durer dix ans davantage'.[32]

---

[29] Beugnot, 'Apologétique et mythe moral', 71. See Ch. 5 above.

[30] The Augustinian foundation of these fragments on the human condition is underlined by the fact that L151 was written on the same page as L629 ('cette duplicité de l'homme est si visible qu'il y en a qui ont pensé que nous avions deux âmes'), as Ernst's reconstruction work has shown (Album, 190).

[31] 'Apologétique et mythe moral', 63; see also 71–2. Nowhere is *repos* in its sense of lack of vigilance more strikingly found than in L919: 'Jésus les [les disciples] trouvant encore dormants sans que ni sa considération ni la leur les en eût retenus, il a la bonté de ne pas les éveiller et les laisse dans leur repos.'

[32] In *De l'esprit géométrique*, *repos* is similarly conceived simply as motionlessness as opposed to movement. See Seuil 354. Cf. L682.

The tension between man's desire for restfulness and his essential instability is inherent in Pascal's conception of the two natures of man. Whereas a writer like Bourdonné sees man's instability as ordained by divine Providence, where 'la foy nous enseigne qu'il doit y avoir quelqu'autre lieu plus tranquille que celuy-cy, où nous pourrions joüir d'un parfait repos',[33] for Pascal the contradictory senses of restlessness and peace act as a permanent reminder both of man's fallen condition and of his original perfect nature. In other words, another kind of instability is engendered by an awareness of these contrasting forms of spurious human *repos*. Indeed, the dialectician manipulates such a sense of agitation so as never to leave the reader in a mindless state of repose, as he stresses at the end of L449: 'quelque parti qu'il [*the searching reader*] prenne, je ne l'y laisserai point en repos'. Restlessness forms an integral part of the persuasive process.

SPIRITUAL *REPOS*

The only hope of eternal restfulness lies, therefore, in the spiritual option, an aspect which is reiterated in both biblical and Augustinian tradition. St Augustine's *Confessions*, for example, begin and end with a plea for deliverance from the agitation of human life towards spiritual rest in God. In the first chapter we find the words, 'vous nous avez créés pour vous, et que notre coeur est toujours agité jusqu'à ce qu'il trouve son repos en vous',[34] and he concludes in the final chapter of book XIII, 'vous êtes toujours dans le repos, parce que vous êtes vous-même votre repos'.[35] A similar sentiment is expressed in L460:

Le Dieu des chrétiens est un Dieu qui fait sentir à l'âme qu'il est son unique bien; que tout son repos [R3] est en lui; qu'elle n'aura de joie qu'à l'aimer;

---

[33] *Le Courtisan desabusé* (Paris, 1658), 406. Bourdonné writes of *repos* only in the sense of R3. For him, 'il n'y a rien de si déraisonnable que de croire pouvoir trouver du repos et de la stabilité dans le monde' (p. 404). See D. C. Potts, 'Pascal's Contemporaries and *Le Divertissement*', *Modern Language Review*, 57 (1962), 33, 35, 36.   [34] I. i. 2.
[35] XIII. xxxviii. 591. Cf. IV. xi. 120: 'c'est en lui que tu trouveras un repos inébranlable'; VI. xvi. 215: 'Vous [= Dieu] seul est son [l'âme] repos' (*et tu solus requies*). See Sellier, *Pascal et Saint Augustin*, 36–8. Cf. also the use of *repos* in L267, L275, L392, and L608, which shows direct inspiration from biblical vocabulary, and where the promised land is referred to as 'un lieu de repos'.

et qui lui fait en même temps abhorrer les obstacles qui la retiennent et l'empêchent d'aimer Dieu de toutes ses forces.

This need to abhor the obstacles to spiritual *repos* transmutes itself into a different attitude towards time. Whereas the unbeliever is always prompted by his inner restlessness to look towards the future and, indeed, to recognize that only death can provide an end to his agitation, the believer becomes indifferent to the past and to the future, and concentrates instead on the present, so that he can achieve final rest with God without being encumbered by the instability of his fallen state. This point is accentuated in a letter which Pascal wrote to Mlle de Roannez:

> Le passé ne nous doit point embarrasser, puisque nous n'avons qu'à avoir regret de nos fautes. Mais l'avenir nous doit encore moins toucher, puisqu'il n'est point du tout à notre égard, et que nous n'y arriverons peut-être jamais. Le présent est le seul temps qui est véritablement à nous, et dont nous devons user selon Dieu. [. . .] Notre Seigneur n'a pas voulu que notre prévoyance s'étendît plus loin que le jour où nous sommes. C'est les bornes qu'il faut garder, et pour notre salut, et pour notre propre repos [R3]. Car en vérité les préceptes chrétiens sont les plus pleins de consolation: je dis plus que les maximes du monde.[36]

However, although the believer is urged to remain content within the present time, that does not mean that he should be entrenched within a mindless stasis. From a Christian standpoint, he must be ever moving towards the final state of repose which God's grace alone can bestow upon him. Indeed, paradoxically, spiritual *repos* is dependent on another kind of agitation, the search for truth, as L599 makes clear:

> Différence entre repos [R3] et sûreté de conscience. Rien ne donne l'assurance que la vérité; rien ne donne le repos [R3] que la recherche sincère de la vérité.[37]

The text of *Sur la conversion du pécheur* perhaps best sums up the different kinds of *repos* which we find in the *Pensées*. Its neo-Platonist characteristics of 'élévation' and its concern with 'refus du périssable, obsession de l'écoulement, désir de la stabilité et du repos par l'union à un Etre immuable' have all been clearly

---

[36] Dec. 1656, Seuil 270.
[37] Cf. the notion of eternal spiritual *repos* and temporary searching with the 'Mémorial', L913: 'Éternellement en joie pour un jour d'exercice sur la terre'.

identified by Philippe Sellier as filtered through various Augustinian writings.[38] The first use of the word evokes the false sense of repose which various 'délices' of the world gave to the believer before his conversion. His conversion gives him first a self-knowledge:

> Cette nouvelle lumière lui [*the soul*] donne de la crainte, et lui apporte un trouble qui traverse le repos [R1 and R2] qu'elle trouvait dans les choses qui faisaient ses délices.[39]

After this come the various steps in his progress towards ultimate salvation, culminating in a spiritual *repos* which is eternal and unsurpassable:

> Elle [*the soul*] traverse toutes les créatures, et ne peut arrêter son cœur qu'elle ne se soit rendue jusqu'au trône de Dieu, dans lequel elle commence à trouver son repos [R3] et ce bien qui est tel qu'il n'y a rien de plus aimable, et qu'il ne peut lui être ôté que par son propre consentement.[40]

On all levels, therefore, the concept of *repos* is informed, paradoxically, by movement. On a human register, man is torn between his natural restlessness and his instinct for a restfulness which is beyond his grasp. On a spiritual level, the believer understands the means, movement through searching, and the end, final rest in God.

Key to *Repos*

R1 *repos*: absence of movement
R2 *repos*: pursued tranquillity
R3 *repos*: spiritual peace

---

[38] *Pascal et Saint Augustin*, 85. See also J. Orcibal, 'Thèmes platoniciens dans l'*Augustinus* de Jansénius', in *Augustinus Magister*, ii (Paris, 1954), 1077–85.
[39] Seuil 290.
[40] Ibid. 291. Cf. François de Sales, *Traité de l'amour de Dieu*, vi. 8 (in *Œuvres*, ed. A. Ravier, Paris, 1969), 633: 'l'âme ainsi tranquille en son Dieu ne quitterait pas ce repos pour tous les plus grands biens du monde'. See also ibid. chs. 9, 10.

7
Bonheur/Félicité

Pour moi, quand je regarde Paris ou Londres, je ne vois aucune raison pour entrer dans ce désespoir dont parle M. Pascal; je vois une ville qui ne ressemble en rien à une île déserte, mais peuplée, opulente, policée, et où les hommes sont heureux autant que la nature le comporte.

(Voltaire)[1]

Following my discussion of words depicting both movement (*inconstance* and *inquiétude*) and rest or stasis (*ennui* and *repos*), all of which interact with and react against each other, it is not surprising to find Robert Mauzi's comment (referring specifically to the eighteenth century) that 'les réflexions sur le bonheur sont fondées [. . .] sur la découverte de la dualité qui partage le cœur humain: mouvement et repos'.[2]

It is difficult to differentiate between the terms *bonheur* and *félicité*, as the seventeenth-century dictionaries show. The Académie dictionary, for example, defines *bonheur* as 'félicité' and *félicité* as 'beatitude' and 'bonheur parfait', whereas the Furetière dictionary defines *bonheur* as 'félicité parfaite'. Moreover, the Académie's addition of numerous qualifiers to *bonheur* in its list of illustrations, such as 'veritable bonheur', 'solide bonheur', 'bonheur parfait', 'bonheur apparent', and 'bonheur éternel', testifies to the problems associated with a precise definition of the word. In the Richelet dictionary, *félicité* is equated with 'souverain bien' and 'bonheur', whereas the Furetière takes pains to point out that 'on confond souvent le souverain bien avec la félicité'. The Furetière for its part interprets 'béatitude' as 'le souverain bien' and 'la félicité éternelle', while the Académie sees it as both 'félicité' and 'bonheur'. However, all three dictionaries are in accord over the mainly spiritual connotations of *béatitude*: 'Il ne se dit guere que de la félicité éternelle' (Académie).

The interchangeability of *bonheur* and *félicité* which we find in

[1] *Lettres philosophiques*, letter 25.
[2] *L'Idée du bonheur au XVIIIe siècle* (Paris, 1976), 432.

the dictionaries informs the use of both terms in the *Pensées*. As far as I can ascertain, they are completely synonymous, with neither word, moreover, being used exclusively in an immanent or transcendent context. Indeed, this interchangeability can serve, in a way similar to the polyvalent meanings of single terms, to reinforce the sense of the instability of language. One possible way of differentiating the two terms is their pairing with antonyms. *Bonheur* is most frequently contrasted with *malheur*, and *félicité* with *misère*. Also, *bonheur/malheur* are terms traditionally connected with fate, as can be seen in the Nicot French–Latin dictionary translation of *malheur* as 'infortunium'. However, as both *malheur* and *misère* are easily interchangeable in the *Pensées*, and as *misère* is more often opposed to *grandeur* than *félicité*, this only serves to accentuate their affinity. Furthermore, the use of *heureux* as an adjective or a noun tends to be directly linked to *bonheur/félicité*; and, except where I state to the contrary, I intend to treat all terms in conjunction with each other.

SUR LA CONVERSION DU PÉCHEUR

The appearances of *bonheur* and *félicité* in *Sur la conversion du pécheur* perhaps best introduce the different levels on which we find that they operate in the *Pensées*. The Augustinian-based neo-Platonism of *Sur la conversion du pécheur* has already been mentioned in Chapter 6, and I shall return briefly to this subject in my discussion of the Stoic notion of happiness. There are three distinct ways in which *bonheur/félicité* seems to be used in *Sur la conversion du pécheur*. On a first level, it is equated with a spurious human sense of happiness (which I shall call B1). On a second plane, man is deemed to seek a happiness which is true and justified in itself but which is only temporary (B2). The third sense relates to eternal spiritual happiness with God (B3) (see the Key at the end of this chapter).

Pascal first details the problems of the soul, 'qui recherche sérieusement à s'établir dans une félicité [B3] aussi durable qu'elle-même'.[3] Such a lasting spiritual happiness cannot be found within the confines of the corrupt world, for 'l'âme, étant immortelle comme elle est, ne peut trouver sa félicité [B3] parmi des choses périssables'. However, although any happiness which relies solely

---

[3] All references to *Sur la conversion du pécheur* come from Seuil 290, except where stated.

on earthly things is necessarily false, man can attain a happiness which in itself is perceived as positive (Pascal calls it 'véritable', which would distinguish it from totally false happiness), but which is essentially temporary:

> De sorte que l'âme s'étant amassé des trésors de biens temporels de quelque nature qu'ils soient, soit or, soit science, soit réputation, c'est une nécessité indispensable qu'elle se trouve dénuée de tous ces objets de sa félicité [B1]; et qu'ainsi, s'ils ont eu de quoi la satisfaire, ils n'auront pas de quoi la satisfaire toujours; et que si c'est se procurer un bonheur véritable [B2], ce n'est pas se procurer un bonheur durable [B3], puisqu'il doit être borné avec le cours de cette vie.

These three forms of happiness will determine my analysis of *bonheur/félicité*. I intend first to consider B1, especially in relation to the fragments concerning *imagination*. I shall then move to the notion of happiness and *divertissement*, especially in conjunction with B1 and B2, before concluding with a study of fragments which deal particularly with happiness in the sense of B3.

FALSE HAPPINESS

It is in the fragment subtitled 'Imagination', L44, that the dialectician defines most clearly the notion of a happiness which is completely fabricated and therefore false:

> L'imagination dispose de tout; elle fait la beauté, la justice et le bonheur [B1] qui est le tout du monde.

In other words, it creates its own world with its own values, 'une seconde nature'. Happiness is therefore defined within the confines of this second nature, in direct opposition to all rational perception. While an initial reading of the text would give the reader an undefined sense of instability, closer analysis reveals the deliberate ways in which the dialectician conveys this destabilization. Concepts, such as happiness, health and wealth, which are ordinarily perceived to be fixed are thrown into flux by the creation of a second reality governed by the imagination:

> Elle [l'imagination] a ses heureux [B1], ses malheureux, ses sains, ses malades, ses riches, ses pauvres. [. . .] Elle ne peut rendre sages les fous mais elle les rend heureux [B1], à l'envi de la raison qui ne peut rendre ses amis que misérables, l'une les couvrant de gloire, l'autre de honte. (L44)

As Richard Parish puts it, 'the unbeliever must be brought to see his ideal of fulfilment as illusory; the *puissances trompeuses*, led by the imagination, create an inauthentic state of happiness which the apologist must annihilate before indicating its permanent replacement'.[4]

This false sense of happiness emanates from man's attempt to place himself and his own state of well-being above all other concerns:

> Quel dérèglement de jugement par lequel il n'y a personne qui ne se mette au-dessus de tout le reste du monde, et qui n'aime mieux son propre bien et la durée de son bonheur [B1] et de sa vie que celle de tout le reste du monde. (L749)[5]

Paradoxically, this spurious happiness is coextensive with what the dialectician calls 'grandeur de l'homme', that is, the Stoic perception of man's inner strengths:

> Grandeur de l'homme.
> Nous avons une si grande idée de l'âme de l'homme que nous ne pouvons souffrir d'en être méprisés et de n'être pas dans l'estime d'une âme. Et toute la félicité [B1] des hommes consiste dans cette estime. (L411)[6]

In a fragment which was originally headed by the words 'Contre les philosophes qui ont Dieu sans J.-C.', certain unnamed 'philosophes'

---

[4] Pascal's 'Lettres provinciales': A Study in Polemic (Oxford, 1989), 106. See also 105–14, where Parish identifies the 'converted meanings' of happiness. I shall refer again to his analysis in this chapter.

[5] Sénault makes a similar point in *L'Homme chrestien ou La Reparation de la Nature par la Grace* (Paris, 1648): 'quelque chose que fassent les hommes, quelques desseins qu'ils conçoivent, quelques entreprises qu'ils executent ils veulent tousjours estre bien-heureux; s'ils s'engagent dans la guerre, ils cherchent leur bon-heur dans la victoire; s'ils s'accordent avecque leurs ennemis, ils cherchent la felicité dans la paix; s'ils amassent des richesses, ils cherchent leur Beatitude dans l'abondance [. . .]. Il est vray qu'ils sont malheureux et criminels, parce qu'ils la cherchent où elle n'est pas, et que par un aveuglement qui est la punition de leur peché, ils veulent trouver dans la varieté des creatures ce qui ne se peut trouver que dans l'unité du Createur' (pp. 764–5). However, whereas Sénault condemns unreservedly this misguided search for happiness, Pascal's approach is more subtle: for him, happiness in the sense of B2 is not entirely negative.

[6] Cf. L470: 'La plus grande bassesse de l'homme est la recherche de la gloire, mais c'est cela même qui est la plus grande marque de son excellence; car, quelque possession qu'il ait sur la terre, quelque santé et commodité essentielle qu'il ait, il n'est pas satisfait, s'il n'est dans l'estime des hommes. Il estime si grande la raison de l'homme que, quelque avantage qu'il ait sur la terre, s'il n'est placé avantageusement dans la raison de l'homme, il n'est pas content [B1].' The adjective *content* appears exclusively in the *Pensées* within a human context.

(specified in the Port-Royal edition as 'les Platoniciens, et même Epictète et ses sectateurs') are perceived to found their happiness on just such a need for the esteem of others. Pascal's knowledge of Platonism stemmed largely from his reading of Augustine, and it seems that for his purposes he equated the Stoics with the Platonists. As Sellier has noted of Pascal, 'il semble qu'il ait rapproché platonisme et stoïcisme, rapprochement que son ignorance de Platon et le choix d'Epictète facilitaient, pour les opposer à l'épicurisme de Montaigne':[7]

> Philosophes.
> Ils croient que Dieu est seul digne d'être aimé et d'être admiré, et ont désiré d'être aimés et admirés des hommes, et ils ne connaissent pas leur corruption. S'ils se sentent pleins de sentiments pour l'aimer et l'adorer, et qu'ils y trouvent leur joie principale, qu'ils s'estiment bons, à la bonne heure! Mais s'ils s'y trouvent répugnants s'[ils] n'[ont] aucune pente qu'à se vouloir établir dans l'estime des hommes, et que pour toute perfection, ils fassent seulement que, sans forcer les hommes, ils leur fassent trouver leur bonheur [B1] à les aimer, je dirai que cette perfection est horrible. Quoi, ils ont connu Dieu et n'ont pas désiré uniquement que les hommes les aimassent, que les hommes s'arrêtassent à eux. Ils ont voulu être l'objet du bonheur volontaire [B1] des hommes. (L142)[8]

The notion of *bonheur volontaire* relates directly to man's self-centred *volonté*, which itself cannot offer true happiness (in the sense of B3). As the dialectician emphasizes in another fragment,

> La volonté propre ne satisfera jamais, quand elle aurait pouvoir de tout ce qu'elle veut; mais on est satisfait dès l'instant qu'on y renonce. Sans elle on ne peut être malcontent; par elle on ne peut être content. (L362)[9]

---

[7] *Pascal et Saint Augustin* (Paris, 1970), 86; see also 84–5. Pascal emphasizes the positive aspects of Epictetus' Stoicism in the *Entretien avec M. de Sacy*. As Sellier puts it, 'cet éloge d'un stoïcien est propre à Pascal, qui ne cesse d'opposer stoïcisme et épicurisme pour révéler ensuite la synthèse chrétienne, conformément au programme précisé à la fin de l'*Entretien*. L'évêque d'Hippone procède différemment: il élève au-dessus des erreurs stoïciennes et épicuriennes la grandeur du platonisme, qui est à ses yeux la meilleure propédeutique à l'Évangile' (p. 86).

[8] For other contemporary responses to the notions of happiness defined by the 'philosophes', see R. Du Pont, *La Philosophie des esprits* (Rouen, 1628; 1st edn. 1602), 236; Du Teil, *Catechisme des Sçavans* (Paris, 1651), 247–8; Sénault, *De l'usage des passions* (Paris, 1641), 'Préface'.

[9] Cf. *De l'esprit géométrique*, Seuil 355, where the role of *volonté* in the need for *agrément* is condemned: 'Cette voie est basse, indigne et étrangère.' See T. Harrington, *Vérité et méthode dans les 'Pensées' de Pascal* (Paris, 1972), 93–4.

HAPPINESS AND *DIVERTISSEMENT*

In addition to its relationship to *ennui*, the notion of *divertissement* is closely connected to the different kinds of happiness in the *Pensées*. Indeed, it plays a central part in the dialectician's deliberate destabilization of the reader's perception of a fixed happiness. In L132, for example, an idealized and pure sense of happiness (B3), identified by the semantic markers 'saints' and 'Dieu', which man cannot attain by himself, is contrasted with an interlocutor's idea of happiness which is provoked by diversion and which in fact is spurious (B1):

> Divertissement—Si l'homme était heureux [B3] il le serait d'autant plus qu'il serait moins diverti, comme les saints et Dieu. Oui; mais n'est-ce pas être heureux [B1] que de pouvoir être réjoui par le divertissement?
> —Non; car il vient d'ailleurs et de dehors; et ainsi il est dépendant, et partout, sujet à être troublé par mille accidents, qui font les afflictions inévitables.

This false sense of happiness which is caused by *divertissement* is clarified in L133:

> Divertissement.
> Les hommes n'ayant pu guérir la mort, la misère, l'ignorance, ils se sont avisés, pour se rendre heureux [B1], de n'y point penser.

Divertissement represents, therefore, evasion from reality and the subsequent creation of a 'happiness' which is not unlike the artificial happiness which the imagination engenders, as we saw in L44. Similarly, lack of awareness of the self leads to false happiness. For man, 'il lui est meilleur de s'ignorer pour être heureux [B1]' (L687). This ignorance can also lead man to be duped by the false happiness posited by others. In the *Lettres provinciales*, for example, the polemicist makes just such a claim against Père Annat:

> Votre bonheur [B1] est digne de compassion, et ne peut être envié que par ceux qui ignorent quel est le véritable bonheur [B3].[10]

It is in the long fragment on *divertissement*, L136, that the dialectician most successfully shifts between different registers of happiness, thus attaining the undefined sense of instability which a

---

[10] Seuil 460.

first reading generates. A closer examination of the methods used to convey this instability reveals the dialectician's skilful interplay between false happiness (B1), justified happiness (B2), and eternal happiness (B3). Throughout the fragment, these different kinds of *bonheur/félicité* are contrasted and linked with *malheur*. The image of a king who, without the distraction of *divertissements*, is 'plus malheureux que le moindre de ses sujets qui joue et qui se divertit' points to a *malheur* which has two main layers. On one level it shows the wretchedness of man's corrupt state ('le malheur naturel de notre condition faible et mortelle'), but on another level it uncovers a misdirected unhappiness which is itself contrasted with a false sense of happiness (B1), that which is produced from the pleasures of diversions. It is interesting to note that the term *félicité* is also assigned to describe a king's state *without divertissements*. But here the words 'cette félicité languissante' would seem to correspond to the later phrase, 'un amusement languissant et sans passion', which provokes *ennui* in man.

The dialectician immediately points out the complexities inherent in assigning a single meaning to *bonheur*. Language must be the extension of man's fallen nature if the true spiritual state of happiness cannot be distinguished from the happiness [B1] which is derived from diversions such as gambling and hunting:

Ce n'est pas qu'il y ait en effet du bonheur [B3], ni qu'on imagine que la vraie béatitude [B3] soit d'avoir l'argent qu'on peut gagner au jeu, ou dans le lièvre qu'on court; on n'en voudrait pas s'il était offert. (L136)[11]

We find a similar ironic awareness of the way in which different interpretations of happiness become distorted in the fourth letter of the *Lettres provinciales*. Montalte is confused that the excesses of men, which he believes would ensure their damnation, in fact, according to the Jesuits, 'rendent leur salut assuré'. At this, he interjects, 'O la bonne voie pour être heureux en ce monde et en l'autre!'[12]

---

[11] Cf. L889: 'Si notre condition était véritablement heureuse [B3], il ne nous faudrait pas divertir d'y penser pour nous rendre heureux [B1].' Cf. Voltaire's rejection of Pascal's perception of *divertissement* and *bonheur* in letter 25 of the *Lettres philosophiques*. As Antony McKenna puts it, for Voltaire, 'le divertissement est un véritable bonheur, car le bonheur ne consiste que dans le plaisir', *De Pascal à Voltaire* (Oxford, 1990), ii. 895. See also Mauzi, *L'Idée du bonheur au XVIIIe siècle*, ch. 10.   [12] Seuil 384.

Thus, the deliberate juxtaposition of these different kinds of happiness serves to unsettle the reader. On one level, *divertissements* relate directly to false happiness, as the following extracts from L136 show:

> Et c'est enfin le plus grand sujet de félicité [B1] de la condition des rois, de ce qu'on essaie sans cesse à les divertir et à leur procurer toutes sortes de plaisirs.
>
> Voilà tout ce que les hommes ont pu inventer pour se rendre heureux [B1] [. . .].
>
> Un amusement languissant et sans passion l'ennuiera. Il faut qu'il s'y échauffe, et qu'il se pipe lui-même en s'imaginant qu'il serait heureux [B1] de gagner ce qu'il ne voudrait point qu'on lui donnât à condition de ne point jouer [. . .].
>
> L'homme, quelque plein de tristesse qu'il soit, si on peut gagner sur lui de le faire entrer en quelque divertissement le voila heureux [B1] pendant ce temps-là, et l'homme quelqu'heureux [B1] qu'il soit s'il n'est diverti et occupé par quelque passion ou quelque amusement, qui empêche l'ennui de se répandre, sera bientôt chagrin et malheureux. Sans divertissement il n'y a point de joie; avec le divertissement il n'y a point de tristesse. Et c'est aussi ce qui forme le bonheur [B1] des personnes [. . .] de grande condition qu'ils ont un nombre de personnes qui les divertissent et qu'ils ont le pouvoir de se maintenir en cet état.

However, on another level, man's need to divert himself inclines him towards a recognition of a different happiness, one that is associated with *repos*,[13] in its meaning of the intuition of spiritual peace. It is this state, man's perception of a happiness which points towards eternal spiritual happiness, which I call B2. In a deleted passage, for example, we find the adjective *heureux* used in this way:

> Dire à un homme qu'il soit en repos, c'est lui dire qu'il vive heureux [B2]. C'est lui conseiller [. . .] d'avoir une condition toute heureuse [B2] et laquelle il puisse considérer à loisir, sans y trouver sujet d'affliction. (L136)

This happiness emanates from man's sense of his original perfect nature, as the dialectician explains in another paragraph:

---

[13] See my discussion of L136 in Ch. 6 above. Mauzi comes near to this positive active dimension of *bonheur* (which I class as B2) in a brief note: 'il existe une *correspondance* entre la recherche active du bonheur terrestre et l'aspiration implicite à l'éternité, la première *figurant* la seconde' (*L'Idée du bonheur au XVIIIe siècle*, 180).

Et ils [les hommes] ont un autre instinct secret qui reste de la grandeur de notre première nature, qui leur fait connaître que le bonheur [B2 and B3] n'est en effet que dans le repos et non pas dans le tumulte.

Sénault, despite not developing the theme of *divertissement*, makes this point even more emphatically, in *L'Homme criminel*: 'ce plaisir qu'il [l'homme] cherche dans tous ses divertissemens est fondé sur le souvenir de sa premiere felicité'.[14]

The reconstruction by Pol Ernst of pages of the original text of the *Pensées* enables us to have further evidence of the close relationship between the notion of happiness and *divertissement*. L408, which contains quotations (taken from Montaigne) of Virgil and Horace on, as Jean Mesnard suggests,[15] the different approaches of various dogmatists towards happiness, was followed immediately by L10:

> Une lettre de la folie de la science humaine et de la philosophie.
> Cette lettre avant le divertissement.
> *Felix qui potuit.*
> *Felix nihil admirari.*
> 280 sortes de souverain bien dans Montaigne. (L408)
> Les misères de la vie humaine ont frondé tout cela. Comme ils ont vu cela ils ont pris le divertissement.[16]

It is evident from the above fragments that Pascal's interest in the differing perceptions of the sovereign good came largely from Montaigne. However, it should be noted that the many different definitions of happiness which form such an integral part of the dialectician's persuasive strategy emanate from a long philosophical tradition. Aristotle, who is named directly only once in the *Pensées*, in L533 (through the medium of Montaigne),[17] wrote notoriously in book 1, chapter 5 of his *Rhetoric* and in the first two books of his *Nicomachean Ethics* of the shifting definitions of happiness. In a 1654 translation by François Cassandre of the

---

[14] *L'Homme criminel* (Paris, 1644), 498. Sénault entitles the 10th Discours of the fifth Traité, 'Que la plus grande part de nos divertissemens sont des occasions de peché', but *divertissement* is not as central or significant a concept as in the *Pensées*.
[15] *Les 'Pensées' de Pascal* (Paris, 1976), 220.
[16] See Ernst, Album, 23. The Latin quotations come via Montaigne in III. x. 998 and II. xii. 562. Ernst's reconstruction of this page shows that Lafuma is clearly wrong to read 'frondé' as 'fondé'. Cf. L76.
[17] *Essais*, II. xii. 488. Cf. the debate in the 4th letter of the *Lettres provinciales* about Aristotle and Bauny, Seuil 386.

Rhetoric (a copy of which we know to have been in de Sacy's library),[18] for example, we find such an awareness of the differing notions of happiness:

> Supposons donc que le souverain Bien, et la Felicité se rencontrent, ou à *Mener une vie dont toutes les actions reussissent au contentement de celui qui les fait sans pourtant s'éloigner en rien du devoir d'un honneste homme ni de la vertu*, ou encore à *Se voir en tel estat qu'on n'ait affaire de rien*, ou bien à *Passer si agreablement ses jours que les plaisirs n'en puissent estre troublez*, ou enfin à *Jouir d'une possession si parfaite de toutes choses, qu'on soit en puissance également et de les conserver dans le besoin, et de les acquerir de nouveau si elles estoient perdues*; car sans doute tout le monde demeure d'accord que le souverain Bien consiste, ou dans la possession de quelqu'une de ces choses, ou de plusieurs ensemble.[19]

The fact that man is torn between contradictory states of happiness and notions of the sovereign good indicates his own instability. However, the sense of true spiritual happiness which man feels instinctively from his original nature can prompt him to search for eternal happiness both within himself and as encapsulated in God. Indeed, only a recognition of the complexity of the notion of happiness can activate such a search. Those who posit all hope of happiness in a single issue, such as those who seek it through diversion or those Stoics who believe they can find it solely within themselves, are clearly misdirected, as the dialectician emphasizes in L407:

> Les stoïques disent: rentrez au-dedans de vous-même, c'est là où vous trouverez votre repos. Et cela n'est pas vrai.
> Les autres disent: sortez dehors et cherchez le bonheur [B1] en un divertissement. Et cela n'est pas vrai, les maladies viennent.
> Le bonheur [B2 and B3] n'est ni hors de nous ni dans nous; il est en Dieu et hors et dans nous.[20]

---

[18] See O. Barenne, *Une grande bibliothèque de Port-Royal: Inventaire inédit de la bibliothèque d'Isaac-Louis Le Maistre de Sacy (7 avril 1684)* (Paris, 1985), 128.
[19] *La Rhetorique d'Aristote en François* (Paris, 1654), I. v. 42. Cf. *Nicomachean Ethics*, trans. H. Rackman (London, 1982), I. iv, vii–xiii. See H. M. Davidson, *Audience, Words and Art* (Columbus, Oh., 1965), 91.
[20] Cf. 'Notre instinct nous fait sentir qu'il faut chercher notre bonheur [B2] hors de nous' (L143), written on the same sheet as L142 (Ernst, *Album*, 170). See also the commentary on the Stoics: 'Le Souverain Bien. Dispute du Souverain Bien. *Ut sis contentus temetipso et ex te nascentibus bonis* [Seneca]. Il y a contradiction, car ils conseillent enfin de se tuer. Oh! quelle vie heureuse [B1] dont on se délivre comme de

This perception of the multivalence of happiness stems directly from Pascal's Augustinian vision of man. Indeed, in a fragment which was written on the same sheet as L407 and which was directly inspired by the famous opening of Augustine's *Confessions*, we find *bonheur* used in the sense of B3, thus accentuating the contrast between the different levels of *bonheur* about which Pascal was writing concurrently: 'Si l'homme n'est fait pour Dieu pourquoi n'est-il heureux [B3] qu'en Dieu' (L399).[21] *Bonheur/félicité* would be univocal if man were in his original perfection; there would be no such thing as false happiness:

> Car enfin si l'homme n'avait jamais été corrompu il jouirait dans son innocence et de la vérité et de la félicité [B3] avec assurance. Et si l'homme n'avait jamais été que corrompu il n'aurait aucune idée ni de la vérité, ni de la béatitude [B3]. Mais malheureux que nous sommes et plus que s'il n'y avait point de grandeur dans notre condition, nous avons une idée du bonheur [B2] et nous ne pouvons y arriver. (L131)

Man, without a recognition of his state, finds himself longing for happiness but unable to attain it: 'Tous les hommes recherchent d'être heureux [B2],' writes the dialectician, 'Cela est sans exception, quelques différents moyens qu'ils y emploient' (L148):

> Qu'est-ce que donc que nous crie cette avidité et cette impuissance sinon qu'il y a eu autrefois dans l'homme un véritable bonheur [B3], dont il ne lui reste maintenant que la marque et la trace toute vide et qu'il essaye inutilement de remplir de tout ce qui l'environne [. . .].[22]

la peste!' (L147); this fragment constitutes a paraphrase of Jansenius (see Sellier, *Pascal et Saint Augustin*, 83). Sénault, in the Preface to *L'Homme criminel*, stresses that 'ils [*Stoics like Seneca and Zeno*] se vantoient que leur felicité dependoit de leur pouvoir, qu'en despit du Ciel ils pouvoient estre bien-heureux, et que si leur bonheur n'estoit pas aussi long, il estoit aussi tranquille que celuy de Dieu.' Cf. L140, where the dialectician refers to 'les vices de Zénon même'. Sénault also points out the differing conceptions which ancients like Aristotle, Seneca, and Epicurus have of happiness: 'Chascun ne s'est-il pas fait une idée differente de la felicité' (p. 158).

[21] See Ernst, Album, 33. Also written, amongst others, on the same sheet were L400, L404, and L405. I shall discuss L399 again in the section on spiritual happiness.

[22] Cf. L134: 'Nonobstant ces misères il [l'homme] veut être heureux [B2] et ne veut être qu'heureux [B2], et ne peut ne vouloir pas l'être'; also cf. L978: 'il veut être grand, il se voit petit; il veut être heureux [B2], et il se voit misérable'. See also L47. Sellier, in *Pascal et Saint Augustin*, 82–3, fully documents Pascal's debt to Augustine in his discussion of happiness; e.g. Sermon 306: 'Omnis autem homo, qualiscumque sit, beatus vult esse.' In the *Confessions*, x. xx–xxiii, Augustine considers the difficulties of understanding the true nature of happiness. In Arnauld d'Andilly's

It is this notion of man's two natures which lies at the foundation of the desire to be happy, and not other conceptions, such as *honnêteté*. Damien Miton, for example, who, as Pascal claims, 'voit bien que la nature est corrompue' (L642),[23] writes of happiness in very similar terms to L148, but he perceives true happiness as coming from a shared quest for *honnêteté* and not from any spiritual source:

> Tous les hommes veulent estre heureux: ce desir ne nous quitte point pendant tout le cours de la vie. C'est une verité dont tout le monde demeure d'accord.
>
> Mais pour se rendre heureux avec moins de peine, et pour l'estre avec seureté, sans craindre d'estre troublé dans son bon-heur, il faut faire ensorte que les autres le soient avec nous: car si l'on pretend songer seulement à soy, on trouve des oppositions continuelles, et quand nous ne voulons estre heureux, qu'à condition que les autres le soient en mesme temps, tous les obstacles sont levez, et tout le monde nous preste la main. C'est ce ménagement de bon-heur pour nous et pour les autres, que l'on doit appeler l'Honnesteté, qui n'est, à le bien prendre, que l'Amour bien reglé.[24]

Miton's inability to project true happiness any further than his humanity shows precisely why, as Pascal goes on to say in L642, 'il ne sait pas pourquoi ils [les hommes] ne peuvent voler plus haut'. Whereas for Miton happiness can be found amongst men, for Pascal the fact that man wishes to be happy must point back to his original perfect happiness.

Yet the fact that man yearns for happiness is no guarantee of spiritual joy. Often these desires are themselves misdirected, and the happiness for which he longs is no different from the false perception which *divertissements* engender:

> La nature nous rendant toujours malheureux en tous états nos désirs nous figurent un état heureux [B1] parce qu'ils joignent à l'état où nous sommes les plaisirs de l'état où nous ne sommes pas et quand nous arriverions à ces

---

translation (Paris, 1659), 'au lieu, qu'encore que nous sachions ce que c'est que la félicité, et que la connoissance que nous en avons nous la fasse aimer, nous ne laissons pas de désirer de l'acquérir, afin d'être heureux' (ch. xxi).

[23] See also L597 and L853, where Miton is named directly.
[24] 'Pensées sur l'honnesteté', in C. de Saint-Evremond, *Œuvres meslées* (Paris, 1680), vi. 1–3. See L. Thirouin, *Le Hasard et les règles: Le Modèle du jeu dans la pensée de Pascal* (Paris, 1991), 90, where a section of this passage is described as 'cette conception réaliste et brutale de l'*honnêteté*'.

plaisirs nous ne serions pas heureux [B1] pour cela parce que nous aurions d'autres désirs conformes à ce nouvel état. (L639)

According to Pascal, true spiritual happiness only comes to those who have found God and who continue to serve him. Those who search for him may possess the potential for happiness [B2], but they are still essentially 'malheureux', as he makes clear in L160:

> Il n'y a que trois sortes de personnes: les uns qui servent Dieu l'ayant trouvé, les autres qui s'emploient à le chercher ne l'ayant pas trouvé, les autres qui vivent sans le chercher ni l'avoir trouvé. Les premiers sont raisonnables et heureux [B3], les derniers sont fous et malheureux. Ceux du milieu sont malheureux et raisonnables. (L160)[25]

SPIRITUAL HAPPINESS

Consequently, man's only hope of true happiness is to understand that joy which is found in God:

> Il faut que pour rendre l'homme heureux [B3] elle [la religion] lui montre qu'il y a un Dieu, qu'on est obligé de l'aimer, que notre vraie félicité [B3] est d'être en lui, et notre unique mal d'être séparé de lui [. . .]. (L149)

Indeed, such happiness was clearly intended to play an integral role in the completed work which Pascal envisaged:

1. Partie. Misère de l'homme sans Dieu.
2. Partie. Félicité [B3] de l'homme avec Dieu. (L6)

Furthermore, the attainment of this spiritual happiness would seem to give man added perceptions. As Richard Parish puts it,

> Man aspires to *bonheur* and may believe he possesses it, in his own terms. But when he truly does possess it (in God's terms), it is entirely different from what he imagined it would be [. . .].[26]

This is precisely the point made in *Prière pour demander à Dieu le bon usage des maladies*, which imitates the style of the Beatitudes in

---

[25] The way in which Pascal continually differentiates between various categories is highlighted by a fragment which appeared on the same sheet as L160 (Ernst, *Album*, 35), L562: 'il n'y a que deux sortes d'hommes, les uns justes qui se croient pécheurs, les autres pécheurs qui se croient justes'.

[26] *Pascal's 'Lettres Provinciales': A Study in Polemic* (Oxford, 1989), 109. Cf. Sellier, *Pascal et Saint Augustin*, who sees Pascal's treatment of happiness as profoundly Augustinian: 'la béatitude augustinienne est inséparable de la connaissance de la vérité totale' (p. 81).

Matt. 5 and Luke 6. The speaker, addressing God, acknowledges that his perception of happiness was very different from what he now sees God's intention to be; the contrast between God's eternal present and the speaker's past corruption is underlined by the use of present and past tenses:

> Vous dites: 'Bienheureux sont ceux qui pleurent, et malheur à ceux qui sont consolés'. Et moi j'ai dit: 'Malheureux ceux qui gémissent, et très heureux ceux qui sont consolés'. J'ai dit: 'Heureux ceux qui jouissent d'une fortune avantageuse, d'une réputation glorieuse et d'une santé robuste'. Et pourquoi les ai-je réputés heureux, sinon parce que tous ces avantages leur fournissaient une facilité très ample de jouir des créatures, c'est-à-dire de vous offenser?[27]

However, the dialectician still makes deliberate use of the secular and transcendent connotations of the term, not only to show to the true believer the reality of his happiness in God but also to make this happiness attractive and understandable to the non-believer. In L357, for example, he writes,

> Nul n'est heureux [B1 and B3] comme un vrai chrétien, ni raisonnable, ni vertueux, ni aimable.

In order to meet the non-believer on his own terms, the dialectician must use a vocabulary which will be discernible on an immanent level. Thus, although the adjectives *heureux*, *raisonnable*, *vertueux*, and *aimable* appear primarily on a transcendent level in L357, they can also be perceived to be attractive on all levels. This strategy is made clear in a fragment headed by the word *Ordre*, L12, where reason is evoked, together with the adjectives *vénérable* and *aimable*:

> Les hommes ont mépris pour la religion. Ils en ont haine et peur qu'elle soit vraie. Pour guérir cela il faut commencer par montrer que la religion n'est point contraire à la raison. Vénérable, en donner respect.
> La rendre ensuite aimable, faire souhaiter aux bons qu'elle fût vraie et puis montrer qu'elle est vraie.
> Vénérable parce qu'elle a bien connu l'homme.
> Aimable parce qu'elle promet le vrai bien.[28]

---

[27] Seuil 364. Cf. 'faites-moi la grâce, Seigneur, de réformer ma raison corrompue, et de conformer mes sentiments aux vôtres. Que je m'estime heureux dans l'affliction, et que, dans l'impuissance d'agir au-dehors, vous purifiez tellement mes sentiments qu'ils ne répugnent plus aux vôtres' (p. 364).

[28] Cf. *Lettres provinciales*, 11th letter, p. 419, and Parish's commentary in *Pascal's 'Lettres Provinciales'*, 84.

As we find in another fragment, 'Il n'y a que la religion chrétienne qui rende l'homme aimable et heureux [B3] tout ensemble' (L426). Happiness is translated to a transcendent level by the acceptance of Christianity, for it is through Christ that virtue and true felicity can be restored:

> Sans J.-C. il faut que l'homme soit dans le vice et dans la misère. Avec J.-C. l'homme est exempt de vice et de misère.
> En lui est toute notre vertu et toute notre félicité [B3].
> Hors de lui il n'y a que vice, misère, erreur, ténèbres, mort, désespoir. (L416)

It is precisely this level of eternal *bonheur* which is at stake in the Wager fragment (L418). The dialectician uses language which can be taken on a human level in order to communicate the necessity of spiritual salvation. Where 'béatitude' [B3] is concerned, the reader is urged to wager on God's existence and so on 'une éternité de vie et de bonheur' [B3], for there is the chance of 'une infinité de vie infiniment heureuse [B3] à gagner'.

There remains one further stage of awareness of spiritual *bonheur*, and that is within the context of the Church. Man's happiness proves his difference from inanimate objects, which cannot feel such joy. Yet, by keeping this happiness to himself, man cannot grow; he must be able to impart it to others. Pascal makes use of the Pauline image of the mystical body of Christ to show that individual happiness cannot be whole without its incorporation into a fully conscious unity:

> Dieu ayant fait le ciel et la terre qui ne sentent point le bonheur [B3] de leur être, il a voulu faire des êtres qui le connussent et qui composassent un corps de membres pensants. Car nos membres ne sentent point le bonheur [B3] de leur union, de leur admirable intelligence, du soin que la nature a d'y influer les esprits et de les faire croître et durer. Qu'ils seraient heureux [B3] s'ils le sentaient, s'ils le voyaient, mais il faudrait pour cela qu'ils eussent intelligence pour le connaître, et bonne volonté pour consentir à celle de l'âme universelle. Que si ayant reçu l'intelligence ils s'en servaient à retenir en eux-mêmes la nourriture, sans la laisser passer aux autres membres, ils seraient non seulement injustes mais encore misérables, et se haïraient plutôt que de s'aimer, leur béatitude [B3] aussi bien que leur devoir consistant à consentir à la conduite de l'âme entièr[e] à qui ils appartiennent, qui les aime mieux qu'ils ne s'aiment eux-mêmes. (L360)

Even at this stage of his argument, the dialectician plays with the different meanings of *bonheur*. Although all instances of the word

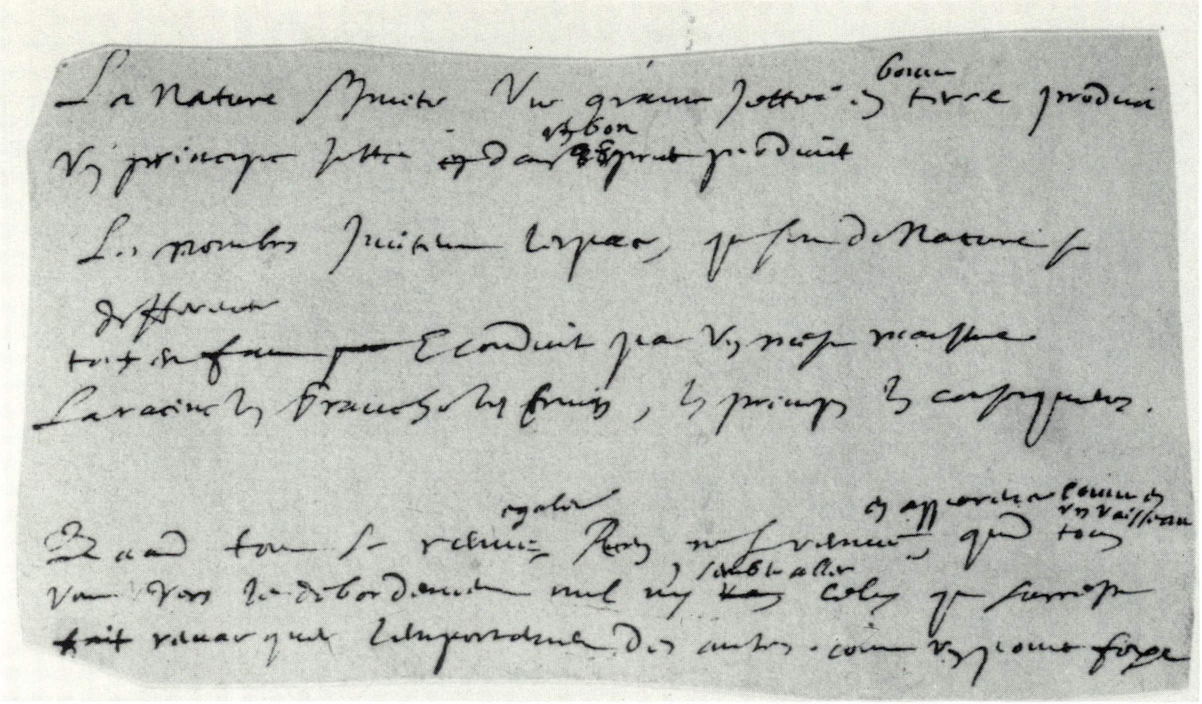

Fig. 4. L698

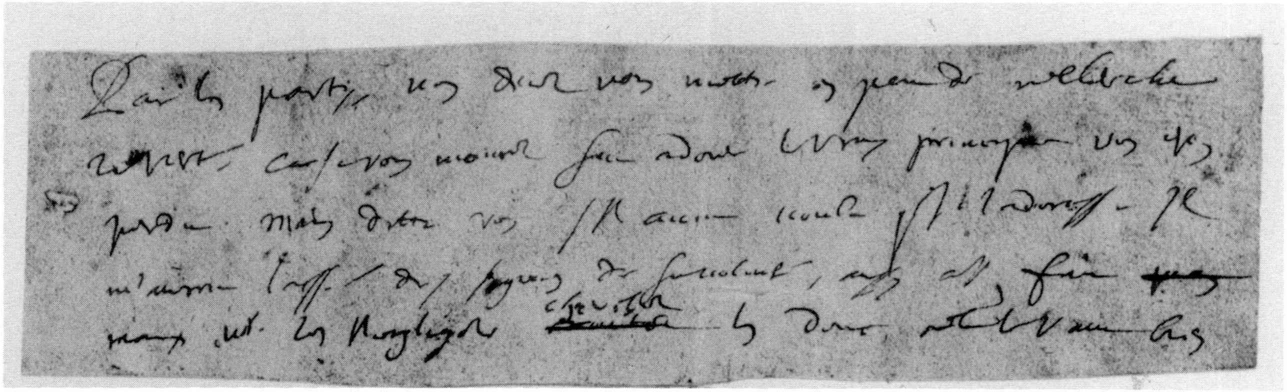

FIG. 3. L158

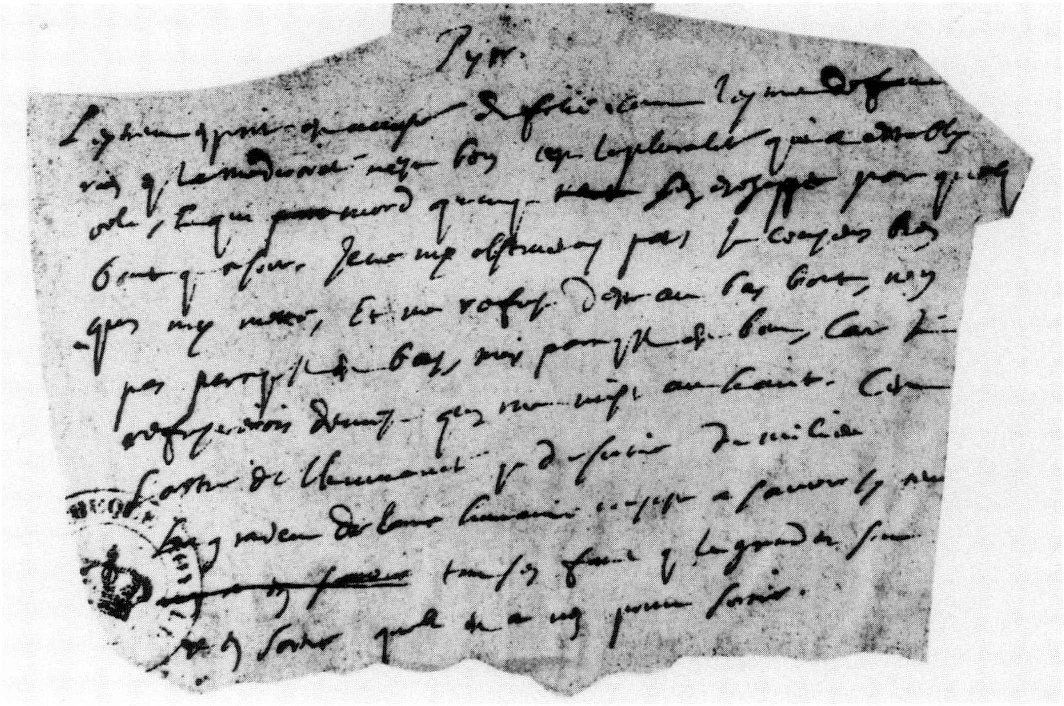

FIG. 2. L518

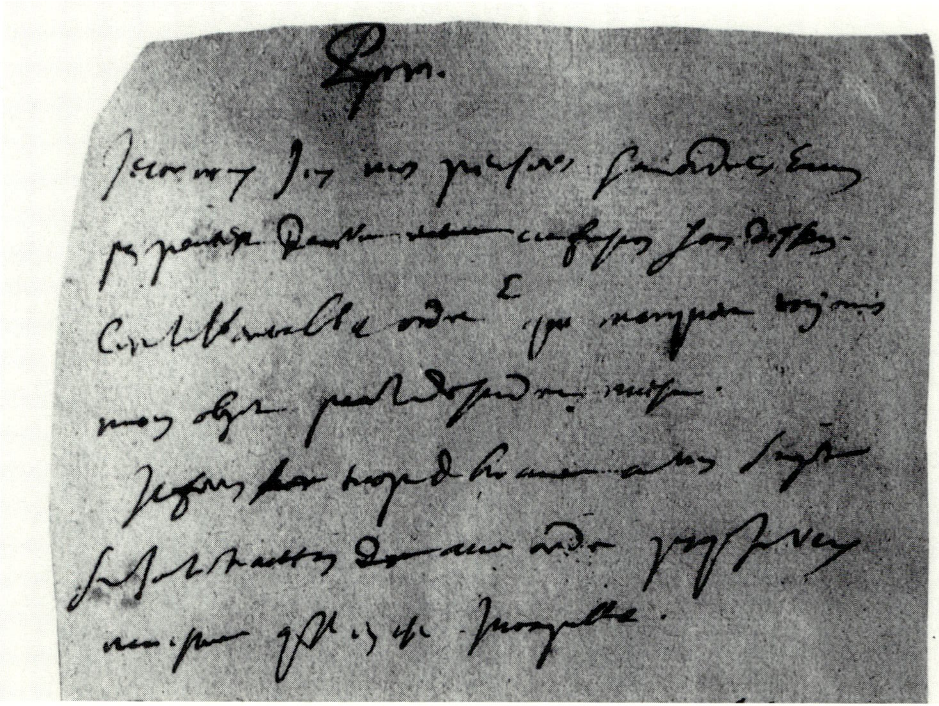

FIG. 1. L532

in the above fragment refer through imagery to eternal happiness, as I have indicated, we find by implication the absurdity of false kinds of *bonheur*. Insentient beings cannot grasp the concept of true happiness. Man needs 'intelligence' and 'bonne volonté' in order to appreciate it. Those who have misdirected their search for happiness are as uncomprehending and alone as those without senses.

Happiness, then, retains its complexity at all levels. Man cannot help but search for happiness, and yet, because of his fallen state, he cannot assume that he will find it. This seeming paradox is mirrored in a fragment which I have mentioned already and which poses two apparently contradictory questions:

> Si l'homme n'est fait pour Dieu pourquoi n'est-il heureux [B3] qu'en Dieu.
> Si l'homme est fait pour Dieu pourquoi est-il si contraire à Dieu. (L399)

Even after the attainment of spiritual happiness, man must be continually wary. Perhaps a concluding section from *Sur la conversion du pécheur* effectively sums up this need:

> Elle [l'âme] se résout de conformer à ses volontés [de Dieu] le reste de sa vie; mais comme sa faiblesse naturelle, avec l'habitude qu'elle a aux péchés où elle a vécu, l'ont réduite dans l'impuissance d'arriver à cette félicité [B3], elle implore de sa miséricorde les moyens d'arriver à lui, de s'attacher à lui, d'y adhérer éternellement...[29]

True happiness in man can only be attained through a knowledge of his fallen state: as Sénault puts it, 'la source de nostre misere estant celle de nostre bonheur'.[30]

Key to *Bonheur/Félicité*

B1 *bonheur*: spurious happiness
B2 *bonheur*: pursued happiness
B3 *bonheur*: spiritual happiness

---

[29] Seuil 291.   [30] *L'Homme criminel*, opening 'Epistre'.

8
Justice

> Les idées que nous avons de ce qui est juste ou injuste, sont étrangement bornées, puisqu'enfin il ne s'agit entre nous que d'une justice d'homme à homme [...].
>
> (Filleau de la Chaise)[1]

The complexities of the vernacular use of *Justice* can be seen in the thirteen pages of the 1757 edition of the *Encyclopédie* devoted to the term. The three major dictionaries of the seventeenth century may all concur in their initial definition of *justice*, as 'vertu morale' or 'volonté ferme', 'qui rend à chacun ce qui luy appartient';[2] but allied to this meaning, which concerns the common rights of man, we find a profusion of other senses. Not all of these are pertinent to this study, although it is worthwhile pointing to some distinctions which are widely referred to: both the Académie and Furetière dictionaries, taking Aristotle's *Nicomachean Ethics* as their source, divide this form of justice into two sorts, 'commutative' and 'distributive'.[3] Both kinds of justice are placed on a specifically human level, and a distinction is made between that justice which is natural and that which is necessary to curb those people who contravene natural laws.[4] Both the Académie and Furetière

---

[1] *Discours sur les 'Pensées' de M. Pascal* (Paris, 1672), 46.

[2] This definition can be linked to that in Justinian's *Digest*, 1. 1. 10: 'iustitia est constans et perpetua voluntas ius suum cuique tribuendi' (Justice is a steady and enduring will to render unto everyone his right).

[3] Furetière, who gives a fuller definition of the 2 terms, misinterprets them. More accurate is the definition offered by the *Encyclopédie* (D. Diderot and J. D'Alembert, *L'Encyclopédie ou Dictionnaire raisonnée des sciences, des arts et des métiers*, New York, 1969, facsimile of the 1757 Paris edn.): 'Justice Commutative est cette vertu et cette partie de l'administration de la justice, qui a pour objet de rendre à chacun ce qui lui appartient dans une proportion arithmétique. [...] Justice Distributive signifie quelquefois cette vertu dont l'objet est de distribuer à chacun selon ses mérites, les graces et les peines, en y observant la proportion geometrique' (vii. 94). See *Nicomachean Ethics*, trans. H. Rackman (London, 1982), v. i–v.

[4] Cf. Aristotle, *La Rhetorique d'Aristote en françois*, trans. F. Cassandre (Paris, 1654), I. xiii: 'il y a deux sortes de Loix, les unes Particulieres, les autres Communes. J'appelle Loix Particulieres celles qui servent de regle dans un Estat, et que châque

dictionaries then go beyond a definition of human justice to identify a spiritual justice which they term 'la justice originelle', elaborated by the Académie as 'Cette rectitude interieure causée par la grace de Dieu'.

The definition of these different types of justice offered by the dictionaries will act as an outline to the different categories into which it is convenient to divide the different usages of the word *justice* in the *Pensées*. As with my analysis of all other terms, I shall apply symbols to designate the different forms of justice, but, as we shall see, there are different levels to be found within each category. The distinction between the different kinds of justice is based on terms as they are used by Pascal (see Fig. 5). In my analysis of this hierarchy in uses of the word *justice* in the *Pensées*, I intend first to deal briefly with *injustice* before considering natural justice and established justice (J1), then to move to an examination of *les justes* (J2), and finally to discuss the different forms of divine justice (J3) (see the Key at the end of this chapter).[5]

la justice divine (= justness + retribution) (J3)
|
la justice éternelle/véritable/essentielle/originelle
|
la justice/les justes (= righteousness) (J2)
|
la justice humaine (J1)
| |
la justice naturelle (J1a)   *la justice politique* (J1b)
|
injustice

FIG. 5

peuple s'impose à lui-même; [. . .] J'appelle Loix Communes celles que la lumiere naturelle nous découvre, et qu'il semble que la Nature même nous ait dictées' (p. 157).

[5] R. Taveneaux, in *Jansénisme et politique* (Paris, 1965), 65, follows J. Chevalier, in his edn. of Pascal's *Œuvres complètes* (Paris, 1954), 1504, in establishing 3 main meanings of *justice* used by Pascal: 'A. La vertu surnaturelle élevant les hommes au rang de fils adoptifs de Dieu; B. La vertu qui nous porte à rendre aux autres ce qui leur est dû; C. Le pouvoir divin d'ordre et de répression.' As I hope to show, further distinctions need to be made, especially concerning human justice (meaning B). See also Chevalier's *Pascal* (Paris, 1922), 352–6.

INJUSTICE

Perhaps the most significant point about *injustice* is that it is used exclusively as an implicit or explicit contrast to either human or spiritual justice. As I suggested in Fig. 5 *injustice* is linked directly to human justice and not to spiritual justice. Even though the polemicist in the *Lettres provinciales* evokes the injustices of the Jesuits, they are unjust not in a spiritual sense but in their very fallibility as human beings; this view is made forcefully in the fourteenth letter, which concerns homicide, where God, 'étant la justice et la sagesse même [...] est aussi incapable d'injustice que d'erreur'.[6] Similarly, in the *Pensées*, the dialectician accentuates the chasm which lies between the purity of Christianity and the injustice of men:

Avant que d'entrer dans les preuves de la religion chrétienne, je trouve nécessaire de représenter l'injustice des hommes qui vivent dans l'indifférence de chercher la vérité d'une chose qui leur est si importante, et qui les touche de si près. (L428)

Furthermore, true Christians are perceived as people who 'espèrent la sainteté, l'exemption de l'injustice' (L917).[7]

The reference to 'la lettre de l'injustice' in L9 suggests that injustice as a term might have played a more central role in the finished work; but, as most of the points raised in L9 are amply developed in L60, it is more likely that injustice would be used as a counterfoil to the analysis of legal and political justice.[8] Elsewhere, *injustice* is shown to be closely related to man's *concupiscences* and self-love: 'ainsi nos devoirs nous obligeant d'aimer Dieu et nos concupiscences nous en détournant nous sommes pleins d'injustice' (L149).[9]

Because of the complexities inherent in the term *justice*, as we shall see, *injustice* by contrast lacks the tension which distinguishes

---

[6] Seuil 436. Cf. L885: 'Il est bon qu'ils fassent des injustices, de peur qu'il ne paraisse que les molinistes ont agi avec justice, et ainsi il ne les faut pas épargner. Ils sont dignes d'en commettre.'

[7] Cf. C. Jansenius, *Traduction d'un discours de la reformation de l'homme interieur* (Paris, 1659), 74: 'Je sçay bien qu'il n'y a non plus d'injustice que d'impuissance en Dieu.'

[8] Cf. L66, L67, L85, where the term *injustice* appears in conjunction with matters of legal and political justice.   [9] Cf. L410, L595, L597, L617.

other 'negative' terms such as *ennui*, *inquiétude*, and *inconstance*. Where it is not placed in direct opposition to *justice*, it is coupled with other terms, such as *bassesse* (L410), *ambition*, *concupiscence*, *faiblesse*, and *misère* (L595).[10]

HUMAN JUSTICE (J1)

The relative simplicity of *injustice* in the *Pensées* can be attributed partly to the intricacy of Pascal's treatment of human justice. Injustice is unambiguous in that it can only be associated with the innate corruption of man. Human justice, on the other hand, shows itself to be divided between man's fallen state, which inevitably provokes false justice, and an intrinsic rightness, which would seem to point to that 'instinct secret qui reste de la grandeur de notre première nature', as the dialectician describes it in L136.

As we have seen, the contemporary dictionaries distinguish between two sorts of human justice, that which is natural and that which is established to counter offenders of natural justice. Pascal makes a similar distinction between what I shall call natural justice (J1*a*) and established (or political) justice (J1*b*). It is in the second of his *Trois discours sur la condition des grands* that he defines most clearly natural and established greatness, both of which contain an inner justice:

> Il y a dans le monde deux sortes de grandeurs; car il y a des grandeurs d'établissement et des grandeurs naturelles. Les grandeurs d'établissement dépendent de la volonté des hommes, qui ont cru avec raison devoir honorer certains états et y attacher certains respects. Les dignités et la noblesse sont de ce genre. En un pays on honore les nobles, en l'autre les roturiers, en celui-ci les aînés, en cet autre les cadets. Pourquoi cela? Parce qu'il a plu aux hommes. La chose était indifférente avant l'établissement: après l'établissement elle devient juste, parce qu'il est injuste de la troubler.
>
> Les grandeurs naturelles sont celles qui sont indépendantes de la fantaisie des hommes, parce qu'elles consistent dans des qualités réelles et effectives de l'âme ou du corps, qui rendent l'une ou l'autre plus estimable, comme les sciences, la lumière de l'esprit, la vertu, la santé, la force.[11]

The inclusion of *la force* as one of 'les grandeurs naturelles' puts it into direct opposition with established justice, and this is clearly a

---

[10] See also L847, where the word *injustice* is used ironically to indicate the corruption of magistrates.   [11] Seuil 367.

central preoccupation in the *Pensées*, as we shall see.[12] Gérard Ferreyrolles, in a reference to the above passage, states that 'la justice ici est de proportionner les devoirs aux qualités',[13] qualities which can be seen in their most positive light. Only 'des respects de l'établissement' should be accorded to 'les grandeurs de l'établissement', just as only 'les respects naturels' should be granted to 'les grandeurs naturelles'.[14] The word *justice* is central to this second *Discours*, and both kinds of justice, as separate from each other as they may be, are viewed on a human level: the 'grandeurs d'établissement', for example, demand 'une reconnaissance intérieure de la justice (J1b) de cet ordre', the *ordre* being that human order which is the establishment. As Pascal reiterates, 'Voilà en quoi consiste la justice [J1b] de ces devoirs. Et l'injustice consiste à attacher les respects naturels aux grandeurs d'établissement, ou à exiger les respects d'établissement pour les grandeurs naturelles'.[15] Aspects of the natural order, such as geometry (an example which Pascal uses in this *Discours*), contain a natural justice or truth, and cannot be tainted by human imagination ('la fantaisie des hommes') as can 'les grandeurs d'établissement'. But they cannot be seen as on the same level as those 'vérités divines' which are 'au-dessus de la nature', and which God alone can 'mettre dans l'âme', as he puts it in *De l'esprit géométrique*.[16]

Before I consider natural justice, a brief overview of various critical approaches to human justice in the *Pensées* would be useful as a starting-point. Generally, Pascal's view of human justice is perceived as entirely negative. Lucien Goldmann, for example, writes that, 'Pour Pascal, à l'époque des *Pensées*, il n'y a pas de loi humaine juste et valable.'[17] Similarly, René Taveneaux asserts: 'Aucune loi humaine ne peut être tenue pour juste ou pour raisonnable.'[18] This is reiterated by Thomas Harrington, who states that 'la vraie justice [...] est perdue à jamais par la chute originelle', adding that, except for perfect Christians, 'c'est à l'état d'idéal inaccessible pour tous'.[19] Most of these opinions are derived

---

[12] The terms *force* and *justice* are juxtaposed in the following fragments: L81, L85, L86, L103.   [13] *Pascal et la raison du politique* (Paris, 1984), 159.
[14] Seuil 367.
[15] Ibid. 367. See also Ferreyrolles, *Pascal et la raison du politique*, 159–60.
[16] Seuil 355.
[17] *Le Dieu caché: Étude sur la vision tragique dans les 'Pensées' de Pascal et dans le théâtre de Racine* (Paris, 1955), 304.   [18] *Jansénisme et politique*, 22.
[19] *Vérité et Méthode dans les 'Pensées' de Pascal* (Paris, 1972), 44.

from a reading of L60, which itself is directly inspired by Montaigne's *Apologie de Raimond Sebond* and which I shall discuss shortly. Philippe Sellier, on the other hand, questions 'le scepticisme moral des *Pensées*' and makes a comparison with St Augustine's writings, concluding that both Pascal and Augustine affirm a positive aspect of human justice, through 'l'existence de lois naturelles'. As Sellier stresses, 'l'homme n'est pas assez corrompu pour être incapable de percevoir où est la vraie morale quand on la lui montre'.[20] However, in a more recent article, Sellier adds that for Pascal, in the tradition of the *De Civitate Dei*, 'seule la foi est accès à la connaissance de la vraie justice (*justitia*): privés de cette connaissance, les groupes humains ne possèdent que *des sortes de droits*'.[21] Gérard Ferreyrolles accentuates even further the acceptance of natural justice in Catholic tradition. Fragments such as L60 should not, he proposes, be viewed individually, but rather should be seen as forming part of 'une stratégie d'ensemble hors de laquelle leur signification et leur portée ne peuvent être correctement appréciées'.[22] He discerns Pascal's attitude towards human justice in a much more optimiste light, and finally asserts man's '*participation* à la justice divine qui est la définition même de la loi naturelle'.[23] Most recently, Laurent Thirouin has reacted strongly against what he terms 'la seule dimension contestable' of Ferreyrolles's book, which is 'son obstination à réconcilier la pensée politique avec la notion de loi naturelle'.[24] Thirouin points out instead that 'la vraie nature des lois est ludique',[25] and that 'les lois politiques, en se substituant à la loi naturelle irrémédiablement perdue, transforment l'espace social en espace de jeu'.[26] I shall return to some of these critical views during the course of this chapter.

NATURAL JUSTICE (J1*a*)

Before I discuss the place of natural justice in the *Pensées*, it is necessary to recognize the difficulties which are associated with the

---

[20] *Pascal et Saint Augustin* (Paris, 1970), 103.
[21] 'Vous êtes embarqués ...: Où prendrons-nous un port dans la morale?', *Papers on French Seventeenth-Century Literature*, 14–15 (1981), 19.
[22] *Pascal et la raison du politique*, 183.   [23] Ibid. 185–6.
[24] *Le Hasard et les règles: Le Modèle du jeu dans la pensée de Pascal* (Paris, 1991), 58.   [25] Ibid. 49.   [26] Ibid. 60.

noun *nature* and adjective *naturel*. As Pierre Magnard emphasizes,

Quand le dix-septième siècle parle de nature, ce sont moins des assonances qu'une telle idée évoque, que des oppositions ou plus exactement des différences: nature-condition, nature-établissement, nature-coutume, nature-art, nature-naturel, nature-prud'homie, nature-loi, nature-grâce, nature-miracle, nature-surnaturel. Ce jeu diacritique donne toute sa valeur différentielle à une notion qui s'enrichit et se précise de ces multiples différenciations.[27]

These complexities are evident in the *Pensées* and are indeed compounded by the Augustinian doctrine of two natures, 'deux états dans la nature humaine', as defined in the *Écrits sur la Grâce*.[28] Man retains an instinct of his first nature, but that is corrupted by his fallen nature: 'La concupiscence nous est devenue naturelle et a fait notre seconde nature. Ainsi il y a deux natures en nous, l'une bonne, l'autre mauvaise' (L616). Thus, when we consider 'la justice naturelle', it is always necessary to question whether that justice comes from a perception of our pure nature or from our corrupt state.[29]

For the purpose of this discussion, I have chosen to incorporate various categories within the single heading 'natural justice', but it is worth pointing out the distinctions which can be made. On one level, there exists *iustitia naturalis* (or *ratio naturalis*), which is the conscience of natural justice. On another level, we find *ius naturale* (natural law) and *leges naturales* (instances of the former), which I will understand as meaning the application of natural justice.

L60, which represents a very close reworking of passages from Montaigne's *Apologie de Raimond Sebond*,[30] has generally been

---

[27] *Nature et histoire dans l'Apologétique* (Paris, 1975), 400.
[28] Seuil 312.
[29] I have deliberately chosen not to go into the topic of 'nature' in any great depth, as it is too complex to analyse completely in this chapter, and it has been discussed thoroughly by many commentators. See Magnard's book, cited above. Also, for *nature* and *coutume*, see ch. 3 of H. Davidson, *The Origins of Certainty: Means and Meanings in Pascal's Pensées* (Chicago, 1979), and B. Norman, *Portraits of Thought: Knowledge, Methods, and Styles in Pascal* (Columbus, Oh., 1988), 30–7. For an interpretation of the positive side of nature, see G. Ferreyrolles, 'Pascal et la rédemption de la nature', in *Méthodes chez Pascal*, 285–95.
[30] See Montaigne's *Essais* (in *Œuvres complètes*, ed. M. Rat, Paris, 1962), II. xii. esp. 562–5.

accepted as indicative of Pascal's rejection of natural justice in the *Pensées*. René Taveneaux, for example, before citing L60, calls Pascal 'tributaire du scepticisme de Montaigne', and states, using the term 'droit naturel' (*ius naturale*), 'Admise, au moins implicitement, par *Les Provinciales*, l'existence d'un droit naturel accessible à la raison et contestée par les *Pensées*'.[31] Similarly, Erich Auerbach asserts that 'Pascal n'a rien de commun avec la théorie du droit naturel'.[32] Ferreyrolles counters this interpretation. In addition to his plea to consider fragments such as L60 within a wider strategy, it seems clear that, although the shortcomings of human political justice are set down in L60, the existence of natural laws (*leges naturales*) is not thrown into doubt. Thus, although the instability and inconstancy of human justice are exposed, and indeed made fun of,[33] the fact that men accept the existence of common natural laws and yet do not share any common *political* justice ('les lois universelles') highlights the paradoxes of the human condition:

> Ils confessent que la justice [J1a] n'est pas dans ces coutumes, mais qu'elle réside dans les lois naturelles communes en tout pays. Certainement ils le soutiendraient opiniâtrement si la témérité du hasard qui a semé les lois humaines en avait rencontré au moins une qui fût universelle. Mais la plaisanterie est telle que le caprice des hommes s'est si bien diversifié qu'il n'y en a point. (L60)

Indeed, later in the same fragment, we find the assertion, 'Il y a sans doute des lois naturelles, mais cette belle raison corrompue a tout corrompu.' It is significant that, instead of 'cette belle raison corrompue', Pascal originally wrote 'cette belle raison dogmatique', for he was clearly thinking of the opposition of the Sceptics to the arrogance of the dogmatists. Although such reasoning has corrupted

---

[31] *Jansénisme et politique*, 60.
[32] 'La Théorie politique de Pascal', in A. Lanavère (ed.), *Pascal* (Paris, 1969), 143. See also J. S. Spink, *French Free-Thought from Gassendi to Voltaire* (London, 1960), 71–3.
[33] See L. Thirouin, 'Conservatisme et dérision: L'Analyse pascalienne des lois', *Cahiers de littérature du XVII*ᵉ *siècle* (1987), 112–19, who points out the reiteration of the words *plaisant* and *plaisanterie* in fragments like L60 and L9 and stresses 'une jubilation devant la force comique des lois' (p. 113). With a fragment like L60, Thirouin argues, 'l'effet immédiat est le rire: les lois humaines, qui prétendent recevoir leur autorité de la nature même de l'homme, sont dénoncées par leur instabilité comme des fruits du hasard' (p. 114). See also Thirouin, *Le Hasard et les règles*, 44. I would argue that such instability is indeed mocked but that the existence of natural justice is not denied completely.

everything, the existence of natural laws is not doubted. People like the dogmatists may have corrupted all interpretation of human justice, but that does not negate the existence of certain natural laws. If we compare this section with the passage from Montaigne which inspired it, a subtle but important distinction can be made. Where Montaigne writes, 'Il est *croyable* qu'il y a des loix naturelles',[34] Pascal asserts, 'Il y a *sans doute* [= sans aucun doute] des lois naturelles' (L60).[35] Moreover, where Montaigne does not differentiate greatly in this passage between different kinds of justice, a close study of the *Recueil original* shows that in L60 Pascal was at pains to make a clear distinction between human political justice (J1*b*), natural justice (J1*a*), and *la véritable justice* (J3). In the first paragraph, for example, the words *la véritable justice* are deleted twice and *l'essentielle justice* once. Clearly he was reserving the adjectives *véritable* and *essentielle* for a higher spiritual justice (J3), and found that he could not apply them to human political justice (J1). In fact, he solves the problem here by replacing *justice* with *équité* ('l'éclat de la véritable équité aurait assujetti tous les peuples'), a word which is closely associated with *human* justice.[36] As the Richelet dictionary defines *équité*, it is '[une] sorte de justice qui consiste à reparer les defauts des loix'. *La véritable équité* would mean here, then, a common interpretation of human justice. *Cette justice constante* in the next sentence would therefore be a reference to that fictitious state of universal political justice. *Justice* is used in the first paragraph primarily to denote *political* justice and as a contrast to natural justice (*les lois naturelles*) in the succeeding paragraphs:

[34] *Essais*, II, xii. 564. My italics.
[35] The use of *sans doute* to designate a certainty was commonplace in the 17th c. See Ferreyrolles, *Pascal et la raison du politique*, 167.
[36] Cf. L978, where *équité* and *justice* are clearly interrelated but also distinct from each other: 'Voilà les sentiments qui naîtraient d'un cœur qui serait plein d'équité et de justice.' Cf. Aristotle's distinction in Cassandre's translation of the *Rhetoric*, I. xiii. 163: '*l'Équité au reste n'est autre chose qu'une certaine raison de Justice qui supplée au defaut de la Loy écrite, parce que cette loy n'en fait aucune mention*'. Cf. also in the 1553 translation of the *Nicomachean Ethics*, v. x: 'l'équité, qui est meilleure que quelque droict, est droict aussi: et n'est, comme estant quelque autre genre, meilleur que le droict. Le droict donques, et l'equité sont une mesme chose: car bien qu'ils soyent tous deux bons, de beaucoup meilleure toutesfois est l'equité' (pp. 90–1). For a full account of the complexities of the term 'equity' in the Renaissance, see I. Maclean, *Interpretation and Meaning in the Renaissance: The Case of Law* (Cambridge, 1992), 175–8.

Sur quoi fondera[-t-]il l'économie du monde qu'il veut gouverner? Sera-ce sur le caprice de chaque particulier? Quelle confusion! sera-ce sur la justice [J1b]? il l'ignore. Certainement s'il la connaissait il n'aurait pas établi cette maxime, la plus générale de toutes celles qui sont parmi les hommes, que chacun suive les mœurs de son pays. L'éclat de la véritable équité aurait assujetti tous les peuples. Et les législateurs n'auraient pas pris pour modèle, au lieu de cette justice constante [J1], les fantaisies et les caprices des perses et allemands. On la verrait plantée par tous les états du monde, et dans tous les temps, au lieu qu'on ne voit rien de juste ou d'injuste qui ne change de qualité en changeant de climat, trois degrés d'élévation du pôle renversent toute la jurisprudence, un méridien décide de la vérité. En peu d'années de possession les lois fondamentales changent, le droit a ses époques, l'entrée de Saturne au Lion nous marque l'origine d'un tel crime. Plaisante justice [J1b] qu'une rivière borne. Vérité au-deçà des Pyrénées, erreur au-delà. (L60)

It is significant that the paradoxes inherent in the different kinds of justice are reinforced by the use of tenses in this paragraph and indeed elsewhere in L60. Whereas absolute values (such as 'l'éclat de la véritable équité') are immediately diminished by their association with the subjunctive or conditional, relative values are accompanied by the present indicative.

Thus it would clearly be wrong to assume, from the dominant scepticism of L60, that Pascal rejected all notions of natural justice. Certainly he would have been aware of the Catholic tradition's, and indeed his fellow Jansenists', acceptance of natural laws. Jansenius himself wrote of the existence of natural laws, in conjunction with divine providence, showing how even within corruption signs of natural law can be found:

C'est un ordre de la nature et de la providence divine, que tout ce qui est sujet à leurs loix, et renfermé dans leurs bornes, retourne à son origine par un mouvement perpetuel. De là vient que tout ce qui naist de la terre, se va rejoindre à la terre d'où il a esté tiré; que tous les fleuves rentrent dans la mer d'où ils sont sortis; et que tout ce qui est composé des élemens se resout en ces mesmes élemens. Et cet ordre est estably par une loy si immuable et si universelle, que l'on en void mesme quelques marques et quelques traits en la corruption des choses, dans laquelle elles perdent leurs premieres qualitez, et sortent de leur estat naturel.[37]

Jansenius' friend, Jean Duvergier de Hauranne, the future abbé de Saint-Cyran, also attests to the presence of natural laws, such as (in

[37] *Traduction d'un discours de la reformation de l'homme interieur*, 3–4.

this case) the rights of men of the church to defend themselves with arms:

> Car si les essences des creatures sont immuables, par ce qu'elles ne sont autre chose que les éternelles idées de la nature de Dieu qui contient et represente necessairement toutes les choses qui peuvent estre produites; il faut que cette loy naturelle de se deffendre par les armes et par toute autre sorte de moyens, qui est comme le premier rayon et la premiere idée naissante de l'esprit de l'homme, soit aussi necessaire et immuable que ceste mesme nature raisonnable et c'est [sic] esprit dont elle derive, qui est veritablement comme une loy, pour le dire ainsi, en l'esprit de Dieu.[38]

Pascal himself makes a strong affirmation of natural justice in the *Lettres provinciales*, especially letter 14, where the polemicist condemns the Jesuits' acceptance of homicide in certain circumstances:

> je serai obligé d'employer la plus grande partie de cette lettre à la réfutation de vos maximes, pour vous représenter combien vous êtes éloignés des sentiments de l'Église et même de la nature. Les permissions de tuer que vous accordez en tant de rencontres, font paraître qu'en cette matière vous avez tellement oublié la loi de Dieu, et tellement éteint les lumières naturelles, que vous avez besoin qu'on vous remette dans les principes les plus simples de la religion et du sens commun.[39]

We need now to examine the extent to which natural justice is God-given, as the quotation above from the *Lettres provinciales* undoubtedly implies. In L520, to which I shall return in the section on divine justice, the dialectician asserts the existence of a certain justice, 'selon que Dieu nous l'a voulu révéler'. This justice must be distinguished from human nature which 'n'était qu'un continuel changement', for it is inspired by God, but it would seem to be different from *la véritable justice* (J3), actual divine justice. If human nature is so corrupt, can we call this justice 'natural'? I venture to suggest that we can, in so far as it can be the mark or the figure of man's prelapsarian nature. Ferreyrolles, in his article, 'Pascal et la rédemption de la nature', despite coming rather close to

---

[38] *Apologie pour Messire Henry-Louis Chastaigner de la Rochepozay* (Paris, 1615), 72–3. Ferreyrolles gives other detailed examples of both traditional and Jansenist acceptance of natural laws in *Pascal et la raison du politique*, ch. 4.

[39] Seuil 435. The theme of political justice and killing is common in the *Pensées*. See L60, L9, L20, L51.

a Thomist and even Jesuit conception of nature, as he admits,[40] ascertains that in the *Pensées* 'la nature peut parler de la surnature et être sauvée par et dans elle'.[41] As we find in L662, where the Pelagians, who believed that man can be saved naturally without grace, thus constituting those of 'la première naissance', are contrasted with Catholics, who form part of 'la grâce de la seconde naissance', 'La grâce [...] est en quelque sorte naturelle'.[42] Pierre Magnard reinforces this view in his book on nature in the *Pensées*:

> Faute de rendre l'homme à son origine, l'idée de nature semble l'orienter vers son destin, incapable de se recommander de l'innocence native, elle anticipe la grâce dont elle s'avérera la figure.[43]

Thus it would seem justifiable to use the term 'natural justice' to describe that justice which is given to men by God. This aspect of justice contrasts markedly with the way in which other words function in the *Pensées*, as I have shown in previous chapters, and I shall consider this problem at the end of this section on human justice.

However, it must be added here that, although some sort of God-given natural justice exists, man's fundamental corruption will cloud his judgement. He may therefore have an innate sense of natural laws, but his weakness will prevent him from maintaining total order. Thirouin admits that 'Pascal croit en l'existence de la loi naturelle mais, par réalisme, il abandonne l'espoir qu'on puisse, ici-bas, s'appuyer sur son autorité'.[44] I would argue that Pascal does not abandon all hope of entrusting oneself to natural laws, but rather that he maintains a profound scepticisme. Ferreyrolles's repeated insistence on the centrality of natural laws leads him to underestimate the Augustinian dimension and to imagine an order on earth which does not exist for Pascal. Man's original perfection cannot be recaptured on earth. As Jean-François Sénault stresses,

> toutes ces bonnes inclinations qui nous restent apres la perte de la Justice originelle, sont desreglées; et l'homme est si universellement corrompu, que

---

[40] See the discussion after his article, in *Méthodes chez Pascal*, 290–5.
[41] 'Pascal et la rédemption de la nature', 290.
[42] Cf. *Écrits sur la grâce*, Seuil 318: 'ils [les Pélagiens] avancent que Dieu a eu une volonté générale, égale, et conditionnelle, de sauver tous les hommes (en la masse corrompue) comme en la création'.
[43] *Nature et histoire dans l'Apologétique*, 402.
[44] *Le Hasard et les règles*, 67.

ses avantages mesme luy sont pernicieux [...], et si nous en tirons maintenant quelque profit, nous le devons à la Grace et non pas à la Nature.⁴⁵

POLITICAL JUSTICE (J1b)

If natural justice is in some way linked to God, then political (established) justice would appear to be indistinguishable from man's fallen state. Sénault in *L'Homme criminel*, for example, shows how man's notion of justice is closely linked to the deception of language: 'pendant qu'ils [les hommes] avoient le nom de Justice en la bouche, on remarquoit qu'ils n'avoient que la vanité dans le cœur'.⁴⁶ Similarly, Pascal makes clear in the *Trois discours sur la condition des grands* that, whereas 'les grandeurs naturelles sont celles qui sont indépendantes de la fantaisie des hommes',⁴⁷ the 'grandeurs d'établissement', such as political laws, are based upon the deceptive powers of man's corrupt imagination. In the first *Discours*, for example, Pascal informs the young nobleman that his privileged status is due to 'la fantaisie des lois'.⁴⁸ Yet, this kind of justice is not completely divorced from God's will:

Je ne veux pas dire qu'ils [les biens] ne vous appartiennent pas légitimement, et qu'il soit permis à un autre de vous les ravir; car Dieu, qui en est le maître, a permis aux sociétés de faire des lois pour les partager; et quand ces lois sont une fois établies, il est injuste de les violer.⁴⁹

Thus, although political justice is not *essentially* just, it is God's wish that laws, once established, should not be violated, for 'le plus grand des maux est les guerres civiles' (L94). This theme is echoed throughout the *Pensées*. The definition of political justice is therefore closely allied to the need for peace, 'qui est le souverain bien' (L81). L66 gives us the clearest definition of this justice:

Injustice.
Il est dangereux de dire au peuple que les lois ne sont pas justes, car il n'y obéit qu'à cause qu'il les croit justes. C'est pourquoi il faut lui dire en même temps qu'il y faut obéir parce qu'elles sont lois, comme il faut obéir aux supérieurs non pas parce qu'ils sont justes, mais parce qu'ils sont

---

⁴⁵ *De l'usage des passions* (Paris, 1641), 'Préface'.
⁴⁶ *L'Homme criminel* (Paris, 1644), 276.   ⁴⁷ Seuil 367.
⁴⁸ Ibid. 366.   ⁴⁹ Ibid. 366.

'JUSTICE'

supérieurs. Par là voilà toute sédition prévenue, si on peut faire entendre cela et que proprement [c'est] la définition de la justice [J1b].[50]

The adjective *juste* here would seem to be used throughout this fragment in its purest sense, that of true, essential justice in opposition to flawed political justice. As we can deduce from the *liasse* entitled 'Raisons des effets' (and which I have discussed at length in previous chapters), in order to understand the fundamental corruption of such political laws and yet to preserve peace, one must have 'une pensée de derrière' (L91), otherwise termed 'une double pensée' in the first *Discours*:

> Que s'ensuit de là? que vous devez avoir [. . .] une double pensée; et que si vous agissez extérieurement avec les hommes selon votre rang, vous devez reconnaître, par une pensée plus cachée mais plus véritable, que vous n'avez rien naturellement au-dessus d'eux.[51]

Human justice is difficult to ascertain, as the reference to the need for 'une pensée plus cachée' shows. Unlike *force* (might) which is tangibly present, human political justice has no such attributes. It is within this context that Pascal calls this justice 'spirituelle' in L85; it is airy and intangible:

> Si l'on avait pu l'on aurait mis la force entre les mains de la justice [J1b], mais comme la force ne se laisse pas manier comme on veut parce que c'est une qualité palpable, au lieu que la justice [J1b] est une qualité spirituelle dont on dispose comme on veut.[52]

---

[50] The fact that this fragment, which is concerned substantially with human justice, is entitled 'Injustice' supports my earlier point that *injustice* has no function other than in connection with human justice and the corruption of man. It appears on the same page as L67, also entitled 'Injustice'. See Ernst, Album, 119. The fact that these 2 fragments were accompanied on the same page by L34, which accentuates 'la faiblesse de l'homme', suggests that, even within this form of human justice, Pascal was not forgetting the theme of the fundamental corruption of humanity.
[51] Seuil 366. Nicolas Faret, in *L'Honneste-Homme ou L'Art de plaire à la Cour* (Paris, 1630), recognizes the important need to preserve peace: 'la vraye et legitime puissance des Souverains n'est qu'un noeud d'authorité et de justice pour la conservation du bien public' (p. 77). But his evaluation lacks the subtlety and complexity of Pascal's notion of justice: for him, 'la voye de la nature et de la justice est facile, seure, et innocente, et tout project qui s'esloigne des regles de la raison a l'erreur qui le guide' (pp. 79–80).
[52] L85 is headed by a quotation from Terence's *Heautontimoroumenos*, 4. 5. 47, 'Summum jus, summa injuria' (the most sublime law leads to the greatest injustice), and is quoted by Charron in *De la sagesse*, 1. xxxvii. 5: 'voilà comment la Justice non

The dialectician goes on to stress that 'on appelle juste ce qu'il est force d'observer'. Human justice is subject to the manipulation of language. As Laurent Thirouin puts it, 'c'est dorénavant par abus de langage que les lois sont dites justes'.[53]

As a result of its difficulties, 'la justice [J1b] est sujette à dispute. La force est très reconnaissable et sans dispute' (L103). Force is 'une grandeur naturelle', as named in the *Trois discours*; political justice is only 'une grandeur d'établissement'. In order to achieve stability on earth, the two must coexist. Justice by itself is powerless because of its undefined state. Force by itself, on the other hand, leads to tyranny:

> Justice [J1b], force.
> Il est juste que ce qui est juste soit suivi; il est nécessaire que ce qui est le plus fort soit suivi.
> La justice [J1b] sans la force est impuissante, la force sans la justice [J1b] est tyrannique.
> La justice [J1b] sans force est contredite, parce qu'il y a toujours des méchants. La force sans la justice [J1b] est accusée. Il faut donc mettre ensemble la justice [J1b] et la force, et pour cela faire que ce qui est juste soit fort ou que ce qui est fort soit juste.
> La justice [J1b] est sujette à dispute. La force est très reconnaissable et sans dispute. Aussi on n'a pu donner la force à la justice [J1b], parce que la force a contredit la justice [J1b] et a dit qu'elle était injuste, et a dit que c'était elle qui était juste.
> Et ainsi ne pouvant faire que ce qui est juste fût fort on a fait que ce qui est fort fût juste. (L103)

The use of syllepsis in this fragment, where the adjective *juste* at the beginning appears in a different sense from the later use of *juste* and *justice*, accentuates that very intimation that 'la justice est sujette à dispute'. At the beginning, the dialectician makes a deliberate pun on the meaning of *juste* as 'correct', contrasting it with the human justice of the remainder of the fragment. Yet this latter use of justice, as unstable as we perceive it to be, suggests the existence of

---

seulement heurte la charité, mais elle mesme s'entrave et s'empesche, dont est tresbien dit et au vray, *summum jus, summa injuria*' (p. 116). Cf. the heading to L86, 'Veri juris', which comes from Cicero's *De Officiis*, 3. 17 ('we do not possess any solid and exact model of true laws and perfect justice'), found in Montaigne, *Essais*, II. i. 773.

[53] 'Conservatisme et dérision', 117. See Ch. 1 above for a discussion of the use of the words *dire* and *contredire* in the political fragments.

some form of ideal human justice. As Erich Auerbach, somewhat reluctantly, states in his discussion of this fragment, 'nous devons alors admettre qu'est ici reconnue l'existence d'une justice objective, distincte de la force et indépendante d'elle du moins dans l'idéal'.[54]

To consider human justice as a whole, therefore, we discover facts which would appear to contradict the ways in which Pascal treats other words. On a human scale, through natural justice, there is a direct link with God. Moreover, man's very fallen nature, his *concupiscence*, has achieved a certain coherence which amounts to a form of justice. But the presence of human justice does not negate other fragments which accentuate man's fallen state, a point which is made clear in L211:

> On a fondé et tiré de la concupiscence des règles admirables de police, de morale et de justice [J1b].
> Mais dans le fond, ce vilain fond de l'homme, ce *figmentum malum* n'est que couvert. Il n'est pas ôté.[55]

Nevertheless, a final question concerning human justice must be answered. Why does Pascal allow for a different interpretation concerning human justice? All terms which I have considered thus far show that, on a human scale, their very incoherence prompts the reader to look towards the constancy of a Christian God, but they differ from human justice in that their 'natural' state is not directly inspired by God. It would seem that Pascal's reasons for approaching justice in this way are strongly motivated by his insistence on peace as a sovereign good and on civil disorder as the worst of all possible ills. By negating all forms of human justice, he would be

---

[54] 'La Théorie politique de Pascal', 141.
[55] Cf. 'Factum pour les curés de Paris', where the Casuists are blamed for attempting to justify 'les dérèglements'. According to the 'curés' (for whom it is probable that Pascal was writing), as long as some form of human law maintains stability, 'concupiscence' is kept in check and can maintain a certain order: 'Ce qu'il y a de plus pernicieux dans ces nouvelles morales [proposed by the Casuists], est qu'elles ne vont pas seulement à corrompre les mœurs, mais à corrompre la règle des mœurs, ce qui est d'une importance tout autrement considérable. Car c'est un mal bien moins dangereux et bien moins général d'introduire des dérèglements en laissant subsister les lois qui les défendent, que de pervertir les lois, et de justifier les dérèglements, parce que la nature de l'homme tend toujours au mal dès sa naissance, et qu'elle n'est ordinairement retenue que par la crainte de la loi, aussitôt que cette barrière est ôtée, la concupiscence se répand sans obstacle, de sorte qu'il n'y a point de différence entre rendre les vices permis, et rendre tous les hommes vicieux' (Seuil 471–2).

implicitly encouraging revolution.[56] Clearly, he acknowledges the need for political stability, and, although human justice is essentially tainted and not questioned, established laws are needed to preserve peace:

> La justice [J1b] est ce qui est établi; et ainsi toutes nos lois établies seront nécessairement tenues pour justes sans être examinées, puisqu'elles sont établies. (L645)

It is within this context too that we should regard the *Raisons des effets*, and Pascal's acknowledgement of the right of succession. Because civil war is so dangerous, he sees any form of natural succession as preferable:

> Opinions du peuple saines.
> Le plus grand des maux est les guerres civiles.
> Elles sont sûres si on veut récompenser les mérites, car tous diront qu'ils méritent. Le mal à craindre d'un sot qui succède par droit de naissance n'est ni si grand, ni si sûr. (L94)

This desire for peace thus validates the more direct link between human and divine justice. Man on his own is incapable of stability. Only God can ordain this need for peace on earth in the Christian republic, as adumbrated in L380, where 'Dieu ayant fait le ciel et la terre qui ne sentent point le bonheur de leur être, il a voulu faire des êtres qui le connussent et qui composassent un corps de membres pensants'.[57]

LES JUSTES (J2)

At this point it would be appropriate to develop Pascal's definition of *les justes*, which I shall translate as 'righteous men', for they

---

[56] It is this aspect which L. Thirouin terms Pascal's 'conservatisme' in 'Conservatisme et dérision'.

[57] It is important to distinguish between the pragmatism of this need for peace on earth, following Montaigne's recognition of the destructive effect of civil wars and Descartes's 'morale provisoire', and true peace, which can only be found in God. Cf. the 'Réponse des curés de Paris', where the Casuists are accused of promoting false peace. True peace can only be linked to God, whereas false peace is inherent in the corrupt world: 'les vrais enfants de l'Eglise savent bien discerner la véritable paix que le Sauveur peut seul donner, et qui est inconnue au monde, d'avec cette fausse paix que le monde peut bien donner, mais qui est en horreur au Sauveur du monde. Ils savent que la véritable paix est celle qui conserve la vérité en la possession de la crédulité des hommes' (Seuil 478). See my discussion of this passage in Ch. 6 above.

clearly represent a link between human and divine justice. The instability of language underlies the term *juste*, for it can refer to both nouns *justice* and *justesse*. Indeed, one definition of *justesse* by Richelet as 'le temperament qui se trouve entre l'excés [*sic*] et le defaut' captures well the sense of *les justes* providing a link between wretchedness and salvation. As the Académie dictionary describes *le juste*, he is a person who has taken a step away from his post-lapsarian humanity towards eternal communion: 'celuy qui est en la grace de Dieu'. The biblical use of the term *justi* also refers largely to the future salvation of the righteous, as shown in de Sacy's translation of Matt. 13: 49: 'C'est ce qui arrivera à la fin du monde: les anges viendront, et sépareront les méchants du milieu des justes.'[58] However, as we shall see, the salvation of *les justes* is, for Pascal, no foregone conclusion.[59]

Perhaps the best indication of Pascal's conception of the term comes from two fragments, L725 and L864, which refer to what the dialectician sees as the Jesuits' corrupt interpretation of religion. In both fragments, *les justes* are perceived as being for the Jesuits 'sans charité'. Thus, it would seem likely that for Pascal, contrary to the Jesuits, *les justes* must be blessed with the order of 'la charité'.

In 'Le Mystère de Jésus (L919), *les justes* are equated with the disciples of Jesus, those who had been chosen by God:

Jésus pendant que ses disciples dormaient a opéré leur salut. Il l'a fait à chacun des justes [J2] pendant qu'ils dormaient et dans le néant avant leur naissance et dans les péchés depuis leur naissance.

Although Jesus has effected the salvation of *les justes*, the fact of their humanity, of their sins, is not denied. Indeed, this would support the argument in the *Écrits* (as we shall see) that grace should not be considered an automatic gift to *les justes*. Similarly, false human justice engenders false *justes*, as we find later in L919:

La fausse justice [J1] de Pilate ne sert qu'à faire souffrir J.-C. Car il le fait fouetter par sa fausse justice [J1] et puis le tue. Il vaudrait mieux l'avoir tué d'abord. Ainsi les faux justes [J1]. Ils font de bonnes œuvres et de méchantes pour plaire au monde et montrer qu'ils ne sont pas tout à fait à J.-C., car ils en ont honte et enfin dans les grandes tentations et occasions ils le tuent.

[58] Cf. Luke 1: 17; 14: 14; Acts 24: 15; 1 Peter 3: 18.
[59] There are clearly other problems in the *Pensées* pertaining to the *justi* which I have not discussed here, such as the identity of 'les bons' in L12.

Thus, true *justes* are interpreted as human beings who are blessed by charity, whereas false *justes* are inextricably linked to the corrupt aspects of human justice (J1). Indeed, Christ's death, which took place under the trappings of human justice, accentuates the failings of that very justice, and, by implication, points to the unchanging and true nature of God's justice:

> J.-C. n'a pas voulu être tué sans les formes de la justice [J1], car il est bien plus ignominieux de mourir par justice [J1] que par une sédition injuste. (L940)

Overall, therefore, *les justes* are those humans who, although members of a sinful and corrupt world, have been blessed with a will to follow God:

> elle [la seule religion chrétienne] apprend aux justes [J2] qu'elle élève jusqu'à la participation de la divinité même, qu'en ce sublime état ils portent encore la source de toute la corruption qui les rend durant toute la vie sujets à l'erreur, à la misère, à la mort, au péché, et elle crie aux plus impies qu'ils sont capables de la grâce de leur rédempteur. (L208)[60]

DIVINE JUSTICE (J3)

At the highest level Pascal places that spiritual justice which is termed alternately *la justice divine* (L418), *la justice de Dieu* (L418, L774, L948), and *la justice éternelle* (L269, L485). Similarly, *la véritable justice* or *une justice véritable* is used mainly in a spiritual context (L520, L85).[61] Within the category of divine justice, there are two distinctions to be made. Not only does *la justice de Dieu* contain the sense of God's justness (J3*a*), but it can also have the meaning of retribution which God has the power to impose on man (J3*b*). This latter meaning is clear in L418:

---

[60] It should be noted here that the related noun *les bons*, as it appears in L12, indicates men who still need to be persuaded of the truth of religion and who consequently are still to attain salvation: 'La [la religion] rendre ensuite aimable, faire souhaiter aux bons qu'elle fût vraie et puis montrer qu'elle est vraie.'

[61] Cf. the juxtaposition of the adjective *juste* with *véritable* in L931, where again the terms are closely linked to spiritual justice: 'J'essaye d'être juste, véritable, sincère et fidèle à tous les hommes et j'ai une tendresse de cœur pour ceux à qui Dieu m'a uni plus étroitement'. The use of *la véritable justice* in L44 occurs, however, as a contrast to the false justice which imagination promotes, and therefore in this instance denotes human justice.

Il faut que la justice de Dieu [J3b] soit énorme comme sa miséricorde. Or la justice [J3b] envers les réprouvés est moins énorme et doit moins choquer que la miséricorde envers les élus.

Both senses, justness and retribution, can be applied to Pascal's use of *justice* in a passage from the *Écrits sur la Grâce*, where man's two natures are compared:

> Dans l'état d'innocence, Dieu ne pouvait avec justice [J3] damner aucun des hommes, Dieu ne pouvait même leur refuser les grâces suffisantes pour leur salut.
>
> Dans l'état de corruption, Dieu pouvait avec justice [J3] damner toute la masse entière; et ceux qui naissent aujourd'hui sans en être retirés par le baptême sont damnés et privés éternellement de la vision béatifique, ce qui est le plus grand des maux.[62]

Significantly, all instances of divine justice (with both senses) are introduced in order to counteract the fallibility of human justice. As Pascal wrote in a letter to his sister Gilberte on 1 April 1648, man's 'captivité' on earth comes as a direct result of God's justice, in both its senses:

> nous devons bien ménager l'avantage que la bonté de Dieu nous donne de nous laisser toujours devant les yeux une image des biens que nous avons perdus, et de nous environner dans la captivité même où sa justice [J3] nous a réduits, de tant d'objets qui nous servent d'une leçon continuellement présente.[63]

Moreover, man by himself cannot hope to have any understanding of spiritual justice, for it is 'la volonté de Dieu qui est seule toute la bonté et toute la justice [J3a]' (L948). Thus, God's grace alone can bestow, through faith, knowledge of divine justice: 'Que l'homme sans la foi ne peut connaître le vrai bien, ni la justice [J3]' (L148). Yet this latter use of 'justice' also implies man's understanding of natural justice, which, as we saw, is directly linked to spiritual justice. As Jacques Chevalier suggests with reference to L148, 'C'est peut-être que la pratique de la véritable *justice naturelle* est inséparable de la *charité*, au sens plein, qui est surnaturelle.'[64]

Thus, in L85, after the evocation of 'l'injustice de la Fronde, qui élève sa prétendue justice [J1b] contre la force', the dialectician

---

[62] Seuil 312.   [63] Ibid. 273.   [64] *Pascal*, 356.

asserts: 'Il n'en est pas de même dans l'Église, car il y a une justice véritable [J3] et nulle violence.' Indeed, God's justice is perceived as the major way to counter the sins of man, as can be seen in a fragment which recalls Pascal's discussion of Epictetus and Montaigne in the *Entretien avec M. de Sacy*: 'Comme les deux sources de nos péchés sont l'orgueil et la paresse Dieu nous a découvert deux qualités en lui pour les guérir, sa miséricorde et sa justice [J3*b*]' (L774). In the *Entretien*, Pascal contrasts the sin of pride with spiritual justice, and shows that even *une véritable justice* can be corrupted by an arrogant and, by implication, rational acceptance of justice without the channel of faith: 'Montaigne est incomparable pour confondre l'orgueil de ceux qui, hors la foi, se piquent d'une véritable justice' [J1].[65] Another term which differentiates spiritual justice from other forms of justice is that of 'essential justice'. I derive the word 'essential' from a fragment in which the dialectician (whom I take to be the 'je') conveys his discovery that human justice (J1), as opposed to divine justice (J3), is not *essentially* just:

J'ai passé longtemps de ma vie en croyant qu'il y avait une justice [J1 + J3] et en cela je ne me trompais pas, car il y en a selon que Dieu nous l'a voulu révéler, mais je ne le prenais pas ainsi et c'est en quoi je me trompais, car je croyais que notre justice [J1] était essentiellement juste, et que j'avais de quoi la connaître et en juger, mais je me suis trouvé tant de fois en faute de jugement droit, qu'enfin je suis entré en défiance de moi et puis des autres. (L520)[66]

As I mentioned earlier, this fragment offers an interesting insight into the possibility that human justice, despite not being in essence just, can be just where God chooses to give it to man.

It is clear that the notions of God's justice (retribution) and mercy are integral to the question of grace. Indeed, in the *Écrits sur la Grâce*, the word *justice* is repeated often. As we saw, Pascal shows that, for fallen man, 'Dieu pouvait avec justice condamner

---

[65] *Entretien avec M. de Sacy*, Seuil 297. See also p. 296. It would seem that Pascal intends no change of meaning when placing the adjective *véritable* before or after the noun. Similarly, there appears to be no discernible difference of meaning when the indefinite and definite articles are used with *véritable justice*, as in L520 and L85.

[66] The whole of this fragment was crossed out by Pascal. I should point out that Ferreyrolles makes use of the term 'l'essentielle justice' to distinguish it from other forms of justice. See *Pascal et la raison du politique*, 184–5, 191, 195, 200, 278–9.

toute la masse entière' (Seuil 312–13). Elsewhere in the *Écrits*, he reiterates that God can quite justifiably abandon all men:

> Tous les hommes étant dans cette masse corrompue également dignes de la mort éternelle et de la colère de Dieu, Dieu pouvait avec justice [J3*b*] les abandonner tous sans miséricorde à la damnation.[67]

God's justice as retribution is largely equated with abandonment, 'délaissement', as Philippe Sellier points out,[68] and is set against God's mercy:

> Si la justice divine [J3*b*] se manifestait par le *délaissement*, la miséricorde se révèle par le *discernement*. Dieu 'discerne' dans la masse ceux qu'il décide de sauver.[69]

Clearly, Pascal's perception of divine justice and mercy comes directly from St Augustine, and it would be useful to quote extensively from a passage from *De Civitate Dei* where retribution and mercy are compared:

> Mais la peine eternelle semble dure et injuste au sens de l'homme, parce que dans la foiblesse de nostre petit esprit, nous n'avons pas cette pure et treshaute sagesse, qui descouvre la pesanteur et la laideur de la premiere desobeïssance d'Adam. Car plus l'homme joüissoit parfaitement de Dieu, plus il l'a injustement abandonné; et il s'est rendu digne d'un mal eternel, ayant estouffé en soy un bien qui le pouvoit estre. De là toute la masse des hommes a esté condamnée; parce que celuy dans lequel elle estoit comme antée et paistrie, a esté puny; et personne n'eschappe à cette peine, que celuy que la misericorde et une grace indue en esloignent: et le genre humain est tellement partagé, qu'il paroist en quelques uns ce que peut la grace misericordieuse, et dans le reste la juste vengeance. Car l'un et l'autre ne paroistront pas en tous; car si tous demeuroient dans les peines d'une juste condamnation, personne ne descouvriroit la grace du Redempteur; et si tous passoient des tenebres à la lumiere, la severité du Juge ne seroit manifestée en aucun. Et certes la rigueur de la vengeance en chastie beaucoup davantage, que la clemence n'en espargne, afin que nous comprenions ce qui estoit deu à tous les hommes. Et quand ce chastiment s'estendroit à tous, personne n'accuseroit justement la justice du Vengeur: et parce qu'il y en a tant de sauvez de cette masse perdue, nous avons sujet de rendre des actions de graces immortelles au bien-fait gratuit du Liberateur.[70]

---

[67] Seuil 318. Cf. 'il pouvait avec justice abandonner tous les hommes' (p. 318), 'il pouvait avec justice les abandonner tous' (p. 318).
[68] *Pascal et Saint Augustin*, 258–68.
[69] Ibid. 269.
[70] *De la Cité de Dieu*, trans. Le Sieur de Ceriziers (Paris, 1655), XXI. xii. 730.

As early as 1648, Pascal came close to the Augustinian perception of the function of grace, viewing spiritual justice in men as essentially part of God's grace. In a letter to Gilberte, he wrote that 'la continuation de la justice [J3] des fidèles n'est autre chose que la continuation de l'infusion de la grâce, et non pas une seule grâce qui subsiste toujours; et c'est ce qui nous apprend parfaitement la dépendance perpétuelle où nous sommes de la miséricorde de Dieu'.[71]

It is within this context that Pascal opposes the Molinists in the *Écrits sur la Grâce*. Because the Council of Trent did not specify whether grace is always bestowed on the righteous (*les justes*) or not, the Molinists interpreted this silence as meaning that all righteous men would be saved, whereas Pascal chose to follow the Augustinian tradition that God alone has the power to grant grace. The debate concentrates on whether the Council has declared that God directly gives the righteous the power to fulfil the commandments, or precepts, of the Church.[72] As Pascal points out, 'le Concile déclare que les justes [J2] ne sont pas toujours exempts de péchés véniels, mais qu'ils ne détruisent pas la justice [J3]'.[73] *Justice* here would perhaps be best translated as 'righteousness', distinct from divine justice itself. Indeed, Pascal's quotation of St Augustine in the same passage demonstrates the differentiation which he wishes to make between God's justice and man's attempt to establish his own justice:

Après avoir entendu ces témoignages légitimes, évangéliques et apostoliques, soyons-en édifiés pour la grâce, laquelle n'entendent pas ceux qui, ignorant la justice de Dieu [J3] et voulant établir la leur [J1], n'ont point été soumis à la justice de Dieu [J3].[74]

---

[71] 5 Nov. 1648, Seuil 274.
[72] See Sellier, *Pascal et Saint Augustin*, 279–80: 'Comme Jansénius et Arnauld, Pascal reconnaissait aux justes différents pouvoirs de pratiquer les commandements: le premier procède de la puissance naturelle du libre arbitre; le second, de la grâce habituelle qui consiste en un état présent, mais n'assure pas à elle seule la persévérance sans un secours actuel; le troisième, de ces grâces simplement excitantes que Dieu a voulues trop faibles pour qu'elles triomphent des concupiscences déchaînées et qu'il donne selon son bon plaisir, soit pour disposer ensuite à des secours plus forts qui orienteront vers la conversion, soit pour empêcher l'excès des crimes, soit pour faire percevoir à l'homme de quelle maladie il doit être guéri. Seul le pouvoir plein et entier d'agir, qui ne peut naître que de la grâce actuelle et efficace, peut manquer aux justes, comme l'enseigne saint Augustin.'
[73] Seuil 346.   [74] Ibid. 347.

The problem of the interpretation of the Council of Trent comes from whether the righteous man (*le juste*) can persist in righteousness (*la justice*) without divine help:

> le Concile condamne d'anathème ceux non seulement qui disent que le juste [J2] persévère dans la justice [J2] sans un secours spécial, mais même ceux qui disent que le juste [J2] a le pouvoir de persévérer dans la justice [J2] sans un secours spécial. Et par conséquent le Concile a aussi condamné d'anathème cette dernière proposition.[75]

Pascal's conclusion in the *Écrits* strongly indicates the way in which he views divine justice. Although God alone is capable of true justice, his judgement is not consequently discernible to all men. Indeed, to use the terminology which is applied to human justice in the *Trois discours sur la condition des grands*, God's judgement is effected 'par une pensée plus cachée mais plus véritable'.[76] Yet, where man must have 'une double pensée' in order to understand his fundamental corruption, God's thought remains hidden because of the gulf which exists between God and man in his postlapsarian state. Only God can be *truly* just:

> Concluons donc de ces décisions toutes saintes: que Dieu par sa miséricorde donne quand il lui plaît, aux justes [J2], le pouvoir plein et parfait d'accomplir les préceptes, et qu'il ne le donne pas toujours, par un jugement juste quoique caché.[77]

Finally, Pascal's depiction of divine justice in the *Pensées* is strongly coloured by either direct quotation from or explicit reference to the Bible.[78] Perhaps the most interesting biblical allusion comes in L489, where Pascal refers widely to the Book of Isaiah, for it emphasizes again the chasm which the fall of man has brought about between human justice and spiritual justice. Perfect justice was once integral to man's first nature, but 'c'est pour nos crimes que la justice [J3] s'est éloignée de nous'. Furthermore, 'Nous avons attendu la justice [J3] et elle ne vient point. Nous avons espéré le salut et il s'éloigne de nous' (L489).

---

[75] Ibid. 347–8. [76] Ibid. 366.
[77] Ibid. 348. Cf. L781: 'Elle [l'Écriture] dit [. . .] que Dieu est un Dieu caché et que depuis la corruption de la nature il les a laissés dans un aveuglement dont ils ne peuvent sortir que par J.-C., hors duquel toute communication avec Dieu est ôtée.'
[78] See e.g. L483, 'Écoutez-moi, vous qui suivez la justice et qui cherchez le Seigneur' (Isa. 51), and L485, '70 semaines sont prescrites et déterminées sur votre peuple et sur votre sainte cité, pour expier les crimes, pour mettre fin aux péchés et abolir l'iniquité et pour introduire la justice éternelle' (Dan. 9: 20).

This emphasis on man's inability to attain spiritual justice by himself tempers, therefore, the strong links which exist between natural justice and supernatural justice. There is no room for complacency. Although God has placed certain forms of justice on earth in order to maintain peace, his essential justice underlines the fallibility of human justice. Man must strive towards this perfection, but only God's grace can grant him true justice. As long as he searches, man can hope for the time that eternal justice, rather than human legal justice, will reign, as Pascal is at pains to point out:

Le péché prendrait fin et le Libérateur, le saint des saints amènerait la justice éternelle [J3], non la légale [J1*b*], mais l'éternelle [J3]. (L269)

Now that I have considered the different levels within the use of *repos*, *bonheur*, and *justice* (I shall call them 'saved' terms), certain parallels can be drawn between each of them. Moreover, comparisons can now be made with *inconstance*, *ennui*, and *inquiétude* (to be called 'fallen' terms).

For each of *repos*, *bonheur*, and *justice*, the meaning fluctuates between three registers. On the first level, R1, B1, and J1 are all depicted as spurious and innately corrupt, but with differing nuances. While R1, for example, represents a false sense of restfulness which man believes himself to be avoiding, B1 stands for the happiness which man thinks he possesses in the world. J1 is more complex, owing to the belief that natural justice is needed to avoid total chaos, but fundamentally it shows man's flawed notion of justice. On the second level, both R2 and B2 show man's inner sense of peace and happiness which he believes himself to be seeking and which relates to an instinct of his pre-lapsarian perfection, whereas J2 indicates a similar instinct of righteousness. On the third level, R3, B3, and J3 all depict directly eternal spiritual perfection, as epitomized in God, but also implicitly pointing back to their human counterparts as a continual reminder of human corruption.

In the partial conclusion to the chapters on *inconstance*, *ennui*, and *inquiétude*, I proposed the notion of the three orders as a comparative model for the three main levels of meaning of each term. The three orders can similarly be applied to *repos*, *bonheur*, and *justice*. While the first category of each term is linked exclusively to the materiality of man's fallen existence ('chair'), the second level incorporates 'esprit' and 'cœur' in their association with the rational and intuitive grasp of self-knowledge; the third order of 'charité' also corresponds directly to the third category of meaning. However, the similarities and differences between the shifting registers of saved and fallen terms dictate a more complex analysis which the three orders do not adequately reflect.

If we now compare the use of the saved terms to the fallen ones, we find some quite startling similarities and illuminating differences. For the fallen terms, Inc. 1, E1, and I1 epitomize the wretchedness of the human condition, whereas for the saved words, R1, B1, and J1 reflect a spurious state which is also a strong sign of man's wretchedness and corruption. The second category in both fallen and saved vocabulary acts crucially as a hinge between the first and third registers of each term: all the words show a movement away from wretchedness and towards a sense of perfection. Indeed, the notion of movement underlies Inc. 2, E2, and I2 as well as R2, B2, and J2. More specifically, it is the concept of *divertissement* which appears central to both fallen and saved terms in this category. As I showed with *ennui*, *divertissement* embodies its active state, and it is this aspect which links it to the restlessness inherent in the terms *inconstance* and *inquiétude*. For *repos* and *bonheur*, *divertissement* (as shown especially in L136) is of major importance. Although the connection between *justice* and *divertissement* is not as direct, the movement of the *justes* from their corruption towards the hope of salvation is mirrored in the positive movement within *divertissement*.[79] Also, as Ferreyrolles points out, 'la vie sociale', with its customs and laws, 'est une machine à produire du divertissement', and 'la société tout entière roule sur le divertissement'.[80] As far as the third category is concerned, an interesting distinction can be made. Inc. 3, E3, and I3 all remain within their scope as fallen terms, but they point directly towards the saved register; in fact, believers experience Inc. 3 and

---

[79] Moreover, it is interesting to note that L269, which makes a firm distinction between human and divine justice (J1 and J3), was written on the same paper-type (FN/PH) as L136, which would indicate that both fragments were more or less contemporary, written, according to Ernst (Album, 152), in Apr. 1658. It is also significant that some important political fragments, L89–93, were written at about the same time (May–June 1658, according to Ernst) on another type of paper (FNIC). All this shows that Pascal was formulating some notions of justice at the same time that he was writing on *divertissement*.

[80] *Pascal et la raison du politique*, 128. See this close connection between social life and *divertissement* in e.g. L139.

especially E_3 and I_3 as an integral part of their endeavours to attain God's perfection. Conversely, R_3, B_3, and J_3 depict a state of true spiritual perfection as encapsulated in God's peace, happiness, and justice (Inc. 3, E_3, and I_3 have no such direct divine referent), but they all point back to the fallen register. The Fall is never forgotten, and truth can never be taken for granted.[81] Fig. 6 sums up some of the preceding comparisons.

'Fallen' terms		'Saved' terms
Inc. 1, E_1, I_1	wretchedness	R_1, B_1, J_1
Inc. 2, E_2, I_2	movement (*divertissement*)	R_2, B_2, J_2
Inc. 3, E_3, I_3	<..................>	R_3, B_3, J_3

FIG. 6

A detailed analysis of these terms shows, therefore, how all of them fit a similar pattern. Concepts firmly entrenched within the wretchedness of man's corruption are transformed through the hinge-like second category to a higher plane. But it is through the fragmentary text that the dialectician juxtaposes the varying meanings of the terms, leaving the reader in a continual state of flux, which itself acts as a reminder of fallen man's instability. Those terms which represent the varying and contradictory aspects of the human condition are carefully manipulated as means to an effective persuasive end.

It is clear, therefore, how Pascal differs from other writers of the time in his deliberate juxtaposition of differing registers of meaning. In the final analysis, we can see how dictionary definitions, the influence of various sources, and even the study of certain epistemological terms do not reflect fully his radical methods of persuasion. Only a close examination of words which for him encapsulate the human condition reveals the integral role which shifting meanings play in the text. If the different registers of meaning of each term had been placed in a conventionally ordered sequence, the reader would have had the freedom to omit certain sections of the text which were central to the argument. By

---

[81] For a summary of the different meanings of all the terms, see the Table of Terms at the end of the book.

mingling the different levels of meaning within single fragments, the dialectician forces the reader to take into account all categories.

CHRIST AS MEDIATOR

The movement from the fallen to the saved has now been discussed within central concepts in the *Pensées*, but the key figure of Christ as mediator between human and divine should not be ignored. Indeed, it is significant that L253, a fragment devoted to the 'deux avènements' of Christ and his death overcoming human death, should have appeared on the same sheet as part of the long *divertissement* fragment, L136,[82] for clearly Pascal was considering both the importance of Christ and the centrality of *divertissement* concurrently.

Throughout the *Pensées*, the dialectician repeats the Old Testament prophecies that, as he puts it in L260, 'J.-C. serait Dieu et homme'. Christ is perceived as an incarnate instance of the paradoxicality of revealed religion. His life on earth provides the vital link between human wretchedness and knowledge of God:

> La connaissance de Dieu sans celle de sa misère fait l'orgueil.
> La connaissance de sa misère sans celle de Dieu fait le désespoir.
> La connaissance de J.-C. fait le milieu parce que nous y trouvons et Dieu et notre misère. (L192)[83]

Moreover, Christ provides the key to man's self-awareness in life and understanding of death:

> Non seulement nous ne connaissons Dieu que par Jésus-Christ mais nous ne nous connaissons nous-mêmes que par J.-C.; nous ne connaissons la vie, la mort que par Jésus-Christ. Hors de J.-C. nous ne savons ce que c'est ni que notre vie ni que notre mort, ni que Dieu, ni que nous-mêmes. (L417)

It is in this respect therefore that 'en J.-C. toutes les contradictions sont accordées' (L257) and that he is 'l'objet de tout, et le centre où tout tend' (L449), for he both assumes and resolves the contradictions of man's fallen nature. Without Christ, man is unable to

---

[82] See Ernst, *Album*, 156.
[83] Cf. L189: 'nous ne connaissons Dieu que par J.-C. Sans ce médiateur est ôtée toute communication avec Dieu.'

achieve communication with God.[84] Significantly, the word *condition* is used in L946 to show how Christ was an integral part of the human condition and yet transcended that wretched state:

> Considérer J.-C. en toutes les personnes, et en nous-mêmes. J.-C. comme père en son père. J.-C. comme frère en ses frères. J.-C. comme pauvre en les pauvres. J.-C. comme riche en les riches. J.-C. comme docteur et prêtre en les prêtres. J.-C. comme souverain en les princes, etc. Car il est par sa gloire tout ce qu'il y a de grand étant Dieu et est par sa vie mortelle tout ce qu'il y a de chétif et d'abject. Pour cela il a pris cette malheureuse condition pour pouvoir être en toutes les personnes et modèle de toutes conditions.

In the concluding chapter, I shall consider the implications of the manipulation of language by the dialectician. Is it an elaborate conceit and deceit? Or is there an unerring sense of truth which guides the dialectician in his exploitation of the instability of meanings?

Key to *Justice*

J1   *justice*: human justice
      J1*a*: natural justice
      J1*b*: political justice

J2   *justice*: *les justes* (righteousness)

J3   *justice*: divine justice
      J3*a*: justness
      J3*b*: retribution

---

[84] Cf. L781: 'L'Écriture dit au contraire que Dieu est un Dieu caché et que depuis la corruption de la nature il les a laissés dans un aveuglement dont ils ne peuvent sortir que par J.-C., hors duquel toute communication avec Dieu est ôtée.'

Part III

Playing with Truth

9
Playing with Truth

THEOPHILE. Comme le jeu [...] est une espece de divertissement, on n'en sçauroit avoir une juste idée, qu'on ne sçache auparavant ce qu'on appelle divertissement en general. Pour vous dire donc ce que je pense du divertissement, je croy ... que ...

EUGENE. D'où vient, Theophile, que vous hesitez, et que vous semblez avoir de la peine à vous exprimer?

THEOPHILE. Je croyois, Eugene, vous dire facilement ce que je croyois avoir bien pensé; et tous les termes m'échappent lorsque je m'efforce de vous donner une definition reguliere du divertissement.

(Jean Frain du Tremblay)[1]

We have now seen how the dialectician, in establishing the fallenness of both language and order in the world, exploits this awareness through his use of key terms depicting the human condition. The instability generated by the fluctuation between different registers of meaning serves as a means of persuasion in itself, for the fact of being unsettled represents an important step away from indifference. The reader is caught in a search to which he is irrevocably committed. Moreover, just as the fragmentary composition of the *Pensées* shows a carefully constructed disorder ('non pas peut-être dans une confusion sans dessein'—L532), the analysis of particular terms will have revealed, beneath the apparent confusion of shifting meanings, the dialectician's precise manipulation of words.

At the end of the previous chapter, I noted the centrality of the notion of *divertissement* to those words depicting the human condition. The wide sense which Pascal wished to apply to the term is clear in L478: 'sans examiner toutes les occupations particulières, il suffit de les comprendre sous le divertissement'. It would

---

[1] *Conversations morales sur les jeux et les divertissemens* (Paris, 1685).

therefore be useful here to consider more closely the implications of such a concept.

Divertissement is directly related to the notion of play in the *Pensées*. David Jaymes, for example, takes Jacques Henriot's statement that 'si l'homme joue, c'est parce qu'il y a du jeu dans l'être de l'homme',[2] and goes on to associate *jeu-divertissement* with *jeu-dialectique*:

> For Pascal, 'play' is initially a problem: a defect in being, it is both the source of man's disquietude and the means by which he distracts himself from that disquietude. Yet, at the same time, Pascal sought to render play dialectical, that is, to channel and direct the movement and freedom inherent in play in order to transform it into a constructive quality of being.[3]

As I have shown, *divertissement* emanates from man's corrupt nature and acts as an impetus to redirect him towards spiritual perfection. However, there still remains the question why play and *divertissement* should be so central to the human condition in the first place. Pascal is not unique in the seventeenth century in the importance which he attached to the notion of play. Jean Frain du Tremblay, for example, who himself was closely associated with Port-Royal, writes in his *Conversations morales sur les jeux et les divertissemens* that 'le Jeu est une matiere qui regarde tout le monde; car on ne voit personne de quelque âge, de quelque profession, de quelque sexe, et de quelque condition qu'elle soit, qui ne joue, et qui ne croye pouvoir jouer à toutes sortes de jeux'.[4]

In a masterly study of what he calls 'le modèle du jeu' in Pascal's thought, Laurent Thirouin shows how fallen man finds himself in a world regulated entirely by chance, 'où les rôles sont distribués au

---

[2] Henriot, *Le Jeu*, 98, quoted in Jaymes, 'Play in Pascal's *Pensées*', *Papers on French Seventeenth Century Literature*, 14–15 (1981), 40.

[3] Ibid. 41.

[4] (Paris, 1685), 2. Cf. p. 7, where gambling in particular is evoked: 'la passion du jeu est un poison qui infecte tout le monde'. Cf. also the English theologian Thomas Gataker in *Of the Nature and Use of Lots* (London, 1619): 'considering that those things that are most in use, are by meanes of mans corruption most subject to abuse; it ought not to seem strange, if the like hath among the rest befallen Lots; it having been so much in use, they have not beene free from much abuse' (p. 1). See H. de Ley's *Le Jeu classique: Jeu et théorie des jeux au grand siècle* (Paris, 1988), for an analysis of play in various 17th-c. texts.

hasard et tenus par convention'.⁵ As Thirouin sees it, for Pascal 'la vraie nature des lois est ludique'.⁶ Man must obey the rules of different laws as if they were the rules of a game:

> Obéir à des règles auxquelles on ne reconnaît aucune valeur, mais que l'on s'interdit de modifier, c'est la définition que nous avons donnée du jeu. L'homme asservi aux vanités est donc un homme condamné à jouer.⁷

A recognition of these rules as those of a game which fallen man is condemned to play distinguishes the true Christian from the 'peuple', 'demi-habiles', 'habiles', and 'dévots' in L90. The 'demi-habiles' might realize the part that chance plays in life, but it is the perfect Christian who discerns the true 'raison des effets',⁸ the rules of the game, and so is able to rise above the others through 'une autre lumière supérieure':

> Raison des effets.
> Gradation. Le peuple honore les personnes de grande naissance, les demi-habiles les méprisent disant que la naissance n'est pas un avantage de la personne mais du hasard. Les habiles les honorent, non par la pensée du peuple mais par la pensée de derrière. Les dévots qui ont plus de zèle que de science les méprisent malgré cette considération qui les fait honorer par les habiles, parce qu'ils en jugent par une nouvelle lumière que la piété leur donne, mais les chrétiens parfaits les honorent par un[e] autre lumière supérieure. (L90)

However, although man is condemned to play on earth, this game is finite. Death puts an end to all games of chance.

It is in this context that we should view L418, the Wager fragment. The central fact of the Wager is that 'on est forcé à jouer'. Chance gives way to the necessity of the game. Whether he likes it or not, man is caught in a game over which he has no control. In deciding not to commit himself to a wager, therefore, man is forcibly interrupting the game. In other words, by opting out of a game of which he is a player, he is in effect wagering against the existence of God. Some recent studies have revealed how the Wager is not concerned with proving the existence of God. Thirouin, for

---

⁵ *Le Hasard et les règles: Le Modèle du jeu dans la pensée de Pascal* (Paris, 1991).
⁶ Ibid. 49. ⁷ Ibid. 84.
⁸ Cf. Thirouin's 'Raison des effets: Essai d'explication d'un concept pascalien', *XVIIᵉ siècle*, 134–7 (1982), 47: 'la raison d'un effet est tout à la fois sa cause (l'explication de cet effet) et sa légitimé'.

example, through a copious analysis of the mathematical aspects of L418, shows how mathematical proofs are used precisely to show their invalidity in religious persuasion: 'le pari c'est la preuve que les preuves ne valent pas'.[9] Bernard Howells comes to a similar conclusion in his examination of the *pari*, making the important point from the mathematical analyses in L418 that 'concepts, as Pascal insists elsewhere, are never simple and unambiguous like numbers'.[10]

Related to the notion of play is that of the theatre, an important aspect largely ignored by Thirouin.[11] In an article on the notion of play in La Rochefoucauld, Philip E. Lewis equates games of strategy with the theatre. As he puts it, 'games of strategy require the player to assume a *rôle* which he conceives and acts out with regard to other players, who are likewise rational actors playing their roles'.[12] Man's submission to the rules of chance is mirrored within the conventions of the theatre. Death interrupts both the game and the theatrical representation of life, as is shown most vividly in L165: 'le dernier acte est sanglant quelque belle que soit la comédie en tout le reste'. In the *Entretien avec M. de Sacy*, Pascal had already, in a passage devoted to the positive side of Epictetus' writings, evoked the comparison of man's role in life to that of an actor on stage:

Souvenez-vous, dit-il [Epictetus] ailleurs, que vous êtes ici comme un acteur, et que vous jouez le personnage d'une comédie, tel qu'il plaît au maître de vous le donner. S'il vous le donne court, jouez-le court; s'il vous le donne long, jouez-le long, s'il veut que vous contrefassiez le gueux, vous le devez faire avec toute la naïveté qui vous sera possible; ainsi du reste.

---

[9] Thirouin, *Le Hasard et les règles*, 181.

[10] 'The Interpretation of Pascal's *Pari*', *Modern Language Review*, 79/1 (1984), 56. Howells offers a very useful study of the different stages of the fragment's composition. He comes to the conclusion that Pascal 'began toying with the popular wager argument, seeking first of all to use it to impress upon the reader the urgency of commitment. The novel idea of putting the argument into detailed mathematical form grew out of the metaphor in a kind of brainstorm and was marginal to his intentions. He finally saw that the argument could be put to more devastating use as part of a strategy aiming to show up the irrationality of the *libertin*'s reluctance to countenance religion' (p. 62).

[11] Thirouin makes only passing reference to theatrical imagery in *Le Hasard et les règles*, 59.

[12] 'La Rochefoucauld: The Rationality of Play', *Yale French Studies*, 41 (1968), 138.

C'est votre fait de jouer bien le personnage qui vous est donné; mais de le choisir, c'est le fait d'un autre.[13]

Moreover, it is significant that the term *divertissements* was commonly used to refer to the theatre in the seventeenth century; Pascal himself uses the word in this sense in L764. It is significant too that all references to the theatre, such as in L413 and L897 (where Corneille is named), L628, L773, L581, and L505, are associated with the depiction of the human condition.[14]

The reader is therefore forced to take part in a game on various levels. The rules of play allow for the illusion of order. As J. Huizinga has described in his *Homo Ludens*, play 'creates order, *is* order. Into an imperfect world and into the confusion of life it brings a temporary, a limited perfection.'[15] However, for Pascal, that 'perfection' is completely deceptive. As a fallen being, man has no choice but to submit himself to 'le hasard' and to play the game of the Wager. As a reader, he is caught in the game of trying to discern stability through the continually shifting meaning of key terms within a fragmentary text. The positive function of searching which is implicit within the movement associated with *divertissement* points towards the possible attainment of an eternal truth. However, can that truth be reached by man on earth? Does the word *vérité* escape the instability which informs the other terms in the *Pensées*?

TRUTH AND PLAY

In the Wager fragment, we find immediately the problem of truth subsumed within the paradigm of the game. The dialectician questions the existence of an absolute truth: 'N'y a[-t-]il point une vérité substantielle, voyant tant de choses vraies qui ne sont point la vérité même?' (L418). At a later stage in his argument, he concludes that a certain truth can be attained through the exercise of reason, but that this is inadequate as a means of conversion: 'cela est

---

[13] Seuil 293. The source of this allusion to Epictetus is the 1609 Paris translation by Jean de Saint-François (Goulu) of his *Manuel*, 654. See P. Courcelle's edn. of the *Entretien* (Paris, 1960), 12–13.
[14] I have discussed this aspect fully in ' "Levez le Rideau": Images of the Theatre in Pascal's *Pensées*', *French Studies*, 47/3 (July 1993).
[15] *Homo Ludens: A Study of the Play-Element in Culture* (London, 1949), 10.

démonstratif et si les hommes sont capables de quelque vérité celle-là l'est':[16] in other words, the truth obtained from demonstration is a relation between a subject and its predicate, and not a 'vérité substantielle'. On a human level, reason can attain the former, but cannot aspire to the latter.

Vérité, like the other terms I have discussed, must function on different planes. Indeed, in a human context, the search for a truth is likened to a game, which adds a further dimension to the notion of play. It also serves as a warning to those who search for a transcendent truth. As positive as the movement generated by *divertissement* may be, often the search provides more interest than the attainment of truth. In other words, if *divertissement* is self-perpetuating it only serves to intensify man's state of wretchedness, and in this respect is 'la plus grande de nos misères' (L414). The dialectician's direct juxtaposition of truth and play finds its most vivid representation in L773:

> Rien ne nous plaît que le combat mais non pas la victoire.
> On aime à voir les combats des animaux, non le vainqueur acharné sur le vaincu. Que voulait-on voir sinon la fin de la victoire et dès qu'elle est arrivée on en est saoul. Ainsi dans le jeu, ainsi dans la recherche de la vérité. On aime à voir dans les disputes le combat des opinions mais de contempler la vérité trouvée? point du tout. Pour la faire remarquer avec plaisir il faut la faire voir naître de la dispute. De même dans les passions il y a du plaisir à voir deux contraires se heurter, mais quand l'une est maîtresse ce n'est plus que brutalité.
> Nous ne cherchons jamais les choses, mais la recherche des choses.

From an Augustinian standpoint, truth on earth is corrupted by the Fall. Sénault, for example, states that, if man 'n'avoit perdu la supréme verité, il ne seroit pas en queste de son ombre'.[17] Pure truth is undermined by the presence of error which in turn manifests itself through language: 'la verité [. . .] est environnée d'erreurs qui la surprennent si elle s'esgare, et qui luy ravissent sa pureté si elle escoute leurs paroles'.[18] Indeed, for Pascal, words and error are closely related just as lack of words and divine truth are equated, as we see in L99:

---

[16] This is a major point made by Thirouin in his extensive analysis of L418: 'il ne s'agissait pas pour l'apologiste de convertir par un raisonnement mais de montrer qu'un raisonnement [. . .] est impropre à convertir' (pp. 176–7).

[17] *L'Homme criminel* (Paris, 1644), 142.   [18] Ibid. 404.

Il faut se tenir en silence autant qu'on peut et ne s'entretenir que de Dieu qu'on sait être la vérité, et ainsi on se le persuade à soi-même.

However, the fact that in the *Pensées* the word *vérité* appears more than 200 times in its singular form and 30 times in its plural form, in addition to the more than 20 occurrences of the related noun *le vrai*, testifies to its significance in the dialectical framework. Indeed, Jean Mesnard has pointed out that in the *Pensées* 'le problème de la vérité [...] devient problème de vie'.[19] Moreover, Pol Ernst, in his reconstruction of the dates of the composition of the *Pensées*, has shown that a great number of fragments from the early paper-type bearing the watermark RCDV (dating from the end of 1656 to March 1657) were already centrally concerned with *vérité*.[20] The extreme complexity of the notion of truth pervades all aspects of the human condition.

VÉRITÉ

In the long fragment on 'imagination', the dialectician shows that because of our human and therefore fallen status, we cannot hope to attain truth, conceived here as an abstract ideal or 'souverain bien', through human means:

> La justice et la vérité sont deux pointes si subtiles que nos instruments sont trop mousses pour y toucher exactement. S'ils y arrivent ils en écachent la pointe et appuient tout autour plus sur le faux que sur le vrai. (L44)

Human faculties, such as reason and the senses, cannot be relied upon as infallible scientific instruments to register this aspect of truth. In this respect Pascal differs most markedly from Descartes. In his *Discours de la méthode pour bien conduire sa raison et chercher la vérité dans les sciences*, Descartes affirms that 'la puissance de bien juger et distinguer le vrai d'avec le faux, qui est proprement ce qu'on nomme le bon sens ou la raison, est naturellement égale dans tous les hommes',[21] and that all truth can

---

[19] 'Pascal et la vérité', *Chroniques de Port-Royal*, 17–18 (1969), 21. Cf. C. Falcucci in *Le Problème de la vérité chez Pascal* (Paris, 1939), who emphasizes Pascal's 'attachement à la vérité par-dessus toutes choses' (p. 7).
[20] See Ernst, 'Géologie et stratigraphie des *Pensées* de Pascal', (thesis, Univ. of Paris IV, 1990), 153.
[21] *Discours de la méthode*, 1ère partie, from *Œuvres et lettres*, ed. A. Bridoux (Paris, 1952), 126.

be attained through reason. For Pascal, on the other hand, reason and common sense are inadequate by themselves to ascertain justice or truth. In L21, for example, where with painting 'il n'y a qu'un point indivisible qui soit le véritable lieu', in truth and morality such a 'point' cannot so easily be found: 'La perspective l'assigne dans l'art de la peinture, mais dans la vérité et dans la morale qui l'assignera?'

Moreover, in his acknowledgement of the difficulties which are inherent in his use of the term *vérité*, Pascal differs from previous apologists. Two works which include the word in the title, Charron's *Les Trois veritez* and Silhon's *Les Deux veritez*, demonstrate no such subtlety. Charron declares in the preface to his book that 'je me suis advisé d'essayer à prouver, l'une après l'autre, trois propositions, comme trois veritez grandes, et trois degrez de bastiment et establissement de la vraye et certaine religion contre tous ses ennemis'.[22] He then proceeds to specify these three Truths: that men are obliged to have a religion, that Christianity is the only true religion, and that the Catholic faith is the best choice within the Christian spectrum. Charron acknowledges that several truths can be found in the world, but he does not recognize their problematic nature; rather, they spring directly from divine truth:

Ne faut il pas par necessité, qu'il y ayt une premiere, souveraine et universelle verité et bonté, source premiere de toutes ces singulieres et particulieres veritez et bontez, dispersees inegalement par toutes les choses?[23]

Jean de Silhon at the beginning of *Les Deux veritez* is as inflexible as Charron: he defines his two Truths as 'l'une de Dieu et de sa providence, l'autre de l'immortalité de l'ame'.[24] Pascal's choice not to spell out such 'truths' but rather to consider aspects of human truth avoids an intransigence which delineates the works of Charron and Silhon, and allows for different layers of meaning in the word *vérité*. Although, like Charron and Silhon, he would understand *les vérités* as constitutive parts of an ultimate Truth, he would also assess those levels on which *vérité* is equivocal.

Thomas Harrington categorizes seven types of method which

---

[22] *Œuvres* (Geneva, 1970; facsimile of 1635 Paris edn.), ii. 2.
[23] Ibid. i. 26–7.
[24] Silhon, preface to *Les Deux veritez* (Paris, 1626).

Pascal uses for the discernment of truth in works other than the *Pensées*:

La première est celle qui permet de se convaincre de certaines vérités terrestres [*by which I take Harrington to mean mainly scientific truths, separate from any spiritual truths*]: elle s'adresse à la raison et Pascal lui donne le nom de *méthode géométrique*. La seconde, c'est celle que Pascal appelle *l'art d'agréer*. Cet art permet de faire croire des opinions sur les choses terrestres en faisant appel aux passions humaines; Pascal nous dit que cette méthode est trop subtile pour qu'il puisse en décrire les principes ou même l'appliquer. La troisième méthode est celle qui sert à faire passer les vérités divines dans l'âme par les voies du cœur. Cette troisième méthode dépasse évidemment les puissances humaines. La quatrième méthode est celle qui consiste à s'appuyer sur l'autorité, soit des livres, soit des personnes. Cette méthode, écrit Pascal dans la *Préface pour le Traité du Vide*, convient surtout aux matières qui relèvent de la mémoire. La cinquième méthode consiste à appliquer les sens et le raisonnement, comme en physique. La sixième méthode, employée dans les *Écrits sur la Grâce*, consiste à passer, par le raisonnement, des points non contestés aux points contestés et à présenter la vérité chrétienne comme intermédiaire entre deux erreurs. La septième et dernière méthode, employée dans ces mêmes *Écrits*, consiste à démêler les divers sens des propositions de la théologie afin de trouver le bon, celui qui s'accorde avec l'ensemble de la tradition chrétienne.[25]

Harrington goes on to reject the adequacy of these methods when applied to *vérité* in the *Pensées*, but offers instead the *liasse* entitled 'Raisons des effets' as the key to understanding truth in the *Pensées*. However, without questioning the undoubted value of Harrington's analysis, we must be wary of attempting to resolve the contradictory problems involving truth in such a neat way. In addition to the 'Raisons des effets', which indeed are as central as Harrington suggests, many of the other methods which he lists also play an integral part in the *Pensées*. The value of reason, for example, which is encapsulated in the 'esprit géométrique', is not denied completely, as can be seen in L513 ('la finesse est la part du jugement, la géométrie est celle de l'esprit'); the method of relying on tradition and authority is clearly set out in, for example, fragment L865 ('la vraie source de la vérité [. . .] est la tradition'); and L733 presents seemingly contradictory truths which one must 'démêler' (to use Harrington's term). I shall discuss more fully some of these fragments at a later stage in this chapter.

[25] *Vérité et Méthode dans les 'Pensées' de Pascal* (Paris, 1972), 9–10.

As we have seen already, *vérité* is not used as a univocal concept. Indeed, the model which I have applied to the other key terms can be employed equally well with *vérité*. Moreover, it is no coincidence that *vérité* is often paired with those 'positive' terms concerning the human condition, most particularly *bonheur* and *justice*.[26] On a human scale, *vérité* (V1—see Table of Terms and Fig. 7) is portrayed as inherently corrupt and illusory, usually equated with legitimacy (V1*a*), with the related concept of the veracity of a proposition (V1*b*) or with the depiction of reality (V1*c*). Relating to the notion of play and the illusion of truth (V1), it is striking that the word 'illusion' means literally 'in-play', stemming from the Latin 'illudere' or 'inludere'. Man's corruption is inseparable from a world governed by play.[27] The most notable example of V1*a* is used in L60 (which I quoted extensively in Chapter 8), where *vérité* is arbitrarily conceived ('un méridien décide de la vérité') and where it, like justice, is ironically depicted, in a paraphrase of Montaigne's words, as totally inconsistent: 'Vérité au-deçà des Pyrénées, erreur au-delà' (L60). *Vérité* in the sense of V1*b* is best exemplified in L92, where the belief of the 'peuple' in the truth of a proposition is shown to be illusory and misplaced:

Raison des effets.
Il est donc vrai de dire que tout le monde est dans l'illusion, car encore que les opinions du peuple soient saines, elles ne le sont pas dans sa tête, car il pense que la vérité est où elle n'est pas. La vérité est bien dans leurs opinions, mais non pas au point où ils se figurent.

Truth in the sense of reality (V1*c*) occurs most often with the noun *le vrai*. In L131, for example, the dialectician asserts that 'nous n'avons aucune idée du vrai, tous nos sentiments étant alors des illusions'.

However, truth for man in his fallen state rests on a fundamental contradiction: he desires truth but cannot attain it. This disparity can be found initially in L71, where Pascal first wrote after the heading 'Contradiction' the words, 'désir de vérité, justice', before crossing them out. As we saw with the concepts of *repos*, *bonheur*,

---

[26] The combination of *bonheur* and *vérité* is found especially in the expression *vrai bien*, as seen in fragments like L12, L148, L149, L393, L453, L537, L626, and L631. See P. Sellier, *Pascal et Saint Augustin* (Paris, 1970), 80–1, for a discussion of the pairing of *vérité* and *bonheur*. [27] See Huizinga, *Homo Ludens*, 11.

and *justice*, this sense of truth shows a move away from the fundamental corruption of man and points to an awareness of a higher truth, and belongs to the second category, V2. The dialectician develops this situation in L75:

> L'Ecclésiaste montre que l'homme sans Dieu est dans l'ignorance de tout et dans un malheur inévitable, car c'est être malheureux que de vouloir et ne pouvoir. Or il veut être heureux et assuré de quelque vérité [V2]. Et cependant il ne peut ni savoir ni ne désirer point de savoir. Il ne peut même douter.

Man in his wretched state cannot know truth, and yet he is unable *not* to wish for it.[28] The restlessness which this paradoxical situation provokes represents a first step towards the acceptance of the existence of a spiritual truth (which I shall call V3):

> Qu'il [l'homme] se haïsse, qu'il s'aime: il a en lui la capacité de connaître la vérité [V2] et d'être heureux; mais il n'a point de vérité [V3], ou constante, ou satisfaisante. (L119)

At its highest level, *vérité* is unequivocally equated to God (V3), as we saw earlier in L99. Closely related to this stable truth is that exemplified by Christ ('la vérité du Messie'—L826), V3*a*, which in turn contains the truths of the Christian religion (V3*b*) and the orthodox truths of the Catholic Church (V3*c*). It is within this context that most examples of the plural form *vérités* occur.[29] Only in L44, where *vérités* is used solely as the plural of the truth of a proposition, and L449, where geometric truths are evoked, do we find *vérités* appearing with an explicitly different sense. Some uses of *le vrai* are also related to the truths of religion.[30] The truths of Christianity and the Church provide a vital link between man and God.

The different levels of *vérité* are summarized in Fig. 7.

Now that we have an outline of the structures within which truth functions, I shall move to an analysis of truth within the context of man's corrupt state, particularly the notion of truth and falsity, before assessing the importance of the 'Raisons des effets' in man's progression towards the possibility of absolute truth.

It should be noted at this stage that Pascal differs to some extent

---

[28] Cf. L401: 'Nous sommes incapables de ne pas souhaiter la vérité et le bonheur et sommes incapables ni de certitude ni de bonheur.'
[29] See e.g. L733, L189, and L604.   [30] e.g. L692, L721, L758, L856.

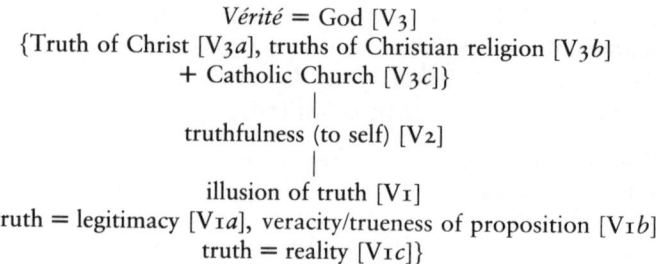

FIG. 7

from Arnauld and Nicole in the treatment of *vérité*. Although they acknowledge the fallibility of human judgement of truth,[31] they come nearer to the Cartesian value of reason than does Pascal, although the senses are given more prominence than with Descartes,[32] and they place more emphasis on reason as being one of two possible ways of assessing the truth of a statement:

> Car il y a deux voies generales qui nous font croire qu'une chose est vraie. La premiere est la connoissance que nous en avons par nous-mêmes, pour en avoir reconnu et recherché la verité, soit par nos sens, soit par notre raison; ce qui se peut appeller generalement *raison*, parceque les sens mêmes dépendent du jugement de la raison; ou *science*, prenant ici ce nom plus generalement qu'on ne le prend dans les écoles, pour toute connoissance d'un objet tirée de l'objet même.
>
> L'autre voie est l'autorité des personnes dignes de creance, qui nous assûrent qu'une telle chose est, quoique par nous-mêmes nous n'en sachions rien; ce qui s'appelle foi, ou creance [. . .].[33]

Arnauld and Nicole go on to specify that, as there can be two kinds of authority, from God and from men, so too can there be two

---

[31] See A. Arnauld and P. Nicole, *La Logique ou L'Art de penser* (1662), ed. P. Clair and F. Girbal (Paris, 1981), III, xx, b, 6, p. 282.

[32] Arnauld and Nicole place their view of reason and the senses between that of Descartes, who rejects all value of the senses, and Gassendi, who ascertains that it is not the senses themselves but rather the judgements formed from those senses which deceive us.

[33] *La Logique*, IV. xii. 335. Cf. I. 22: 'il faut rendre son esprit capable de découvrir la verité, lors même qu'elle est cachée et enveloppée'. H. Davidson points out that Arnauld and Nicole 'would have had a higher opinion of rhetoric if they had not held so high an opinion of truth, so firm a conviction of its attainability, and such confidence in its power to impose itself once grasped', *Audience, Words, and Art* (Columbus, Oh., 1965), 82.

kinds of faith, divine faith, which is never subject to error, and human faith, which can indeed be fallible. Indeed, in many cases, Arnauld and Nicole use the word *foi* where Pascal uses *vérité*. Although human faith can attain certainty as if 'nous en avions des demonstrations mathematiques', it is true that 'il est souvent assez difficile de marquer précisément quand la foi humaine est parvenue à cette certitude, et quand elle n'y est pas encore parvenue'.[34] According to Arnauld and Nicole, 'la foi suppose toûjours quelque raison', and, 'à l'égard de la foi divine, parce que la vraie raison nous apprend que Dieu étant la vérité même, il ne nous peut tromper en ce qu'il nous revele de sa nature ou de ses mysteres'.[35]

TRUTH AND CORRUPTION

In fragment L45, truth is presented on two different levels. In the first use of the word, *vérité* operates from both a transcendent and human standpoint: all truth remains hidden from fallen man's blinkered vision. The second occurrence of the term is used specifically in a human context: the very principles of human perception of truth—reason and the senses—are shown to be faulty, a view which distinguishes Pascal from Arnauld and Nicole:

> L'homme n'est qu'un sujet plein d'erreur naturelle, et ineffaçable sans la grâce. Rien ne lui montre la vérité [V1, 2, and 3]. Tout l'abuse. Ces deux principes de vérité [V1], la raison et les sens, outre qu'ils manquent chacun de sincérité, s'abusent réciproquement l'un l'autre; les sens abusent la raison par de fausses apparences. Et cette même piperie qu'ils apportent à l'âme, ils la reçoivent d'elle à leur tour; elle s'en revanche. Les passions de l'âme les troublent et leur font des impressions fausses. Ils mentent et se trompent à l'envi. (L45)

At the end of this fragment, Pascal wrote, 'Il faut commencer par là le chapitre des puissances trompeuses.' Clearly at this point the dialectician intends to consider those 'puissances', like *imagination*,

---

[34] *La Logique*, IV. xii. 336.
[35] Ibid. 337. As Pascal sees it, faith is above all reason and can only be a gift from God: 'La foi est différente de la preuve. L'une [la preuve] est humaine et l'autre est un don de Dieu. [. . .] C'est de cette foi que Dieu lui-même met dans le cœur, dont la preuve est souvent l'instrument' (L7). However, in some cases, discernment of the genuine nature of faith is needed by the Church. Cf. L975: 'les hommes prennent souvent leur imagination pour leur cœur; et ils croient être convertis dès qu'ils pensent à se convertir'.

coutume, and *amour-propre*, which deceive and corrupt man's already flawed perception of truth. Significantly, both *imagination* and *coutume* relate directly to the notion of play and are identified as creating their own set of rules, 'une seconde nature' (L44 and L126).³⁶

In the long fragment devoted to *amour-propre*, L978, self-love is depicted as the cause of man's aversion for truth, a truth which can be equated here to self-knowledge (V2), as is evident in the examples which are used, but which does not preclude a sense of man's blindness to transcendental truths. In the following extract from L978, the speaker introduces the analogy of the Protestant churches' reaction against confession in order to show man's desire to avoid truth, thereby also implying a further spiritual truth within the Catholic law (V3c):

> Car n'est-il pas vrai que nous haïssons la vérité [V2 and V3c] et ceux qui nous la disent, et que nous aimons qu'ils se trompent à notre avantage, et que nous voulons être estimés d'eux autres que nous ne sommes en effet?
> En voici une preuve qui me fait horreur. La religion catholique n'oblige pas à découvrir ses péchés indifféremment à tout le monde; elle souffre qu'on demeure caché à tous les autres hommes; mais elle en excepte un seul, à qui elle commande de découvrir le fond de son cœur, et de se faire voir tel qu'on est. Il n'y a que ce seul homme au monde qu'elle nous ordonne de désabuser, et elle l'oblige à un secret inviolable, qui fait que cette connaissance est dans lui comme si elle n'y était pas. Peut-on s'imaginer rien de plus charitable et de plus doux? Et néanmoins la corruption de l'homme est telle qu'il trouve encore de la dureté dans cette loi; et c'est une des principales raisons qui a fait révolter contre l'Église une grande partie de l'Europe.

Man's hatred of truth contains, paradoxically, an acknowledgement of the existence of another human truth, in this case self-knowledge (V2). This is how the reader, while caught in the game of searching for shifting truths which are a continual sign of his corruption, is always faced with the possibility of another, more stable truth. By stressing that man knowingly wishes others to be deceived, the dialectician places in the reader's mind the idea of a truth which lies beyond the wretchedness of self-deception.

---

³⁶ J. Huizinga in his *Homo Ludens* calls custom, in its sense of ritual, 'a spirit of pure play truly understood' (p. 5). See also pp. 19–20.

Moreover, the reaction which the belligerent and hyperbolic tone of the dialectician will inevitably provoke in the reader only adds to the elaborate game of enticing some form of commitment:

> Il y a différents degrés dans cette aversion pour la vérité [V2], mais on peut dire qu'elle est dans tous en quelque degré, parce qu'elle est inséparable de l'amour-propre. [...]
> L'homme n'est donc que déguisement, que mensonge et hypocrisie, et en soi-même et à l'égard des autres. Il ne veut donc pas qu'on lui dise la vérité [V2 and 3]. Il évite de la dire aux autres; et toutes ces dispositions, si éloignées de la justice et de la raison, ont une racine naturelle dans son cœur.[37]

Through this deliberate self-deception, it is evident that, in a fallen world, truth and falsity coexist. Indeed, as a passage from the third letter of the *Lettres provinciales* shows, there exists on all levels a very thin line between truth and error:

> La vérité est si délicate, que si peu qu'on s'en retire, on tombe dans l'erreur: mais cette erreur est si déliée, que, sans même s'en éloigner, on se trouve dans la vérité.[38]

In the long fragment which deals with Imagination in its role as one of the 'puissances trompeuses', just such an interchangeability of truth and error is evident:

> Imagination.
> C'est cette partie dominante de l'homme, cette maîtresse d'erreur et de fausseté, et d'autant plus fourbe qu'elle ne l'est pas toujours, car elle serait règle infaillible de vérité [V1], si elle l'était infaillible du mensonge. Encore—
> Mais, étant le plus souvent fausse elle ne donne aucune marque de sa qualité marquant du même caractère le vrai et le faux. (L44)

This fluctuation between truth and falsity in turn explains Pascal's ironic statement in L60, quoted earlier, of the fact that what passes for truth, in other words legitimacy (V1*a*), on one side of a border is viewed as error on the other. Truth becomes so obscured that, by

---

[37] Cf. L617: 'Qui ne hait en soi son amour-propre et cet instinct qui le porte à se faire Dieu, est bien aveuglé. Qui ne voit que rien n'est si opposé à la justice et à la vérité.'

[38] Seuil 380. It should be noted that the notion of truth containing falsehood and vice versa is a medieval and Renaissance commonplace about the effect of the use of 'probable' premisses. See I. Maclean, *Interpretation and Meaning in the Renaissance: The Case of Law* (Cambridge, 1992), 73–5.

contrast, lies appear to gain the upper hand. The words 'en ce temps' in L739 reveal the sense of truth as legitimacy changing not only through geographical space, as in L60,[39] but also through temporal dimensions; what may pass for truth at one time may well be perceived as lies at another:

> La vérité [V1] est si obscurcie en ce temps et le mensonge si établi qu'à moins que d'aimer la vérité [V1, 2, and 3] on ne saurait la connaître.[40]

Furthermore, in *De l'esprit géométrique*, Pascal moves away from the central discussion, concerning geometric truth, to a depiction of the human condition which is close to that found in the *Pensées*, where he shows that by nature man can only accept what he understands. In other words, he is often able to embrace lies more readily than the truth, whether it be self-knowledge or the existence of God:

> C'est une maladie naturelle à l'homme de croire qu'il possède la vérité [V1, 2, and 3] directement: et de là vient qu'il est toujours disposé à nier tout ce qui lui est incompréhensible; au lieu qu'en effet il ne connait naturellement que le mensonge, et qu'il ne doit prendre pour véritables que les choses dont le contraire lui paraît faux.[41]

Man's reluctance to love truth leads to an indifference which in turn results in a confusion between truth and falsity. In L428, for example, the speaker upbraids those men 'qui vivent dans l'indifférence de chercher la vérité [V3] d'une chose qui leur est si importante, et qui les touche de si près', namely eternal life. Yet this indifference reaches the point where 'ils ne savent s'il y a vérité [V1] ou fausseté dans la chose.'

This juxtaposition of corrupt and spiritual truth, as well as the

---

[39] Cf. L840: 'Ce n'est pas ici le pays de la vérité; elle erre inconnue parmi les hommes.' As R. Parish puts it in *Pascal's 'Lettres Provinciales': A Study in Polemic* (Oxford, 1989), 'this *pays* represents the areas of secular or indeed erroneous religious thought which deny or suppress the role of the crucifixion in Christian teaching because they deny or suppress the areas of human experience to which it corresponds: pain, suffering, sin, death—*misère* in other words' (p. 80).

[40] As in many fragments, spiritual truth is implied here also. It is probable that Pascal is referring to the condemnation of Jansenius and that of the *Lettres provinciales*. L740, written on the same page as L739 and also in Gilberte's hand (and included in the same fragment by Sellier and Le Guern in their edns.), implies the Jesuits' abuse of their knowledge of the truth: 'Les malingres [*as spelt by Gilberte, but probably 'malins'*] sont gens qui connaissent la vérité mais qui ne la soutiennent qu'autant que leur intérêt s'y rencontre mais hors de là ils l'abandonnent' (L840).

[41] Seuil 352.

mingling of the concepts of truth and falsity, serve to unsettle the reader's belief in his ability to attain truth on earth. The dialectician plays with the different notions of truth both to dislodge preconceived opinions and to pose further questions about man's condition in a fallen context. In L691, for example, the words 'le pyrrhonisme est le vrai' throw into doubt both the status of scepticism and the nature of *le vrai*. On one level, Pyrrhonism can be taken to combat dogmatic rationalism, which is described by the dialectician in L896 as 'ce mal': 'pyrrhonisme est le remède à ce mal et rabattra cette vanité'. Moreover, within this context, Pyrrhonism can lead the formerly arrogant rationalist to question his beliefs and possibly to reassess his thoughts on religion. In this way, 'le pyrrhonisme sert à la religion' (L658). If we consider scepticism in this light, then it can indeed point towards a spiritual truth. But, on another level, scepticism epitomizes man's fallen state; he is certain of nothing and is unable to find truth in any context. Thus *le vrai* must represent a false or flawed form of truth. As Mesnard puts it, 'le pyrrhonisme n'est le vrai que pour l'homme sans Dieu'.[42] Mesnard, perhaps unconsciously, then introduces the theme of the game: 'dans le pyrrhonisme poussé à l'extrême, il entre une part de jeu'.[43] It is part of the dialectician's game to destabilize all notions of human truth.

To take L131, a central fragment devoted to Pyrrhonism, we find immediately the shifting values of truth. Initially, in Pascal's characterization of Pyrrhonism, the dialectician accedes to the Sceptics that 'nous n'avons aucune certitude de la vérité [V1*b*] de ces principes' (first principles). Moreover, he states (in a deleted section) that 'Qu'on accorde donc aux pyrrhoniens ce qu'ils ont tant crié, que la vérité [V1, 2, and 3] n'est pas de notre portée'.[44] Yet the dialectician goes on to reject the Sceptics' belief that man cannot attain any *sense* of truth, and shows by contrast the way in which the doctrine of the Fall explains man's confusion of *vérité* and *mensonge*:

Car enfin si l'homme n'avait jamais été corrompu il jouirait dans son innocence et de la vérité [V3] et de la félicité avec assurance. Et si l'homme

---

[42] 'Pascal et la vérité', 24.   [43] Ibid. 25.
[44] E. Limbrick, 'Le Pyrrhonisme est le vrai', in *Mélanges à la mémoire de V.-L. Saulnier* (Geneva, 1984), chooses mainly to concentrate on this aspect only. See p. 448.

n'avait jamais été que corrompu il n'aurait aucune idée ni de la vérité [V3], ni de la béatitude. Mais malheureux que nous sommes et plus que s'il n'y avait point de grandeur dans notre condition, nous avons une idée du bonheur et nous ne pouvons y arriver. Nous sentons une image de la vérité [V2] et ne possédons que le mensonge. (L131)

In L905, another fragment concerning the Sceptics, Pascal distinguishes between a truth, which is partially true and partially false (in other words, truth in a fallen world, V1), and 'la vérité essentielle', truth in its purest and most transcendent form (V3):

> Pyrrhonisme.
> Chaque partie est ici vraie en partie, fausse en partie. La vérité essentielle [V3] n'est point ainsi, elle est toute pure et toute vraie. Ce mélange la détruit et l'anéantit. Rien n'est purement vrai et ainsi rien n'est vrai en l'entendant du pur vrai.

From the standpoint of essential truth, nothing in this world can be purely true. It is evident that this fragment refers to Montaigne's 'Nous ne goustons rien de pur' (II. xx), hence explaining the heading, 'Pyrrhonisme'.[45] Pascal diverges from the sceptical viewpoint that nothing can be pure by emphasizing the contradictory aspects of human existence, as can be seen in the examples which he uses in L905. In this world, we can possess only partial truth, but the perception of this fragmented truth, this 'instinct secret qui reste de la grandeur de notre première nature' (L136), distinguishes it from the agnosticism of the Sceptics. Indeed, a truth which is fragmentary is matched by the fragmentation of the text:

> On dira qu'il est vrai que l'homicide est mauvais: oui, car nous connaissons bien le mal et le faux. Mais que dira[-t-]on qui soit bon? La chasteté? Je dis que non, car le monde finirait. Le mariage? non, la continence vaut mieux. De ne point tuer? non, car les désordres seraient horribles, et les méchants tueraient tous les bons. De tuer? non, car cela détruit la nature. Nous n'avons ni vrai, ni bien qu'en partie, et mêlé de mal et de faux. (L905)

Furthermore, partial truth and partial falsity can be manipulated by the dialectician to encourage his reader to acknowledge the existence of many levels of truth. In this way, whereas a reader can reject the peremptory statement of 'truths' of a Charron or a Silhon with an equal degree of presumption, here one's response must be

---

[45] See my discussion of the 3 fragments headed by 'Pyrrhonisme' in Ch. 2 above. All 3 fragments, L518, L532, and L905, contain references to the *Essais*.

attuned to the layers of possibility which are offered by the dialectician. Fragment L701 is crucial in this regard:[46]

> Quand on veut reprendre avec utilité et montrer à un autre qu'il se trompe il faut observer par quel côté il envisage la chose, car elle est vraie ordinairement de ce côté-là et lui avouer cette vérité [V1b], mais lui découvrir le côté par où elle est fausse. Il se contente de cela car il voit qu'il ne se trompait pas et qu'il y manquait seulement à voir tous les côtés. Or on ne se fâche pas de ne pas tout voir, mais on ne veut pas être trompé, et peut-être cela vient de ce que naturellement l'homme ne peut tout voir, et de ce que naturellement il ne se peut tromper dans le côté qu'il envisage, comme les appréhensions des sens sont toujours vraies.

In this passage, truth (V1b) is perceived as justifiable in the mind of the beholder. In other words, the dialectician does not question the validity of another person's impression of truth. It is in this respect that 'les appréhensions des sens sont toujours vraies': we believe our perceptions to be true. On one level, this fragment would seem to constitute a psychological ploy of flattery in order to engage the other person's sympathy. However, on all other levels it cannot be interpreted simply as a covert statement of intent to win over one's opponents. Rather, it should be seen as a plea to look beyond one's immediate impressions and, above all, to recognize that truth is neither one-dimensional nor static.

Contrary to Descartes, who holds the notion that 'n'y ayant qu'une vérité de chaque chose, quiconque la trouve en sait autant qu'on peut savoir',[47] Pascal acknowledges the existence of differing truths in a fallen world, such as in L443:

> Tous errent d'autant plus dangereusement qu'ils suivent chacun une vérité [V1]; leur faute n'est pas de suivre une fausseté, mais de ne pas suivre une autre vérité [V1, 2, or 3].

Within the context of man's fallen nature, therefore, truths can differ from each other and can be ambivalent in themselves. The fragments devoted to *La raison des effets* both augment and provide a key to these complexities.

---

[46] I believe that T. Harrington seriously underestimates the value of this fragment when he asserts that it 'ne donne qu'un pâle reflet' of the depiction of *vérité* which can be found in the *liasse*, 'Raisons des effets'. See his *Vérité et Méthode dans les 'Pensées' de Pascal*, 12.

[47] *Discours de la méthode*, 2ᵉ partie, 139.

RAISON DES EFFETS

Recent scholarship has done much to redefine the importance of the *raison des effets*.[48] Jean Molino in his article links Pascal's use of *effet* in the *Pensées* to the recurrence of the word in his scientific works, such as the *Traités de l'équilibre des liqueurs et de la pesanteur de la masse de l'air*. *Effet* is associated with the seventeenth century use of the term *phénomène*. However, as Laurent Thirouin points out and develops, the narrow and exclusively scientific sense which Pascal applied to *effet* in his scientific treatises cannot be used when discussing the very different concerns of the *Pensées*. It should be added here that the occurrences of *effet* in the *Lettres provinciales* contain no evidence of its scientific meaning. As informative as these scientific roots may be, they can only be seen as interesting starting-points in a full understanding of the *raison des effets*. One must move from the scientific to the moral value of *effet*. As Thirouin elaborates,

> Le sens que prend le mot 'effet' dans les *Pensées* apparaît bien comme un décalque métaphorique de sa valeur scientifique. En science comme en morale, l'effet est le fondement, le départ de l'interrogation; on affecte de le considérer comme une donnée brute mais l'on sait ce qu'il représente déjà d'élaboration intellectuelle. De plus, il est toujours marqué d'une importance stratégique: on choisit de questionner précisément tel effet car on le considère comme l'expression privilégiée d'une loi. L'effet, enfin—et cela nous ramène au sens le plus commun du terme—a pour unique valeur le pouvoir qu'on lui attribue de démasquer une loi: ce n'est que le résultat d'une réalité fondamentale qu'il nous permettra peut-être d'atteindre. L'effet est constitutivement incomplet, transitoire. Si le divertissement est un effet, ce ne peut donc pas être l'aboutissement de la quête: le moraliste doit chercher au-delà une réalité plus fondamentale qui se cache derrière l'effet.[49]

This 'realité' lies in the *raisons des effets*, where, as Thirouin shows, 'la raison d'un effet est tout à la fois sa cause (l'explication de cet effet) et sa légitimité, ce en quoi cet effet est la situation la plus conforme à la raison'.[50]

---

[48] In addition to Harrington's analysis of the *raisons des effets*, I have consulted in particular J. Molino, 'La Raison des effets', in *Méthodes chez Pascal*, and, above all, L. Thirouin's 'Raison des effets: Essai d'explication d'un concept pascalien', *XVIIe siècle*, 134–7, (1982), 31–50. I have chosen to limit my discussion here to the way in which the *raisons des effets* relate to *vérité*. [49] Ibid. 41.
[50] Ibid. 47.

While in L701 truth is perceived to function on different levels, the fragments devoted to *raisons des effets* show the way in which a 'renversement continuel du pour au contre' (L93) can be applied to truth. One must have 'une pensée de derrière' (L91) in order to grasp a truth (V1*b*) which is hidden, complex, and profound. Although 'le peuple' may find truth in their opinions, their perception of that truth is misplaced, as we saw earlier in L92.

In L93, the dialectician applies the 'renversement continuel du pour au contre' to these arguments, showing how the opinions of the people are both 'saines' and 'vaines'.[51] By exploiting the contradictions of man through this depiction of truth, Pascal differs markedly from an apologist such as Silhon, who asserts that

la verité pouvant aussi bien se trouver en l'affirmative, qu'en la negative; on doit par maxime de prudence embrasser l'affirmative, et se tenir aux consequences d'icelle.[52]

The significance of the role of truth and the *raison des effets* can, so far, be resumed as follows. On the one hand, the *raison des effets* offers further proof of the instability of truth in a fallen world. As Thirouin puts it, the *raison des effets*, with the meaning of 'le fait que les effets ont raison, [. . .] vient de la déraison du monde'.[53] The many levels of truth and indeed the need for the interpretation of truth testify to the corruption of this world. Yet, on the other hand, through this very 'pensée de derrière', there exists the possibility of a fixed truth. Fragment L99, which clearly is closely related to the major concerns of 'Raisons des effets', shows the inadequacy of man's perception of truth, and yet also offers at the end a truth which indicates a greater stability (V3):

Ce qui cause cela est que nous sommes bien certains que nous n'avons pas mal à la tête, et que nous ne sommes pas boiteux, mais nous ne sommes pas si assurés que nous choisissons le vrai [V1]. De sorte que, n'en ayant d'assurance qu'à cause que nous le voyons de toute notre vue, quand un autre voit de toute sa vue le contraire, cela nous met en suspens et nous étonne. Et encore plus quand mille autres se moquent de notre choix, car il faut préférer nos lumières à celles de tant d'autres. Et cela est hardi et difficile. Il n'y a jamais cette contradiction dans les sens touchant un boiteux.

---

[51] T. Harrington gives a cogent analysis of the way in which 'renversement du pour au contre' is applied to vocabulary, such as the meanings of *raison* and *monde* in L101, *Vérité et méthode dans les 'Pensèes' de Pascal*, 34–5.
[52] *Les Deux veritez*, 14–15.   [53] 'Raison des effets', 48.

L'homme est ainsi fait qu'à force de lui dire qu'il est un sot il le croit. Et à force de se le dire à soi-même on se le fait croire, car l'homme fait lui seul une conversation intérieure, qu'il importe de bien régler. *Corrompunt bonos mores colloquia prava.* Il faut se tenir en silence autant qu'on peut et ne s'entretenir que de Dieu qu'on sait être la vérité [V3], et ainsi on se le persuade à soi-même.

Within the context of the Christian religion, Pascal defines two contrasting truths (V3*b*): a truth which implies man's capacity for greatness and a truth which emphasizes his state of corruption:

Elle [la religion chrétienne] enseigne donc ensemble aux hommes ces deux vérités [V3*b*]: et qu'il y a un Dieu, dont les hommes sont capables, et qu'il y a une corruption dans la nature, qui les en rend indignes. (L449)[54]

It is significant that, unlike Charron and Silhon who name their truths as '*les* trois veritez' and '*les* deux veritez', Pascal calls the above '*ces* deux vérités', which makes his assertion more plausible and less all-embracing. Moreover, through his depiction of the fundamental contradiction between man's corruption and his possible worthiness of God, these *vérités* extend the notion of the game in attaining a double tension which the inflexible 'truths' of his predecessors do not possess.

Through God, the reader is shown that he can attain a sense of real truth (as exemplified in Christian dogma) which appears stable and constant (V3). As Christ himself states in John 14: 6, 'Je suis la voie, la vérité et la vie.' Yet, although man is capable of attaining a higher truth, the dialectician stresses that one should never forget that that truth does not emanate from his own corrupt nature, for, as we saw earlier, man 'n'a point de vérité, ou constante, ou satisfaisante' (L119). Moreover, only God can give man 'vérités divines'. As Pascal emphasizes in *De l'esprit géométrique*, these 'vérités divines [. . .] sont au-dessus de la nature'.[55] The dialectician can only destabilize the reader's sense of human truth in order to indicate the necessity of other higher truths. Human reason is further humiliated when it is accentuated that only through the

---

[54] Cf. the letter written on the death of Pascal's father: 'Que notre volonté ne sépare donc pas ce que Dieu a uni; et étouffons ou modérons, par l'intelligence de la vérité [V3], les sentiments de la nature corrompue et déçue qui n'a que les fausses images, et qui trouble par ses illusions la sainteté des sentiments que la vérité [V3*b*] et l'Évangile nous doit donner', Seuil 277.   [55] Ibid. 355.

'cœur' can man gain intuitive understanding of divine truths from God:

> Je sais qu'il [Dieu] a voulu qu'elles [vérités divines] entrent du cœur dans l'esprit, et non pas de l'esprit dans le cœur, pour humilier cette superbe puissance du raisonnement [. . .].[56]

FIGURES AND MIRACLES

Thus, when we discuss the presence of a fixed truth as represented by God, it always remains only a possibility as long as we are of this earth. God's grace alone can ordain unambiguous truth, as the line from L45 implies: 'l'homme n'est qu'un sujet plein d'erreur naturelle et ineffaçable *sans la grâce*' (my italics). Just as in the *raison des effets*, where one must be aware of the 'renversement continuel du pour au contre', man cannot adhere to a narrow set of rules; he must acknowledge and indeed make positive use of the existence of truths which appear to contradict each other. In other words, in both a human and a transcendent context, man finds himself engaged in a game of truth:

> Les deux raisons contraires. Il faut commencer par là: sans cela on n'entend rien, et tout est hérétique. Et même à la fin de chaque vérité [V1 and 3] il faut ajouter qu'on se souvient de la vérité opposée [V1 and 3]. (L576)

Moreover, in L733, after depicting the contrary errors which abound in the Church, the dialectician asserts that faith embraces many seemingly contradictory truths (V3c):

> Il y a donc un grand nombre de vérités [V3c], et de foi et de morale qui semblent répugnantes et qui subsistent toutes dans un ordre admirable.
> La source de toutes les hérésies est l'exclusion de quelques-unes de ces vérités [V3c].
> Et la source de toutes les objections que nous font les hérétiques est l'ignorance de quelques-unes de nos vérités [V3c].[57]

---

[56] Ibid. It must also be noted that man's flawed use of his *volonté* as well as his reason leads to 'un balancement douteux entre la vérité et la volupté' (p. 356).

[57] The complexity of the notion of truth within the Church is further emphasized in the *Projet de mandement contre 'l'Apologie pour les Casuistes'*, where Pascal admits that all the 'abus qui se glissent dans l'Église puissent rendre suspecte la vérité des promesses de Jésus-Christ' if it were not for the fact that Christ 'a déclaré que plusieurs y jetteraient le trouble', Seuil 484.

Beyond man's inability to attain coherent order, there exists in the orthodox interpretation of Christian theology an 'ordre admirable' which is divinely inspired. In the same fragment, Pascal gives an example of these seemingly contradictory truths, the figure and reality of the Eucharistic Sacrament:

Sur le sujet du Saint-Sacrement nous croyons que la substance du pain étant changée et transubstanciée en celle du corps de Notre Seigneur, Jésus-Christ y est présent réellement: voilà une des vérités [V3c]. Une autre est que ce sacrement est aussi une figure de celui de la croix, et de la gloire, et une commémoration des deux. Voilà la foi catholique qui comprend ces deux vérités [V3c] qui semblent opposées. (L733)[58]

As Pierre Force explains, 'en tant que figure, l'Eucharistie est représentation de choses absentes. En tant que réalité, elle est présence voilée du Christ.'[59] This point is emphasized in the sixteenth letter of the *Lettres provinciales*, where the polemicist sees Christians as being the middle point between those 'bienheureux' who are in heaven and the Jewish people:

Les bienheureux possèdent Jésus-Christ réellement, sans figures et sans voiles. Les Juifs n'ont possédé de Jésus-Christ que les figures et les voiles, comme étaient la manne et l'agneau pascal. Et les chrétiens possèdent Jésus-Christ dans l'Eucharistie véritablement et réellement, mais encore couvert de voiles.[60]

Pascal specifies the Protestant inability to conceive of the Sacrament as being both a figure and the actual presence of Christ:

L'hérésie d'aujourd'hui ne concevant pas que ce sacrement contient tout ensemble et la présence de Jésus-Christ, et sa figure, et qu'il soit sacrifice, et commémoration de sacrifice, croit qu'on ne peut admettre l'une de ces vérités [V3c] sans exclure l'autre, pour cette raison. (L733)

We find therefore that truth in its transcendent sense can easily be confused with a more superficial common opinion. In other words, truth exists on a level deeper than mere external appearances:

---

[58] I have followed M. Le Guern's punctuation in this passage. L. Brunschvicg, in the introduction to his edn. of the *Pensées* (Paris, 1904), i, notes how 'la vérité de la religion se concevra [. . .] par voie d'opposition' (p. cxiii).
[59] *Le Problème herméneutique chez Pascal* (Paris, 1989), 117. Force also makes pertinent comparisons between the *Pensées* and Arnauld and Nicole's *La Logique*, I. iv. See also ibid. IV. xii. 337–8, where the Eucharist and transubstantiation are discussed.
[60] Seuil 450.

Comme J.-C. est demeuré inconnu parmi les hommes; ainsi la vérité [V3] demeure parmi les opinions communes sans différence à l'extérieur. Ainsi l'Eucharistie parmi le pain commun. (L225)

Furthermore, those who try to seek a truth which is obscure rather than blatant are engaging their *volonté* rather than their *esprit*, and, in so doing, are demonstrating a faith which cannot be proved purely by rational means:

> Dieu veut plus disposer la volonté que l'esprit, la clarté parfaite servirait à l'esprit et nuirait à la volonté.
> Abaisser la superbe. (L234)

Yet the very fact that such a truth remains hidden implies a pure truth which need not be figured in heaven. The necessity of interpretation of mysteries at least shows that figures are founded upon an original uncovered truth:

> La religion des Juifs a donc été formée sur la ressemblance de la vérité du Messie [V3a] et la vérité du Messie a été reconnue par la religion des Juifs qui en était la figure.
> Dans les Juifs la vérité [V3] n'était que figurée; dans le ciel elle est découverte.
> Dans l'Église elle est couverte et reconnue par rapport à la figure.
> La figure a été faite sur la vérité [V3].
> Et la vérité [V3] a été reconnue sur la figure. (L826)

It would seem then that figures point towards truth as their end. As Jean Mesnard puts it,

> La distinction fondamentale demeure celle de *figure* et *vérité*. Mais, si la vérité est modèle, elle est, plus essentiellement encore, fin. Non seulement la figure la représente comme en creux, mais elle invite à tendre vers elle.[61]

Miracles are also clearly linked to figures and truth, and they play their part in directing man towards the truth: 'les miracles et la vérité [V3b] sont nécessaires à cause qu'il faut convaincre l'homme entier en corps et en âme' (L848). Yet many of the fragments devoted to miracles pose the problem of distinguishing between true and false miracles as well as of how to interpret them.[62] Indeed, it seems that the dialectician would choose the apologetic force of figures above that of miracles, not only for the greater

---

[61] *Les 'Pensées' de Pascal*, 248.
[62] See L832, L839, L840, L843, L865, L878, L881, L894, for a link between miracles and *vérité*.

subtlety of figurative interpretation but also because the rational proof demanded by miracles would not lend itself to the many-faceted nature of truth; the realization of this problem is evident in L574:

> Un miracle, dit-on, affermirait ma créance, on le dit quand on ne le voit pas.
>
> Les raisons qui, étant vues de loin, paraissent borner notre vue, mais quand on y est arrivé on commence à voir encore au-delà. Rien n'arrête la volubilité de notre esprit. Il n'y a point, dit-on, de règle qui n'ait quelque exception ni de vérité si générale qui n'ait quelque face par où elle manque. Il suffit qu'elle ne soit pas absolument universelle pour nous donner sujet d'appliquer l'exception au sujet présent, et de dire, cela n'est pas toujours vrai, donc il y a des cas où cela n'est pas. Il ne reste plus qu'à montrer que celui-ci en est et c'est à quoi on est bien maladroit ou bien malheureux si on ne trouve quelque joint.[63]

The inadequacy of miracles in an apologetic argument is shown particularly in L184, where the absence of miracles would seem to validate non-belief in Christ, a view which the dialectician certainly does not countenance in the *Pensées*: 'On n'aurait point péché en ne croyant pas Jésus-Christ sans les miracles.'

Ultimately, therefore, man must strive, having acknowledged through the game which marks his fallen state the existence of several truths and indeed many layers of truth, towards a truth which is pure and encapsulated by God's order and charity. Any truth beyond that charity is not of God:

> On se fait une idole de la vérité même [V1 and 3], car la vérité hors de la charité [V1] n'est pas Dieu, et est son image et une idole qu'il ne faut point aimer ni adorer, et encore moins faut-il aimer ou adorer son contraire, qui est le mensonge.
>
> Je puis bien aimer l'obscurité totale, mais si Dieu m'engage dans un état à demi obscur, ce peu d'obscurité qui y est me déplaît, et parce que je n'y vois pas le mérite d'une entière obscurité il ne me plaît pas. C'est un défaut et une marque que je me fais une idole de l'obscurité séparée de l'ordre de Dieu. Or il ne faut adorer qu'en son ordre. (L926)

According to the dialectician, it is the duty of the Christian Church to uphold that truth which is of God, a truth which is pure and eternal, the beginning and end of all endeavour, as we find in L974:

---

[63] I read the 1st 'dit-on' as the voice of a sceptical interlocutor, and the 2nd as a general voice.

Comme la paix dans les États n'a pour objet que de conserver les biens des peuples en assurance, de même la paix dans l'Église n'a pour objet que de conserver en assurance la vérité [V3c] qui est son bien, et le trésor ou est son cœur. Et comme ce serait aller contre la fin de la paix que de laisser entrer les étrangers dans un État pour le piller, sans s'y opposer, de crainte d'en troubler le repos (parce que la paix n'étant juste et utile que pour la sûreté du bien elle devient injuste et pernicieuse, quand elle le laisse perdre, et la guerre qui le peut défendre devient et juste et nécessaire); de même, dans l'Église, quand la vérité [V3c] est offensée par les ennemis de la foi, quand on veut l'arracher du cœur des fidèles pour y faire régner l'erreur, de demeurer en paix alors, serait-ce servir l'Église, ou la trahir? serait-ce la défendre ou la ruiner? Et n'est-il pas visible que, comme c'est un crime de troubler la paix où la vérité [V3] règne, c'est aussi un crime de demeurer en paix quand on détruit la vérité [V3c]? Il y a donc un temps où la paix est juste et un autre où elle est injuste. Et il est écrit qu' 'il y a temps de paix et temps de guerre' et c'est l'intérêt de la vérité [V3] qui les discerne. Mais il n'y a pas temps de vérité [V3], et temps d'erreur, et il est écrit, au contraire, que 'la vérité de Dieu [V3] demeure éternellement'; et c'est pourquoi Jésus-Christ, qui dit qu'il est venu apporter la paix, dit aussi qu'il est venu apporter la guerre; mais il ne dit pas qu'il est venu apporter et la vérité [V3] et le mensonge. La vérité [V3] est donc la première règle et la dernière fin des choses.[64]

Thus, although fallen man's perception of truth, human and spiritual, is necessarily flawed, all lesser truths are subsumed in an essential truth which is 'la première règle et la dernière fin des choses' and which offers a resolution to the search for truth in all its forms.

However, again as with the other terms which I have explored, the different levels of truth which are questioned by the dialectician can only be discerned from a detailed examination. The reader, despite the explicit reference to an eternal truth, finds himself caught between shifting levels of truth. The game of searching for truth is consistent only in its inconsistency. For man on earth, any stability which he may believe himself to have found is immediately subverted by the dialectician. As he stresses in L177, 'ni la

---

[64] We find a variation of this fragment in the *Écrits des curés de Paris*, where Pascal, the presumed author of the second 'Factum', distinguishes between the time for war and peace as the means of the faithful and truth as the end: 'toutes ces choses sont nécessaires chacune en leur temps pour le bien de la vérité, qui est la dernière fin des fidèles, au lieu que la paix et la guerre n'en sont que les moyens, et ne sont légitimes qu'à proportion de l'avantage qui en revient à la vérité', Seuil 478.

contradiction n'est marque de fausseté ni l'incontradiction n'est marque de vérité'. As long as man remains in his flawed state, the possibility of eternal truth will remain trapped within the fragmentary text. All normal conventions of truth are thrown into disarray by what Sara Melzer calls an 'anti-rhetoric'. But, as she explains, 'this new rhetoric, by leading us farther away from the conventions of truth, paradoxically, will bring us closer to the truth of a higher order: the distance that separates us from truth'.[65]

If we return to the model of the game, we find how the differing and indeed contradictory notions of truth fit into the dialectician's conception of play. Thirouin in *Le Hasard et les règles*, while not discussing Pascal's juxtaposition of shifting notions of truth, acknowledges the problematic status of the term:

Concevoir, même obscurément, la vérité est pour Pascal une tâche redoutable. Proférer la vérité dépasse le plus souvent les forces humaines. Car la vérité est, dans les *Pensées*, un objet structurellement paradoxal: elle est le point mystérieux où convergent les contraires, où peuvent être tenus simultanément les jugements inconciliables. [. . .] La notion de jeu a cette valeur essentielle d'imposer à l'esprit simultanément des vérités contraires. Ce n'est pas un concept philosophique, ni même une métaphore que Pascal appliquerait à l'existence humaine, mais bien un modèle, un prisme à travers lequel un certain nombre de réalités incompatibles apparaissent solidaires.[66]

But the model of the game only works within the context of the doctrine of the Fall. Every game is temporary and can only point towards a higher, more permanent reality. It is this higher being which has been posited in the mind of the reader throughout the *Pensées* in what I have identified as the third category of each term. At the time of death, the non-believer's life is shown to have been governed by chance, but for the saved Christian, God's ordered plan is revealed. This is the point which Pascal makes in the letter upon his father's death:

nous devons chercher la consolation à nos maux, non pas dans nous-mêmes, non pas dans les hommes, non pas dans tout ce qui est créé; mais dans Dieu. [. . .] Que si nous suivons ce précepte, et que nous envisagions cet événement, non pas comme un effet du hasard, non pas comme une nécessité fatale de la nature, non pas comme le jouet des éléments et des

---

[65] '*Invraisemblance* in Pascal's *Pensées*: The Anti-Rhetoric', *Romanic Review*, 73 (1982), 36.   [66] pp. 210–11.

parties qui composent l'homme (car Dieu n'a pas abandonné ses élus au caprice et au hasard), mais comme une suite indispensable, inévitable, juste, sainte, utile au bien de l'Église et à l'exaltation du nom et de la grandeur de Dieu [. . .].[67]

On earth, the dialectician, in encouraging his reader to play with truth, is himself taking part in a game which reminds him of his own fallibility, and which, like the occasional lost train of thought, 'me fait souvenir de ma faiblesse que j'oublie à toute heure' (L656). Indeed, just as the reader can be played, so too can the dialectician in his role as the player be played. In Jacques Ehrmann's words, 'as an object in the game, the player can be its stakes (*enjeu*) and its toy (*jouet*)'.[68] Moreover, the game is contained within the fragmentary text which itself recalls man's fallen nature. In this respect, I differ fundamentally from Thirouin's argument. He concludes that the 'détour inattendu' of Pascal's unfinished and fragmentary work has made the study of the text into another game for scholars. As he puts it, 'les *Pensées* sont une apologie que la Providence a transformée en jeu'.[69] However, despite the further mystery which Pascal's premature death brought to the *Pensées*, their fragmentariness is in no way due entirely to his inability to finish them. Fragmentation is the very structure by which the dialectician continues the game of truth with his readers.

[67] Seuil 275.
[68] '*Homo Ludens* Revisited', *Yale French Studies*, 41 (1968), 55.
[69] 'Raison des effets', 215.

Conclusion

> C'est un grand éloge de dire d'un Livre, qu'il fait penser; et c'est un grand plaisir que la lecture d'un pareil Livre. Or tels sont sur-tout les bons Livres de pensées détachées. Un Lecteur, homme d'esprit et de réflexion, devient Auteur, en lisant Pascal, [...].
>
> (Abbé Nicolas Charles Joseph Trublet)[1]

The above eighteenth-century discussion of 'pensées détachées' sums up particularly well the central concerns of this book. The persuasive process of the *Pensées* is energized by the reader's active participation in sorting through both the fragmentary ordering and the shifting meanings of the text. Indeed, the involvement of the reader becomes creative in itself. The dialectician's role as persuader is therefore subverted as, through the medium of the *Pensées*, the reader operates as his own persuader:

> On se persuade mieux pour l'ordinaire par les raisons qu'on a soi-même trouvées que par celles qui sont venues dans l'esprit des autres. (L737)

In rhetorical terms, the reader becomes master of the *inventio* and *dispositio* of the text. Moreover, as I discussed in Chapter 2, the fourth part of traditional rhetoric, *memoria*, plays an important part in the *Pensées*. The dialectician is concerned with the way of writing 'qui s'insinue le mieux, qui demeure plus dans la mémoire et qui se fait le plus citer' (L745). He recognizes also the importance and the intricacy of maintaining the attention of his reader:

> Langage.
> Il ne faut point détourner l'esprit ailleurs sinon pour le délasser mais dans le temps où cela est à propos; le délasser quand il le faut et non autrement. Car qui délasse hors de propos il lasse et qui lasse hors de propos délasse, car on quitte tout là. Tant la malice de la concupiscence se plaît à faire tout le contraire de ce qu'on veut obtenir de nous sans nous donner du plaisir qui est la monnaie pour laquelle nous donnons tout ce qu'on veut. (L710)

---

[1] 'Sur la manière d'écrire par pensées détachées', in *Essais sur divers sujets de littérature et de morale* (Paris, 1735), 9.

The fragmentariness of the text, the maxim-like simplicity and the poetic qualities of certain fragments remain in the memory to an extent which full prosaic sentences do not. But beyond even these aspects, the reader's memory is made receptive to the continually shifting meaning of terms, as I showed in the central sections of this thesis. Once the notion of the Fall is fully comprehended, the instability of those terms depicting the human condition becomes integral to the reader's search beyond the inadequacies of language and order. In another fragment, the dialectician stresses that 'je trouve d'effectif que depuis que la mémoire des hommes dure, voici un peuple qui subsiste plus ancien que tout autre peuple' (L793). The impermanence of human wretchedness is transposed through *memoria* to the permanence of God's chosen race. Indeed, in the appropriately named *Mémorial*, L913, Pascal urges himself to forget everything of the world ('oubli du monde et de tout, hormis Dieu'), and to remember only God's word, as is shown in the quotation from Ps. 118: 16, *Non obliviscar sermones tuos* (translated by de Sacy as 'je n'oublierai point vos paroles').

As I have stressed throughout, the doctrine of the Fall underlies all aspects of language and truth in the *Pensées*. In a deleted section of L131, Pascal wrote of 'deux vérités de foi également constantes':

L'une que l'homme dans l'état de la création, ou dans celui de la grâce, est élevé au-dessus de toute la nature, rendu comme semblable à Dieu et participant de la divinité. L'autre qu'en l'état de la corruption, et du péché, il est déchu de cet état et rendu semblable aux bêtes. Ces deux propositions sont également fermes et certaines.

Immediately after this passage, the dialectician adds that 'l'Écriture nous les déclare manifestement', giving a number of fragmentary quotations from the Bible, headed by the words *deliciae meae esse cum filiis hominum*, from Prov. 8: 31. The image of wisdom playing in the world in the full sight of God, conclusively translated by de Sacy, points to a game played in harmony with God:

J'étais chaque jour dans les délices, me jouant sans cesse devant lui [Dieu];
Me jouant dans le monde; et mes délices sont d'être avec les enfants des hommes.[2]

Although God stands above the game which marks man's

---

[2] *Proverbes*, 8: 30–1.

corrupt condition, the Fall itself made God embark on his own 'game'. Steven Brams goes so far as to call God 'a superlative strategist'.³ Indeed, the words in L242, 'Que Dieu s'est voulu cacher', show God's decision to hide himself from fallen man as a supreme strategic move. The true Christian strives to heal the rift which the Fall brought about, as is made clear in the *Mémorial*: 'Que je n'en sois pas séparé éternellement' (L913).

We saw in L99 that, although man's 'conversation intérieure' acts as a sign of his corruption, it is also 'une conversation intérieure, qu'il importe de bien régler'. By keeping God ('qu'on sait être la vérité') as the central focus of attention, the reader's process of self-persuasion can be perfected: 'et ainsi on se le persuade à soi-même'. In this way, a transformation from 'conversation intérieure' to 'conversion intérieure' is effected.

By playing with language and order, both dialectician and reader are continually reminded of man's flawed state. But the possibility of transcendence within the very concepts which indicate his fallenness points always to a God who is both stable and constant. Playing with shifting notions of truth becomes an eternal truth played through God.

[3] *Biblical Games: A Strategic Analysis of Stories in the Old Testament* (Cambridge, Mass., 1980), 170. He also states that 'since God does not always get His way, He can properly be viewed as a participant, or *player*, in a game' (p. 5). Concentrating on the Creation and the Fall in ch. 2, Brams distinguishes 5 different 'games': '1. The creation game (player: God). 2. The constraint game (players: God v. Adam and Eve). 3. The temptation game (players: serpent v. Eve). 4. The sharing game (players: Eve v. Adam). 5. The punishment game (players: Adam and Eve v. God.' In Plato's *Laws*, 7. 803, man is perceived as 'a plaything of God', but, unlike with Pascal, he is encouraged to partake in certain 'noble' pastimes so as to gain Heaven's favour.

Table of Terms

The abbreviated form of each word is placed in the left-hand margin after each term. Column 1 refers to Inc. 1, E1, I1, etc. Column 2 concerns Inc. 2, E2, etc. Column 3 corresponds to Inc. 3, E3, etc.

	1	2	3
inconstance (Inc.)	*inconstance*: wretchedness	*inconstance*: restlessness	*inconstance*: spiritual searching
ennui (E)	*ennui*: *néant*	*ennui*: *divertissement*	*ennui*: possible salvation
inquiétude (I)	*inquiétude*: anxiety of fallen state	*inquiétude*: searching	*inquiétude*: spiritual endeavour
repos (R)	*repos*: absence of movement	*repos*: pursued tranquillity	*repos*: spiritual peace
bonheur/ félicité (B)	*bonheur*: spurious happiness	*bonheur*: pursued happiness	*bonheur*: spiritual happiness
justice (J)	*justice*: human justice 1*a* natural; 1*b* political	*justice; les justes*: righteousness	*justice*: divine justness + retribution
vérité (V)	*vérité*: illusory truth 1*a* legitimacy; 1*b* veracity; 1*c* reality	*vérité*: truthfulness to self	*vérité*: God 3*a* Christ; 3*b* Christianity; 3*c* Catholicism

Bibliography

I. TEXTS BY PASCAL

Œuvres complètes, ed. L. Brunschvicg, 14 vols. (Paris, 1904–14).
Œuvres complètes, ed. J. Chevalier (Paris, 1954).
Œuvres complètes, ed. L. Lafuma (Paris, 1963).
Œuvres complètes, ed. J. Mesnard, 3 vols. (Paris, 1964–91).
Le Manuscrit des 'Pensées' de Pascal, ed. L. Lafuma (Paris, 1962).
Pensées, ed. L. Brunschvicg, 3 vols. (Paris, 1904).
Pensées, ed. M. Le Guern, 2 vols. (Paris, 1977).
Pensées, ed. P. Sellier (Paris, 1976 and 1991).
Pensées, ed. Z. Tourneur, 2 vols. (Dijon, 1938).
Discours sur la religion et sur quelques autres sujets, ed. E. Martineau (Paris, 1992).
Pensées, ed. L. Lafuma, trans. A. J. Krailsheimer (London, 1988; first published 1966).

II. DICTIONARIES

COTGRAVE, R., *A Dictionarie of the French and English Tongues* (London, 1611 and 1673).
Dictionnaire de l'Academie Françoise, 2 vols. (Paris, 1694).
FURETIÈRE, A., *Le Dictionnaire universel* (The Hague and Rotterdam, 1690).
NICOT, J., *Le Grand Dictionnaire François–Latin* (Paris, 1614).
RICHELET, P., *Dictionnaire François* (Geneva, 1680).

III. PRIMARY TEXTS

ARISTOTLE, *Les Ethiques d'Aristote à son filz Nicomache*, trans. P. L. of the household of le Conte d'Aran (Paris, 1553).
—— *Nicomachean Ethics*, trans. H. Rackman (London, 1982).
—— *La Rhetorique d'Aristote en François*, trans. F. Cassandre (Paris, 1654).
ARNAULD, A. and NICOLE, P., *La Logique ou L'Art de penser* (1662), ed. P. Clair and F. Girbal (Paris, 1981).
AUGUSTINE, *Confessions*, trans. R. Arnauld d'Andilly (Paris, 1659).
—— *De la Cité de Dieu*, trans. le Sieur de Ceriziers (Paris, 1655).

BARCOS, M. DE, *Correspondance*, ed. L. Goldmann (Paris, 1956).
Bible, trans. LeMaître de Sacy, ed. P. Sellier (Paris, 1990).
BOUCHER, J., *Les Triomphes de la religion chrestienne* (Paris, 1628).
BOURDONNÉ, C., *Le Courtisan desabusé, ou Pensées d'un gentil-homme qui a passé la plus grande partie de sa vie dans la cour et dans la guerre* (Paris, 1658).
CAMUS, J.-P., *Les Diversitez* (Paris, 1609).
CHARRON, P., *Œuvres*, 2 vols. (Geneva, 1970, facsimile of the 1635 Paris edn.).
CONDORCET, J. A. N., *Éloge de M. Pascal* (London and Paris, 1776).
COURCELLE, P., *L'Entretien de Pascal et Sacy* (Paris, 1960).
DESCARTES, *Œuvres et lettres*, ed. A. Bridoux (Paris, 1952).
DIDEROT, D., and D'ALEMBERT, J., *L'Encyclopédie ou Dictionnaire raisonnée des sciences, des arts et des métiers*, 5 vols. (New York, 1969, facsimile of the 1757 Paris edn.).
Digest of Justinian, The, ed. N. Mommsen and P. Krueger, trans. A. Watson, i (Philadelphia, Penn., 1985).
DU PONT, R., *La Philosophie des esprits* (Rouen, 1628; 1st edn. 1602).
DU TEIL, *Catechisme des sçavans* (Paris, 1651).
EPICTETUS, *Les Propos et Le Manuel*, trans. J. Goulu (Paris, 1609).
FARET, N., *L'Honneste-Homme ou l'Art de plaire à la Cour* (Paris, 1630).
FRAIN DU TREMBLAY, J., *Conversations morales sur les jeux et les divertissemens* (Paris, 1685).
FRANÇOIS DE SALES, *Œuvres*, ed. A. Ravier (Paris, 1969).
GARASSE, F., *Apologie du Père François Garasse* (Paris, 1624).
—— *La Doctrine curieuse des beaux esprits* (Paris, 1624).
GASSENDI, P., *Disquisitio Metaphysica*, trans. and ed. B. Rochot (Paris, 1962).
—— *Exercitationes Paradoxicae Adversus Aristoteleos*, trans. and ed. B. Rochot (Paris, 1959).
GATAKER, T., *Of the Nature and Use of Lots* (London, 1619).
HILLERIN, J. DE, *Les Grandeurs et Mystères du St Verbe Incarné*, 3 vols. (Paris, 1635-42).
JANSENIUS, C., *Traduction d'un discours de la reformation de l'homme interieur* (Paris, 1659).
LA CHAISE, F. DE, *Discours sur les 'Pensées' de M. Pascal* (Paris, 1672).
LA HARPE, J.-F., *Lycée ou Cours de littérature* (Paris, 1798-9), iv, vii.
LAFAYETTE, MME DE, *La Princesse de Clèves*, ed. A. Adam (Paris, 1966).
LANCELOT, C. and ARNAULD, A., *Grammaire générale et raisonnée* (Merston, 1967, facsimile of the 1660 Paris edn.).
LE FAUCHEUR, M., *Traité de l'action de l'orateur ou de la prononciation et du geste* (Paris, 1676, first published 1657).
MÉRÉ, CHEVALIER DE, *Œuvres*, ed. C. Boudhours, 3 vols. (Paris, 1930).
MERSENNE, M., *L'Impiété des déistes refutée* (Paris, 1624).

MITON, D., 'Pensées sur l'Honnesteté', in Saint-Evremond, Œuvres meslées (Paris, 1680), vi.
MOLIÈRE, Œuvres complètes, ed. P.-A. Touchard (Paris, 1962).
MONTAIGNE, M. DE, Œuvres complètes, ed. M. Rat (Paris, 1962).
NICOLE, P., Essais de morale (Paris, 1733–71; repr. Geneva, 1971).
—— Traité de la comédie, ed. G. Couton (Paris, 1961).
PLATO, Laws, trans. R. G. Bury, 2 vols. (London, 1926).
SAINT-CYRAN, ABBÉ DE (JEAN DU VERGER DE HAURANNE), Apologie pour Messire Henry-Louis Chastaigner de la Rochepozay (Paris, 1615).
—— Maximes saintes et chrestiennes tirées des lettres de Messire Jean du Verger de Hauranne, Abbé de Saint Cyran (Paris, 1648).
SAINT-EVREMOND, C. DE, Œuvres meslées (Paris, 1680), vi.
—— Œuvres mêlées, ed. L. de Nardis (Rome, 1966).
SÉNAULT, J.-F., De l'usage des passions (Paris, 1641).
—— L'Homme chrestien ou la reparation de la nature par la grace (Paris, 1648).
—— L'Homme criminel (Paris, 1644).
SENECA, Les Œuvres Meslees, trans. S. Goulart (Paris, 1598).
SÉVIGNÉ, MME DE, Correspondance, ed. R. Duchêne, 3 vols. (Paris, 1972–8).
SILHON, J. DE, De l'immortalité de l'âme (Paris, 1634).
—— Les Deux veritez (Paris, 1626).
SIRMOND, A., La Deffense de la vertu (Paris, 1641).
THOMAS AQUINAS, Summa Theologiae, ed. Blackfriars (London, 1963).
VOLTAIRE, Lettres philosophiques (Paris, 1964; first published 1734).
YVES DE PARIS, De l'indifference (Paris, 1638).
—— La Theologie naturelle ou Les Premieres veritez de la foy sont eclaircies par raisons sensibles et morales (Paris, 1633).

IV. SECONDARY TEXTS

ADAM, A., Sur le problème religieux dans la première moitié du XVIIe siècle (Oxford, 1959).
—— 'Sur les Pensées de Pascal', Information littéraire, 9 (1957), 6–8.
ANDRÉ, R., 'Pascal et la question du style', Europe, 597–8 (1979), 78–81.
BAIRD, A. W. S., Studies in Pascal's Ethics (The Hague, 1975).
BARENNE, O., Une grande bibliothèque de Port-Royal: Inventaire inédit de la bibliothèque de Isaac-Louis le Maistre de Sacy (7 avril 1684) (Paris, 1985).
BARNES, A., 'La Table des titres de la copie des Pensées est-elle de Pascal?', French Studies (1953), 140–6.

BARNETT, R. L., *Dynamics of Detour: Codes of Indirection in Montaigne, Pascal, Racine, Guilleragues* (Tübingen, 1986).
BAUDIN, E., *Pascal, les libertins et les jansénistes*, 2 vols. (Neuchâtel, 1946).
BAYLEY, P., 'A Reading of the First *Liasse*', in D. L. Rubin and M. B. McKinley (eds.), *Convergences* (Columbus, Oh., 1989), 196–207.
BERR, H., *Du scepticisme de Gassendi*, trans. B. Rochot (Paris, 1960).
BEUGNOT, B., 'Apologétique et mythe moral: La Méditation pascalienne sur le repos', in L. M. Heller and I. M. Richmond (eds.), *Pascal thématique des 'Pensées'* (Paris, 1988), 57–78.
—— 'Morale du repos et conscience du temps', *Australian Journal of French Studies*, 13 (1976), 183–96.
BIANCHINI FALES, A., 'Le Développement du mot *ennui* de la Pléiade jusqu'à Pascal', *Cultura Neolatina*, 12 (1952), 223–8.
Blaise Pascal: L'Homme et l'Œuvre (Paris, 1956).
BOUCHEZ, M., *La Valeur de l'ennui* (Paris, 1971).
BRAMS, S. J., *Biblical Games: A Strategic Analysis of Stories in the Old Testament* (Cambridge, Mass., 1980).
BRÉMOND, H., *Histoire Littéraire du sentiment religieux en France* (Paris, 1928), 7 vols.
BRIMO, A., *Pascal et le droit* (Paris, 1942).
BRINKMANN, H., *Mittelalterliche Hermeneutik* (Tübingen, 1980).
BROMBERT, V., 'Pascal's Happy Dungeon', *Yale French Studies*, 38 (1967), 230–42.
BRUNSCHVICG, L., *Descartes et Pascal, Lecteurs de Montaigne* (Neuchâtel, 1945).
BUSSON, H., *La Pensée religieuse française de Charron à Pascal* (Paris, 1933).
CARR, T. M., *Descartes and the Resilience of Rhetoric: Varieties of Cartesian Rhetorical Theory* (Carbondale, Ill., 1990).
CARRAUD, V., *Pascal et la philosophie* (Paris, 1992).
CHADWICK, H., *Augustine* (Oxford, 1986).
CHEVALIER, J., *Pascal* (Paris, 1922).
CHRISTODOULOU, K., 'Le Stoïcisme dans la dialectique apologétique des *Pensées*', in *Méthodes chez Pascal*, 419–26.
COGNET, L., *La Spiritualité moderne* (Paris, 1947).
—— 'Le Jugement de Port-Royal sur Pascal', in *Blaise Pascal: l'homme et l'œuvre*, 11–45.
COLLINET, J.-P., 'La Critique littéraire selon Pascal', in *Méthodes chez Pascal*, 391–400.
CONDORCET, J. A. N., *Éloge de M. Pascal* (London and Paris, 1776).
COURCELLE, P., 'De Saint Augustin à Pascal', in *Pascal présent*, 131–46.
—— *Les Confessions de Saint Augustin dans la tradition littéraire* (Paris, 1963).
—— *L'Entretien de Pascal et Sacy* (Paris, 1960).

CRONK, N., 'The Enigma of French Classicism: A Platonic Current in Seventeenth-Century Poetic Theory', *French Studies* (1986), 269–86.
CROQUETTE, B., *Pascal et Montaigne* (Geneva, 1974).
CROSS, F. L., and LIVINGSTONE, E. A., *The Oxford Dictionary of the Christian Church* (Oxford, 1988).
DAUPHINÉ, J., 'Quelques aspects de l'imagination dans les *Pensées*', *Europe*, 597–8 (1979), 86–91.
DAVIDSON, H. M., *Audience, Words, and Art* (Columbus, Oh., 1965).
—— *The Origins of Certainty: Means and Meanings in Pascal's 'Pensées'* (Chicago, 1979).
—— 'Le Pluralisme méthodologique chez Pascal', in *Méthodes chez Pascal*, 19–26.
—— 'Remarques sur la *Concordance des Pensées*', in *Méthodes chez Pascal*, 175–9.
—— and DUBÉ, P., *A Concordance to Pascal's Pensées* (Ithaca, NY, 1975).
—— —— *A Concordance to Pascal's 'Les Provinciales'*, 2 vols. (New York, 1980).
DELASSAULT, G., *La Pensée janséniste en dehors de Pascal* (Paris, 1963).
—— 'La Source des *Pensées* de Pascal', *Revue de sciences humaines* (1958), 213–16.
DE MAN, P., *Blindness and Insight: Essays in the Rhetoric of Contemporary Criticism* (New York, 1971).
DEMOREST, J., *Dans Pascal: Essai en partant de son style* (Paris, 1953).
—— 'Pascal's Sophistry and the Sin of Poesy', in J. Demorest (ed.), *Studies in Seventeenth-Century French Literature* (Ithaca, NY, 1962), 132–52.
DEPRUN, J., 'Pascal et le Purgatoire', in *Missions et Démarches de la Critique: Mélanges Offerts à J. A. Vier* (Haute-Bretagne, 1973), 209–16.
—— *La Philosophie de l'Inquiétude en France au XVIIIe Siècle* (Paris, 1979).
DESCOTES D., *L'Argumentation chez Pascal* (Paris, 1993).
—— 'Fonction argumentaire de la satire dans les *Provinciales*', in H. Baader (ed.), *Onze études sur l'esprit de la satire* (Tübingen, 1978), 43–65.
—— 'Pascal, rhétoricien de la géométrie', *Cahiers de l'Association Internationale des Études Françaises*, 40 (1988), 251–71.
—— 'Piège et paradoxe chez Pascal', in *Méthodes chez Pascal*, 509–24.
—— 'Réflexions sur l'art de persuader', in Y.-M. Bercé (ed.), *Destins et enjeux du XVIIe siècle* (Paris, 1985), 323–31.
DESCRAINS, J., *Jean-Pierre Camus (1584–1652), et ses Diversités (1609–1618), ou La Culture d'un évêque humaniste*, 2 vols. (Lille, 1985).
DIJKSTERHUIS, E. J. (ed.), *Descartes et le Cartésianisme hollandais* (Amsterdam, 1951).
DUBOIS, E., 'Le Père le Moyne et *La Dévotion aisée*', in G. G. Demerson *et*

al. (eds.), *Les Jésuites parmi les hommes au XVIe et XVIIe siècles*, Actes du Colloque de Clermont-Ferrand, Apr. 1985 (Clermont-Ferrand, 1987), 153–62.

DUMONCEAUX, P., *Langue et sensibilité au XVIIe siècle: L'Évolution du vocabulaire affectif* (Geneva, 1975).

EHRMANN, J., 'Homo Ludens Revisited', *Yale French Studies*, 41 (1968), 31–57.

ERNST, P., *Approches pascaliennes* (Gembloux, 1970).

—— 'Géologie et Stratigraphie des *Pensées* de Pascal', 4 vols., thesis, Univ. of Paris IV (Paris, 1990).

—— 'Pascal au travail au jour le jour', in *Méthodes chez Pascal*, 141–54.

FALCUCCI, C., *Le Problème de la vérité chez Pascal* (Paris, 1939).

FERREYROLLES, G., 'Activité de Pascal', in Y.-M. Bercé (ed.), *Destins et enjeux du XVIIe siècle* (Paris, 1985), 301–10.

—— *Blaise Pascal, Les Provinciales* (Paris, 1984).

—— 'L'Imagination en procès', *XVIIe siècle*, 177 (Oct.–Dec. 1992), 469–79.

—— *Pascal et la raison du politique* (Paris, 1984).

—— 'Pascal et la rédemption de la nature', in *Méthodes chez Pascal*, 285–96.

FORCE, P., *Le Problème herméneutique chez Pascal* (Paris, 1989).

FRAISSE, J.-C., *Saint Augustin* (Paris, 1968).

FUMAROLI, M., 'Pascal et la tradition rhétorique gallicane', in *Méthodes chez Pascal*, 359–72.

GALLUCCI, J. A., 'Pascal and Kenneth Burke: An Argument for a Logological Reading of the *Pensées*', *Papers on French Seventeenth Century Literature*, 20/38 (1993), 123–50.

—— 'Politique et écriture: La *Disposition* pascalienne comme principe de liberté', in G. Ferreyrolles (ed.), *Justice et force: Politiques au temps de Pascal (Actes du colloque de Clermont-Ferrand)* (Paris, 1993).

GARANDERIE, A. DE LA, *La Valeur de l'ennui* (Paris, 1968).

GLAUSER, A., 'Montaigne et le roseau pensant de Pascal', *Romanic Review*, 66 (1975), 263–8.

GOLDMANN, L., *Le Dieu caché: Étude sur la vision tragique dans les 'Pensées' de Pascal et dans le théâtre de Racine* (Paris, 1955).

GOLLIET, P., 'Théologie de la foi et méthode apologétique dans les *Pensées*', in *Méthodes chez Pascal*, 53–62.

GOUHIER, H., *L'Anti-humanisme au XVIIe siècle* (Paris, 1987).

—— *Blaise Pascal: Commentaires* (Paris, 1966).

—— *Blaise Pascal: Conversion et apologétique* (Paris, 1986).

—— *Cartésianisme et Augustinisme au XVIIe siècle* (Paris, 1978).

—— *La Pensée métaphysique de Descartes* (Paris, 1962).

GOYET, T., 'La Méthode prophétique selon Pascal', in *Méthodes chez Pascal*, 63–74.

GOYET, T. et al. (eds.), *Pascal, Port-Royal, Orient, Occident*, Actes du Colloque de l'Université de Tokyo, Sept. 1988 (Paris, 1991).

HACKING, I., *The Emergence of Probability: A Philosophical Study of Early Ideas about Probability, Induction and Statistical Inference* (Cambridge, 1975).

HAIGHT, J., *The Concept of Reason in French Classical Thought 1635–90* (Toronto, 1982).

HAMMOND, N., '"Levez le Rideau": Images of the Theatre in Pascal's *Pensées*', *French Studies*, 47/3 (July, 1993).

—— 'The Theme of Ennui in Pascal's *Pensées*', *Nottingham French Studies*, 26/2 (1987), 1–16.

HARRINGTON, T., 'La Notion de simplicité chez Pascal', *Dix-septième siècle*, 154 (1987), 25–37.

—— 'Pascal et la Philosophie', in *Méthodes chez Pascal*, 37–44.

—— *Vérité et Méthode dans les 'Pensées' de Pascal* (Paris, 1972).

HARRIS, R., *The Language Makers* (London, 1980).

HELLER, L. M., 'La Folie dans l'Apologie pascalienne', in *Méthodes chez Pascal*, 297–308.

—— 'Montaigne, Pascal et le thème: À petites causes grands effets', *Bulletin de la Société des Amis de Montaigne*, 27–8 (1978), 11–19.

—— and RICHMOND, I. M. (eds.), *Pascal, thématique des 'Pensées'* (Paris, 1988).

HEYNDELS, R., *La Pensée fragmentée: Discontinuité formelle et question du sens* (Brussels, 1985).

HONG, R.-E., 'Le Paradoxe dans les premières liasses de l'Apologie pascalienne', *Cahiers de l'Association Internationale des Études Françaises*, 40 (1988), 273–83.

HOSSAIN, M., 'A False Antithesis in Pascal's *Pensées?*', *French Studies Bulletin*, 8 (1983), 1–3.

HOWE, V. K., '*Les Pensées*: Paradox and Signification', *Yale French Studies*, 49 (1973), 120–31.

HOWELLS, B., 'The Interpretation of Pascal's *Pari*', *Modern Language Review*, 79/1 (1984), 45–63.

HUBERT, Sister M. L., *Pascal's Unfinished Apology: A Study of his Plan* (New Haven, Conn., 1952).

HUIZINGA, J., *Homo Ludens: A Study of the Play-Element in Culture*, unnamed translator (London, 1949).

JAMES, E. D., *Pierre Nicole, Jansenist and Humanist* (The Hague, 1972).

JANKÉLÉVITCH, V., *L'Alternative* (Paris, 1938).

—— *L'Aventure, l'ennui, le sérieux* (Paris, 1963).

JAYMES, D., 'Play in Pascal's *Pensées*', *Papers on French Seventeenth Century Literature*, 14–15 (1981), 39–49.

JULIEN-EYMARD D'ANGERS, *Pascal et ses précurseurs, L'Apologétique en France de 1580 à 1670* (Paris, 1954).

Jungo, Dom M., *Le Vocabulaire de Pascal* (Paris, 1950).
Kawamata, K., 'Les Deux abbés de Saint-Cyran inspirateurs de Pascal', *Chroniques de Port-Royal* (1979), 125–32.
—— 'Pascal et Saint-Cyran', in *Méthodes chez Pascal*, 433–42.
—— 'Saint-Cyran inspirateur de Pascal', *Journal of Social Sciences and Humanities*, 63 (Tokyo, 1968), 1–118.
Kaye, F., *Charron et Montaigne: Du plagiat à l'originalité* (Ottawa, 1982).
Kenny, A., *Descartes: A Study of his Philosophy* (New York, 1968).
Klein, Z., *La Notion de dignité humaine dans la pensée de Kant et de Pascal* (Paris, 1968).
Koch, E., 'Rhetorical Aesthetics and Rhetorical Theory in Pascal', *Papers on French Seventeenth Century Literature*, 20/38 (1993), 151–70.
Krailsheimer, A., *Pascal* (Oxford, 1980).
Kretzmann, N., Kenny, A., and Pinborg, J. (eds.), *The Cambridge History of Later Medieval Philosophy* (Cambridge, 1982).
Kritzman, L. D. (ed.), *Fragments: Incompletion and Discontinuity* (New York, 1981).
Kuentz, P., 'Le Rhétorique ou la mise à l'écart', *Communications*, 16 (1970), 143–57.
Lagarde, F., 'Le différement de Pascal', *Papers on French Seventeenth Century Literature*, 20/38 (1993), 183–92.
Lanavère, A. (ed.), *Pascal* (Paris, 1969).
Laporte, J., *Le Cœur et la raison selon Pascal* (Paris, 1950).
Lavelle, L., *Psychologie et spiritualité* (Paris, 1967).
Leake, R. E., *Concordance de Montaigne*, 2 vols. (Geneva, 1981).
Le Guern, M., *L'Image dans l'Œuvre de Pascal* (Paris, 1969).
—— *Pascal et Descartes* (Paris, 1971).
—— 'Pascal et la métonymie', in *Méthodes chez Pascal*, 383–90.
Le Guern, M.-R. and Le Guern, M., *Les 'Pensées' de Pascal: De l'anthropologie à la théologie* (Paris, 1972).
Leveillé-Mourin, G., *Le Langage chrétien, anti-chrétien de la transcendance: Pascal–Nietzsche* (Paris, 1978).
Levi, P., *French Moralists: The Theory of the Passions 1585–1649* (Oxford, 1964).
Lewis, G., 'Augustinisme et Cartésianisme à Port-Royal', in J. Dijksterhuis (ed.), *Descartes et le Cartésianisme hollandais* (Amsterdam, 1951).
Lewis, P. E., 'La Rochefoucauld: The Rationality of Play', *Yale French Studies*, 41 (1968), 133–47.
De Ley, H., *Le Jeu classique: Jeu et théorie des jeux au grand siècle* (Paris, 1988).
Limbrick, E., 'Le Pyrrhonisme est le vrai', *Mélanges à la mémoire de V.-L. Saulnier* (Geneva, 1984), 439–48.
Lyons, J., *Language, Meaning and Context* (Bungay, Suffolk, 1981).

McBride, R., *Aspects of Seventeenth-Century French Drama and Thought* (London, 1979).
McKenna, A., 'L'Argument *infini-rien*', in *Méthodes chez Pascal*, 497–508.
—— *De Pascal à Voltaire*, 2 vols. (Oxford, 1990).
—— 'Filleau de la Chaise et la réception des *Pensées*', *Cahiers de l'Association Internationale des Études Françaises*, 40 (1988).
—— 'Pascal et le corps humain', *XVIIe siècle*, 177 (Oct.–Dec. 1992), 481–94.
Mackenzie, L. A. Jnr., 'To the Brink: The Dialectic of Anxiety in the *Pensées*', *Yale French Studies*, 66 (1984), 57–66.
Maclean, I., *Interpretation and Meaning in the Renaissance: The Case of Law* (Cambridge, 1992).
Magendie, M., *La Politesse mondaine et les théories de l'honnêteté en France au XVIIe siècle, de 1600 à 1660*, 2 vols. (Paris, 1925).
Maggioni, Sister M. J., *The Pensées of Pascal: A Study in Baroque Style* (Washington, DC, 1950).
Magnard, P., *Nature et histoire dans l'Apologétique* (Paris, 1975).
—— 'Pascal dialecticien', in *Pascal présent*, 259–89.
Maingueneau, D., *Sémantique de la polémique: Discours religieux et ruptures idéologiques au XVIIe siècle* (Lausanne, 1983).
Marin, L., *La Critique du discours: Sur la 'Logique' de Port-Royal et les 'Pensées' de Pascal* (Paris, 1975).
—— '*Pascal*: text, author, discourse . . .', *Yale French Studies*, 52 (1975), 129–51.
Mariner, F., 'The Order of Disorder: The Problem of the Fragment in Pascal's *Pensées*', *Papers on French Seventeenth Century Literature*, 20/38 (1993), 171–82.
Matoré, G., *La Méthode en lexicologie: Domaine français* (Paris, 1953).
Mauzi, R., *L'Idée du bonheur au XVIIIe siècle* (Paris, 1976).
Melzer, S. E., 'Classicism and Conventions of Meaning in the *Pensées*', *Papers on French Seventeenth Century Literature*, 14–15 (1981), 71–84.
—— *Discourses of the Fall: A Study of Pascal's 'Pensées'* (London, 1986).
—— '*Invraisemblance* in Pascal's *Pensées*: The Anti-Rhetoric', *Romanic Review*, 73 (1982), 33–44.
Mermier, G., 'Inconstance et relativité, Pièces maîtresses de la modernité de Montaigne', *Bulletin de la Société des Amis de Montaigne*, 25–26 (1978), 51–6.
Mesnard, J., 'A la recherche de la bibliothèque de Pascal', *Société des Amis de Port-Royal* (1952), 33–46.
—— 'De la *diversion* au *divertissement*', *Mémorial du Premier Congrès International des Études Montaignistes* (1964), 123–8.
—— 'Discontinuité, contrariété, répétition: Un modèle de l'écriture

pascalienne', in P. Aquilen, J. Chupeau, and F. Weil (eds.), *L'Intelligence du passé: Hommage à Jean Lafond* (Tours, 1988), 409–27.
—— 'Martin de Barcos et les disputes internes de Port-Royal', *Chroniques de Port-Royal*, 26–8 (1977–9), 73–94.
—— *Pascal* (Paris, 1967, 1st edn. 1951).
—— 'Pascal et la musique', in *Textes du Tricentenaire* (Paris, 1963), 195–205.
—— 'Pascal et la vérité', *Chroniques de Port-Royal*, 17–18 (1969), 21–40.
—— *Les 'Pensées' de Pascal* (Paris, 1976).
—— 'Pourquoi les *Pensées* de Pascal se présentent-elles sous forme de fragments?', *Papers on French Seventeenth Century Literature*, 18–19 (1983), 635–49.
—— 'Nombres et textes figurés chez Pascal', *XVIIe siècle*, 177 (Oct.–Dec. 1992), 521–32.
—— 'L'Universalité de Pascal', in *Méthodes chez Pascal*, 335–56.
Méthodes chez Pascal (Paris, 1979): proceedings of a colloquium organized by J. Mesnard, T. Goyet, P. Sellier, and D. Descotes.
MEURILLON, C., 'La Narration dans les *Pensées*', *XVIIe siècle*, 177 (Oct.–Dec. 1992), 507–19.
—— 'Un concept problématique dans les *Pensées*: *Le Moi*', in *Méthodes chez Pascal*, 269–84.
MIEL, J., 'Les Méthodes de Pascal et l'épistème classique', in *Méthodes chez Pascal*, 27–36.
—— *Pascal and Theology* (Baltimore, 1969).
—— 'Pascal, Port-Royal, and Cartesian Linguistics', *Journal of the History of Ideas*, 30 (1969), 261–71.
MOLINO, J., 'La Raison des effets', in *Méthodes chez Pascal*, 477–96.
MONOD, A., *De Pascal à Chateaubriand: Les Défenseurs du Christianisme de 1670 à 1802* (Paris, 1916).
MORFORD, M., *Stoics and Neostoics: Rubens and the Circle of Lipsius* (Princeton, NJ, 1991).
MORGAN, J., 'Pascal's Three Orders', *Modern Language Review*, 73 (1978), 755–66.
MORIARTY, M., *Taste and Ideology in Seventeenth-Century France* (Cambridge, 1988).
MOROT-SIR, É., 'Du nouveau sur Pascal?', *Romance Notes*, 18 (1977), 272–9.
—— 'Remarques sur la lexicologie pascalienne', in *Méthodes chez Pascal*, 181–8.
MOUTSOPOULOS, E., 'De quelques réminiscences platoniciennes dans l'esthétique de Pascal', in *Méthodes chez Pascal*, 411–18.
NADLER, S. M., *Arnauld and the Cartesian Philosophy of Ideas* (Manchester, 1989).
NELSON, R., 'Pascal devant ses lecteurs', in *Méthodes chez Pascal*, 309–18.

NORMAN, B., 'L'Idée de règle chez Pascal', in *Méthodes chez Pascal*, 87–100.
—— *Portraits of Thought: Knowledge, Methods, and Styles in Pascal* (Columbus, Oh., 1988).
—— 'Thought and language in Pascal', *Yale French Studies*, 49 (1973), 110–19.
ORCIBAL, J., 'Thèmes platoniciens dans l'*Augustinus* de Jansénius', in *Augustinus Magister*, ii (Paris, 1954), 1077–85.
PADLEY, G. A., *Grammatical Theory in Western Europe 1500–1700: The Latin Tradition* (Cambridge, 1976).
PARIENTE, J. C., *L'Analyse du langage à Port-Royal: Six études logico-grammaticales* (Paris, 1985).
PARISH, R., 'Mais Qui Parle? Voice and Persona in the *Pensées*', *Seventeenth-Century French Studies*, 8 (1986), 23–40.
—— *Pascal's 'Lettres Provinciales': A Study in Polemic* (Oxford, 1989).
Pascal Présent (Clermont-Ferrand, 1962).
PINEAU, J., 'Les Relations humaines dans l'Apologétique de Pascal', in *Méthodes chez Pascal*, 319–32.
PINTARD, R., *Le Libertinage érudit dans la première moitié du XVIIe siècle* (Paris, 1943).
—— 'Pascal et les libertins', in *Pascal présent* (Clermont-Ferrand, 1962), 107–30.
POTTS, D. C., 'Pascal's Contemporaries and *le Divertissement*', *Modern Language Review*, 57 (1962), 31–40.
PRICE, M., *To the Palace of Wisdom: Studies in Order and Energy from Dryden to Blake* (Edwardsville, Ill., 1964).
PUCELLE, J., 'La Dialectique du renversement du pour au contre et l'antithétique pascalienne', in *Méthodes chez Pascal*, 445–62.
PUGH, A. R., *The Composition of Pascal's 'Apologia'* (Toronto, 1984).
ROHOU, J., *L'Évolution du tragique racinien* (Paris, 1991).
ROUSSET, J., *Anthologie de la poésie baroque française*, 2 vols. (Paris, 1961).
—— *La Littérature de l'Âge Baroque en France* (Paris, 1953).
RUBIN, D. L., and MCKINLEY, M. B. (eds.), *Convergences: Rhetoric and Poetic in Seventeenth-Century France* (Columbus, Oh., 1989).
RUSSIER, J., *La Foi selon Pascal* (Paris, 1949).
SCHÄRER, K., 'Pascal und das Problem der Sprache', in *Romanische Forschungen*, 92 (1980), 74–87.
SELLIER, P., 'Imaginaire et théologie: Le Cœur chez Pascal', *Cahiers de l'Association Internationale des Études Françaises*, 40 (1988), 285–95.
—— 'L'Ouverture de l'apologie pascalienne', *XVIIe siècle*, 177 (Oct.–Dec. 1992), 437–49.
—— *Pascal et Saint Augustin* (Paris, 1970).
—— 'Rhétorique et apologie: Dieu parle bien de Dieu', in *Méthodes chez Pascal*, 373–81.
—— 'Vous êtes embarqué ...: Où prendrons-nous un port dans la

morale?', *Papers on French Seventeenth Century Literature*, 14–15 (1981), 13–37.

SHIOKAWA, T., *Pascal et les miracles* (Paris, 1977).

—— 'Persuasion et conversion: Essai sur la signification de la rhétorique chez Pascal', in Y.-M. Bercé (ed.), *Destins et enjeux du XVIIe siècle* (Paris, 1985), 311–21.

SPINK, J. S., *French Free-Thought from Gassendi to Voltaire* (London, 1960).

STANTON, D. C., 'The Ideal of *Repos* in Seventeenth-Century French Literature', *L'Esprit créateur*, 15 (1975), 79–104.

—— 'Pascal's Fragmentary Thoughts: Dis-order and its Overdetermination', *Semiotica*, 51 (1984), 211–35.

SUEMATSU, H., 'Développement formel de la dialectique pascalienne', in *Méthodes chez Pascal*, 463–76.

TANS, J. A. G., 'Les Idées politiques des Jansénistes', *Neophilologus*, 30 (1956), 1–18.

TAVENEAUX, R., *Jansénisme et politique* (Paris, 1965).

THIROUIN, L., 'Conservatisme et dérision: L'Analyse pascalienne des lois', *Cahiers de littérature du XVIIe siècle*, 9 (1987), 111–34.

—— *Le Hasard et les règles: Le Modèle du jeu dans la pensée de Pascal* (Paris, 1991).

—— 'Pascal et *L'Art de conférer*', *Cahiers de l'Association Internationale des Études Françaises*, 40 (1988), 199–218.

—— 'Les Premières Liasses des *Pensées*: Architecture et signification', *XVIIe siècle*, 177 (Oct.–Dec. 1992), 451–68.

—— 'Raison des effets: Essai d'explication d'un concept pascalien', *XVIIe siècle*, 134–7 (1982), 31–50.

—— 'Le Réalisme de Pascal', in G. Ferreyrolles (ed.), *Justice et force: Politiques au temps de Pascal (Actes du colloque de Clermont-Ferrand, 1990)* (Paris, 1993).

TOCANNE, B., 'Flottements méthodologiques chez Pascal', in *Méthodes chez Pascal*, 45–52.

TOPLISS, P., *The Rhetoric of Pascal* (Amsterdam, 1966).

ULLMANN, S., *Semantics: An Introduction to the Science of Meaning* (Oxford, 1970, first published 1962).

—— *Words and their Use* (London, 1951).

VIGOUROUX, M., *Le Thème de la retraite et de la solitude chez quelques épistoliers du XVIIe siècle* (Paris, 1972).

WARNER, M., *Philosophical Finesse: Studies in the Art of Rational Persuasion* (Oxford, 1989).

WETSEL, D., *L'Écriture et le reste: The 'Pensées' of Pascal in the Exegetical Tradition of Port-Royal* (Columbus, Oh., 1981).

—— (ed.), *Meaning, Structure and History in the 'Pensées' of Pascal* (Paris, 1990).

—— 'Pascal's *Pensées* and Recent Critical Theory: Illumination or

Deformation of the Text?', *Papers on French Seventeenth Century Literature*, 20/38 (1993), 117–22.

WIND, E., *Pagan Mysteries in the Renaissance* (Oxford, 1980; first published 1958).

WOSHINSKY, B., 'Pascal's *Pensées* and the Discourse of the Inexpressible', *Papers on French Seventeenth Century Literature*, 14–15 (1981), 57–65.

Index of Pascal's Works

Pensées (Numbering according to Lafuma edition):

2: 51 n. 5, 61, 70
3: 54
4: 61
5: 51 n. 5, 61, 70
6: 162
7: 61, 70 n. 39
8: 51 n. 5, 70
9: 61, 70, 168, 173 n. 33, 176 n. 39
10: 158
11: 51 n. 5, 61, 70
12: 51 n. 5, 70, 163, 183 n. 59, 184 n. 60, 206 n. 26
14: 56 n. 22
17: 86, 94–5
20: 176 n. 39
21: 46, 204
24: 22, 78, 81–2, 86, 103, 105, 118, 119, 132
27: 88
29: 143 n. 24
33: 83 n. 9
34: 179 n. 50
35: 83 n. 7
36: 105, 108, 113 n. 19
44: 37 n. 32, 76, 121 n. 12, 152, 155, 184 n. 61, 203, 207, 210, 211
45: 61, 77, 209, 219
47: 98, 160 n. 22
51: 176 n. 39
54: 86, 90, 91–2, 95 n. 34, 97
55: 86, 89, 90–1, 95, 97, 100
58: 5, 34, 51 n. 5, 52
60: 98, 100 n. 44, 168, 171, 172–5, 176 n. 39, 206, 211, 212
66: 168 n. 8, 178–9
67: 168 n. 8, 179 n. 50
68: 57, 58
70: 83
71: 206
73: 86, 92
75: 207
76: 141, 158 n. 16
77: 39, 129 n. 34
79: 104, 106

81: 143, 170 n. 12, 178
85: 33, 168 n. 8, 170 n. 12, 179, 184, 185–6
86: 170 n. 12
89: 191 n. 79
90: 53, 191 n. 79, 199
91: 38, 179, 191 n. 79, 217
92: 191 n. 79, 206, 217
93: 68, 134, 191 n. 79, 217
94: 38, 178, 182
98: 5, 38
99: 5, 38–9, 202–3, 297, 217–18, 228
103: 37–8, 170 n. 12, 180
106: 54 n. 16
109: 29–30
110: 15, 30 n. 15
113: 31 n. 18
117: 83 n. 8
118: 54 n. 16
119: 100, 207, 218
122: 36
123: 39 n. 40
126: 210
131: 39, 65, 84–5, 97, 100–1, 160, 213–14, 227
132: 155
133: 155
134: 160 n. 22
136: 83 n. 7, 84, 95 n. 35, 104, 105, 106, 109–14, 135, 136–9, 140, 145, 146, 155–8, 169, 191, 193, 214
137: 31 n. 18
139: 191 n. 80
140: 160 n. 20
142: 154, 159 n. 20
143: 159 n. 20
146: 101
147: 39 n. 39, 159–60 n. 20
148: 54, 83 n. 7, 160, 161, 185, 206 n. 26
149: 54, 162, 168, 206 n. 26
150: 145
151: 146

158: 64
160: 162
165: 200
177: 223–4
184: 222
185: 39 n. 37
189: 193 n. 83, 207 n. 29
190: 129
192: 193
198: 39
199: 13, 44 n. 50, 47, 54 n. 16, 87 n. 4, 95 n. 34, 98, 99, 100, 101, 129 n. 34, 146
200: 31 n. 18
208: 83, 84, 184
211: 181
225: 221
234: 40, 221
242: 228
252: 42
253: 193
257: 40, 193
260: 193
267: 147 n. 35
269: 184, 190, 191 n. 79
270: 130
272: 25 n. 1
274: 42
275: 147 n. 35
281: 57, 113 n. 19
298: 14, 51–2, 133
302: 75
303: 40
308: 51, 52, 129, 133
309: 40 n. 41, 69
328: 40 n. 41
329: 57 n. 23
357: 163
360: 164
362: 154
374: 57
380: 182
387: 51 n. 5, 70 n. 64
392: 147 n. 35
393: 206 n. 26
399: 137 n. 10, 160, 165
400: 125, 137 n. 10, 160 n. 21
401: 207 n. 28
403: 40 n. 41
404: 160 n. 21
405: 137 n. 10, 160 n. 21
407: 137, 140, 159, 160
408: 158
410: 143, 168 n. 9, 169
411: 153
413: 201
414: 104, 114, 202
417: 193
418: 13, 164, 184–5, 199–200, 201–2
421: 57
426: 164
427: 51 n. 5, 69 n. 60, 81, 83, 124, 142
428: 26, 125, 140 n. 17, 145, 168, 212
429: 123
430: 125
434: 81 n. 1, 83
439: 49
443: 215
444: 85
445: 33
449: 54, 55, 56, 69 n. 60, 147, 193, 207, 218
451: 57 n. 23
453: 58, 206 n. 26
454: 95–6
460: 147–8
463: 54
467: 51 n. 5
470: 153 n. 6
477: 125
478: 197
483: 25 n. 1, 113 n. 19, 189 n. 78
485: 25 n. 1, 42, 143 n. 24, 184, 189 n. 78
489: 57 n. 23, 58, 189
503: 58
505: 65 n. 48, 101, 201
511: 51 n. 5, 53
512: 13, 44–5, 53, 65 n. 48
513: 53, 67, 205
518: 64, 66, 214 n. 45
520: 176, 184, 186
522: 119, 124 n. 15
525: 65
528: 44, 45
529: 39 n. 36
530: 45, 68
532: 51 n. 5, 57, 63–9, 132, 197, 214 n. 45
533: 142, 158
534: 106
537: 206 n. 26
542: 10
544: 83 n. 7
545: 87 n. 4

INDEX OF PASCAL'S WORKS

553: 18
558: 47
560: 145
562: 162 n. 25
574: 222
576: 219
581: 201
583: 123
584: 34–5
594: 56, 57
595: 168 n. 9
597: 161 n. 23, 168 n. 9
599: 148
603: 101
604: 207 n. 29
606: 36
608: 147 n. 35
609: 58
616: 172
617: 168 n. 9, 211
620: 31 n. 18, 51 n. 5
621: 143 n. 23
622: 104, 105, 107, 111, 113 n. 19, 139 n. 15
625: 206 n. 26
627: 10, 45
628: 201
629: 146 n. 30
631: 206 n. 26
634: 83 n. 7
637: 124
639: 161–2
641: 145
642: 161
645: 182
646: 75
651: 75
655: 37
656: 10, 41, 225
658: 213
662: 177
665: 35 n. 28
682: 146 n. 32
683: 51 n. 5
684: 51 n. 5
687: 155
688: 75
691: 213
692: 207 n. 30
693: 83 n. 7
694: 51 n. 5, 70–1, 83 n. 7
696: 32 n. 20, 71–2, 73
697: 27, 33, 34
698: 64

700: 57
701: 215, 217
706: 58
708: 73
710: 226
714: 39 n. 38
721: 207 n. 30
725: 183
729: 42
733: 51 n. 5, 77, 205, 207 n. 29, 219–20
734: 88
737: 226
739: 212
740: 212 n. 40
744: 75, 119, 128
745: 7, 75, 76, 226
749: 153
750: 143 n. 24
756: 31 n. 18
758: 207 n. 30
764: 201
767: 100
771: 88, 105
773: 201, 202
774: 184, 186
780: 35, 64 n. 45, 66, 67, 71, 106
781: 189 n. 77, 194 n. 84
784: 29 n. 13, 32, 46, 62
788: 31 n. 18
789: 29 n. 13, 30–1
793: 227
800: 83 n. 7
803: 95 n. 34, 96, 97, 100
805: 91, 95
806: 142
808: 82
826: 207, 221
830: 27 n. 5
832: 221 n. 62
836: 73
839: 221 n. 62
840: 26–7, 212 n. 39, n. 40, 221 n. 62
843: 221 n. 62
846: 58
847: 169 n. 10
848: 221
853: 161 n. 23
856: 207 n. 30
864: 183
865: 205, 221 n. 62
878: 221 n. 62
885: 168 n. 6

887: 18
889: 83 n. 8, 138, 156 n. 11, 221 n. 62
896: 213
897: 201
901: 5
902: 5
904: 5
905: 57, 64, 66, 214
913: 4, 131, 144, 148 n. 37, 227, 228
917: 168
918: 87 n. 4
919: 4, 25 n. 1, 56 n. 22, 105, 115, 125, 129 n. 34, 144 n. 27, 146 n. 31, 183
922: 5
923: 5
924: 5, 143–4
926: 56, 222
928: 37
929: 119, 130
930: 31 n. 18
931: 184 n. 61
933: 51, 129, 133
940: 184
941: 106
945: 56 n. 22, 58
946: 85, 194
948: 184, 185
950: 31 n. 18, 58
954: 39 n. 38
962: 5, 39 n. 38
965: 25 n. 1, 56 n. 22
968: 32–3
970: 51 n. 5
974: 77, 144, 222–3
975: 209
976: 71
978: 36, 37, 160 n. 22, 174 n. 36, 210
991: 58
1001: 18

Lettres Provinciales:
GENERAL REFERENCES:
7, 11, 14, 42, 58–9, 69 n. 59, 105 n. 7, 155, 168, 176, 216.
INDIVIDUAL REFERENCES:
LETTERS
2: 59 n. 29
3: 211
4: 156, 158 n. 17
5: 58 n. 25, 59 n. 28
6: 39 n. 38, 43, 58 n. 25
7: 58 n. 25
8: 54 n. 16, 59 n. 28
9: 58 n. 25
10: 34, 58 n. 25
11: 58 n. 25, 163 n. 28
12: 59 n. 28
13: 58 n. 25, 59 n. 28
14: 59 n. 28, 176
15: 59 n. 28, 59 n. 29
16: 27–8, 54 n. 16, 58 n. 25, 59 n. 28, 220
18: 58 n. 25, 98 n. 41, 119 n. 5

Des caractères de divisibilité des nombres déduits de la somme de leurs chiffres:
14 n. 41

Sur la conversion du pécheur:
87, 108–9, 126 n. 16, 148–9, 151–2, 165

Correspondence:
5, 52, 119 n. 4, 130–1, 148, 185, 188, 218 n. 54, 224–5

Écrits des curés de Paris:
144, 182 n. 57, 223 n. 64

Écrits sur la Grâce:
19, 30, 172, 177 n. 42, 183, 185, 186–7, 188–9, 205

Entretien avec M. de Sacy:
16, 48, 140–1, 142, 186, 200–1

De l'esprit géometrique:
10–18, 32, 37 n. 33, 40, 45–6, 48–9, 53–4, 59–60, 67, 69, 76, 93–4, 146 n. 32, 154 n. 9, 170, 212, 218–9

Lettres de A. Dettonville:
15 n. 46

Préface sur le traité du vide:
52, 90, 205

Prière pour demander à Dieu le bon usage des maladies:
87, 126 n. 16, 128 n. 28, 162–3

Sommation des puissances numériques:
14 n. 41

Traité des ordres numériques:
14 n. 41

Traités de l'équilibre des liqueurs et de la pesanteur de la masse de l'air:
216

Trois discours sur la condition des grands:
52, 83 n. 7, 169–70, 178–80, 189

Index of Names

Académie Françoise 9, 25–27, 35, 41, 51, 68, 82, 83, 95, 101, 104, 118, 136, 143, 150, 166, 167, 183
Adam 19, 187, 228 n.
Adam, A. 70 n.
Arnauld, Angélique 68
Arnauld, Antoine 10–19, 28, 34, 40, 59, 60, 188 n., 208–9, 220 n.
Arnauld d'Andilly, R. 19, 160 n.
Augustine, St. 17–21, 35, 51, 52, 55 n., 58, 68–9 n., 72, 74, 87, 109 n., 118, 126–9, 133, 135, 137 n., 147, 149, 154, 159, 160 162, 171, 187, 188, 206

Baird, A. 51 n.
Barcos, M. de 11, 68–9, 129
Barenne, O. 127 n., 159 n.
Barnes, A. 60 n.
Bayley, P. 50 n., 70 n.
Beugnot, B. 131–2 n., 135, 136 n., 142 n., 145 n., 146
Bianchini Fales, A. 103 n.
Bible 25, 30, 40, 42, 46, 58, 74, 87, 130, 189, 227
Bouchez, M. 103 n.
Bourdonné, C. 33, 88, 121, 147
Bourgeois, Mme 116
Brams, S. 228
Brébeuf 86
Brémond, H. 87 n.
Brinkmann, H. 20 n.
Brunschvicg, L. 61, 89 n., 131 n., 220 n.

Camus, J.-P. 34, 73 n., 87–8
Carr, T. 14
Carraud, V. 62 n., 66 n., 82–3 n.
Cassandre, F. 158, 166 n., 174 n.
Charron, P. 21, 66, 67, 71, 87–90, 92, 99 n., 106, 112, 119, 121–2, 179–80 n., 204, 214, 218
Chevalier, J. 12, 167 n., 185
Christ 4, 20, 27 n., 28, 30, 40, 52, 54, 58, 69, 75 n., 85, 115, 116, 125, 131, 133, 145, 146 n., 153, 164, 183–4,
189 n., 193–4, 207, 218–20, 221, 222, 223
Christina, of Sweden 52
Cicero 21, 180 n.
Cognet, L. 14 n., 127
Condorcet, J. 4 n.
Cotgrave, R. 123
Courcelle, P. 16 n., 118, 140 n., 201 n.
Croquette, B. 21 n., 66 n., 88, 95 n.

Davidson, H. 2, 10, 11, 13 n., 14 n., 33 n., 50 n., 53 n., 86 n., 159 n., 172 n., 208 n.
De la Forge, L. 18
De Ley, H. 198 n.
De Man, P. 46 n.
Delassault, G. 19 n.
Demorest, J. 1, 8 n., 82 n.
Deprun, J. 81 n., 118, 126 n., 127 n.
Des Barreaux 143 n.
Descartes, R. 12, 14, 16 n., 17–18, 26 n., 29 n., 54, 64, 68, 97, 182 n., 203, 208, 215
Descotes, D. 15 n., 43 n., 50 n.
Descrains, J. 87 n.
Dogmatism 9, 29–30, 97, 100–1, 158, 173–4
Du Pont, R. 9, 73, 154 n.
Du Teil 154 n.
Du Vair 87
Dubé, P. 33 n., 50 n., 86 n.
Dumonceaux, P. 103 n., 105, 109 n.
Duvergier de Hauranne, J. 19, 54, 103, 135, 175

Epictetus 16, 75, 97 n., 101, 140, 154, 186, 200, 201 n.
Epicurean 143 n.
Epicurus 160 n.
Ernst, P. 4 n., 5–6, 16 n., 29 n., 39 n., 50 n., 64., 66 n., 70, 88 n., 137 n., 146 n., 158, 160 n., 162 n., 179 n., 191 n., 193 n., 203
Eve 228 n.

Falcucci, C. 203 n.
Faret, N. 121 n., 179 n.

INDEX OF NAMES

Ferreyrolles, G. 51 n., 52 n., 57, 73 n., 170–74, 176–7, 186 n., 191
Force, P. 28–31, 42, 44, 72, 220
Frain du Tremblay, J. 197, 198
Fraisse, J.-C. 20
François de Sales 115–16, 122 n., 126–7, 149 n.
Furetière 8, 9, 25 n., 65, 73, 82 n., 86 n., 95, 96, 103, 104, 118, 136, 150, 166

Gallucci, J. 73
Garanderie, A. 103, 118
Gassendi, P. 173 n., 208 n.
Gataker, T. 198 n.
Goldmann, L. 3 n., 6, 7 n., 11, 61, 63, 68 n., 129, 170
Gouhier, H. 16, 17–18, 29 n., 30 n., 70 n.
Goulart, S. 110, 137

Harrington, T. 54 n., 154 n., 170, 204–5, 215 n., 216 n., 217 n.
Heyndels, R. 72–3
Howells, B. 200
Hubert, M.-L. 4 n.
Huizinga, J. 201, 206 n., 210 n.

James, E. D. 18
Jansenius, C. 19, 28, 55 n., 129, 149 n., 160 n., 168 n., 175, 188 n., 212 n.
Jaymes, 109 n., 198
Julien-Eymard D'Angers 19 n.
Jungo, D. 1, 82 n., 98 n.
Justinian 166 n.
Justus Lipsius 86

Kawamata, K. 54
Klein, Z. 31 n.
Krailsheimer, A. 66, 70 n.
Kritzman, L. 4 n.
Kuentz, P. 72 n.

La Harpe, J.-F. 76, 78 n.
Lafayette, Mme de 121
Lafuma, L. 4, 5, 12, 51 n., 56, 61, 103, 158 n.
Lanavère, A. 173 n.
Lancelot, C. 10, 59
Le Guern, M. 1–2, 14 n., 18 n., 26 n., 29 n., 52 n., 64, 66, 82 n., 94 n., 212 n., 220 n.
Leake, R. 98 n.

Leveillé-Mourin, G. 7 n.
Levi, P. 87
Lewis, G. 17 n., 18
Lewis, P. 200
Limbrick, E. 213 n.

McKenna, A. 11 n., 12, 14 n., 16, 51 N., 60 n., 156 n.
MacKenzie, L. 122, 128
Maclean, I. 20 n., 174 n., 211 n.
Maggioni, M. 1, 63 n., 82 n.
Magnard, P. 8–9, 172, 177
Marin, L. 3 n., 7, 11, 32, 65 n.
Mariner, F. 63 n.
Matoré, G. 21 n.
Mauzi, R. 150, 156 n., 157 n.
Melzer, S. 2–3, 11, 41, 49 n., 63, 68, 224
Méré, C. de 36 n., 40 n., 67
Mersenne, M. 55, 90 n., 110 n.
Mesnard, J. 4 n., 9, 11, 12 n., 16, 33 N., 50 n., 51, 56 n., 61–3, 65, 69 n., 81 n., 90 n., 92 n., 109, 158, 203, 213, 221
Meurillon, C. 7 n.
Miel, J. 18 n.
Miton, D. 161
Molière 25
Molino, J. 32 n., 216
Montaigne, M. de 14, 21, 27 n., 35, 37, 46–8, 66, 72, 74, 75, 81 n., 86–96, 98, 109, 110–12, 119–21, 123, 137, 138, 140, 154, 158, 171, 172–4, 180 n., 182 n., 186, 206, 214
Morford, M. 87 n.
Morgan, J. 52
Morot-Sir, E. 2 n., 3

Nicole, P. 10–19, 40, 59, 60, 113–14, 208–9, 220 n.
Nicot, J. 151
Norman, B. 2, 11, 12, 45 n., 53, 60 n., 63, 67 n., 75, 77, 172 n.

Orcibal, J. 149 n.

Parish, R. 7, 10, 28 n., 153, 162, 163 n., 212 n.
Pascal, Gilberte 3, 56 n., 90, 185, 188, 212 n.
Pascal, Jacqueline 33 n., 131
Paul, St. 55 n., 133
Périer, E. 3, 40 n., 50
Plato 21, 142, 228 n.

INDEX OF NAMES

Port-Royal 10–12, 14, 17, 18, 40 n., 53 n., 55 n., 69 n., 71 n., 127 n., 154, 159 n., 198
Postel, G. 94
Potts, D. 109, 147 n.
Price, M. 60
Pugh, A. 4 n., 29 n., 50 n., 52 n., 63–4, 70, 71 n.
Pyrrhonism, see Scepticism

Richelet 25 n., 31, 68, 82 n., 95, 103, 136, 150, 174, 183
Roannez, Charlotte de 5, 148
Roannez, Monsieur de 50
Roannez family 130
Rohault, J. 18
Rohou, J. 104 n.
Rousset, J. 87
Russier, J. 6, 7 n.

Sacy, M. de 16, 48, 55 n., 116, 127 n., 129 n., 138 n., 140, 142, 154 n., 159, 183, 186 n., 200, 227
Saint-Ange 87
Saint-Evremond, C. de 110 n., 161 n.
Salomon de Tultie 7, 75
Scepticism 29–30, 63–9, 77, 83, 97, 100–1, 137 n., 140–2, 171, 173–5, 177, 213–14, 222 n.
Schärer, K. 7 n.
Sellier, P. 2 n., 4, 19 n., 21 n., 35 n., 38, 40, 51 n., 52, 60 n., 68 n., 70 n., 73, 74–5, 82, 87, 89 n., 109 n., 126 n., 129 n., 135 n., 147 n., 149, 154, 160 n., 162 N., 171, 188 n., 206 n., 212 n.

Sénault, J.-F. 21, 35, 36, 74, 122, 123, 139 n., 153 n., 154 n., 158, 160 n., 165, 177, 178, 202
Seneca 110, 136–7, 140, 160 n.
Sévigné, Mme de 118
Sévigné, Marquis de 113
Silhon, J. de 34 n., 55 n., 113, 129 n., 140 n., 204, 214, 217, 218
Sirmond, A. 34
Spink, J. 173 n.
Stanton, D. 4 n., 66 n., 135, 136 N., 137 n., 145 n.
Stoicism 86–7, 99, 101, 136–7, 139–42, 151, 153

Tavernier 94
Terence 179 n.
Thirouin, L. 32 n., 34 n., 37 n., 53 n., 56 n., 62 n., 161 n., 171, 173 n., 177, 180, 182 n., 198–200, 202 n., 216, 217, 224, 225
Thomas Aquinas 55
Topliss, P. 1, 13 n., 72 n., 82 n.

Ullmann, S. 21 n.

Vigouroux, M. 135 n.
Voltaire 4 n., 150, 156 n.

Warner, M. 52 n., 67 n.
Wetsel, D. 4 n., 43 n., 55 n., 129 n.
Woshinsky, B. 43 n.

Yves de Paris 55, 113

Zeno 160 n.

B
1901
.P43
H36
1994
70665f